Trail Riding

Trail Riding
Train, Prepare, Pack Up & Hit the Trail

Rhonda Hart Poe

Illustrated by Elayne Sears

Storey Publishing

*The mission of Storey Publishing is to serve our customers
by publishing practical information that encourages personal independence
in harmony with the environment.*

Edited by Deborah Burns
Art direction and design by Vicky Vaughn
Text production by Eugenie Delaney and Liseann Karandisecky
Illustrations by Elayne Sears
Indexed by Eileen M. Clawson

Printed in the United States by Von Hoffmann
10 9 8 7 6 5 4 3 2 1

LIBRARY OF CONGRESS CATALOGING-IN-PUBLICATION DATA
Poe, Rhonda Hart, 1959–
   Trail riding / Rhonda Hart Poe.
      p. cm.
   Includes index.
   ISBN-13: 978-1-58017-560-9; ISBN-10: 1-58017-560-0 (pbk. : alk. paper)
   ISBN-13: 978-1-58017-561-6; ISBN-10: 1-58017-561-9 (hardcover : alk. paper)
   1. Trail riding. I. Title.

SF309.28.P64 2005
798.2'3—dc22
                                        2005004050

DEDICATION

For Jillane (Anderson Pike) and Jasper.

Thanks for the miles, the memories, and everlasting friendship. No matter where else life takes us, the woods between Hopper's and Deep Creek are always close to my heart and fresh in my mind.

CONTENTS

ACKNOWLEDGMENTS

Are horse-crazy kids born or made? And do they ever grow up? I owe my undying affection for horses to a childhood surrounded by horses of all kinds, thanks to my horseman father, Richard Massingham, and incredibly tolerant mother, Jeanne Massingham. My brother, Brian Massingham, is also an accomplished horseman, a competitive amateur team roper — along with his wife, Karen — and a professional, full-time farrier and trainer for the past 20-some years. My daughter, Kailah Hart, hasn't caught the bug as bad as her mother, but she was a game rider when she was younger and accompanied me on many horseback adventures. And my son, Lance Hart, has ridden with his uncle, granddad, and even mom on occasion. It's in the blood.

I also thank my friends Beverly Frick and Doanna Gross, dynamic Competitive Trail Riders, for their help in that section (Doanna was the model for many of the illustrations); Colleen Cates, a breeder of McCurdy Plantation Horses with an interest in field trialing, and June and Barry Snook, longtime field trailers, for their help on that topic; friends and gifted equine clinicians Lee Ziegler and Elizabeth Graves for multitudes of suggestions and unflagging moral support, as well as their expertise in the finer points of English riding;

saddle maker par excellence David Genedak, for insights to what I've been sitting on all these years; business partners and friends Alyson Stockham and Lynne Pomeranz for ideas I just wouldn't have thought of in the scope of the project; The Backcountry Horsemen of Washington, for published material that lent credibility to my own ideas; and my friends James Clapp II and Chris Culbertson for their stories and suggestions. I also thank my husband, Daymond Poe, for his patience and suggestions and for not running screaming every time he hears the words *trail horse*.

Of course no book like this would ever come to life without the help and support of great team of professionals. My profound thanks to Deb Burns, my long-suffering and diligent editor, for her patience, insight, and expertise, and to Elayne Sears, whose illustrations breathe life into the concepts words alone can't really explain.

And finally, my heart wouldn't be where it is today without Toby, Tabby, Salty, Sis, Banner, Speck, Molly, Red, Pete, Angel, Spot, Shawn, May (alias Crazy Mabel), Mariah, Buster, Rudy, Snickers, Spud, Shaker, Frosty, Daisy, Damascus, Lady-Hawke, and all the other kind, tough, honest, and wonderful teachers who have given so much to my life. May their trails be forever smooth.

PREFACE: JUST A TRAIL HORSE

Every time, someone says "Aw, he's just a trail horse," I want to scream.

The best horses I have ever known have been trail horses. They have been sound, smart, and willing. Luckily for me, they also have been forgiving. They have been my friends and confidants through childhood, adolescence, teen traumas, a rather shaky hold on adulthood, and, so far, well into middle age. All the while they managed to carry me safely out of every bit of trouble I have ever encountered.

Even today, trail riding is not just something I do; it's a touchstone for my life. When I don't ride, I backslide. Life's joys fade a little. Trail riding lets the rest of the world slip away for a while, until there is nothing but the feel of the horse beneath me, the sound of his hooves on the trail, and the smells and sights of the trail itself. It brings me back to earth and to nature. And it seems to do that for every trail rider I know. On a group trail ride last year, a bald eagle swooped down into the trailhead camp. Eagles are more common in that area than they once were, but every rider there felt as if that eagle was a special gift meant just for us.

Trail riding will take you places and show you things you might otherwise have missed: high country, backcountry, ghosts of 12-foot-wide tree stumps from another era, moss-covered paths, desert sunsets, pristine forests, and sparkling snow-covered fields. In the final moments, when my life passes before my eyes, I look forward to seeing images of the trails behind me, as well as the one ahead.

To trail riders, a horse covers more than just distance. The horse is our time machine. He delivers us to our rustic past, to raw nature, and to basic values of horsemanship that were once the very measure of a man. He simplifies, purifies, and sanctifies.

Writing a book about trail horses is a dream come true for me. It has made me think back to some awesome and awful moments in my life, to recall horses long gone and to remember on old friends. It summed up my life. I've certainly had the benefit of some hard-won learning, from which I hope to spare you. But more than nostalgia has prompted me to write a book just for trail riders. I felt that if trail horses were to get their due, it had to come from someone who knew them well.

My qualifications start with a true horseman for a dad and a true horseman for a brother. Dad was a bit of a horse trader, so every horse on the place had to be in good shape and ready to ride. Good horsemanship was demanded and excuses not tolerated. I learned to put my horse's well-being first, and I discovered that in doing so I'd ensure my own, especially when on the trail. I learned almost as much from my dad and brother as I did from the many horses that have come and gone through my life.

Over the years, I've trained dozens of horses and even done a little showing, but I always preferred to be out on the trail. Growing up in western Washington in the 1960s, I had access to hundreds of miles of trails, logging roads, and quiet country back roads. Most of my riding in those days was done solo, not something I would recommend today but still something I do. Like a lot of trail riders who enjoy the peace and quiet of the trail, I wasn't much of a "joiner," but I did enjoy ten years in the Washington state 4-H horse program, which stressed such important factors as horsemanship, herdsmanship (keeping the barn area tidy), and sportsmanship. This is a program I would recommend to anyone, since even adults can learn a lot from kids and horses.

As I "grew up," I was never able to shake the horse habit and almost always found ways to keep my hand in the equine industry, in one way or another. Working for horse vets allowed me to learn a lot from other people's mistakes, especially regarding what it takes to keep a horse healthy and sound, and how easy it is to jeopardize that health and soundness. Most cases of breakdown we saw could have been easily avoided with better conditioning and preparation.

For years, I dabbled in freelance writing for horse magazines. Eventually, I managed to turn my lifelong love affair with horses and obsessive nature into a dream job, helping to start and run a horse magazine called *The Gaited Horse*. This was the icing on the cake for me: I learned from the best horse people in the business and had the opportunity to explore issues with a variety of professionals, from exhibitors to judges, from veterinarians to research scientists. After more than seven years, I'm very fortunate to count some of the best brains in the horse industry among my friends and colleagues. They have certainly expanded my horizons and improved my judgment.

It has been said that good judgment comes from experience, most of which is the result of bad judgment. I've earned some pretty good judgment. So when I say *don't*, it's most likely because I already did it and it didn't turn out so well. You'll read some embarrassing stories that I hope will spare you the same misfortune. If I can save just one unsuspecting trail rider from a smack in the face by a tree limb, it will all have been worthwhile.

Because trail horses have not been afforded their due respect, I figured a little clarification was in order as to what it really takes to make a good trail horse. I've included information to help you understand how and why they respond as they do, as well as specific ideas for teaching your horse to

do what you want him to do and to stop doing what you don't want him to do. I've also thrown in some tips about staying in one piece on the trail, from the high country to the highway.

If you are considering investing in a trail horse, take your time and don't be misled by pretty eyes, a pretty color, or impressive names on the registration papers. This book will tell you exactly what to look for, what to avoid, and why. Some flaws are relatively unimportant, but others will leave you with a long walk home. If you are working to get a horse ready for the trail, or if you have a trail horse that is not performing up to par, check out the chapters on trail training and trail vices. Some of the worst outlaw horses I've known reformed into model citizens out on the trail.

Once a good saddle horse was so valued that horse theft was a hanging offense. Now racehorses and show horses bring top dollar while the leftovers are priced by the pound. When a horse that "cleans up good" and prances around an arena in circles is perceived as more valuable and "better" than one that reliably carries his rider through all kinds of terrain and obstacles, forward, backward, and — yes — sometimes even in circles, our perception of "value" needs some fine tuning. Of the nearly 7 million horses in the United States, it is the backyard horses that comprise the vast majority of trail/pleasure horses. They allow more than 4 million people to enjoy riding just for the fun of it and provide 317,000 full-time jobs with a $23.8 billion impact on the U.S. economy.

This book is for those owners and their horses, both to lift up that undeserved lowly image and to help develop the many and varied skills required to truly earn that most respectable of titles: Trail Horse.

CHAPTER 1

Get Ready to Ride

BEFORE YOU AND YOUR HORSE HIT THE TRAIL, HERE are some basics to think about. Just about any rider can enjoy trail riding (even riders with physical, mental, or emotional challenges), but not every horse has what it takes to be a trail horse. Before tackling this new adventure, it's essential to take inventory of your strengths and weaknesses. You may be surprised to find hidden treasures within your own abilities, or you may come face-to-face with your own limitations. Assessing your own and your horse's current level of ability will give you a realistic starting point for trail riding.

Why Trail-Ride?

If you are considering trail riding as a healthy, fun, wholesome, family-oriented outdoor activity, you will not be disappointed. It is, however, so much more than that!

Physical activity in the fresh air offers a chance to commune with nature, connect with your horse and other horsemen, and explore wilderness areas more extensively than on foot and more intimately than with a dirt bike. Adventure awaits you on the trail. You can start today, wherever you live. People trail-ride through Central Park in Manhattan, along the beaches and swamps of Florida, in the wide-open spaces of Montana and Wyoming, on bridle paths from California to New Jersey, in the rain forests of Washington state, through the high deserts of Arizona and New Mexico, and just about everywhere in between. Trails throughout Canada also offer diversity, from the temperate hills of British Columbia, through the high country of the Canadian Rockies of Alberta, to the lake-strewn regions of Ontario.

Trail riding will significantly improve your horse's condition and mental stability.

The Pacific Crest Trail offers the best (and worst!) of all terrains as it threads from the Cascade Mountains of Canada south through Washington, Oregon, and California and ends up in sunny Mexico. However, there is an easier way to enjoy international trail riding. Tours are booked almost any time of year around the globe: in England, Ireland, Spain, and Italy; in India, Iran, and Mongolia; in Australia and New Zealand; in South America and Iceland. One company boasts tours in more than 40 countries! (Check the appendix for specific information.)

The physical, mental, and emotional health benefits of trail riding are remarkable. As part of a regular regimen, it develops improved muscle tone, cardiac health, and mental clarity. It's amazing how troubles fade as you travel down the trail. You are much more likely to find yourself daydreaming about trail riding in the middle of an IRS audit than the opposite — worrying over your taxes when you are out on the trail.

Finally, trail riding is useful as a way to improve a horse's performance in the show ring. Relentless ring work can become boring for horse and rider. However, practicing the same maneuvers a few miles down the trail that he normally would practice along the rail adds interest to a horse's life.

Pick a tree down the trail and ride toward it in a straight line; ask for half halt; come to a complete stop; or transition from one gait to another. Stop in mid-trail and ask for a turn on the haunches. Cantering will bring new attention to form with no arena to guide (or slow) his progress. Ask for a trot, halt, or walk after short spurts of cantering. This variety accustoms a horse to working more off the haunches and not weighting the forehand; the constantly changing cues command his attention. Practice leg yields around trees. Look for hills to help build up your horse's hindquarters and carriage. Even at a walk, trail work builds muscle tone and endurance. The most skittish show horse gains confidence along with muscle tone over the miles.

But stuff happens on the trail. Your horse could get scratched or scraped, resulting in scars or white hair regrowth over an injury. He or she could lose a shoe, resulting in tender-footedness, which might alter his gait or leave him lame. Worse, it takes only one misstep to lame a horse.

This chapter is designed to help you understand what it takes for horse and rider to negotiate and safely enjoy the rigors of the trail. Read on to see where you both stand. Let's begin with the best horse for you.

Matching Horse and Rider

Undoubtedly, the most important decision you make as a trail rider is which horse to ride. Whether you already have a horse and are seeking to determine his suitability for the trail or are looking to buy, the same caveats apply. Limit the qualities you value to what works for you. This means ignore the pedigree and show-ring training in favor of those things you truly cherish — a gentle nature or an energetic demeanor, for example. Above all, for trail riding to be any fun for either of you, you and your horse must get along. You must have, or be able to develop, a real bond. The best horse is the best horse for you.

If you are not an expert trail rider, try to match yourself up with a horse with lots of miles under his or her hooves, or if your horse is young or inexperienced, be sure you have the skills to safely guide him or her through whatever the trail may hold, or ride with an experienced trail-riding partner.

PERSONALITY FIT

An indefinable something may draw you to a particular horse, but be on guard for false promises. Sweet eyes and a pretty head do not always make for a good ride. Be strict in your practical assessment, but in the end, go with the horse that just seems to click with your personality.

For instance, if you are an energetic person, eager to conquer the world, find a horse to match. Leave the plow horse behind. On the other hand, if you like to take it slow, the high-strung Park Horse may not be the best choice for a leisurely ride (however, the benefits of trail riding on this horse could do wonders for *his* mind and attitude). Be aware that some traits are best compensated for, not matched. A timid horse and a timid rider generally add up to a long walk home, but a timid rider who rides off on a dominant horse might be lucky to make that walk back. A laid-back, friendly, willing companion is best for those still working on their confidence around horses.

Suffice it to say, if you don't get along with your horse, or if one of you is in a hurry and the other desires to dawdle, personalities can be as important as any physical attributes or training.

RELATIVE SIZE

One of the most obvious physical characteristics to consider is the size of your horse. Good things

To Estimate a Horse's Weight

Be sure the horse stands still with his head up in a normal position.
1. Measure the girth area, about 4 inches behind the elbows.
2. Measure from point of shoulder to point of buttocks.
3. Plug the measurements into the following formula:
   (heart girth^2 x length) ÷ 330 = weight in pounds

come in small packages. Most horses can pack up to one quarter of their own weight in combined rider and gear, but should be asked to carry only about 20 percent for any length of time. This means an "average-sized" horse of 1,000 pounds should be able to haul a 150-pound rider, a 35 to 40-pound saddle, and 10 pounds of snack food or gear on a day trip with ease. However, there are always exceptions. Icelandic Horses are fabled for their ability to carry proportionately more weight than other horses, and donkeys and mules are renowned for their incredible strength and hardiness.

A tall horse can be a challenge for a short person, since trail stops are inevitable, and mounting blocks can be hard to find on the trail. Yarding yourself up the side of your horse can be inconvenient, embarrassing, and a strain on your horse's back.

Common sense says to match a big rider with a big horse and a smaller rider with a smaller horse. A heavy rider can tire a too-small horse and stress muscles, ligaments, and vertebrae. Too much weight, especially going downhill, can easily throw a horse off balance and further strain his legs and back, or cause him to lose his footing and slip, stumble, or fall. A rider who is too small or too light can be intimidated by a big horse, and may not be able to make effective cues, especially if the rider's legs are shorter the legs of than someone the horse is used to carrying. A small person

| Horse too big for rider | Horse too small for rider | Horse just right for rider |

Common sense says to match a big rider with a big horse and a smaller rider with a smaller horse, though exceptions abound.

astride a broad-backed horse will find the width forces her legs so far apart that it can be painful for even moderately long rides.

However, if you and your horse happen to be an odd couple size-wise, there are ways to make it work. Gadgets are available to make mounting easier, and your horse can be taught to take advantage of natural mounting blocks by sidling over to stumps and other aids (see chapter 5). As a rather unathletic kid, I was pretty good at finding logs, ditches, and stumps from which to climb aboard.

Evaluate Your Horsemanship

Understanding your own personal strengths and weaknesses is critical. You never know, in a trail situation, when your life may depend on them. Better horsemanship skills mean safer and more relaxing trail rides. Before you hit the trail, consider what you have to work with and make any necessary adjustments. Don't be intimidated if you don't have years in the saddle behind you, but don't overestimate your abilities if you have ridden nothing other than schooling horses in the confines of an arena.

The following section will help you to rate your horsemanship objectively and determine your own starting point. Almost anyone can hit the trail — today — provided both the horse and the trail suit the rider's abilities. But if you need to change some things or improve some skills, it's better to find out before you are miles from home.

PERSONAL ATTITUDE

Your outlook may not be *everything*, but it does affect every aspect of your horsemanship. The first thing to score is your comfort level. Do you already enjoy riding and just being around horses, or is the very thought intimidating?

Anyone with common sense will recognize that there is a significant chance of injury when trying to control 1,000 pounds of muscle with a horse-hair-trigger reaction time. Fear is the first thing most people must overcome just to approach a horse, let alone to mount one. But there is no better antidote for fear and apprehension than a comprehensive understanding of your abilities. If you are afraid, it's okay to admit that, especially to yourself.

Trail riding presents a tremendous opportunity to build self-confidence (for your horse as well as yourself, but we'll get to that in the next section). You have more to gain than just a fulfilling, healthy, fun hobby. Trail riding can literally change your life. Everything from the rhythms of your horse's movements and the rituals of preparation to the smell of the beast and the trail immerses you in a world all its own. With your attention concentrated on your mount and the trail, you soon find other concerns brushed aside. As your skills and confidence grow and you spend more and more time on the trail, you will find your attitude changing. The pace of life on the trail is exactly as fast as your horse's feet.

On the other hand, if you are already gung-ho for the trail, continue with this evaluation anyway. Caution yourself to be realistic about your abilities. A positive attitude is a great asset on the trail, as long as it is based on reality. If you are a show-ring marvel but don't have experience in the uncontrolled environment of the trail, you may need a reality check. The ring and the wilds (especially suburban wilds, where the laws of nature are skewed and the native *Squawkus bike ridus* can be your worst nightmare), are two different worlds.

Another aspect to attitude inventory is gauging your mind-set. Are you open to learning more? Every ride will have its lessons. Be willing to keep an open mind about what your horse and the trail can teach you.

BASIC KNOWLEDGE

Hopping onto the back of a horse with no prior knowledge is not much different from piloting a plane without first learning to fly. You stand a good chance of a crash landing.

While experience is definitely the best teacher, in this age of abundant information there is no excuse not to acquaint yourself with the basics of horsemanship before you ever touch a horse. In the same vein, even the most experienced horsemen appreciate the value of continuing to learn as much as possible about their mounts.

Do you know how to approach a horse properly? How to bridle, saddle, lead, cue, and restrain a horse? Do you understand *why* things are done as they are? Have you studied equine nature, physi-

Fit to Ride

Not everyone has a perfect body, but that doesn't mean you can't enjoy trail riding. It is the ideal equestrian sport for the physically challenged, and among the few sports that allow participants to start at any level and proceed at their own pace. Here are some examples for inspiration.

- Andy Mills, of Ellensburg, Washington, has been missing part of his right arm since early childhood, yet he is an accomplished horseman, avid backcountry trail rider, and top-notch Dutch-oven trail cook!
- Janey Blevins, of Springtown, Texas, learned to ride as a youngster, following a bout with polio that left her right side severely atrophied. More than 30 years later, the desire to ride was still there, but back surgery threatened to keep her off a horse for the rest of her life. She found the answer she needed in the smooth gait of the Peruvian Paso.
- Susie Wright, of Eolia, Kentucky, suffers from debilitating arthritis, yet she is a world-class rider both in Speed Racking competition and on the trail.
- In Minnesota, Tammy (last name withheld) was paralyzed from the chest down by a fall from a horse when she was 14. She has been trail riding on an Arabian ever since in a special packsaddle fitted with a brace. Just recently she had a Rocky Mountain Horse specially trained to her cues, such as raising and lifting her shoulders instead of moving her seat or legs.

For more information, contact the North American Riding for the Handicapped Association (NARHA). (See the appendix.)

ology, and psychology? Understanding the basic needs, motivations, and reactions of the species is fundamental in order to communicate effectively and ultimately work together as safely and happily as possible.

A rudimentary understanding of the nature of the beast and the best way to work with him is a prerequisite to turning yourself and your horse loose together on the trail. See the appendix for a list of general horsemanship books. You can't depend on your horse if he can't depend on you.

RIDING EXPERIENCE

For trail riding, horse-training experience is invaluable. If you have ever taught a horse a new behavior, you have insight into his mind that simply riding an already trained horse does not provide. You have had to plan ahead, read his reactions, adjust, reward, and possibly try different methods of teaching. These are the habits you want to foster on the trail. You never know when a strange obstacle or circumstance will require getting in touch with your inner Horse Trainer.

Even those with years of experience around horses can find the unstructured environment of the trail to be a challenge. Lessons in the ring do not prepare riders for the inconsistencies, obstacles, and wear of the trail. Show trophies won't prevent saddle sores miles down the trail. I'm not knocking show experience (any experience with horses is a definite plus), but I've seen too many capable ring riders overestimate their abilities and find themselves in trouble on the trail. So again, be realistic.

There are many ways to gain riding experience. Even the masters had their first ride. Many people find the relaxed atmosphere of the trail to be the perfect place to begin their equestrian careers. A calm, experienced trail horse, an easy trail, and an experienced riding partner can indeed be the ideal way to start "riding lessons." Others feel more confident with formal riding lessons in the confines of an arena. A good lesson horse has a feel for novices and can be very forgiving, while the enclosed area makes it easier for a beginning rider to focus on the horse, without having to keep an eye on what may be going on down the trail or coming up the trail. Horse camps are another a good way to gain experience and confidence in the saddle. (For more information, see the appendix.)

Some people feel more confident taking formal riding lessons in the confines of an arena before heading out on the trail.

SKILL LEVEL

Proficiency — or what the cowboy calls "handiness" — is where experience and knowledge come together. The higher your skill level, the more you will enjoy any sport; trail riding is no exception.

One of the nicest things about trail riding, however, is that there is a horse and trail for *any* skill level. You can start with the skills you have. Every trail will add to your attitude, knowledge, experience, and skill. Just be realistic about the horse and trail you choose.

Because learning is a very individual experience, some of us develop skills with much less experience than others, and some of us take longer to integrate all that information and experience into "second nature." For a true horseman, no move is accidental. Every shift of weight, movement of the leg, bend of the fingers, or tilt of the chin has its planned and foreseen consequence.

If your skills are lacking or rusty, be sure to ride out with an experienced buddy at first. If you are already an accomplished horseman in other disciplines, just remember that there is no ring like the trail.

NATURAL ABILITY

I believe horses can be in your blood. I've known people with no previous experience, who professed to know nothing about horses, to bond as naturally and instinctively with a horse as the farm kid who grew up with them.

Some people are empathetic. They "read" the horse, watching and gauging the animal's behavior and reactions. They seem intuitively to understand the horse's thought processes. Where one rider has to be told that when a horse raises his head, tenses his neck, and pricks his ears forward, he is focusing on something that may suddenly elicit a "flight response," another will register all that in the split second it takes for the horse to snort.

Experience hones natural ability, but some of us just start out with more ability than others. Horsemanship demands a keen ability to observe and connect the dots. It also requires a great deal of patience. Though nerves of steel are not a must, steadiness is a definite plus.

A self-absorbed, nervous, high-strung person will have a harder time accessing his or her natural ability to work with horses, but doing so can open up a new world of thinking. In short, you may have more natural ability than you know if you slow down and give it a chance.

PHYSICAL CONDITIONING

Fitness counts. You and your horse will definitely enjoy riding more if you are physically up to the demands of the trail.

Slack muscles tire easily. Tired muscles hurt. And hurting is no fun. Tired muscles also don't always do what we — or our horses — expect or intend. You shift your weight to ease an ache and unwittingly cue your horse to turn on the haunches or launch into a canter. Your shoulders slouch or arms ache and the tension translates through the reins, making your horse **jig** (trot in short, rough steps) or toss his head.

Approach trail riding as a physically demanding sport because it is. Lack of physical conditioning not only dampens enjoyment, but also can put a rider in jeopardy. Although your physical strength will never compare to that of even the puniest horse, your ability to control your horse depends in part on your strength and physical conditioning. Every aspect of riding a horse — balance, equitation, executing cues, and staying on a horse that shies, spins, or bucks — is affected by the rider's physical condition.

Self-Assessment

The next two pages present a chart so that you can evaluate your own ability based on the criteria we've discussed. Having an objective way to summarize your skills is important to your comfort, safety, and advancement in the sport. On pages 14 and 15 you'll find a similar "scorecard" for you and your horse.

Are You Ready for the Trail?

Use this scorecard to evaluate your strengths and weaknesses. For each area, circle the number that most closely reflects your ability, ranging from 1 (almost none) to 10 (expert). Then add up your score and figure out where you fit into the categories on the opposite page.

1. Attitude. The good news is that attitude is an area where you have complete control; if you don't like the score you start with, you can change it. If you are justifiably confident and eager to learn, give yourself a 10. If you are scared spitless and wonder why you were ever talked into getting near a horse in the first place, you score 1. Otherwise, average attitude scores a 5; adjust up or down as you see fit.

1   2   3   4   5   6   7   8   9   10

2. Knowledge. Score yourself according to how much you have learned, through either experience, observation (such as clinics or watching a trainer), or books, videos, and other media. If you are a walking encyclopedia of horse trivia, give yourself a high score of 10. If you are just starting your formal education into equine-ology, score a 1 and hit the booklist in the appendix.

1   2   3   4   5   6   7   8   9   10

3. Experience. Consider your actual level of riding experience and score yourself accordingly. If you have ridden for years, on more horses than you can remember, have trained several horses on your own and seen the results you wanted and expected, have ridden in all sorts of environments — show ring, trail, city streets, parades — then you are a 10. If you are preparing yourself for your first ride, you score 1. If you have ridden, but only on a limited number of horses or in a confined environment, such as a show ring or on supervised rides, give yourself a mid-range score of 5.

1   2   3   4   5   6   7   8   9   10

4. Skill. Rate your skill level according to how much of your knowledge you have routinely put into practice. If you instinctively navigate your mount around obstacles before the horse is aware of them, can rate your horse's speed or direction with a shift of weight or touch of your leg, and perform all the routine duties of horsemanship (feeding, tacking, loading, and medicating) without so much as a second thought, you score 10. If you have yet to figure out which side of his head the halter buckle belongs on, start with a 1.

1   2   3   4   5   6   7   8   9   10

5. Natural ability. The more easily horsemanship comes to you, the higher your score should be. Are you a "natural"? Do you sense what a horse is thinking or feeling, whether by direct observation or by just "gut instinct"? If you are patient, empathetic, and observant, you may well deserve a rating of 10. On the other hand, if the mind and body of a horse is a perplexing, large, and hairy mystery to you, start off with a 1.

1   2   3   4   5   6   7   8   9   10

6. Physical conditioning. Here is yet another category where you are in complete control of your score. Triathletes score 10, couch potatoes score 1. If you work out, walk on a regular basis, or generally stay fit, start at 5 and adjust accordingly.

1   2   3   4   5   6   7   8   9   10

Add up your score here. _____

Self-Assessment Scorecard

Using your score from above, you can now rate yourself in terms of riding ability and trail readiness.

0–12 *Tenderfoot.* Start with a well-trained horse, a well-groomed bridle path, and a good riding instructor or guide. Don't ride alone. Read, attend clinics, work out, and build up to challenges gradually.

13–24 *Tinhorn.* Stick with a horse that knows the ropes, but feel free to take on minor to moderate challenges that he is familiar with, such as fallen logs, light traffic, brush, hills, and longer rides. Ride with a companion.

25–36 *Brush Popper.* You are on your way to becoming an old hand, but exercise caution. You should be able to introduce your horse to new environments and obstacles, and take most surprises in stride. Be careful not to overestimate either yourself or your horse.

37–48 *Ranger.* At this stage, you should be able to ride your choice of trails on any good horse and work with young or inexperienced horses to some degree. Don't forget to prepare for long rides in advance and to carry emergency items.

49–60 *Old Hand.* Hills, water, fire, traffic, wild animals, rude or dangerous trail users, young horses, scared horses, or scared riding companions will not deter you from the trail. Be prepared to help others less confident or experienced.

Evaluate Your Horse

Horses can be confounding. They are generally similar and predictable in their habits and reactions. As prey animals, for example, they are pre-programmed to react in specific ways to avoid being eaten. They all hate to be off balance and fear few things more than being knocked off their feet. When they sense danger, instinct tells them to run first and ask questions later. Most will back down from an aggressive or dominant herd member (and that had better be you!) but some — mares that rank high in their own social order, and stallions — will strike back if you cross them.

Horses vary tremendously from one individual to the next, however, and you can't expect the identical performance, reactions, attitude, or ability from each. Some are nervous and never settle down to enjoy the trail or allow you to enjoy it. Others are so lazy they make a good beginning mount, and eventually they help build up riders' thigh muscles from the constant urging required to keep them moving up the trail. Some horses are reliable and gentle, others unpredictable and dangerous.

Most "problem horses" were not born that way, but were created by poor training, handling, or riding. A horse whose teeth were banged every time a bit was placed in his mouth, or whose ears were constantly mangled by the headstall, may be even more head-shy than the horse who has never been schooled to accept a bridle, or the unruly horse that just doesn't want to cooperate. While the cause is human error in the first case, lack of education in the second, and natural disposition in the third, the result for the rider is the same: a problem that will require time, patience, and hard work to overcome, *if* it can be overcome at all.

CONFORMATION, SOUNDNESS, AND PHYSICAL ABILITY

Conformation (or physical structure) is one of the fundamental things on which horses are judged. Not only is a horse's conformation directly related to our perception of equine beauty, but it is also critical to his functionality. A well-put-together horse can outperform a poorly built one, for a longer time, with less stress to his body. Little does it matter if his color is gorgeous, his pedigree impeccable, and his training worth thousands of dollars if he can't physically handle the demands of long miles under saddle facing unpredictable footing, hills, and obstacles, under the stress of a rider's weight. Before you consider anything else about a potential trail mount, you must determine whether or not he is physically able to do the job (see chapter 2).

Condition and thus physical ability can be improved, but you still have to work within the confines of what the horse's skeletal structure allows. Soundness is in part dictated by how those parts are pieced together and also involves such factors as past injuries and illnesses. For example, a horse that has been "winded" (suffers from heaves or chronic obstructive pulmonary disease) will never be able to handle the same stresses as a horse with a healthy set of lungs.

TEMPERAMENT

What's more important, a sound body or a sound mind? When the rocks slide out beneath you on the trail, you won't be debating one versus the other; you'll be darned glad you had the good sense to choose a horse with both attributes.

A good mind is in trouble if the body can't make good on its demands, and a perfect body is useless if directed by a fractured mind. Each is crucial and depends on the other.

Though all horses are basically natural-born cowards, some are more skittish than others, and a few start out life without a fear or care in the world. Though you can work with a nervous horse and build his confidence, you can't change his basic personality. It's the same way with a dud. No amount of prodding, threatening, or bribes will transform a dull-witted, slow-moving horse into an alert, active, energetic mount.

A good trail horse is willing and able to think on his feet (as well as being mindful and careful of where he places them), willing to take your direction, even over his own instincts, and doesn't panic and react in one fell swoop. Some horses, when startled, spin and disappear into the stratosphere faster than you can say, "It's just a pheasant." Others may snort, stop, stand still, and stare, and these "spook-in-place" horses are the ones you want. A truly bombproof horse has been trained to ignore sudden movements, loud noises, and traffic, but he will be expensive. So plan on starting with a horse with a quiet mind and building up from there.

It's also smart to consider how a prospective trail mount gets along with other horses. If a horse is turned loose with other horses, how does he react? Does he huddle in a corner, dive in after the other horses with ears laid back and teeth bared, or just hang out and appear comfortable? A horse with a nasty attitude toward other horses is no fun when you're miles from home on the trail. He may be banished to the back of a group to avoid conflict with and possible injury to other horses or riders, and he can wreak havoc when tied with or near other horses at the end of the ride or in camp.

It's important to consider how a prospective trail mount gets along with other horses.

The best way to tell how a horse will react when faced with new situations is to expose him to some and then stand back and watch. Obviously, this is easier to do with a horse you already own than with a horse you are considering for purchase. However, if everything else on your shopping list checks out thus far and you are serious about a prospect, many sellers will go along with temperament testing.

Begin with the horse at liberty in a pen and see how readily he accepts your presence. A horse that approaches you curiously is the best prospect; one that can't be caught may have had bad experiences or just a bad attitude.

Setting up the horse can reveal a lot. One potential buyer of one of my horses snuck out a balloon, blew it up, then suddenly popped it without warning (to me or the horse!). The horse didn't react badly, but I did. Plastic bags from the grocery store are also considered especially fearsome by a lot of horses. Rustle one, wave it in the air, caress the horse's neck with it. If the horse ignores it to begin with, he may already be an old hand, or just very quiet by nature. If he startles at first but quickly calms down and comes to investigate he's wary but curious and probably a great trail candidate. If he freaks out, clears the fence, and you never see him again, he's not the trail horse for you anyway.

PREVIOUS HANDLING

Probably the most important thing to consider, other than what you can see standing in front of you, is what you cannot see unless you've owned the horse all his life: the horse's past experience, positive or negative, with humans. A horse that has been mishandled, abused, or neglected may have ghosts you might not recognize, but that you will ultimately have to face.

In assessing a horse you don't already own, or have just recently purchased, find out who has trained and ridden the horse. Meet them if possible and go for a ride. Watch how they handle their current mounts. If you don't feel confident to assess their handling skills, take along someone who can make that assessment.

When considering purchasing a horse, don't be afraid to ask questions. How is he to bridle? Does he stand to be saddled or groomed? Does he bolt or run off when frightened? Better yet, try to observe these things in a prospect, and be brutally honest with yourself in assessing your own horse. A horse that tries to evade contact has been made uncomfortable and is trying to avoid further discomfort. For instance, when a horse raises his head to avoid the bit, steps away (or jumps!) when you try to saddle him, and either pulls his feet away or refuses to lift them, he is telling you that his previous handling wasn't the greatest. See chapter 8 for tips on dealing with specific problems.

The sum total of your horse's previous experience adds up to what you can expect from him until you can significantly add to that experience. If it has been excellent, you are in good standing. If it has been amateurish, inconsistent, unfair, or cruel, consider a different horse. No, it's not fair. Nor is it fair, though, for you to correct someone else's mistakes at your own risk. Unless you are a very experienced horseman, with the time, patience, and facilities to work with a "problem" horse, toss any tendency to feel sorry for him and move on to a horse you can enjoy.

MANNERS

Not long ago I bought a mare that was a stunning beauty on the outside and the witch from Helena on the inside. She was a half sister to my favorite mare, so my expectations ran high for her to be bold, curious, willing, and sweet.

She wasn't. She was bold and curious, but also oblivious to human frailty or requests, vicious toward other horses, destructive of fences, trees, and equipment, and just generally a real night*mare*. If you are faced with a horse that treads on your

toes, bumps into you when you are leading it, crowds you into fences or trees, or, worse, tries to kick or bite at feeding time, you have a serious problem. Horses like this can be extremely dangerous to the novice and nothing short of horrid even to an old hand.

Never let a horse walk into or on you. This is one of the few times it is absolutely acceptable to smack it. No horse would think of being so disrespectful to a dominant herd member — for fear of getting clobbered — so be sure you make your position clear: Don't tread on me. Moreover, seriously reconsider spending your quality trail-riding time with any horse that either doesn't know any better or doesn't care. When basic ground manners go bad, see this as a very clear, big, bright red flag. Think twice before you buy such a horse; he'll be a project from the start. If you already own one, take the time to increase your horsemanship skills so you can improve this basic relationship with your horse before you head out on the trails.

LEVEL OF TRAINING

Your next step is to assess your horse's level of training. A "broke" horse will:
* move forward without resistance;
* back on cue by bending at the poll, not bracing and stiffening his neck and body;
* quietly move away from leg pressure;
* turn as directed;
* stop on cue;
* go faster or slower as cued, and maintain an even gait in between;
* stand quietly for mounting, grooming, etc.

A well-trained horse will understand giving to the bit, collection, and lateral movement. Sound like dressage moves? They are also crucial components of the education of a good trail horse.

In evaluating a new horse, or your own horse with a newly critical eye, there are many things his behavior can tell you before you ever set foot in the stirrups. How is he to halter, lead, and tie? A horse that resists or crowds a handler on the ground needs a refresher course on manners. Such behavior can signify a lack of respect or just a general lack of experience. Often, frightened horses will crowd their handlers in search of security: not a good attribute in a trail horse being led down a steep embankment when thunder suddenly cracks. A horse that stands quietly to be groomed, allows you to lift, inspect, and pick his feet, and doesn't try to move off when being saddled or bridled is telling you he has a good bit of experience, and that it has been good.

Test riding will give you a good idea of what a horse knows and how well he knows it. Begin with the slightest cues possible and see how much pressure it takes, either on the reins, legs, or seat or with whip or spurs, to elicit the response you seek. If it takes multiple cues to move forward, there is either something wrong with the horse (ill, injured, mentally disturbed) or he is not trained to a base level of "broke." If he doesn't respond to slight neck pressure of the reins, he does not neck-rein, a convenient and easily taught trail trait (see chapter 5). If he moves forward or doesn't respond to leg pressure just behind the girth as you cue him to move laterally, it is likely he has not been trained for this. If you are considering buying a horse, ask the owner or trainer to exhibit his range of training. If you are evaluating your own horse, be sure your cues are clear.

ABSOLUTES: GENDER AND AGE

A few years ago I discovered how much fun stallions are to ride. They are bold, forward, and powerful. But only well-trained, well-mannered, naturally quiet stallions make reliable trail mounts. Any unruly horse on the trail can be a pain, but add a good dose of male hormones and "unruly" can quickly turn into "uncontrollable." Stallions are best left to experienced horsemen.

Mature female horses, called mares, can also be hormonally unpredictable. They cycle roughly every month or so and some display all the signs of PMS when they do. Their moods change, their energy level peaks and wanes, and their minds go on temporary leave. Riding a mare in season requires that you know your horse, and that she knows, respects, and believes in you enough to obey your cues against her own whims and moods.

Mares also tend to have very established places in the herd's hierarchy. An alpha mare claims her place in the herd by asserting herself. If you happen to ride an alpha mare and *don't* assert yourself more than she does, odds are you are going where she wants to go, not where you want to go. Mares at the bottom of the pecking order are pushovers, most of the time. They are used to taking orders and acquiescing simply to keep the peace and not get hurt. But be aware that if an established "lower-class" mare is suddenly moved to a different group of horses, especially geldings, she may suddenly decide to assert herself, sometimes with a vengeance. "No more, Ms. Nice Mare . . . I'm done being kicked around." Sometimes that attitude gets tested on a rider. Discourage any such testing quickly and decisively.

Even though many riders avoid mares because of their inherent quirkiness, others prefer them. They are interesting and emotional and tend to bond deeply with their riders if handled with fairness. Alpha-type mares in particular can be almost as bold and forward as any stallion and are a joy for the experienced rider.

The hands-down favorite mount for most riders, however, is a gelding. A gelding is a male horse that has been surgically altered by having his testicles removed. This is often done at a fairly young age (from six months to one year), interrupting the horse's natural development. Hormonal fluctuations are thus avoided. Growth is changed: Evidence exists that geldings tend to grow taller but less massive than their studly counterparts. Secondary sex characteristics, such as a full jaw and arched, powerful neck, never develop.

Because geldings are much steadier in their moods than either stallions or mares, most riders

Is Your Horse Trailworthy?

Use this scorecard to evaluate your horse. For each area, circle the number that most closely reflects his qualities, ranging from 1 (weakest) to 10 (strongest). Then add up his score and figure out where he fits into the categories on the opposite page.

1. Conformation, soundness, and physical ability. If you don't already have a solid understanding of equine engineering, refer to chapter 2 for a quick primer. If your horse is a poster child for appropriate construction, score him 10. If he looks like he was a put together by committee, assign him 1 point. The most severe conformational flaws are pointed out in chapter 2, so score accordingly.

1   2   3   4   5   6   7   8   9   10

2. Temperament. A horse that reacts to a new stimulus with bold curiosity, is willing and compliant, and just generally is fun to work with is a 10. A horse that bolts in fear, pins his ears, and threatens to strike, bite, or kick is a 1. A nice horse with limited "issues" falls somewhere in between.

1   2   3   4   5   6   7   8   9   10

3. Previous handling. The best-case scenario — you learn that your horse's previous owner was a well-educated, experienced horseman who put his own safety first and his horse's well-being a close second — scores 10. If it's the worst case — you find out your horse has been abused — score him 1 point. Average owners with average skills will rate somewhere in the middle.

1   2   3   4   5   6   7   8   9   10

4. Manners. A horse with a pleasant outlook on life does not walk out on you, complies willingly with requests, and generally has good manners. He gets a 10. A horse that drags you at the end of the lead, stiffens up when you pull the reins or the lead, turns his rump to you, or steps into you or on you needs some work before he'll be a safe companion out on the trail. He gets a 1.

1   2   3   4   5   6   7   8   9   10

5. Level of training. A well-broke horse that gives to the bit, moves away from pressure, moves forward, back, and laterally when asked, collects, extends, and responds to different levels of requests with different degrees of response is a 10. A horse that arches his back when you go to mount, refuses to stand for mounting or to go forward, or bolts in response to quiet cues is a 1. A horse that knows the basics (go, stop, turn) earns 5 points.

1   2   3   4   5   6   7   8   9   10

6. Absolutes — gender and age. This is the least subjective category here. If your horse is a gelding, odds are in his favor before he ever mouths a bit. Unless you have strong reasons to feel otherwise about your particular horse, score geldings 10, mares 5, and stallions 1. Score horses aged five to fifteen at 10 points, horses under the age of five score 5 points, and deduct 1 point per year for horses over the age of fifteen. If you have an older horse that is in superb condition, adjust his score accordingly.

1   2   3   4   5   6   7   8   9   10

Add up your horse's score here. _____

Horse Assessment Scorecard

Using your horse's score from the previous page, you can now rate his trail readiness and determine what additional preparation he will need.

0–12 *For Sale.* A horse with a score this low has little to recommend it as a trail mount. Consider the show ring or the sale barn, but please do not put such an animal in a breeding program. The only phrase worse than "He's just a trail horse" is "Well, at least we can breed her."

13–24 *Packhorse.* Horses in this category might actually make decent pack or pony horses while they develop enough physically and/or mentally to be trusted with a rider. Perhaps time on the trail will develop some of the characteristics required of a good trail horse.

25–36 *Rough Stock.* This is a horse for a rider with a wide range of experience, including training experi-

ence. He may have potential, depending on where he lost points, but he is borderline in his present state.

37–48 *Rookie.* Hop on and ride. Horses in this score range should be able to take on most trails with little trouble and accommodate a range of riders. This score represents many good qualities and is a direct reflection on those who have bred, raised, and handled the horse to date.

49–60 *Trail-Horse Prospect.* This is the horse everyone wants. He may often lead the group, pony young horses across streams, drag obstacles from the path, and generally just make himself useful. He will also be the envy of your riding partners and is worth his weight in gold.

If you and your horse have a combined total of less than 60, think very seriously about finding a different horse for you or a different rider for the horse. Matching inexperience or lack of natural ability with more inexperience or lack of natural ability will at best provide challenges that will require hard work and determination to overcome; at worst, it can get you or your horse hurt. It all depends on where you find your weaknesses. It may be possible to compensate for each other and develop a deep, respectful, abiding relationship. Listen to your gut instincts and proceed with open eyes and an open mind.

For those with a very low combined score, stop now, before you hit the trail, and have an experienced trail rider help you evaluate your needs. Lessons for you, training for your horse, or a different mount — now — before you ever set foot or hoof on the trail, could well save you monumental disappointment.

A combined score of more than 80 is a strong sign that you and your horse are ready to hit the trail with confidence, given the preparation this book will provide.

prefer them as saddle mounts, especially on the trail, where a sudden unexpected reaction could leave a rider on foot far from home — or worse.

AGE Another unchangeable horse fact is his age. Horses younger than three should not be under saddle. Neither their bodies nor their brains have developed sufficiently to carry a rider's weight while learning cues, but unfortunately, sometimes the commercial preference is to get them under saddle as early as possible. Time is money to horse breeders and trainers. If you are offered a "seasoned three-year-old trail horse," the best you can hope for is that the seller is wrong about his age. If the horse really has many miles on him at that age, he is unlikely to hold up well in the long run. The damage has been done.

A horse's body matures from the ground up. The hooves grow and harden first, then the lower limbs, and last the vertebrae in the spine and neck. These do not fully mature and harden for most horses until the age of five or six. Yet these most vulnerable parts of the horse's body are the ones most severely stressed by pushing them too hard at too young an age. A three-year-old can handle short jaunts on easy trails and work up over the next two to three years to more demanding work. The North American Trail Riding Conference (see appendix) will not allow horses younger than three to compete in its Competitive Trail Rides.

By the age of five most horses are mature enough for serious trail riding. Though it used to be thought that a horse was washed up by age twelve or so, now that is considered the prime of equine life. There are many reasons for this. Horses that are not pushed too hard at too young an age hold up longer to the stresses of a longer career. Most horses enjoy superior feed and veterinary care as compared to their counterparts of yesteryear. Perhaps the best reason is that horses are not generally considered "disposable," as they once where. Whereas the cowboy could always grab another mount from the remuda should his falter, the average horse owner develops a deep and lasting bond with her horses and wants to keep them, in good health and useful condition, for as long as possible. Fit horses in their mid-twenties can still be found out on the trail covering the miles as heartily as ever.

There are, however, limits for an aging horse. Just like humans, horses lose muscle tone, stamina, and balance as they age. Eyesight can fade and hearing can go, but the most common problem is tooth wear and loss, and the loss of body condition that goes with that. Horses that cannot process feed lose flesh and their body systems diminish.

However, as long as a senior horse is in good health and can handle the physical stresses of the trail, there is hardly a better mount to be found, especially for the novice rider. An older horse is more experienced (even if that experience wasn't on the trail). He has likely learned that overreacting doesn't get him anywhere and accepts strange sights and sounds more calmly than in his youth. Older mounts are generally more reliable and wise to the ways of how things work. An older horse may need some leeway in how much activity he can take before tiring, but he still has a lot to offer as a trail mount.

There is a trail and a trail horse for every rider. No matter where you find yourself today as a horseman, you can be assured of two things: Every rider can improve, even the best, and *you* can enjoy trail riding today. Some of us may need more help than others to get started. Some riders face physical or mental challenges that require the help of a fellow horseman to manage while on the trail. But the best thing about trail riding is that virtually any rider and any horse can participate, benefit, and enjoy!

Senior Class

Chris Culbertson, of Deer Park, Washington, has owned Kelly, a Quarter Horse gelding, since the horse was eighteen years old. "Before that," Chris says, "he was used hard. He was roped off from the time he was four years old almost up until the time I bought him." As of this writing, Kelly is thirty-one years old (comparable to ninety-plus years in human age) and is still ridden, albeit sparingly, in the backcountry.

Chris describes his last ride of 2003. "It was 3,000 vertical feet from the trail back up to the truck, so I was stopping every so often to let him breathe," he explains. "But Kelly would start to paw the ground, he was so impatient. He wanted to go." Chris attributes Kelly's vim and vigor at such an advanced age to several things. "For one," he says, "Kelly is a natural athlete. You can chalk that up to good breeding. But I think the most important thing is good care — good oral care, good feed, worming three or four times a year, vaccina-

tions. Horses today can work a lot longer than they used to because we can keep them healthier longer."

As your horse gets older, it's important to pay attention to signs of aging. If he takes shorter strides, moves more slowly, or resists or refuses to move, he may be suffering from arthritis, an ailment that can be caused early in life by hard work.

- Be especially vigilant about warming up an older horse, and slowly cool him down by hand-walking him after a ride.
- If he loses weight or condition, have his teeth checked and be sure he is on a regular parasite-control (worming) program.
- Commercial pelleted feed can meet all your older horse's dietary requirements and keep him comfortable and working years longer than hay or grain.
- Check his vision by seeing if he can follow a carrot or other treat with his eyes.
- Check his hearing by making a sudden noise behind him; see if he "follows" a sound by watching with his ears pricked forward.
- Most of all, allow your older horse to set a pace that is comfortable for him, give him ample rest, and don't push him past his limits.

As long as a senior horse is in good health and can handle the physical stresses of the trail, he can make an exceptional trail mount, especially for the novice rider.

CHAPTER 2

Trail Traits

⊳⊶⊙⊷⊲

W HAT DOES IT TAKE TO MAKE A GOOD TRAIL HORSE? More than he gets credit for. In fact, not just any old nag has the makings of a good trail horse. A lot of good racehorses, show horses, and competition horses wash out on the trail.

A trail horse must be sound in mind, body, and training. No other horse bears the responsibilities he does. He must not shy, spook, or "save himself first" — in other words, he must defy every instinct his ancestors used to survive. He must carry you and your gear through whatever obstacles arise. And he must know his job. Every trail is more training. Every challenge conquered adds to his résumé.

Attributes of a Trail Horse

The attributes of a good trail horse are many. Carrying his owner through trails fraught with unpredictable possibilities is no job for the faint of heart or head. He must be agile, smart, and of sound mind and body. A willing attitude depends on a strong body.

Literally anything can happen on the trail. There is no judge to stop the class and toss an unruly trail mate out of the ring. No steward to shoo off a noisy or nipping dog, should one appear. No arena fence to keep you on one side and the rest of the world on the other. Not even a rodeo clown to distract danger away from you, should it suddenly swerve and charge in your direction. Because you are so completely on your own, trail riding is potentially the most dangerous equine sport.

If you believe statistics, you are better off riding a motorcycle, safety-wise. What equine-related statistics don't take into account, however, is skill level. Every motorcycle rider has been trained, tested, and licensed. That is not the case with horsemen. So don't let statistics scare you off; they throw the experts, horse whisperers, weekend warriors, drunks, and wannabes all into the same lump and draw conclusions. You are educating yourself — that alone already makes you safer than "average." But even so, proceed with appropriate caution. Begin with choosing your trail horse wisely.

Built for the Job

Whether you are shopping for a trail horse or considering for the job a horse you already own, a thorough critique of any prospect's conformation is in order for several reasons. The most practical consideration is whether or not the horse will be physically able to carry you, safely and comfortably, on whatever type of trails you intend to ride. Other considerations involve *how* the horse will carry you. Will he be smooth riding or jar your joints? Will he tire and become cranky? Will he be

A good trail horse . . .

- Is of correct conformation.
- Is quiet minded, curious, and bold.
- Works willingly and shows interest in the trail.
- Is sure-footed and agile.
- Is tough, hardy, and of good wind.
- Moves out freely, alone, in front of, or behind a group of riders.
- Gets along with other horses.
- Stands tied without fussing, pawing, neighing, or weaving.
- Stands for mounting, dismounting, grooming, saddling, and bridling.
- Follows where you lead with confidence and respect.
- Leads behind you without crowding.
- Loads and unloads from a horse trailer on cue.
- Leads from another horse, and will lead other horses.
- Doesn't kick or bite other horses.
- Crosses mud or water without skirting off to the side.
- Navigates uncertain footing, such as steep, narrow, or brush-choked trails, with care.
- Knows WHOA (from the saddle or 100 feet away!).
- Backs one step at a time.
- Moves away from side pressure, one step at a time.
- Crosses bridges, downed trees, and other obstacles calmly and carefully.
- Will carry, drag, or pull whatever is asked of him.
- Accepts surprises on the trail, without panic, including mountain bikes, dirt bikes, hikers, backpackers, wildlife, pack mules, llamas, goats, and dogs.
- Spooks in place.

In truth, most horses labeled "just a trail horse" deserve a lot more respect. Becoming a trail horse is not easy; it does not happen in one ride. It requires excellent raw material in the horse to begin with, combined with your good, steady, consistent horsemanship in the long run.

able to carry extra weight should you encounter something unexpected on the trail that warrants it? Will he look good doing it, and does that matter to you?

A horse's conformation is his structural make-up. We assess this structure based on human needs and perceptions — how it either pleases us aesthetically or serves our purposes, not necessarily on what is best for survival. A horse that looks bad to us may perform admirably in a natural state. Our judgment of good or bad conformation, therefore, revolves around things we decide the horse should do and how we think he should look. A horse that isn't built to take the rigors of carrying weight mile after mile, up, down, over, and around, will suffer physically. That, in turn, will affect his ability, performance, and attitude.

Reliable weight-bearing conformation consists of a mature, strong, appropriately angled skeletal structure (covered with mature, conditioned, sufficient musculature). Think of the skeleton as a framework for the muscles, ligaments, and tendons that make up the rest of the horse. The rest of the horse is only as strong as the framework that supports it. No amount of muscle building can make up for a poorly engineered skeleton. To judge a horse's conformation critically, one must be able to mentally strip him down to the frame, assess each part individually, as well as how well they all fit together cohesively, and determine what can be improved through conditioning and what you're stuck with.

BALANCE AND SYMMETRY

The first thing to consider is whether or not the horse gives an overall impression of symmetry. If he looks good to you, odds are that he is basically balanced in his structure. The human eye prefers symmetry. On the other hand, if you can't put your finger on something that just doesn't seem attractive to you, it is very likely that the horse is unbalanced in some respect — back end too short to match with front end, neck too short, legs too

Conformation Counts

A horse that simply isn't built to take the rigors of carrying weight mile after mile, up, down, over, and around, will suffer physically and that, in turn, will affect his ability, performance, and attitude.

long, and so on. If all the parts of the horse seem to comprise an attractive "package deal," then move on to the next step of assessing one piece at a time.

FROM THE GROUND UP: AN OVERVIEW

My dad taught me never to judge a horse from the head down. I share the all-too-common tendency to look any horse in the eye and fall in love on the spot. Surely those eyes, so full of promise of our adventures yet to come, could never deceive. Somehow, over many years of following my heart and winding up with less-than-perfect trail companions, I have come to realize that those big brown eyes can indeed mislead, and even prevent one from noticing faults or flaws that become all too obvious at some remarkably inopportune time. Start, instead, at his feet. Not only will that prevent objectivity blindness (it's a lot harder to fall in love with feet than with eyes), but it will also give you a solid starting point of elimination.

Good feet are a must. I'll go into greater detail on exactly what to look for later in this chapter in the section called How to Assess the Feet. In a nutshell, they must be appropriately shaped and sized, with a strong hoof wall that is adequate to hold shoe nails, as many types of trail terrain require the horse be shod for protection.

Watch the horse from both sides, front, and back. Observe him at rest and in motion. All should appear balanced. Some horses appear to be "built downhill." This is most common in breeds derived

Damascus the Dream Horse

I was once the proud owner of a registered Peruvian Paso gelding named Damascus. He was my dream horse, for a couple of months. He had a classically handsome Iberian head, a low-slung croup, an elegant arched neck, a long flowing mane, and that smooth Peruvian gait: effortless, sweeping steps that angled out away from the shoulder and ate up the ground. Sitting on his back was like riding a horse on roller skates. He was incredibly willing for a horse that was supposed to be only greenbroke, and I was told he had never been out on the trail.

On our first trail ride, out with a friend on her horse, he was a model of good behavior. He went quietly up the road, ignored dogs barking and other horses calling and galloping around their pastures as we passed, and picked his way carefully through a logged-off area. He even crossed a fast-moving creek with no more hesitation than to put his nose down, sniff, and carefully step in.

The creek, however, proved to be the end of the ride. The other horse flat-out refused to get in the water. We even tried dragging the beast in, using Damascus as a pony horse, which he accepted without question and gave his all — although at one point I landed on the cold, wet, jagged creek bottom.

Admittedly feeling that Damascus was obviously a superior trail prospect compared to my riding partner's horse, I remounted my prize Peruvian and headed back home. Again, he picked his way through slash, passed dogs and horses, and ignored traffic. In fact, rather than rush home, like the barn-sour nag ahead of us, he seemed to be taking his time. Then he was definitely moving slower. Then he was barely moving at all.

Damascus was lame, but I couldn't tell where. I got off and walked the last mile home, stopping every few minutes to let him rest. He wasn't sweating, his respiration and pulse were only slightly elevated, but he was definitely hurting — somewhere.

When I got him home, pulled off the saddle, and started to feel for sore spots, it was hard to find a spot that wasn't sore. Apparently 2 miles was all he had in him. All his legs were sore; the area of his suspensory ligaments was swollen, spongy, and ouchy. His back was a tight, flinching coil. His hindquarters were tense and sore. These were the consequences of putting an unsuitable horse through more than he could handle.

Because I had always wanted a Peruvian, I took a free "rescue" horse and tried to treat him like a saddle horse. He had been happy and healthy in the pasture and had spent a joyous summer on abundant grass (with a creek running through it, come to think of it), never showing the slightest indication of soreness. But a short ride up a very mild grade, lifting his feet to clear snags, and then heading back had been too much for him.

The reason? Aside from that gorgeous head and neck, conformationally Damascus was a train wreck. He had a long back that tied in to short, shallow hips behind the lumbosacral junction (which contributed to that super-smooth gait). His pasterns were long and very low, bending to horizontal with the ground when in gait, another reason for that incredible smoothness. He was post-legged in the rear, and stood with his hind legs tucked under his belly. He was not built to carry his own weight, let alone mine plus a saddle. But I couldn't make myself believe he couldn't handle an easy trail ride until I had seen for myself. He was just too willing, too wonderful, and too incredibly smooth not to make a great trail horse.

Function, however, depends on form. Damascus couldn't stand up to even light work. Sick with guilt for putting him through such pain when I should have known better, I immediately made plans to find him a retirement home, at age eight.

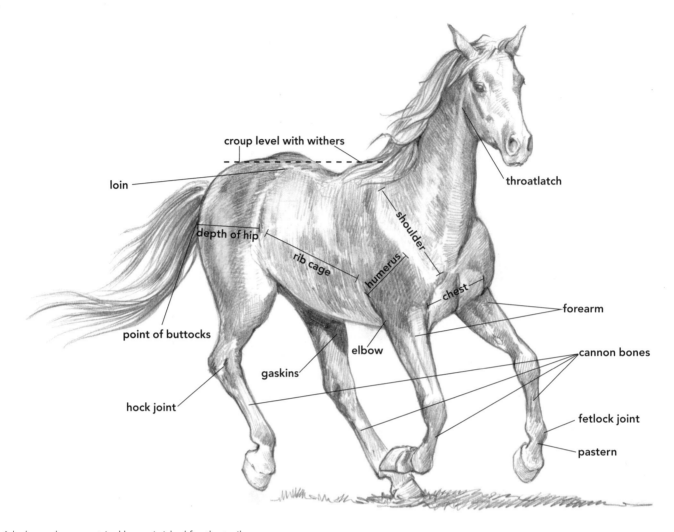

A balanced, symmetrical horse is ideal for the trail.

from the Quarter Horse and is actually a "good thing" in a sprinter, but not so much fun on a steep descent from the high country. Withers and croup should be approximately level and if they aren't, the reason is often in the leg structure. A long, sloping shoulder allows for a smoother ride. Depth of hip (the distance from the point of the hip to the farthest point on the buttocks or stifle) allows for strength in the hind end. A good rule of thumb is for it to be approximately one third the overall body length.

A short, functional back (measured from the withers to the lumbosacral junction) helps to ensure weight-carrying ability, but some leeway exists for certain types of horses in that a slightly longer back may allow for a smoother gait, which is easier on both the horse's body and yours. A functional back of more than 45 percent of the horse's total body length (measured from point of shoulder to point of pelvis) is considered long. In gaited horses, this tends to predispose the horse to pace. A functional back of less than 39 percent of total body length is considered short and inclines a gaited horse toward a trot.

Where the lumbosacral junction lies in relation to the pelvis also affects gait. Placement of the lumbosacral junction toward the front of the pelvis may indicate a strong back but can reduce a horse's tendency to do an easy gait. Behind it tends to allow for more lateral natural gait, but may result in a weaker back in terms of carrying weight. How much strength can/should be sacrificed for gait is one of the most controversial issues in breeding gaited horses.

The hindquarters of the horse are the source of his power. Measured from the point of the hip to the point of the buttocks, they should make up at least 30 percent of the overall length of the animal; shorter is simply weaker. The hind legs should attach to the hindquarters so that if you were to drop a plumb line from the point of the buttocks to the ground, it would fall even with the rear cannon and fetlock. This allows for maximum strength and efficiency in movement.

CONFORMATION CONSEQUENCES

Some aspects of conformation are more important for the trail horse than others. What matters most is whether or not your potential trail mount is built to handle the type of riding you intend to do. A horse doesn't have to have major conformational defects to have problems on the trail related to his structure. It largely depends on the terrain you intend to conquer.

Unfortunately, lots of conformational faults can adversely affect a horse's ability to carry a rider safely and comfortably. These include misshapen feet, long or weak pasterns, crooked legs, long cannon bones, knock-knees, straight shoulders, mutton withers, a too-narrow chest, a too-wide chest, long loins, a sway back, a misshapen rib cage, hip problems, and small or wobbly hocks. Other problems, such as small nostrils, a narrow throatlatch, a slab-sided rib cage, a long back, lack of bone substance, calf knees, small feet, post-legs (too straight through the hocks), contracted heels, and weak hoof walls can stress a horse's structure over time and/or heavy work and lead to a breakdown. The following procedure should give you sufficient information to assess your horsepower.

Before we proceed to judge conformation, I offer a word of caution about critiquing your horse by his breed standard. If you are assessing a horse that is a winner in the show ring or hails from a World Grand Champion bloodline, set that aside in your mind and look objectively at the structure that is actually in front of you. Sadly, what often places in the show ring as the highest representation of how a breed should look and move may not be structurally sound enough to make a good trail horse. Extreme looks can carry extreme consequences.

> *"Do not go from head to toe, but look instead from feet to head."*
> — Horseman's saying

Assessing a Horse

Here's a walkthrough of what, specifically, to watch out for in a prospective trail horse. Some deviations carry more-radical consequences than others. Mild deformities that won't matter on easy trails can make more-difficult trails a painful struggle, and as I learned with Damascus, if a horse isn't built to carry weight, it doesn't matter what else is

Beautiful Inside

Symmetry and image aside, even a horse that looks ugly on the outside can surprise you with what's on the inside. Niki Oliver considered her horse, RC, ugly from the day he was foaled in 1989. She described him as hide stretched over bone and hoped that his looks would improve as he filled out. They didn't. In fact, Niki took a lot of ribbing for how ungainly this colt was. When he reached the age of two, she planned to break him in order to find a home for him and be rid of an animal that just didn't fit her image of a horse.

He was sweet to the point of loving, which equine experts still try to tell us isn't possible. If Niki sat down in the pasture, he would lie down and put his head in her lap.

A registered Tennessee Walking Horse, RC's gait was a rough pace instead of the naturally smooth running walk that is the breed's signature gait. He was spooky on the trail at first, and always, always, ugly.

But RC had more going for him than met the eye. With a year or so of riding, the spookiness went away, and the sweetness stayed. On group trail rides, kids would bring him a pillow and blanket and climb all over him. By four years of age he was 16 hands high, big, black, and still ugly, but his gait had improved. That year he and Niki covered 800 trail miles in a flat-footed walk that left every other horse in the dust. RC went everywhere and became the gentle horse that everyone wanted to ride. His experience with novice riders made him all the more careful. He seemed to know instinctively how to take care of his rider. By the time he was five, he was practically famous. There was a waiting list of people who wanted to borrow him for rides.

In 1994 Niki and her husband, Al, took a 2-week-long break from the world and rode deep into the Smoky Mountains of Tennessee and North Carolina. They struck out on their own and reveled in the pure wilderness experience, far from phones, televisions, radios, and weather reports, riding for 20 miles a day and camping with their horses, RC and Stoney. They had no idea a hurricane was bearing down on the East Coast.

With each horse weighed down by 150 pounds of gear, they set out with light hearts for an overnight ride. It started to rain. They donned rain gear and pressed on. The wind blew, but they were ahead of schedule so they rode on. They found themselves on a section of trail that they later learned had not been ridden, let alone maintained, for years.

The trail was overgrown, on hills that ranged from steep to steeper, and both horses walked with their noses to the path. The going was tough but the only alternative was to backtrack, so they pressed forward. The wind and rain were relentless. At 5,700 feet of elevation the sides of the trail began to wash away. And then things got bad.

At one point there was nothing left of the trail but one strategically placed rock on which the horses had to balance, then cross 4 feet of nothing in one stride. RC managed to perch on the rock. Following the voice command of Al ahead of him, Niki remembered, "on his own, that big ugly horse crossed the expanse." Then things got worse.

They came to a large tree blocking the trail. It was too big to step over or jump. The only way forward was under the tree. The only other alternative was to go back down a dangerous trail that was washing out by the minute. Niki

and Al dismounted and ducked under the tree, twisting to avoid jagged broken limbs. To their utter amazement, both horses dropped to their knees and inched forward beneath the tree, all the while being raked by limbs, until they had cleared the obstacle and stood, pelted by rain, on the other side. They continued on, at one point having to jump over a tree and land on the scant 2-foot-wide trail that remained on the other side.

A little farther down the trail, the shale side of the mountain gave way, sweeping both horses downhill. Niki and Al managed to slide off and, holding on to roots and fingerholds, they watched and listened with amazement as RC and Stoney struggled to climb back up to them.

Just as they began to hope that they would make it out alive, the entire trail gave way beneath Stoney. First the horse, then Al slid out of sight. Al was rescued with a rope, but they had to leave Stoney until rescuers could return for him. It was up to an ugly horse to safely deliver both riders back to camp. With much of the trail washed out, RC, Al, and Niki finally did make their way back, only to learn they had survived Hurricane Alberto. Stoney was rescued the next day.

One moral of this story is to think twice about how you define beauty. For Niki, true beauty is a horse that knows his rider will fall off if he is not careful, that senses if his rider is frightened and carries her ever so slowly to safety, that stops when he hears her crying and waits to be told it's okay, and that, as the trail falls away beneath him, responds when his rider calls.

right with him. We'll start with the feet and go up from there, as my dad recommends.

HOW TO ASSESS THE FEET

Hooves do more than just hold your horse's shoes on: they also act as shock absorbers. Size, shape, and structure all matter. The sole should be well cupped inward, the frog fleshy and healthy, and the underside free from any discharge, greasiness, or off smells. The hoof angle should flow into the pastern angle. Abnormalities of the feet are clues to other things that go awry in the horse's body.

FOOT SIZE Do the size of the feet fit the size of the horse? Feet that are too small for the horse are actually fairly common, especially in Quarter Horses and related breeds (such as Paints and Appaloosas), Thoroughbreds, and gaited breeds.

Since small feet have less surface area over which to disperse the concussion of impact, they are much more subject to bruising, road founder (concussion laminitis), navicular syndrome, and plain old soreness than is a better-proportioned hoof. Too small a hoof reduces its shock absorption ability, stressing limbs, joints, and the rest of the body, and eventually leads to arthritis and ringbone (another degenerative joint disease). Small-footed horses are often sore-footed horses. Their short-strided, choppy steps can make the rider almost as uncomfortable as the horse is.

While special shoeing (egg-bar or polyurethane shoes) may help alleviate pain, it can't change the fact that a horse whose feet are too small for the rest of him is at a practical disadvantage as a trail horse. Lots of miles, hard or rocky ground, and downhill grades will all take their toll on him. In addition, small hooves often set the horse up for other problems, such as contracted heels and thin hoof walls, which again lead to pain and breakdown. If you plan to spend much time on the trail, be sure the feet fit the horse.

Adequate hoof size is relative to the overall size and weight of the horse. The size of a horse's hoof

---

What Will You Ask of Your Horse?

Those who ask no more of their mounts than a casual meander down a level, well-maintained bridle path will probably never find mild conformational flaws to be a problem. On the other hand, those who seek to surmount alpine heights cannot afford to hitch their intentions to any but the soundest of steeds.

---

should be ample enough to support the body of the horse plus the additional weight of tack and rider. For the most part, the bigger the better, except that extremely oversized hooves, often referred to as "dish plate" hooves, are prone to spreading out and flattening of the sole.

One objective way to tell if a horse's hoof size is appropriate is to compare his hoof or shoe size with his weight. (See page 3 to estimate weight.) Here are some guidelines; these will vary by manufacturer.

* Ponies and small horses (500 to 700 pounds) generally fit a 000 size shoe (4⅛ inches wide by 4⅜ inches long).
* Arabians and Cobb-size horses (700 to 1,000 pounds) often take a 00 size horseshoe (4⅜ inches wide by 4¾ inches long).
* An average-size (1,000 to 1,200 pounds) Quarter Horse usually fits a 0 shoe (4⅝ inches by 5 inches long).
* A size 1 (4⅞ inches by 5¼ inches) is most often used on stouter saddle horses (1,200 to 1,300 pounds).
* Size 2 (5¼ by 5⅝ inches) fits large-footed horses, such as those with some draft blood.
* Sizes 3 (5½ by 6 inches), 4 (5⅞ by 6⁵⁄₁₆ inches), and 5 (6¼ by 5¾) are for heavy draft horses.

To apply these estimates to an unshod horse, be sure that his feet have been properly trimmed

Hoof Structure

Hoof structure can be hard to assess because most of it is hidden beneath the **hoof wall**, the tough covering over the surface of the hoof. The hoof wall should be thick, smooth, and without rings, ridges, or cracks, and should usually be thickest at the toe. Rings or ridges can indicate illness or injury that may already have caused permanent damage.

The core of the hoof is the **frog**, which grows out from the heel toward the center of the hoof in an inverted V. Because it works to pump blood throughout the foot structure, it is sometimes called "the heart of the hoof." It is a callus pad that should come in contact with the ground with each step. It aids in traction and is also part of the horse's shock absorption system. A healthy frog should feel spongy when you press it, and should expand across the sole, as shown.

The inner foot consists of the **coffin bone,** a rigid, weight-bearing bone that establishes the shape of the foot; the **navicular bone,** which bears the **deep flexor tendon,** regulating the forward swing of the foot; and the **laminae,** which attach the hoof wall to the coffin bone and provide blood circulation.

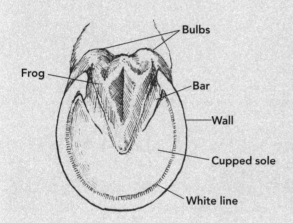

Bulbs
Frog
Bar
Wall
Cupped sole
White line

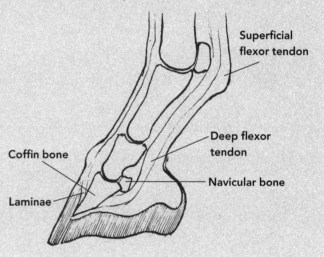

Superficial flexor tendon
Coffin bone
Deep flexor tendon
Navicular bone
Laminae

within the past six weeks, as the hoof can grow more than ⅜ inch per month. (Front hooves tend to grow out more slowly than hind hooves, and shod hooves slower than unshod.) Then measure across the surface of the hoof sole. Overgrown hooves are not the same as "big feet."

FOOT SHAPE The natural shape of a horse's hoof should be nearly round at the base in the front hooves and slightly oval (longer toes) in the hinds. Noticeable deviations may be congenital or the result of poor management, illness, or injury. The hoof wall should be straight from the coronary band to the end of the hoof. **Flares** (bends in the posterior hoof wall) signify that the foot is out of balance. The bend in the hoof wall weakens it and can cause cracks. If flares are not corrected, over time they can realign the structure of the hoof. A flare or inward bend at the front of the toe is called a **dish.** This can cause a horse to **forge** (hit the front feet with the hind).

Hoof angles are critical to a trail horse's soundness. The angle of the hoof is measured from the ground up the slope of the hoof to where it joins with the lower leg (at the coronet band). Too-low angles contribute to a range of hoof, leg, and back problems, due in part to the increased concussion they impart to the limbs. Too-low angles also reduce normal blood flow in the heel and make the toe land first, which can cause stumbling.

Today, the consensus of professional farriers is that in a fully grown horse, an angle of about 54 degrees to 60 degrees is healthiest. An angle of 54 is consistent with the hoof angles reported on wild horses of the American West living under conditions of hard, dry soil. On average, hoof angles of less than this put undue stress on muscles, tendons, and ligaments and shift more weight to the heels, often causing them to contract (see page 29). About the only time a low hoof angle is beneficial is in rehabilitating a horse that has foundered (see page 38).

Hoof shape can affect your horse's surefootedness as well as his soundness. **Coon-footed** horses, in which the degree of slope in the hoof is steeper than that of the pastern, tend to overstress the back of the fetlock, which can lead to structural breakdown. **Club-footed** horses, in which the front of the hoof is steeper than a 60-degree angle (often with high, steep heels as well), are notorious stumblers and quite prone to bruising or laminitis due to the impact of the hoof landing forward on the toe. **Mule feet,** so called because of the steep-walled, narrow, oval-shaped structure commonly seen in mules, are less effective as shock absorbers than properly shaped hooves and can be predisposed to the same litany of concussion-related problems. Mule-footed horses, however, are often

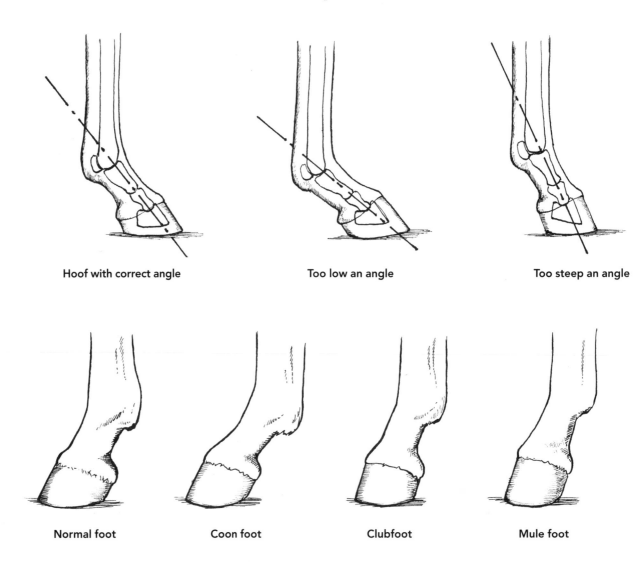

Hoof with correct angle   **Too low an angle**   **Too steep an angle**

Normal foot   **Coon foot**   **Clubfoot**   **Mule foot**

Hoof shape can affect your horse's surefootedness as well as his soundness.

noted for their toughness (even on rocky ground) and surefootedness (certainly mules are).

Hooves in which the walls flare to one side are often the result of angular limb deformities or misalignment of the bones inside the hoof. Beware of any uneven hoof development (often along with an uneven coronet band) as an indicator that something is amiss — perhaps genetic; perhaps due to chronic lameness that caused the horse to land not squarely; perhaps due to inept hoof care.

According to horse lore, white hooves are weaker and softer than dark-colored or black horn. With adequate protective shoeing, however, they don't, in fact, pose a problem.

Lift a hoof and look underneath. Flat soles can be prone to bruising, suffering from each concussion on any but the softest footing. **Contracted heels,** in which the bulbs of the heels pull close together, may be the first clear indicator of long-term unsoundness or stress in the legs. They are a warning sign that something is amiss in the limbs of the horse and can lead to further lameness problems.

Thrush can develop as dirt and moisture get trapped in the narrow space between the heels, and impact-related stress can aggravate sole bruises, navicular disease, and laminitis. Another problem is thin hoof walls, which tend to grow longer in the toe and lead to contracted heels. They tend to crack, don't hold shoes well, and have less shock absorption ability.

Finally, be sure there are no holes through the sole or spots that cause the horse to flinch when you touch them. These signify an abscess, which can put your horse out of commission for weeks. Checking your horse's hooves should be a regular, if not daily, habit.

FEET AT A GLANCE

Look for appropriate size, strong hoof wall, cupped sole.

Avoid clubfeet, coon feet, flat soles, contracted heels, weak or thin hoof walls.

FORELEGS: BALANCED AND STRAIGHT

Most horses naturally carry up to 70 percent of their weight on their front legs. Training a horse to engage the hindquarters brings his hind legs farther underneath his torso (closer to his center of gravity) and lightens the weight on the forehand, but the front legs still bear most of the weight and concussion. Therefore, straight, sound, strong front limbs are essential for a good trail horse.

Take a good look at the lower limbs from the pasterns to the knees and hocks. The legs should appear balanced and straight when viewed from the front. Look for sufficient bone to carry weight and withstand the rigors of climbing up- and downhill, stepping over obstacles, or pulling through plowed fields, sand, or even mud or water. A good test is to measure the cannon bone, just below the knee; on a 1,000-pound horse it should measure 7 to 8 inches around. Cannon bones should be short and straight, both front and rear. The joints should be large and smoothly joined to the lower limb.

Now feel. You should detect no puffy, hot, or spongy spots. This can be especially critical in the area around the suspensory ligaments and up into the branches, where early breakdown can begin.

Continue up the leg and look for length and sufficient muscle development in the forearm and gaskin, all the way through the shoulder and hip. Underdeveloped muscles can be built up, but a horse with visible muscle definition can take more work than a puny one.

STRAIGHTNESS Are your horse's feet aligned, toed in or toed out? Sometimes a horse that stands **pigeon-toed** (toed in) or **splay-footed** (toed out) will have other obvious conformational issues, such as a wide or narrow chest, that cause the hoof to land unevenly, putting uneven force on the hoof and entire leg structure with each stride.

Splay-footed horses often tend to **wing,** meaning that they will fling their hooves to the inside of

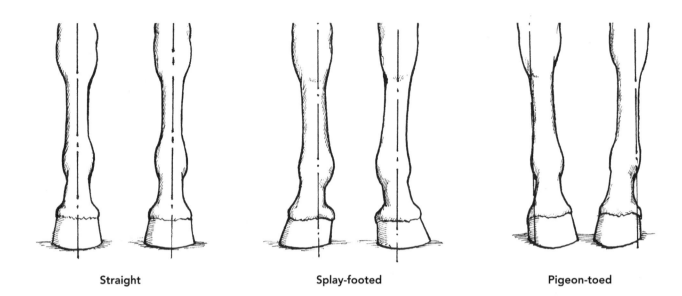

| Straight | Splay-footed | Pigeon-toed |

The straightness of a horse's front legs can affect his stride and motion.

the stride. This in turn causes one front leg to interfere with the other front leg, trip, and even fall. Lameness can be the least of your worries with a horse that falls. Scars on the inside of the fetlock and/or splint bone are clues that a horse strikes himself in motion and is not a great trail candidate for anything other than a slow Sunday saunter.

Pigeon-toed horses tend to **paddle** (fling the hoof to the outside of a straight arch of the stride), and while this poses less problem than a horse that catches itself with its own feet, the wasted motion and added stress can lead a horse to tire more quickly than a straight-legged horse would. Horses that show straight legs only to deviate in or out at the pastern have the added stress of uneven footfall landing that will inevitably lead to arthritic breakdown or laminitis over time and/or hard work.

BONE MASS You must determine whether or not a horse has sufficient bone to hold up to the work of carrying you and your gear. To test for adequate bone substance, measure around the leg just below the knee joint at the top of the cannon bone. The leg of a 1,000-pound horse should measure 7 to 8 inches around.

Again, the type of terrain and riding you choose will have a tremendous impact on the degree of bone you require in your horse. Knights in full chain-mail armor required heavy, draft-blood chargers, but even jockeys like to have the reassurance of a sturdy skeleton beneath them. Some breeds, including Arabians, mustangs of Spanish descent, and Icelandics, claim to have denser bone, meaning they can have less bone volume while still having all the benefits of substantial bone structure, but overall, adequate bone is something you can readily assess visually. An overly "refined" or dainty horse may not hold up to the rigors of life on the trail.

PASTERN The few inches of leg between the coronet band and the fetlock joint offer more insight into a horse's long-term soundness than does almost any other measurement. A general rule of thumb is that the length of the pastern should be no more than three quarters of the length of the cannon bone, but long cannon bones and long pasterns may balance in appearance while doubling the weak points of the horse. Add an extreme slope to those long pasterns and the horse will have a very smooth, cushioned gait, something that has been sought after and bred for by horsemen for generations.

Unfortunately, those long, sloping pasterns do not hold up well, and eventually tendons and

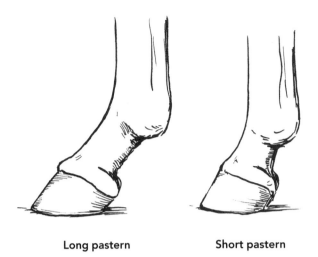

Long pastern **Short pastern**

Both too-long and too-short pasterns are subject to stresses that can lead to breakdown.

muscles become overstressed by the extra effort it takes to rebound from each concussion. So while the ride may be extra smooth, it may also be short and, ultimately, painful for the horse.

Horses with long, weak pasterns tend to develop suspensory ligament weakness (fetlocks drop), ringbone, arthritis, and other degenerative conditions. On the other hand, short pasterns (less than half the length of the cannon bone) make for a better sprinter than trail mount, as these horses tend to be quick but rough-gaited and prone to stumbling on hard surfaces.

CANNON BONE The **cannon bones** are the leg bones between the fetlock and the knees in front and between the fetlock and the hocks behind. Mechanically they can be compared to a lever arm at the end of a pulley system in which the knee or hock is the pulley and the muscles of the upper leg are the levers. The shorter the lever arm, the more efficient the system. Long cannon bones are less efficient in raising and lowering the lower leg and allow for more stress on the tendons and knee or hock joints than do short cannons. Longer bones require longer tendons to hold the muscles in place, which are less effective at keeping the lower limb secure than shorter tendons are. This is especially detrimental to a trail horse, because negotiating broken ground or inclines stresses the leg joints more than ground- or ring work does.

KNEE, FOREARM, AND ARM To function as pulleys, the knees must be in alignment with the rest of the system, strong, flat, and flexible. Legs that tie in below the knee, calf knees, bench knees, and bucked knees are all faults that unduly stress the structure of the joint, predisposing it to injury and lameness. Lack of flexibility in the knee and the hyperextension of the joint in bucked-kneed

Crooked knees will eventually suffer from undue strain with regular use.

Tied-in knee

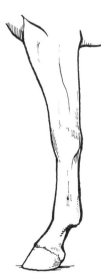

Calf knee

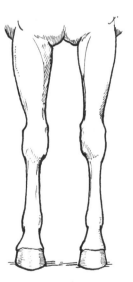

Bench knee

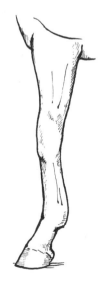

Bucked knee

horses makes them prone to stumbling.

The **forearm,** or radius, of the horse is the length of the front leg from the knee to the elbow. It should be long in comparison to the cannon, providing a good, long scaffolding for the attached muscles. Short forearms are often bred for in horses in which high **animation** (knee lift) is sought for the show ring. Though not a serious problem, the shorter the forearm, the more strides and effort it takes the horse to cover ground.

The **arm,** or humerus, reaches from the elbow to the point of the shoulder. If it is too short, the shoulder angle will be correspondingly narrow (less than 90 degrees), resulting in a short-strided, jarring gait that is uncomfortable to ride and stressful to the legs and forefeet of the horse.

FORELEGS AT A GLANCE

Look for substantial (even "coarse") bone; medium-length pasterns (from one half to three quarters of the length of the cannon bone); short cannons; long forearms and arms; and large, smooth, flatly aligned knees.

Avoid overly refined bone; long, sloping pasterns; long cannons; short forearm and/or arm; and any abnormalities in the knees.

ASSESSING CHEST AND SHOULDERS

Just as big, bulging muscles make a bodybuilder look strong, bulky chest muscles make a horse look powerful. And in both cases, they actually restrict athletic ability and flexibility. Typical of "halter-type" Quarter Horses, a wide, muscular chest is not as efficient as a more average-sized front end.

Just as an oversized chest is not an asset, however, neither is a too-narrow chest. In fact, narrow-chested horses, commonly seen in many gaited breeds such as Saddlebreds, Paso Finos, and Tennessee Walking Horses, may have problems with their legs interfering with each other, simply because the narrow base of their framework has the legs moving so close together. They may also have a tough time bearing up under a heavy rider. A narrow chest may also be a sign of poor development, malnutrition, or lack of condition. The shoulder and neck often reflect the same lack of development.

The chest should allow ample room for a horse to expand his lungs, but not be so wide that it restricts the stride of the front legs. Narrow horses often appear to have both front legs "coming out of the same hole," while wide horses stand with a bulldog stance. Look for a happy medium.

Shoulders play a huge part in the length of stride and quality of ride. A short, steep shoulder makes the horse work harder for every step and jars the rider with each impact. The impact on the front legs and feet is magnified, which puts them at higher risk for wear and injury. A shoulder angle of between 45 and 55 degrees provides a good attachment for the muscles that work the legs, allowing for freedom of motion for a good stride.

CHEST AND SHOULDERS AT A GLANCE

Look for medium width in the chest and a long, laid-back, sloping shoulder.

Avoid too wide or too narrow a chest and/or short, steep shoulders.

HIND LEGS: THE POWERHOUSE

The hindquarters are the powerhouse of the horse's body. They provide impulsion and acceleration. The bigger the hindquarters and supporting structures, the better, although ideally they should balance with the front end of the horse.

The same structural preferences for the pasterns, fetlocks, and cannon bones apply to the hind legs as the front. Things to watch out for include weak or crooked hocks, short or weak gaskins, and small, weak hindquarters.

HOCKS The hocks should be just a bit higher than the knees, but if the cannons are too long and/or the gaskins too short, the hocks will appear

Ideal shoulder conformation

Short, steep shoulder

Shoulder conformation is directly related to length and height of stride.

too high. In the extreme, this causes the whole horse to tilt "downhill" from back to front. This condition frequently accompanies sickle hocks (see below) and commonly leads to **forging** (over-reaching and clipping the front feet with the hinds). Conversely, too-long gaskins make it difficult for the horse to get his hocks underneath himself and often result in the hocks appearing to rest too low, in a sickle- or cow-hocked stance, causing short strides in the hind legs.

It is important for the hocks to be large and smooth, as undersized hocks are weak and subject to wear, injury, and degenerative joint disease. Think of the hocks as the rear-end pulley over which the tendons and muscles pull to operate the lower legs. Small equals weak and inefficient.

How the hocks tie in to the rest of the legs also affects the horse's movement and soundness. **A sickle-hocked** horse is one in which the cannon comes out from the hock at a forward angle. Contrary to horse lore, this does not make for a more nimble horse by mechanically placing the hind legs more underneath him; it makes for a horse subject to distended tendons and/or degenerative joint disease due to the closed angle of the hock and the stress this constantly places on the back of the joint.

The reverse, a horse that is **camped out** behind (stands with the hind legs behind the point of the buttock), is at a practical disadvantage for getting his hind end under himself. This conformation creates extra work and stress on the horse's legs as they kick back behind the horse during each stride before setting down. The lack of support beneath the body also predisposes the horse to back stress and/or injury.

Cow-hocked horses are those in which the hocks point inward, toward each other. Such horses are also subject to uneven stress load on the hock joints and to twisting of the fetlocks each time a hoof hits the ground. They tend toward uneven hoof wear, bruising and cracking, and stress-related wear on the inside hock joint.

Another fault is a **post-legged** horse, common in racing lines and some gaited types, in which the angle of the hock is so wide that the back legs look nearly straight. This puts significant tension on the hock and suspensory ligaments and over time can lead to spavin, cartilage damage, and breakdown of the suspensories.

HINDQUARTERS Even though a trail horse does not face the same demands as a jumper or dressage prospect, a powerful back end is an

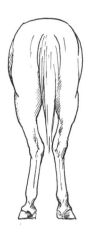

| Normal hocks | Cow-hocked | Camped-out | Sickle-hocked | Post-legged |

Hind-limb conformation affects thrust of stride and long-term soundness.

absolute must for scaling hills and covering miles and miles of trails.

In some horses, especially many of Spanish descent and some draft horses, the pelvis is very steep and the croup drops off in what is called a **goose rump.** Though speed is affected, the bigger problem for the trail horse is the extra load placed on the lumbar spine and the greater risk of injury.

Short hips (and the appearance of high stifles) have been bred for in speed horses, but ultimately result in a short-strided, choppy gait on the trail.

Narrow hips are yet another bred-for characteristic (primarily in speed horses) that can confound the trail horse by allowing his too-close-together legs to interfere with each other, leading to injury or stumbling. Horses who have suffered a traumatic injury sometimes have one hip lower than the other, which is one more reason why it is important to view a prospective trail horse from all angles. Unevenness inevitably leads to soreness.

HIND LEGS AT A GLANCE

Look for short cannons; strong, properly angulated hocks; depth of hindquarters and hip.

Avoid overly long or too-short gaskins; short or too-narrow hips.

WITHERS, BACK, AND RIB CAGE

If you ride with a saddle, then a well-constructed set of withers is important. It's that simple.

The withers are part of the horse's spine, comprising the eighth through the twelfth thoracic vertebrae. They provide the lever that allows the muscles of the neck and back to work together. Poorly developed withers can be more than just an inefficient lever; they can be downright dangerous. Flat, wide withers, often called **mutton withers,** provide no stopping point to anchor the saddle. The angle of a steep downhill grade can thrust the saddle and the rider's weight onto the forehand of the horse, putting tremendous strain on his front legs and throwing him off balance, often in the worst part of a steep, twisting trail. On the other hand, very prominent or high withers can cause saddle-fitting problems that either force the saddle back off the withers or cause it to pinch at the withers, either way resulting in soreness. Some horses have a slight dip behind the withers that can cause the saddle to **bridge** (ride high over the dip) and pinch at the withers, again leading to pain in the back and withers.

A horse's back is considered long if the distance from withers to the highest point of the croup is more than one third of his overall body length. Never forget that your fate (not just your weight)

Normal back, withers, head, and neck

Flat, wide withers

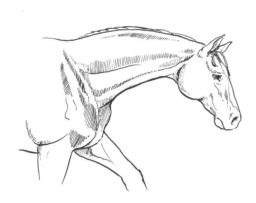

Too long a neck

Prominent withers

rests on the back of your trail horse. It's not realistic to expect a horse with a weak back to carry you home, every time. Be especially leery of a horse with a long or weak back and loins if you ride in the mountains: This stretched-out structure makes it nearly impossible for a horse to balance going downhill.

A horse with a high croup looks like he is built "downhill." Because his weight is shifted forward, such a horse weighs the forehand and can be rough-gaited and off balance, especially on hills. Sore shoulders and withers will be common as the weight of the saddle and rider is forced forward. But don't rule out a high-crouped young horse too quickly, as he is a work in progress and the withers often catch up with the croup by age four.

Also avoid a low-backed or **sway-backed** horse.

Ewe neck

Good withers provide a natural stop for the saddle. The neck acts as a counterbalance to the rest of the body.

This refers to an obvious dip along the spine, which is a sign of weak ligaments in the back. It may be caused by old age, poor condition, injury, or overuse. It is also a common consequence of bearing many foals. Low-backed conformation, as is sometimes seen in Saddlebred Horses, forces the rider behind the horse's center of gravity, leading to back soreness. It is often accepted in gaited horses, since shifting the rider's weight to the rear is one way of manipulating gait.

The depth of the chest and rib cage affects saddle fit and how comfortably you can sit your horse. A wide-bodied horse can force your legs to the side, stressing your hips and pelvic joints. Horses with a pear-shaped rib cage, narrow in front and wider toward the flanks, can make keeping a saddle in place difficult. Constant shifting chafes, making you and your horse weary and uncomfortable, and can be tedious and even dangerous when riding in varied terrain. The same applies to a **slab-sided** horse (one with a narrow rib cage), with the added problems of less lung capacity.

WITHERS, BACK, RIB CAGE AT A GLANCE

Look for average to somewhat prominent withers; a strong, moderately short back; and ample, well-sprung ribs.

Avoid flat, wide "mutton" withers; too-high withers; long, weak, and/or low backs; and pear-shaped or slab-sided rib cages.

NECK AND HEAD: LENGTH AND SHAPE

While admittedly few aspects of your horse's neck and head will have a significant impact on his suitability as a trail horse, there are a few things to be aware of, including what those gorgeous eyes can really tell you.

A horse's neck should be long enough to serve as a graceful counterbalance for negotiating obstacles or tough terrain. Good trail horses like to put their heads down and watch anything on the trail that concerns them. The curve of the throatlatch should be obvious and fairly fine. This allows the horse to breathe easily, whether his head is up or down or his neck is arched.

Too long of a neck, however — significantly longer than the body length of the horse — carries some serious disadvantages. The extra length adds more weight to the front end of the horse, which affects balance, especially on hilly terrain. Long, slender necks are also associated with other problems, including Wobbler's syndrome, in which the vertebral canal compresses the spinal cord.

Another problem to avoid is the **ewe-necked** horse, one whose neck dips along the top and bulges along the bottom. Ewe necks often develop as a result of malnutrition and poor development. However, the lower neck bulge can be a warning sign that the horse has habitually misused his neck, due either to extremely poor riding, whereby he has learned to lean heavily on the bit, or to **stargazing,** in which he carries his head high. Such horses tend to be unpredictable (as the odd head carriage impairs their balance and vision), uncoordinated, and rough to ride.

The shape of a trail horse's head may not seem important, but despite the common adage "You don't ride his head," there *are* some important things to consider. Nostrils should be large enough to draw in air efficiently. Eyes should be clear, bright, and without cloudy spots or "floaters." Horses with eyes that face forward as much as possible have a better range of binocular vision and as a result tend to be more confident.

Other things to watch out for are any neck or head components that can restrict the free flow of air, such as a too-narrow throatlatch and jaw, small nostrils, and an extremely concave (dished) face. Also, avoid **parrot-mouthed** horses, whose upper lip and jaw structure extend forward past the lower, as they can develop eating problems that make it difficult to keep them in condition.

WHAT THE EYES CAN REALLY TELL YOU Finally, it's time to gaze into those soulful eyes. A horse's eyes are expressive and reflect many things, from his health to his state of mind. They should be set fairly well forward in a trail horse to allow for maximum binocular vision toward the front of his range of sight (a range of 60 to 70 degrees). A horse can see in roughly a 350-degree field of vision, with blind spots directly in front of the nose and behind the head, depending on how he carries his head.

In some breeds, such as the Appaloosa, Morgan, and American Saddlebred, quite a bit of the **sclera** (the outer covering of the eyeball, visible surrounding the iris) is normally white and prominent. Otherwise, a "bug-eyed" horse (with white of eye visible) is a stressed, nervous, or hurting individual, and something to avoid, or at least to question.

The eyes should be clear. Occlusions or injuries can lead to permanent impairment that will severely curtail a horse's usefulness on the trail. A horse's eye that has been injured will have a bluish tint to it. **Moon blindness,** or recurrent uveitis, comes and goes, as the name implies, and over a few years renders the horse blind. When active, it appears as a bluish white blob over the surface of the eye.

Your horse can see things in binocular vision for roughly half his ocular scope, which means he sees them the same way you do when looking at them head-on (except for things directly in front of his face at close range). But things in his peripheral vision are perceived differently — and processed in his brain as a separate picture from each eye. Almost anything can look like a monster when it approaches a horse from this field of view. Considering the wide range of a horse's field of vision, it is little surprise that some things that seem really silly can scare the bejeebers out of him if first seen from an angle of poor focus. So lest those eyes lead you on, look at them foremost as a means for processing visual information, and not until you've considered the rest of the horse as the windows to his soul.

NECK AND HEAD AT A GLANCE

Look for a long (but not too long) neck; adequate-sized nostrils; clear eyes.

Avoid a too-narrow throatlatch or jaw; small nostrils; parrot-mouthed horses.

Health Issues

A lot of things can compromise a horse's overall health, some of which are no more important than a cold, others of which can be debilitating. It's wise to have your veterinarian check any horse you are considering for purchase, or even a horse you already own and are considering training for trail. There are plenty of things, however, that you can look for on your own.

A healthy horse looks, well, healthy as a horse. There is a shine to his coat and a light in his eye. There is no discharge from eyes, nose, or genital area. His coat is smooth and glossy in summer, thick and luxurious in winter. He is alert and interested. He moves smoothly and evenly.

Be especially leery of any lameness or back soreness. Feel for swelling or heat in his legs and back. Some injuries heal and leave no permanent damage, save maybe a scar (which can leave the skin tender in the area indefinitely). **Windpuffs** (swellings in the synovial fluid of the fetlock joints) come and go and may never really bother most horses, but in others can be a harbinger of

Evidence of Founder

Watch out for **fever rings**, horizontal ridges that form on the hoof when a horse founders. A horse that has **foundered** (developed an advanced case of laminitis) may be predisposed to repeating bouts.

Founder and laminitis are not exactly interchangeable terms. **Laminitis** is an inflammation of the **laminae** (connective tissue) within the hoof, which leads to detachment of the third phalanx (the main "toe bone" housed within the hoof wall, called PIII by your vet). **Founder** is the "sinking" and forward tipping or rotation of the third phalanx of the foot that accompanies an advanced case of laminitis.

A foundered horse is in extreme pain and may not even be able to stand due to the pressure within his feet. Early phases of the disease show up as tenderfootedness (walking on eggshells) or just a stiff, unnatural gait, with the horse putting as much weight as possible on his hind legs if the fronts are involved (most common).

A chronic case of laminitis can last from nine months (the time it takes to regrow the hoof wall) to the rest of the horse's life. If a horse's gait is off or he walks as though his feet hurt, he is not a trail-horse prospect for the time being. He could just be stiff from a workout or sore from a too-close trim. When in doubt, consult your vet.

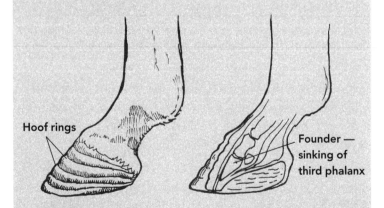

Hoof rings

Founder — sinking of third phalanx

Hoof rings on the outside warn of structural changes in the hoof wall and foot.

things to come. At the very least they indicate that there is a problem somewhere, such as a history of misuse over hard surfaces, improper shoeing or trimming, or faulty structure in the fetlock joint itself. Hocks that wobble from side to side when the horse moves, for example, can indicate crookedness in action. **Shin splints** (bumps along the cannon bone) reveal that the horse has been worked hard on hard surfaces and may be predisposed to arthritic problems down the road. Arthritis can be evident as a slowness to start out or reluctance to move. And just as for us, it tends to worsen in wet, cold weather or before a storm.

If the horse is a mature saddle horse, check to see if he is shod. The shoes aren't important, but knowing that the horse's hooves are adequate to shoe if necessary is a plus. If there are no shoes, check for nail holes, and if there is no evidence of shoeing, ask why. Be cautious of large cracks in the hoof wall or quarter cracks in the heel. These flaws don't mean you can't make an excellent trail horse out of your prospect, but they do mean you will have to spend some time and money rehabilitating his feet first. If a horse has very overgrown feet, find out why. It could be that he has been neglected or is difficult to trim.

Horses that have been ridden poorly (too much weight, weight too far back on the spine, in hollow frame, etc.) often tend to break down over time. Look for early warning signs such as low back (swayback) or back soreness.

Watch for signs of infection or infestation. Lethargy, fever, discharge, or other symptoms foretell disease. A rubbed-off tail head, rough coat, potbelly (also common in youngsters), and exposed ribs all signal parasitic infestation. Be aware that a severely malnourished horse or one that has been undernourished over a long period of time, especially while growing up, may never recover to the degree it takes to make a sound and reliable trail horse. Significant neglect can cause long-term damage to internal organs and leave a horse subject to repeated bouts of colic.

Pay particular attention to a horse's wind. Horses with "broken wind" (see chapter 4) will never be able to handle long or physically challenging trails. Check his wind by warming the horse up, then working hard for a few minutes until he is breathing hard. A winded horse may cough right from the beginning. Warning signs are a nasal discharge and wheezing or whistling as he exhales. His sides will double-heave on exhaling.

Temperament

Your horse reacts to his world, you, training, and the trail in ways that arise from his natural temperament as well as from his experience to date. It doesn't matter whether his reactions are based on inborn characteristics or learned ones — either way, you have to deal with them. But while many things can be altered with training and experience, a horse's temperament, or attitude, is as much a part of his basic makeup as his conformation is. It really won't change much over his lifetime.

Temperament varies tremendously from horse to horse. For example, the flight response is common to all horses, but some tend to bolt the instant something registers on their radar, others stand their ground to watch or even investigate further, and the rare few will challenge (fight) rather than flee. Some horses have more natural confidence than others, some are energetic, some lazy, some sensitive, some thick-skinned, some very interested in new things, others not so curious. Whatever your horse's temperament, it will dictate how he reacts to any given situation before he has time to think about it.

TEMPERAMENT ON THE TRAIL

A horse of any temperament will benefit from time spent on the trail. A shy or nervous horse can gain a tremendous amount of confidence from positive experiences in a relaxed atmosphere. Dominant horses, those that can really test a rider's patience and resolve because they expect to lead and not follow, learn to accept their rider's judgment and guidance mile by mile. Lazy horses often perk up when there is a change in routine and atmosphere (such as arises at each bend in the trail), and the horse that never slows down often relaxes, both mentally and physically, as the miles flow behind him.

Even so, a horse that doesn't have a good natural temperament just doesn't allow you to relax and enjoy the trail as much as one that does. Trail riding should be as much about being out on the trail and communing with nature, leaving your troubles behind, slowing down to a manageable pace, and renewing your mind and sense of peace as it is about "riding." A good trail horse rarely detracts from that precious experience.

This is where temperament is key. A nervous horse is exhausting on the trail. You must be on guard constantly, watching ahead in case something sets him off. A lazy horse will certainly help you to develop your leg muscles as you keep urging him forward. A dominant horse that questions your authority will keep you constantly alert. So while all these types of horses can ultimately benefit from trail riding, they are not as naturally suited to the task as a confident, energetic but laid-back individual.

SENSITIVITY

We've all seen a sensitive horse. He leaps when he gets a shot, quivers in the wind, or withdraws and won't face you after you yell at him. There are degrees of sensitivity, and while no one likes a dud, an oversensitive "stress-case" horse is no fun either.

Sensitive horses are often tense and tend to overreact to stimuli. Translation: They are "spooky." A sensitive horse can be a challenge as a trail horse because often he has tense (sore) muscles due to anxiety, and you never know what he might react to, or how. Strange sights, smells, sounds, or movements are all potential "spooks" to a sensitive horse. Sensitive horses also tend to be more aware of pain.

On the upside, they are also reactive to cues and corrections. While you might have to boot a less sensitive horse to get him moving, a subtle nudge will motivate a more sensitive horse.

The opposite of a sensitive horse is a horse that plods along, seemingly sleepwalking down the trail. Horses like this can make good trail mounts for fearful riders, but to a more experienced rider can be disappointing in their unresponsiveness. While an insensitive horse ignores your mistakes, he ignores a lot of your aids as well.

Test your horse's sensitivity by suddenly clapping your hands loudly or flapping your coat near his head. A sensitive horse may wheel and not stop until he is at a "safe" distance, while an insensitive horse may not even look up. Generally, the most sensitive horses are not the best suited for the trail, but a good rider and good trail experiences can do wonders for their confidence. The entire experience of trail riding, and all of the training exercises that follow to that end, essentially boil down to building confidence, skill, and agility . . . all rolled into one happy trail horse.

PERSONALITY AND INTELLIGENCE

Another consideration is your horse's personality. Whether he is loving or aloof, curious or oblivious, these qualities affect your relationship with him and therefore your enjoyment of time spent with him. A horse that likes people will follow you around the pasture, or follow you with his eyes as you move around the barn. How important is this on the trail? No more important than the personality of the friends you ride with, but it's part of the package deal of your horse. It's always nicer to spend time with someone you get along with.

Intelligence is something that matters more in a trail horse than you might think. A slow-witted horse often reacts more suddenly than a quick thinker because he relies more on instinctive behavior than does a horse that thinks through the situation.

Look for a horse that has a confident, positive outlook on life. An alert, curious, and bold horse will carry you places a scaredy-cat never will. Watch to see how he reacts and responds to various situations. If left tied, does he snooze patiently, relax, but stay interested in his surroundings, or paw frantically? When you ride off, does he move out willingly or try to turn and head back to the barn or trailhead? Does he approach strange, new things without noticing, with curiosity and confidence, tentatively, or not at all?

Test your horse to see how reactive he is, but be sure to set up the experiment so that both you and he are safe should he panic. There are any number of ways to do this, subject to what you have available and how creative you are. The object is to see how your horse reacts, on his own, when something startles him. The ideal horse spooks in place when he does spook, staring at whatever alarms him and eventually stepping toward it for a closer look.

If your horse doesn't pass with standing (as opposed to *flying*) colors, seriously consider how trailworthy he will be in the long run. A dud will distract you from the joys of trail riding by making you constantly urge him forward, but a nervous wreck will soon have you just as rattled as he is.

Gaits on the Trail

Smooth, ground-covering gaits are a must for any good trail horse. One of the most important things you can do in assessing a prospect is to watch him move. Short, choppy gaits are hard on both your spine and your horse's. A horse that doesn't pick up his feet well is prone to stumbling, but one that steps too high is wasting valuable energy that he will need on a long ride.

Gaits are a function of the horse's neurology, conformation, maturity, condition, training, shoeing (in some cases), and the way in which he is ridden. These things influence not only which gaits he will perform, but also how he'll perform them. Training can alter gaits for better or worse.

Horses are "hard-wired" at birth to perform a "big trot," a fast gallop, or a saddle gait, among others. Correct conformation will produce correct gaits. Muscle development based on maturity and/or conditioning will dictate how well and how long a horse performs any gait. Gaits affected by shoeing are iffy at best.

Finally, a good rider always rides a better horse than a bad rider does. If a horse rides more smoothly for someone else than for you, examine your seat and balance. A forward seat will force the horse onto the forehand, which can make for an unbalanced and bumpy ride. An unbalanced seat results in an unbalanced horse, and a nervous rider can restrict the otherwise loose and relaxed movement a smooth gait requires.

THE WALK

Although other gaits are a definite plus on the trail, the most important gait of a good trail horse is a clean, smooth, efficient walk. Horses can normally walk for hours without rest. From the saddle, the walk has a back-and-forth motion with an even rhythm, as the horse's head gently nods up and down. If you feel a hitch or a bump, investigate for lameness or consult with your farrier for any necessary corrections.

A good trail horse can "walk out," covering ground in a plain walk as fast as other horses can at the trot. The body swings from side to side in a loose, easy motion. It's also important for a good

trail horse to be able to **rate** (increase or decrease) his speed, even at the walk. If you ride with friends and like to chat, if you smell wildflowers off the trail and want to savor the scent, if for any reason you want to slow down, a good trail horse should be able to comfortably alter his speed at your whim.

THE TROT

The trot is a great gait with which to cover ground fairly quickly. It is referred to as diagonal because if you were to look at the horse's legs as the four corners of a box, the legs on the diagonal corners move forward in unison with each stride. In this two-beat gait, you can hear two beats for every full stride (each foot moves forward one step). This paired movement results in a brief moment in each stride where the horse is airborne, a moment of suspension in air, followed by the impact of the horse's hooves on the ground. Whether you ride English or Western, it is easier on the horse's back (and, most likely, your fanny) to post to the trot. On the trail, this is as simple as rising and sitting with every other step of the horse's stride.

Riding at the trot helps to break up the ride and is a mind refresher for both horse and rider. Most horses can handle trotting for extended periods. As with the walk, a horse should be able to rate his speed at the trot from a slow, dallying jog to a sweeping extended trot. The horse's body should be loose and swingy as the gait flows freely from the hip and shoulder in smooth strides. The horse's head and croup remain steady, but his entire body rises and drops with each stride with the **flight phase** (moment of suspension) of the gait. In a good, even trot, the hind foot will cover the track left by the front hoof on the same side of the body.

THE CANTER AND GALLOP

Cantering down the trail with the wind in your hair and the sun on your face is one of the great joys of riding. A smooth canter, without **cross-firing** (mixing leads), surging, or lagging, is part of

THE THREE STANDARD GAITS

THE WALK

THE TROT

THE CANTER

THE SADDLE OR EASY GAITS

THE RUNNING WALK

THE STEPPING PACE

THE FOX TROT

THE SADDLE RACK

A variety of gaits will serve well on the trail. Gaited horses offer more and smoother choices.

the repertoire of a well-trained horse, and, though not essential on the trail, a whole lot of fun. This three-beat gait should be somewhat constrained, rather than full-out in speed. A comfortable canter gently rocks the rider and can be sat with a deep seat. It should be kept to moderate distances.

The gallop, a gait of speed, can be risky on a new trail. A misstep at the gallop can break a leg or send the rider flying. Nevertheless, few aspects of horseback riding can match the thrill of galloping a fast horse. In this gait the horse's body stretches forward (in a more aerodynamic frame than cantering) and, unlike a three-beat canter, has four discernible beats. Riders often sit this gait with their weight in the stirrups, leaning forward to remain over the horse's center of gravity to ease the burden of their own weight. Horses can cover a lot of ground quickly at the gallop, but should not be asked to exert themselves at this level for more than a few minutes at a time.

THE SADDLE OR EASY GAITS

Although there are many names for the saddle gaits, they boil down to a handful of basic gaits with a few variations. They are naturally inborn to most horses that perform them (see Gaited Horses, page 48), though they are often modified through training, like the walk, trot, canter, and gallop.

Saddle gaits are classified as square (derivatives of the walk), diagonal (derivatives of the trot), and lateral (derivatives of the pace; see page 44). Until the advent of slow-motion video, these gaits were long mislabeled and misunderstood, and even today those misconceptions linger.

Defining the gaits is actually quite simple. All saddle gaits have the same footfall — right hind, right front, left hind, left front — regardless of where you start in the cycle of a stride. Speed or style of execution does not a separate gait make.

THE SQUARE GAITS The **flat walk** is essentially the same as the regular walk common to all horses, but with extended reach and more speed. It is considered a square gait because each foot lifts up and sets down independently in an even 1-2-3-4 beat. There are always two or three feet on the ground at a time, with one foot setting down just as another is taking off and a third firmly planted on the ground. The motion is similar to a regular walk, with the head nodding deeper to keep time with the faster gait.

The **running walk** is a flat walk with attitude. It is incredibly smooth to ride. Under the name running walk, it is the signature gait of the Tennessee Walking Horse, but is also known as the *paso llano* among aficionados of the Peruvian Paso breed and the obscure and rarely used term *hlanpandc fetgangur* in Iceland. It is a fluid, loose, relaxed gait.

Like the flat walk, each hoof picks up and lifts up independently in an even 1-2-3-4 beat. The differences are increased speed, the transfer of weight between the legs, and, especially in Walking Horse breeds, the action of the hind feet overstepping the tracks of the front feet by at least several inches. At top speed (around 10 miles per hour) the horse hops from one set of feet to the other and there is an instant where both front feet can be in the air at the same time, while still maintaining two feet on the ground at any one time. In the running walk, the horse's head nods deeply, but there is no up-and-down motion of the rear end. In Peruvian Paso Horses, the head nods very little and the hooves swing out from the shoulders (called **termino**).

THE DIAGONAL GAITS The **fox trot** (also known as the *trocha* of the Paso Fino and the *pasitrote* of the Peruvian Paso) is similar to the trot but much smoother to ride. The legs still move forward in diagonal pairs as in the trot, but the front hoof usually hits the ground before the hind, breaking up the diagonal set-down and changing the rhythm to a 1-2—3-4 sequence, with an audible hesitation. This eliminates the moment of suspension because the hind foot hits the ground at the same instant that the opposite front foot picks up, with the result that there is always one or two feet on the ground at a time. It is a relaxed and loose gait, and one that is easy for the horse to maintain while carrying a rider. Both the head and the croup move up and down at the fox trot. A slower version of this gait is called the **fox walk**.

THE LATERAL GAITS An entire group of gaits falls under the heading of **rack**. This gait can be as lofty, animated, and exciting as the show-ring version performed by the American Saddlebred, as low, slow, and humble as the trail gait of the Rocky Mountain Horse, or anywhere in between.

The **true rack** can be a speedy gait. Also known as the *hreina* (pure) *tolt* in regard to Icelandic horses and the *largo* with Paso Finos, individuals can hit speeds of 25 miles per hour while maintaining the true form of the gait. The rack is considered a lateral gait because the hooves on the same side pick up at the same time (laterally). However, they set down individually, so some consider the rack a square gait.

This is also an extremely comfortable gait to ride because there are always one or two feet on the ground. When a horse is racking, his head is carried upright and relatively still, but the croup rises and falls with the rhythm. In this gait there is a hop between the front legs and the hind legs, which creates a split second during which all of the horse's weight is supported by one foot. Because of this, and the fact that the horse carries his head higher and his back somewhat hollow in this gait as a natural consequence of the spine and limb movement, racking gaits are quite stressful to the horse, even though they are remarkably smooth to the rider.

A slower version of the rack is referred to as the **saddle rack** or **stepped rack**. In varying forms, this gait is also known as the *fino* and *corto* to Paso Fino enthusiasts, the Mountain Pleasure Gait in Mountain Horse breeds, or sometimes the **slow gait** or **singlefoot**. (However, the term *singlefoot* is reserved by some aficionados for a speed rack in which only a single foot at a time is in contact with the ground.)

Like the true rack, the saddle rack is an evenly timed gait, but again, even though the hooves set down independently, the gait is sometimes called lateral because the hooves pick up on the same side (laterally) at the same time. (This happens because the front feet lift far enough off the ground to cause a split-second delay in when they set down.) Because of the slower execution, the saddle rack always has either two or three feet on the ground. Perhaps the easiest way to tell a saddle rack from a true rack is that in a saddle rack there is no bobbing of the head and neck, but sometimes a sideways sway instead. The croup moves up and down along with the action of the hocks, flexing at the lumbosacral junction.

In a **broken** or **stepping pace,** the hooves pick up together as they do in the rack and set down almost in unison. It is the minute delay between the set-down of the hind and front hooves on the same side that breaks up the gait and keeps it smoother than a hard pace (see below) because there is still always at least one hoof on the ground. The resulting beat is uneven, 1-2-3-4, which sounds like the "mirror image" of a fox trot. Called a *sobreandando* in Peruvian Pasos and a *skeith tolt* in Icelandics, and sometimes loosely referred to as an **amble,** it is a gait of increased speed from a rack or running walk. Generally, unless very well locked in or trained in gait, most horses tend to set down their lateral hooves closer and closer together in time the faster they gait. When a horse moves in a stepping pace, neither his head nor his croup moves up and down as in a running walk or rack, but his entire body seems to wobble from side to side.

The **pace** represents the opposite end of the gait spectrum from the trot. Whereas a horse in a trot moves his diagonal legs in unison, a pacing horse moves the legs on the same side forward in unison, which is why the gait is described as lateral. A true (hard) pace is rough to ride and not a lot of fun on the trail, but with time, conditioning, patience, skill, and some luck, you can train a pacing horse to break up his gait into a smoother riding stepping pace.

The more lateral the gait, the more stressful maintaining it is to the horse's body. This is because the horse's body moves in increasing hollow form the more lateral the gait becomes. His head rises, his back drops down, and his spine flexes more deeply at the lumbosacral junction the more toward the pace his gait becomes. Unfortunately, due to a lack of understanding of collection (see chapter 5) gaited horses are often ridden in a frame in which the head is cranked up and the neck flexed at the poll, but the back is still hollow and the hind legs string out behind the horse with every stride. This puts incredible strain on the muscles supporting the back and belly of the beast, and over time can lead to excessive soreness and swayback.

SADDLE GAITS ON THE TRAIL Although racking and pacey gaits can take their toll on the horse, you can still enjoy them in moderation on the trail. They are wonderful, fun, incredibly smooth, and comfortable (for the rider), but they can be overdone, especially by enthusiastic novices. Keep the gaiting stretches to a minimum (until the horse is conditioned to maintain them for longer periods), and vary your ride with a collected walk or trot (to stretch and relieve his topline).

Factors that can affect the horse's quality of gait, and thus his ability to hold a gait for any length of time, include his age and development, certain conformational defects, discomfort caused by tack, and the ability and physique of his rider. A too-heavy rider can wear out a racking horse in no time. A rider that doesn't ride with a balanced seat can throw off the horse, force him to compensate constantly for the rider, and not only butcher the quality of the gait, but also tire the horse needlessly in doing so.

Exaggerations of any gaits are not trail gaits. But using the quiet atmosphere of the trail to polish a show horse can work wonders on the quality of his gaits. Just be sure the footing and grade are safe.

Breed and Type

Some breeds have garnered reputations as reliable or hardy on the trail. Arabians, for example, have made their mark in endurance riding because of their supreme staying power and their ability to cover miles and miles of tough terrain yet recover pulse and respiration quickly. Icelandics are staid and surefooted. Quarter Horses, Morgans, Appaloosas, and Mountain Horse breeds have built solid reputations as sound, dependable trail mounts.

Choosing what breed of horse you want as a trail horse can be as simple or confusing as you let it be. As long as you remember to keep the individual horse you are considering in mind and not what his "breed" is "supposed to be," you'll be fine.

The most obvious breed differences are really just differences in looks. A horse is said to be **typey** if he looks the way his breed is supposed to look. If a horse isn't typey, it can be virtually impossible to tell what breed he is without a copy of his registration papers. Unlike dog breeds, where, for instance, a Dachshund is readily distinguishable from a Great Dane, most differences in horse breeds are subtle. While you might easily tell an Arabian from a Clydesdale, many breed distinctions are much tougher to identify.

So what do you expect from a horse because it has been designated a specific breed? Arabians are known for their hardiness and endurance, but what if you get a wimpy one? Tennessee Walking Horses are known for their smooth gaits, but what if yours trots? On the other hand, American Quarter Horses were originally bred for sprinting speed and later for their natural instinct to go after cattle (cow sense), but countless Quarter Horses have become the mount of choice for leisure trail riders.

Your horse's breed can merely offer clues as to what he may be like; it is not a guarantee. In short, regardless of breed, it all centers on the individual.

PONY AND SMALL HORSE BREEDS

A pony is any horse under 14.2 hands (58 inches). Traditionally, ponies have been considered mounts for children and small adults, but some ponies and small horses are more than adequate mounts for full-sized riders. Welsh Cobs, Icelandic Horses, and other stoutly bred ponies have the build and the brains to carry adults through any terrain. Also, breed promoters for Icelandics claim that during centuries of evolution in a harsh environment, these horses learned to rely on each other for protection and body warmth, gathering in close proximity against the frigid, relentless arctic winds. They are reportedly less likely than most other horses to kick out at each other.

Ponies are known for being smart, tough, and surefooted. For smaller riders, ponies make ideal trail partners, as they are relatively inexpensive to keep and are easy to mount and dismount. The disadvantages to a pony mount are that they have a reputation of being smart, easily spoiled by improper handling, and sometimes ornery if mishandled, and some can be rough riding given their draft-horse-in-miniature conformation.

Crossbred horse/pony individuals often offer the best of both types, and then some. Hybrid vigor makes them hardy and tough. The pony/horse cross often mellows out any pony-minded hardheadedness.

COLDBLOOD BREEDS

Known for their large size (up to 20 hands and weighing a ton), pulling strength, and compliant natures, draft horses may not be the first breeds one thinks of when contemplating a trail horse, but they have some impressive characteristics in their favor. Draft horses tend to be less reactive by nature, which is what the term *coldblood* refers to. They are less rattled by things that might send other horses into equine emotional overdrive. Draft types have substantial to massive bone and can certainly handle the workload of trail riding. They are also bigger to manage in every way, from tack and equipment, to mounting and dismounting, to feeding; and they require an adequate-sized trailer as well.

In tight situations, draft horses can have a tougher time negotiating around obstacles simply due to their bigger size, and steep inclines can be a challenge as their conformation (thick, heavy

Icelandic Horse

Norwegian Fjord Horse

neck, short croup, goose-rump) often makes it harder for them to balance going downhill. Also, since they are built to lean forward and pull from the shoulder, drafts tend to be heavy on the forehand and may jar your teeth loose at the sitting trot. And, of course, they are BIG to get your legs around!

WARMBLOOD BREEDS

Most familiar these days as "sport horses" (jumping, dressage, three-day eventing, and driving prospects), the term *warmblood* refers to types developed by crossing coldblood (draft) with hotblood (see below) breeds. There are many evolving Warmblood types, including Dutch, Swedish, Belgian, Danish, Iberian, Hanoverian, Holsteiner, Selle-Français, Danish, and others, which represent a combination of regional native horses and hotblood outcrosses.

Most warmblood "breeds" are in an ongoing process of evolution. Registries continue to accept outcrosses from other approved breeds to maintain hybrid vigor on an ongoing basis as they strive toward their "breed goal." The combination of draft substance and mentality and Thoroughbred, Arab, or Iberian vitality is considered by many (including top Olympic riders) to result in the ideal riding horse. The "hotblood" contributes a lively temperament, while the draft blood keeps its cool. Not surprisingly, the same qualities that make for a good sport horse — soundness, responsiveness, stability of character, hardiness, and intelligence — are also the makings of a truly good trail horse.

Warmbloods tend to be large, substantially built horses, with all the needs of any big horse. Mounting and dismounting them can be a challenge for the petite rider.

HOTBLOOD BREEDS

Regardless of any given individual's temperament, *hotblood* traditionally refers to Arabians and Thoroughbreds. Other groups that also fit this category are the Iberian (Spanish) breeds, including the Andalusian and Lusitano, along with other racing breeds, such as the Standardbred.

Few horses are tougher, more intelligent, and possessed of more sheer determination than those we have come to describe as "hotblooded." Legends abound of the heart and soul of the fearless Arabian courser or the Thoroughbred who races beyond his abilities. Competitive trail and endurance riders set the standard with hotbloods, which continue to dominate these sports.

Warmblood

Arabian

The only caveat in choosing a hotblooded trail horse is that you must be committed to understanding and working with his naturally energetic character. Many horses classified as hotblooded are as laid-back and easy to work with as any draft or Warmblood, but others live up to the designation. Hotblooded horses tend to be sensitive and require an alert and aware rider. The horse interprets every movement to be an instruction from headquarters, even though you were just trying to untie your slicker from the cantle.

STOCK HORSES

Not really Warmbloods in the draft/hotblood-cross sense, stock horses are a designation built around the genetic base of the American Quarter Horse. Foundation Quarter Horse lines are really hotblood/native mare crosses from a variety of lines. Horse people often forget that the Quarter Horse is not a creation of the western United States but originated in the old Virginia horse country of our colonial days. In fact, many other breeds, including Spanish, Morgan, and English types, went into developing this versatile, all-American breed. With such a diverse background, it should be no surprise that there is a different "type" of Quarter Horse for virtually any equine pursuit, from the fast action of racing and cutting to the daily grind of ranch work to the limitless escape of the open trails.

Breeds that developed from heavy crossing with Quarter Horses include the Appaloosa and Paint. Although these breeds include some family lines that are not derived from the Quarter Horse, the overwhelming emphasis by the breed associations has been toward that type. Foundation Appaloosas, however, are actually more closely related to Iberian-type horses, because the early horses of the Palouse (the region in southeastern Washington state, southwestern Idaho, and the northeast corner of Oregon for which the breed was named) were often obtained from Native American raids on Mexican settlements.

American Quarter Horse

Bred for speed and quick responses, it is almost surprising that the Quarter Horse has also come to be accepted as a standard on the trails. Though some lines are notorious for their quickness and sometimes edgy temperaments, the average Quarter Horse is a calm, easygoing, sturdy trail mount. Those bred for the halter show ring, on the other hand, are the equivalent of an equine body builder in physique — including the tendency toward being muscle-bound and having decreased flexibility and range of motion.

GAITED HORSES

Gaited breeds include the American Saddlebred, Icelandic Horse, Kentucky Mountain Saddle Horse, Missouri Fox Trotter, Mountain Pleasure Horse, Paso Fino, Peruvian Paso, Racking Horse, Rocky Mountain Horse, Spotted Saddle Horse, and Tennessee Walking Horse (and derivatives of these breeds); all have their die-hard followings. These breeds are distinguished from all other types of horses by their extra gaits. For many, they are not only the best choice for a trail horse; they are the only choice!

Though popular throughout history until the advent of carriage-worthy roads in Europe, gaited

Tennessee Walker

horses are perceived as something of a modern-day anomaly. Part of this perception is no doubt due to the typical gaited show scene in which horses are shown in built-up shoes, with artificial tail sets and extreme action, by riders in formal, even gaudy, attire.

This slanted representation of these breeds has led many horsemen to misinterpret or even discredit the horse's innate ability. The "extra" gaits are collectively referred to as **easy, soft,** or **saddle gaits** because of their smoothness and ease in the saddle. They include the running walk, rack, stepping pace, and fox trot and are inborn to one extent or another. They may be fine-tuned by training.

Saddle gaits are highly desirable to anyone spending long hours in the saddle because they are much less jarring to the rider and (except for the rack and stepping pace) less tiring to the horse. The reason for this is that there is no moment of suspension — and subsequent landing — in these gaits, unlike in a trot, wherein the horse is literally airborne between each stride. Of course, it's not the moment of suspension that makes the ride of a trotting horse jarring, but the impact of landing after every stride. As mentioned previously, in the

saddle gaits, there is always at least one foot on the ground (or two, or three). No suspension, no landing, no jarring.

What type of gaited horse is best for the trail? The good news is that individual gaited horses have the same potential to make good trail horses that non-gaited horses do, given the same criteria of conformation and temperament already mentioned. And while it is generally true that certain breeds are identified with certain gaits, gaits are by no means guaranteed.

For instance, the Tennessee Walking Horse was originally established as a breed known for the running walk, a brisk (8 to 10 miles per hour) stride that is exceptionally smooth to ride because the horse always has two or three feet on the ground. In this breed, particularly in the show ring, the running walk is further characterized by **overreach,** in which the rear hooves overstep the footprint of the front hooves by 18 inches or more; by the horse nodding his head (sometimes to an extreme) with the rhythm of the gait; and by the horse's ears flicking back and forth and his teeth clacking to the beat.

Not every Tennessee Walker performs this gait, however; in fact, a lot of show horses (dubbed Performance Horses officially, but commonly referred to as Big Lick horses) *can't* do the gait without extremely large shoes and extreme training methods that in some cases are so abusive they are illegal. Yet the running walk is also performed naturally, albeit with much less "flair," by Peruvian Pasos, Missouri Fox Trotters, Mountain Horses, some Morgans, and countless individual gaited horses with or without notable pedigrees. While show-ring extremes (which exist in most breeds, by the way) have no place on the trail, the point here is that generalizing about breeds and gaits reveals more exceptions than rules.

OTHER BREED CONSIDERATIONS

Of course, there are dozens of breeds outside these categories, as well as thousands of individuals

Gait Defects

In searching for a gaited trail horse, keep in mind that what wins in the show ring is often not appropriate out on the trail. Be very particular about conformational faults, and politely bypass any breeder who tries to pawn off serious conformational defects as "necessary to gait." It just isn't so.

Many gaited horses have a more laid-back shoulder (from 51 to 57 degrees) than the typical horse does and a slightly longer functional back (to allow for flexion at the lumbosacral junction). Some may even have slightly camped-out, sickle-hocked, or cow-hocked legs (see page 33). Minor variations are to be expected as a result of the different type of movement these horses perform; glaring flaws, however, are not necessary to gait and are just as damaging to the soundness of a gaited horse as they are to any other horse.

Also, be aware that special saddles, bits, riding styles, and the like are an offshoot of the show ring, and not necessary for the trail rider.

within the categories that don't fit the generalizations. Canadian Horses, Cleveland Bays, Curly Horses, Haflingers, Morgans, Walers, and mules all make superb trail mounts. But the caution remains: If you are shopping for a trail horse and considering a particular breed, consider the "breed standards" to be suggestions, not guarantees.

There is one other aspect of a registered horse that you may find truly valuable. Just as a marriage draws you into a whole new family, owning a registered horse can introduce you into an extended "family" of horsemen with interests similar to your own. Some registries have tremendous trail-riding incentive programs, while others could use some encouragement in recognizing the contributions their trail-riding members make. Most have regional affiliated clubs that may offer organized group rides or privileged access to otherwise limited trails.

Personal Preference

Among the general tendencies of each breed are some aspects that can be defined only as a matter of personal preference: things such as style, color, and carriage. None of these makes a difference on the trail, but they can enhance your overall enjoyment of horse ownership and riding for purely aesthetic reasons. It's like comparing a bright red sports car to a gray luxury car — which one you prefer is based on how you drive and how you see yourself. Horse ownership is a tremendous luxury these days. Own one you can be proud of.

The style of horse you ride might mean nothing to you at all, but to some people it is a genuine concern. Some people just don't see themselves on a pony or draft horse but envision themselves cantering down the trail on an elegant Thoroughbred, Saddlebred, or Warmblood. Others think of the Quarter Horse as the "muscle car" they should have.

Depending on how important style is to you, consider which breeds offer the types of things you are interested in. Want long and lean? Think hot-bloods. Want warm, friendly, and fuzzy? Pony or draft breeds or crosses may be your perfect choice. From the high tail carriage of the Arabian or Saddlebred to the flare of the full mane and tail of Spanish breeds to the incomparable showiness of the Peruvian Paso as he moves out in gait, hooves flashing out in termino from his long, laid-back shoulders, there is an image that goes with every breed. Just remember that to reap the full effect of that image, you need to find a horse that is typey for his breed.

COLOR

Some breeds are considered color breeds, as the gene pool for the horses is limited to certain hues. Norwegian Fjords and Spanish Sorrias are exclusively dun, but other breeds, including the Arabian and Thoroughbred, contain no duns. Percherons are almost always gray or black, Andalusians gray, black, or bay. Haflingers are exclusively sorrel and, not surprisingly, Cleveland Bays are bay. Appaloosas, Walkaloosas, Tiger Horses, and the Pony of the Americas are all known for bright coat patterns, ranging, from spots over a white background (leopard), to a white-spotted "blanket" over a solid color, to a solid coat with white flecks and countless variations in between. Sometimes a breed is merely heavily associated with a color. Many people think of Arabians as gray and Rocky Mountain Horses as chocolate, though both breeds boast a brilliant range of colors.

While coat color may, at first glance, appear to be less than skin deep, it can have more relevance on the trail than you might suspect. Horses of certain colors tend to be "thin-skinned" and subject to **gall** (sores) if tack is not tended with extreme care; other colors have been heralded through generations of horsemen's lore for the durability and toughness of the hide beneath.

This is because coat color is closely tied to skin color. Light-colored horses often have very light to white skin, which can be easily sunburned, especially if a horse is stabled and then taken out for extended periods of time without sun protection. The same goes for white markings and pink skin on exposed areas. Gray horses that have turned white with age are an exception, as they are born with dark skin and hair and only the hair lightens with each successive shedding and regrowth.

Gray-colored horses, however, have a unique issue of their own. Gray horses are subject to melanomas (cancer) of the skin. For the most part, it's not a matter of "if" a gray horse will develop melanoma, but when. Happily, gray horses also have the highest survival rate of any species when it comes to melanoma and are under study for clues to how other species might benefit from their inborn ability to beat this common cancer.

Some colors are believed linked to other characteristics. Palominos gall easily, black coats fade out in the sun, and duns are tough of skin, hooves, and mind. Be cautious of horses from lines that have been bred for their color. They can suffer from seemingly unrelated problems when color takes precedence in a breeding program. Flashy color is not a fair trade-off for sound conformation or a good mind.

Sometimes color breeding reveals genetically linked problems. Horses bred for the silver dapple or chocolate color developed an eye problem known as anterior segment dysgenesis syndrome, or ASD. Researchers confirmed that

> *"A good horse has no color."*
> — traditional saying

this was the unfortunate result of the physical proximity of the gene for coat color and the gene for the eye problem on the DNA strand. Paint Horse breeders sadly discovered the lethal white syndrome (in which foals that inherited two genes for a certain white pattern died before or shortly after birth) by breeding for spectacular coat patterns.

Traditional horse lore holds that the color of the horse holds secrets to his personality. Sorrels tend to be fast and "hot" mentally (very alert), and to mature quickly. Bays are very hardy and solid, while liver chestnuts were valued for their endurance and usefulness. Grays are believed to be quite stoic and gentle, while palominos are thought to be flighty, browns respectably serious, and roans durable and tough under hard work, blue roans being especially valued in German and Spanish tradition. Duns and buckskins (though the colors are under totally separate genetic control) are each believed to be tough, durable, and smart. As with much traditional lore, some of these beliefs are true and others simply myths.

CHAPTER 3

Trail Tack & Gear

>━┼◆━◦━◆┼━

ONE OF THE NICEST THINGS ABOUT TRAIL RIDING AS AN equine pursuit is that you really don't need any special tack or gear; in most circumstances, the basics will do. There are so many nifty options in tack and accessories, however, that it can become overwhelming to figure out what you need, let alone what you want. Your gear can be as rudimentary or as up-to-the-minute high-tech as you wish.

The information in this chapter touches on everything, from the basics on. It should help you to narrow down your choices and figure out what you really need. (For advice on special gear for bad weather, see chapter 9, The Nature of the Trail.)

Saddles and Saddle Fit

With specially designed saddles and bridles available for every equine discipline, the biggest obstacle to having the right tack that fits comfortably and serves its purpose is the retail industry itself. Don't let choosing tack for trail riding turn you into a victim of marketing. You don't need a special trail saddle, just one that fits you, your horse, and the purpose. And there are no "wonder" bits, just educated hands. Less is more, most of the time.

Saddles evolved to help horses carry weight. Since around 200 B.C.E., they have been designed with a wooden frame to keep the rider up off the horse's sensitive vertebrae. This maintained a healthier back for the horse, which kept him in service longer than a mere pelt could, slung across his back. This framework design, known as a **tree,** evenly distributes the rider's weight across the horse's back over a much larger surface than the area under the rider's seat and legs. The larger the bearing surface, the fewer pounds per square inch of weight in any one spot. This is why a saddle is healthier for horse's back than riding bareback, because no matter how much "surface area" you have, it won't distribute your weight away from the horse's spine as well as a saddle tree does.

Not that you can't forgo the saddle entirely on short jaunts. Few joys compare to a summer saunter down a country lane or a charge through a snow-buried field with nothing between you and your horse but your jeans. As long as you and your horse are comfortable and secure, you have the correct tack. Just be aware that over the long haul, a saddle is healthier and more comfortable for your horse than bareback.

SADDLE STYLES

Almost any style of saddle can be a suitable trail saddle. The only saddle that is unacceptable for

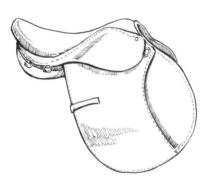

Forward seat

Most styles of saddle will serve well on the trail, with the exception of the Lane Fox cutback saddle.

All-purpose

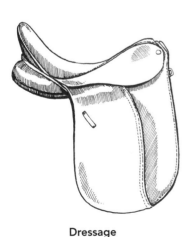

Dressage

Lane Fox — not recommended

trail riding is a Lane Fox cutback show saddle, where the pommel is cut back behind the withers. These are designed to set the rider back over the weakest part of the horse's back in order to elicit a more exaggerated gait in the show ring, and have no place on the trail.

Of course, each style of riding has its pros and cons. Trade-offs in security, comfort, expense, and ease accompany the different types of gear and styles of riding.

WESTERN SADDLES

Beginning trail riders often prefer Western saddles because they are readily available and offer more stability than English types. The swells, cantle, and seat (see illustration) of Western saddles typically allow for a deep, secure seat, especially appreciated over steep or uneven terrain. Though the saddle horn was designed to hold a struggling calf at the end of a lariat, it often serves as a handhold for those learning to balance on horseback. Western saddles offer other practical advantages, such

as broad stirrup leathers that keep sweat and dirt from the horse off the rider's legs, wide stirrups for a comfortable and stable foothold, hoof pick holders, saddle strings, and other handy add-ons.

There are drawbacks, however. Most Western saddles are heavy (commonly 35 to 50 pounds), although saddles made with synthetic materials are surprisingly lightweight. Mass-market saddle manufacturers rely heavily on Quarter Horse bars. On a Western saddle, the **bars** are the weight-bearing parts of the tree that run along the sides of the horse's spine. By "Full Quarter Horse bars," manufacturers generally mean a saddle for a horse that is "long and broad with moderate to low withers"; Standard Quarter Horse Bars are meant for the majority of stock-type horses; and Semi-Quarter Horse bars are for high-withered horses. But there is no set measurement as to what any of this means in the industry, making it a challenge to fit individual horses.

Other downsides are: large, stiff leather skirts (designed to protect the horse's sides from saddlebags or brush rubbing against them) that can interfere with the horse's range of motion; wide, stiff stirrup leathers that can twist against your leg, causing knee and ankle stress; stirrups that may be hung too far forward of the saddle, forcing your weight against the cantle; a prominent horn that can leave a dent in your innards should you duck to avoid low-hanging limbs.

DIFFERENT WESTERN STYLES Western saddles come in styles designed for specific tasks, most of which center on working cattle. The different styles all have the same components — swells (pommel), seat, cantle, skirts, and rigging — but these are customized for the purpose of the saddle.

Cutting saddles have huge **swells** — the padded parts on either side of the saddle horn (see illustration) — and a flat seat to allow the rider to sit securely as his horse rocks back on his hocks and dashes and twists after cows.

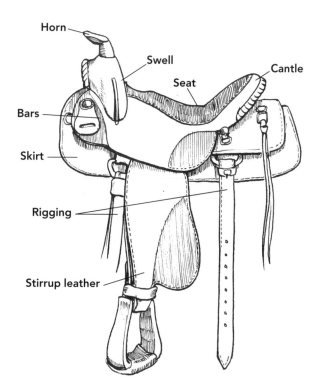

Horn

Swell

Seat

Cantle

Bars

Skirt

Rigging

Stirrup leather

Each part of a Western saddle serves a specific purpose.

It's a Cinch!

The back cinch on a double-rigged saddle is often misunderstood and misused. It is part of an overall rigging system designed to keep the saddle firmly in place. Not all Western saddles are designed for use with a back cinch, so a lot of riders assume it isn't necessary to use one. However, saddles that *are* designed with a back cinch won't fit a horse properly if the back cinch is not used.

The tree on a double-rigged saddle is designed to rest evenly over the horse's back when *both* cinches or girths are properly secured. Using only the front cinch forces excess pressure down toward the front of the saddle, tipping the saddle (and your weight) forward and impinging on the horse's withers and/or shoulders. Without the back cinch, the saddle may be unstable and bounce up and down at the rear (cantle) when the horse trots or canters, shift going down hills, and/or pinch and cause soreness if it doesn't fit well in the first place.

If you use a back cinch, make sure it is snug up against the horse's belly and check it occasionally to be sure it stays snug. It should never be tight, nor should there be daylight between it and the horse. It's far too easy for brush or even a hind foot to get tangled up in a loose back cinch; the most likely time and place for that to happen is halfway down a steep, narrow, winding trail.

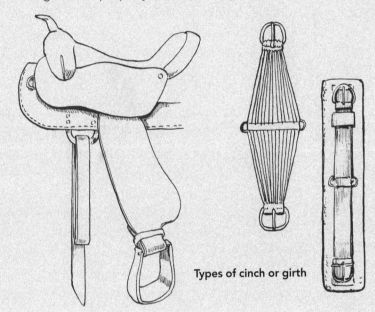

Types of cinch or girth

Roping saddles, built to resist the pull of a steer, have a large horn, a tough tree, and double rigging (see box). Both the fork and the cantle are low.

Reining saddles are built for close contact with a low, non-stomach-gouging horn, and the welled seat dips down to give the rider room to roll back over her pelvis during sliding stops.

Barrel-racing saddles are built for security at speed with wide swells, a very deep seat, a high saddle horn, and minimal skirts to allow for maximum range of motion and extension in the horse.

Pleasure saddles are designed for rider comfort on trails, not speed events or even maximum mobility. They typically have a high fork and cantle to create a deep, secure pocket for the rider and are double-rigged.

RIGGING Rigging refers to the parts that go under the horse's body to hold the saddle in place: the **cinch,** or **girth,** that goes under the horse's belly; and the **latigo** (strap on the near side that holds the cinch in place) or **billet(s)** (straps on the off side to which the cinch or girth is buckled).

A Tale of Two Seats

Since we are using the designation of saddles as Western or English, it's important to understand that there are basically two styles of seats — Jineta and Brida (also called *estradiota)*. Each evolved for a specific purpose. Let's explore why the Jineta seat is better for trail riders and how the saddle you use greatly determines how you sit your horse.

The **Jineta** style developed in the Middle East and was historically referred to as the Moorish style. The Moors preferred to travel light, depending on their swiftness and maneuverability to win in battle.

They designed saddles to accommodate the horse's back in motion by constructing a frame made of two wooden bars connected at the front and rear by arches tied together with rawhide. Stirrups placed just forward of the center of the seat positioned the rider so that his shoulder, elbow, hip, and heel were in alignment. The seat rose slightly in the front and toward the rear, with the lowest point in the center. Two cinches held the saddle firmly in place. (Eventually saddles of this design led to the concepts of rock, twist, and flare that dictate saddle design today.) After the Moors invaded Spain, this style caught on there, was later exported to the New World, and ultimately left its mark on Mexican and "Western" saddles.

The **Brida** style evolved in Europe, whose warriors, the knights, rode to battle in heavy armor aboard the equine equivalent of tanks — heavy, draft-type horses, often themselves covered in armor. The rider couldn't bend his legs much, so he had to sit the horse straight-legged, almost as if he were standing.

Saddle design here focused on a knight keeping his seat while carrying and thrusting a lance, as well as when receiving a blow from a rival. The saddles had huge arches both front and rear, which dug into the horse's back to prevent the saddle from shifting and possibly unloading the overloaded rider. (Once off the horse, a knight was at his enemy's mercy, of which there really wasn't enough to go around.) The seat was flat, with a high cantle and a wide pommel that wedged the rider in place, and also served somewhat as shields. The saddle was held in place by one cinch rigged at the very front. This design allowed the knight to

A Moorish rider in Jineta style

A knight riding in Brida style

brace against impact by shoving his feet forward and leaning back against the cantle, without the saddle shifting backward or to the side. Except for Spain, most of Europe eventually adopted this straight-legged style of riding and continued to produce saddles designed to hold the rider in that position.

Eventually these styles resulted in the types of saddles we know as "Western" and "English," and vestiges of the early influences are still seen in saddles made today. Dressage and most stock saddles (Western and Australian) place the rider in a Jineta seat. This is the best seat for the trail rider, as it is less tiring to the horse and more balanced for the rider. Saddle seat and plantation saddles place the rider in a Brida seat, and hunt seat and jumping saddles put the rider in a variation of it.

The Brida seat, while handy for riding at speed or jousting with knights, makes it difficult for a horse to round its back, which in turn makes it very tough to engage his hindquarters, and it invariably keeps the rider's balance off center. Riding in a Brida seat — with the feet shoved forward and the rider's weight crammed back against the cantle — is a common mistake, often seen regardless of saddle design. Be sure you don't choose a saddle that puts you in this position by design.

Western saddles are often **double-rigged,** meaning there are two cinches, or girths. They can have full double rigging (the front ring for attaching the latigo to the cinch is directly below the middle of the swell), which almost always requires a back cinch in order for the saddle to stay in place; ⅞ rigged (the ring is an inch farther back and also benefits from a back cinch); ¾ rigged (the ring is an additional inch back); ⅝ rigged (another inch back); or center fire, which places the cinch ring in the center of the tree.

There are many types of girths and cinches to choose from, but mohair is the best. The natural hair of Angora goats, mohair is a strong fiber with a certain amount of "give." It is spun into sturdy strands that are grouped together to form the body of the cinch. The individual strands of each cinch spread out across the horse's underside distributing the pull and force of the saddle and rider across a broader area than a solid girth does, and allowing air to circulate through the area. Mohair "breathes" and wicks sweat from the body.

Regardless of the type of cinch or girth you use, be sure to keep it clean. Most materials (except for neoprene) absorb sweat and as a consequence can rot through and weaken. Dirty cinches quickly become stiff and gall the horse's skin, leaving raw, sore spots where the cinch has to hold fast on the next ride.

Other nice touches for your trail horse's comfort include woolen cinch or girth covers and ring keepers that go over the hardware to prevent pinching and chafing.

ENGLISH SADDLES

A lot of riders prefer English-style saddles because these position their legs in the narrow "groove" between the horse's forelegs and his belly, which aids balance and close contact. They weigh less than Western saddles, and the fit can be adjusted by adding or taking away stuffing in the panels, unlike Western saddles, in which the fit is primarily dictated by the tree bars. (Wool stuffing, loosely

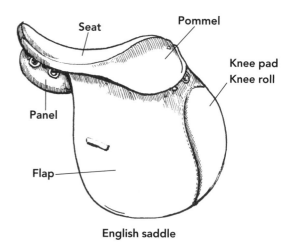

English saddle

placed and not allowed to ball up, is preferred to foam stuffing.) Knee rolls or pads in the saddle flaps (see illustration) help the rider keep her legs in position. Models designed especially for trail riders sport rings for tying on saddlebags and extra seat padding. Because the stirrup irons are attached to narrow, flexible leathers, there is less wear and tear on the rider's knees and ankles.

One shortcoming, however, is that those narrow leathers afford no protection to a rider's legs from a sweaty horse. Another is due to the shorter length of the saddle itself; in many models the bars of the tree are too short to disperse the rider's weight effectively.

DIFFERENT ENGLISH STYLES English saddles come in many styles, including all-purpose, dressage, and hunt-seat/jumper.

The **all-purpose** styles are a hybrid between balanced dressage saddles and more forward hunter types. They afford a slightly deeper seat than other English styles, which moves the rider's legs back for slightly less contact with the horse. The flaps are large and rounded with leather knee pads and large knee rolls beneath.

Dressage saddles — some are better designed than others — are meant to help a rider balance perfectly over the strongest part of the horse's back. They have very deep seats and long, wide flaps, both of which are pluses for the trail rider. The flaps sometimes have kneepads, knee rolls, or thigh rolls (also called **blocks**). Avoid saddles with large, stiff pads or rolls, or any that interfere with the rider's leg position. Dressage saddles usually have an extra billet sewn to the bottom to help position the girth. The panels are rounded and thick.

Hunt-seat and **jumping saddles** have flat seats, soft knee pads on the flaps, and little to no knee roll beneath them. Some saddles have thigh rolls to the rear of the flaps to prevent a rider's legs from slipping too far back, but most riders prefer more freedom of movement in the legs for trail riding than these rolls allow. The flaps are small and rounded. They are designed to keep the rider balanced more toward the horse's forequarters in order to be able to move with the center of gravity upon approaching, clearing, and landing after jumps, but that forward seat can make keeping your balance going down steep hills a challenge.

Another type of English saddle is the **saddle seat** variety, such as the Lane Fox mentioned previously. These saddles have very long, wide flaps with no kneepad. The seat is long and flat. The panels are flat and thin with no sweat flap. The pommel is relatively flat and has a 4-inch gap where it is "cut back" to allow clearance of the horse's withers. They are built to place the rider's weight backward with very little leg contact, and are a poor choice for the trail.

AUSTRALIAN STOCK SADDLES

Another type of saddle that has grown in popularity with trail riders is the Australian stock saddle. Originally designed for chasing cattle through rugged terrain, they combine some of the best attributes of Western and English styles. The seat is secure, like that of a Western saddle, but more forward, as in an English saddle. They weigh less than a Western saddle and offer closer contact with stirrups hung much the same as a dressage saddle. They offer more weight distribution through the bars than an English saddle does. Some have oversized knee rolls, or "poleys," that hold the rider in place: a boon to some, a bust to

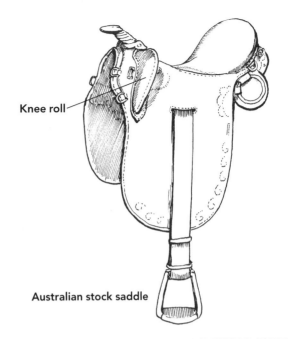

Knee roll

Australian stock saddle

Best of Both Worlds

Tighten a Western cinch by pulling the latigo through the cinch ring and then running it back through a ring that is either attached to the tree or sewn into the skirt. English-type girths, in contrast, are buckled to billets. On the trail, where rest stops can be frequent, in my experience it's a lot quicker and more convenient to loosen and lash a latigo than it is to buckle and unbuckle billets.

The Cashel Company, in Onalaska, Washington, has a number of ingenious and useful innovations for trail riders; one of my favorites is the Cashel Converter. Made of heavy-duty harness leather and hardware, the converter buckles at the top to the billets of an English saddle and has a cinch ring at the bottom to attach a Western style cinch. Using this device, it takes about a minute to change the rigging of an English-style saddle to that of a Western saddle.

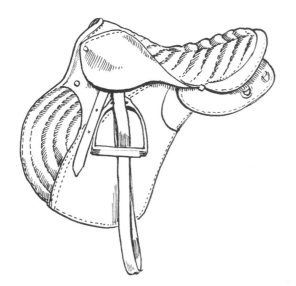

English-type endurance saddle

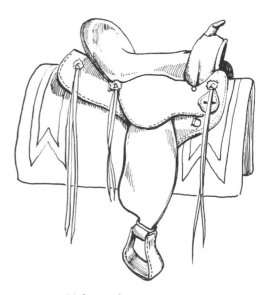

Lightweight Western saddle

others. Although they keep you from sliding forward, they also limit your ability to move forward with your horse over jumps or at speed.

SPECIALTY SADDLES

Other types of saddles are designed with special riding styles in mind and, depending on how you intend to ride, may or may not be worth the extra investment.

ENDURANCE SADDLES Many riders feel that endurance saddles are the ultimate trail saddles. They are lightweight and designed for the comfort of both horse and rider over the long haul. Unnecessary weight has been trimmed from these designs, so skirts and leathers are at a minimum, yet handy tie-ons are usually plentiful for such things as slickers, saddlebags, and other goodies needed on a long ride. They are often designed for smaller-backed horses, since Arabians are so prevalent in the sport of Endurance racing.

GAITED SADDLES Another specialty is the gaited saddle. These come in a variety of styles but most tend toward the Britda seat, making them undesirable as trail saddles. Many are built long and narrow in an effort to fit the "gaited" body style, which is no more a one-size-fits-all proposition

than fitting Quarter Horses. Special Icelandic saddles have been around for decades and Peruvian saddles for centuries, but even though they are steeped in the tradition of the breeds for which they were developed, they are not always — or even *often* — the best choice for trail riding. They can also be expensive. Peruvian saddles especially can be very ornate, heavy, and expensive.

Sidesaddles are another type designed for a very specialized type of riding. Most often used on gaited horses (how do you post to a trot sideways, anyhow?), they are hard to come by these days. They have two horns in the front and a long flap down the left side, with a very short flap on the right.

SADDLE CONSTRUCTION

If you could peek beneath the skirts, you would see how the saddle tree is made. The old-fashioned rawhide-covered trees are the strongest but also the heaviest. Trees made from wood and covered in fiberglass are strong and waterproof; trees made from molded plastic are lightweight, but flimsy by comparison.

In Western saddles, the broader the surface area, the better the weight distribution (fewer pounds per square inch); for the trail horse who may carry saddle and rider day in and day out, a tree made with broad bars is a real blessing.

Treeless Saddles

Treeless saddles are a fairly new option on the saddle market. Several brands have been developed for everything from dressage to endurance racing. Manufacturers proudly acclaim the pluses as lightweight; soft, comfortable, body-molded fit; and free range of motion for the horse. They are most often touted as the best option for a custom fit, especially on hard-to-fit horses.

Indeed, lots of horses do show improvement as soon as their rider switches from their old "tree" saddle to a new "treeless" saddle. It's important to realize, however, that if changing from one saddle to another significantly improves a horse's performance or even just his attitude (all other factors remaining constant), it's likely that the old saddle was either uncomfortable or at least limited the horse's range of motion. Riders often report that the treeless saddle is very comfortable for them as well.

Unfortunately, a treeless saddle proposes several problems for the horse and rider. Without that rigid tree floating along either side of the horse's spine, there is little to distribute the rider's weight away from it. Vertebrae are fragile and easily damaged, often with long-term consequences.

In order to protect them, the saddle must be designed to create an empty channel immediately over the spine, and it takes a rigid material to maintain the integrity of that channel.

Some really fat, wide horses have a back with a natural channel along the spine as their back muscles rise above it on either side. For them a treeless saddle may be fine in terms of back health.

However, another common problem is that due to the lack of rigid support, riders tend to over-tighten the cinch or girth. That's because without that stabilizing framework, a treeless saddle is more likely to shift. This can be a real surprise when mounting, or when the saddle slips over the withers heading down a steep hill. Of course, a lot of this has to do with the shape of the horse, and with other equipment used. A crupper (see page 76) can help stabilize any saddle on a horse with insufficient withers.

Finally, independent equine professionals report that many horses that show remarkable improvement when first switched to a treeless saddle eventually develop back pain. Over time, the lack of support — and rider compensation for the lack of stability — takes its toll.

Even though the market is fairly new, the idea of treeless design isn't; the earliest forms of saddles had no rigid framework. It took horsemen centuries to develop that technology. The gauchos of South America developed one form of treeless saddle that does keep the rider's weight off the horse's spine. Rolled-up rawhide was soaked, fitted to the back of the horse, and allowed to dry. Once dry, the tough and rigid rawhide tubes held the shape of the horse's back. They were built into the bottom of the saddle for a custom-fit, "treeless" saddle that still provided a rigid support off the horse's spine.

Over time, as the saddle maker's art and equine science advanced, the rigid tree was adopted worldwide as the best method for protecting the horse's spine and stabilizing the saddle. Why go back?

Rough It with Roughout

A clue as to how well a leather saddle is made is in the edges. Well-made leather saddles have smooth finished edges, while cheaply made ones will be rough and unfinished.

Roughout leather is an exception. Hide is tacked onto the saddle with the rough side out; this provides a little friction to help you keep your seat and not slip, as you might on smooth leather. Meant more for speed events, roughout can add a sense of security on steep trails. Those riding in thick brush or cactus also prefer Roughout because it doesn't show scratches the way smooth, polished leather does.

MATERIALS

Most traditionalists prefer a saddle made from leather and a wooden tree. The best leather is strongest, lasts longest, and costs the most. It has a smooth, supple feel to it, never crackly or spongy.

Traditionally, trees were built from a variety of available woods. Light hardwoods such as yellow poplar or the strong, flexible softwood of Douglas fir are preferred now. Layering the wood in different directions makes the tree stronger because there is no one grain direction to allow a split. Trees were traditionally wrapped in wet rawhide and dried under controlled conditions to prevent the wet leather from warping the wood. Some saddle makers still use this technique.

SYNTHETICS Synthetic saddle materials are common these days. Those to look for include such innovations as the heavy-duty fabric Cordura and leatherlike materials Equi-leather, Biothane, and Equi-suede. Precast fiberglass or polymer trees are common as well.

As long as the saddle fits your horse well, a synthetic saddle can be a great bargain. Fabric-covered saddles cost about a half to a third of what comparable leather saddles run. They are lightweight and will serve the pleasure trail rider well for at least 5 years, depending on how often and/or rough the riding. This is a lot less than the life expectancy of a traditional leather saddle, however, as synthetics are generally less durable. Most synthetic trees are not as rugged as the traditional wooden trees either, but when combined with a synthetic covering, they usually outlast the rest of the saddle so the combined package works out well.

Western saddles often come with nylon latigos, which can be replaced with leather. Nylon doesn't hold as fast and can chafe the horse as it moves back and forth. Synthetic billets may also need to be replaced over time, as they can crack and become weak and unsafe.

Synthetic girths made from neoprene, felt, faux fleece, polyester, elastic, and other fabric blends are remarkable for easy maintenance and longevity, but less comfortable than natural materials for the horse. Solid girths with a heavy nylon backing don't flex and can restrict a horse's breathing. Neoprene causes more sweating without allowing the skin to breathe, and a lot of riders complain that it galls their horses. However, slick synthetics don't collect burrs and bits of brush the way natural fibers and even fluffy synthetics do.

SADDLE FIT

Saddle fit is essential to your horse's comfort and performance, especially on the trail, where hours, miles, and constant changes in terrain and footing can take their toll if a saddle is rubbing your horse the wrong way. If a saddle doesn't fit, it hurts the horse. It may pinch here or rub there, causing soreness. Horses with sore backs and shoulders don't perform at their peak and at times can be downright grumpy. You would be too if you were in their saddle. Resist the temptation, however, to attribute all behavioral problems to pinched withers or a sore back. If your horse's behavior is an issue in every saddle you try and you are sure the fit is adequate, go back to training basics.

Saddle fit is more important than style. Whatever style of saddle you use, be sure it fits both you and your horse. One size does not fit all. No matter what the retail industry claims, saddles with Quarter Horse bars aren't guaranteed to fit Quarter Horses, and Arab trees won't fit all Arabs. Moreover, since gaited horses range in size from short, broad-backed Icelandics and petite, short-coupled, narrow Pasos to loose and lanky 16-hand Walking Horses and Saddlebreds, one size barely fits *some*. And as much as I wish I could make it so, my seat will never fit in the same size saddle as a fashion model's would, any more than it would in a saddle fit for a linebacker. Each and every horse and rider has custom-fit needs in an off-the-rack tack world.

A poorly fitted saddle can cause enough discomfort to ruin a good horse's performance and/or attitude and even cause long-term physical damage. Similarly, a well-fitted saddle, improperly placed on your horse's back, or a properly fitted, properly placed saddle topped off with an out-of-balance rider, can also cause back soreness and all the problems that go with it.

Horses are a lot like ladies in a shoe store; some are harder to fit well than others. Poor conformation doesn't help. Horses with very high or very low or broad withers can be as tricky to fit as someone with flat feet. So can very wide or narrow horses, or horses that are noticeably uneven from one side to the other, which is very common. Long sloping shoulders need more room for freedom of motion than steep shoulders do. Horses with "downhill" conformation need to be fit so that the saddle isn't constantly jammed into their shoulders, making them sore and stiff. Short-coupled horses need shorter trees; long-backed horses need more length in the bars.

How often, how hard, and how long you ride, your weight, the terrain you tackle, and your horse's condition will all contribute to how critical saddle fit is for your horse. A 200-pound rider covering 100 miles a day of rough country will definitely need the best fit possible, whereas an 85-pound girl who rides only for an hour at the walk on weekends won't have to be as careful. Of course, we all want a perfectly fitted saddle, but realistically, some of us get more leeway than others.

WHAT IS PROPER FIT? A properly fitted saddle distributes the rider's weight evenly along the *longissimus dorsi* muscles on either side of the horse's spine (see illustration page 67). It does not contact the spine at any point, clears the withers, and allows for free range of motion in the horse's shoulders and hips. It places the rider's weight over the strongest part of the horse's back (roughly over the center of the thoracic vertebrae) and balances the rider, rather than tipping her forward (over the forehand) or backwards (against the cantle). It allows both horse and rider to move freely and comfortably.

Be aware that saddle fit will change over time as the horse gains or loses weight, muscle bulk, or tone, and even to some extent when he moves, such as when he rounds his back in collection or hollows it out in a saddle gait. Fitting adjustments or even a new saddle may be needed to accommodate the long-term changes in your horse's body. Saddle fit is an ongoing commitment.

TREE FIT AND CONDITION You can tell a lot about how a saddle will fit before you put it on the horse. If it has been damaged or twisted, or if the tree is broken, pass it by or replace it. You will be able to see or feel these things better off the horse than on him. The tree should be solid, not bend, hinge, or give in any direction. Some saddle

The Tree's Job

The job of the tree is to disperse weight evenly over a moving surface. It should not move at all.

How to Saddle a Horse

To check saddle fit correctly, first be sure the horse is saddled properly.

1. Begin with your horse standing quietly on a level surface. It's next to impossible to gauge fit when the horse is leaning up or downhill or fidgeting from side to side.

2. Place the saddle forward on the withers and gently slide it back so the hair lies flat and won't irritate the horse (see drawing).

3. Once it is in the best position, pull any mane hair out from under the saddle so it doesn't tug. (Imagine walking along with someone yanking your hair with every step . . .)

4. Tighten the cinch.

Always tighten the front cinch on a Western saddle first. When unsaddling, always loosen the front cinch last. That way, if anything spooks a horse while you are saddling him, he is less likely to wind up with a saddle dangling from under his belly.

The girth should be snug enough so that if you grasp the saddle by the pommel and cantle and pull toward you (as if to mount), the saddle stays in place. You should still be able to slide a finger between the girth and the horse.

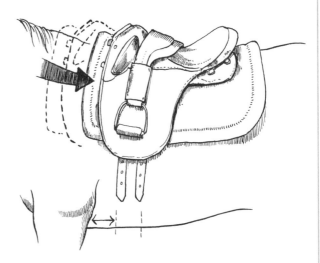

Place the saddle forward on the withers and slide it back into the "sweet spot," where it most naturally fits the horse (step 2).

makers have experimented with flexible trees, but because the job of the tree is to disperse weight evenly over a moving surface, it should not move at all.

Any flex in the tree translates into instability. This can magnify discomfort to the horse if he is crooked (almost all horses are more developed on one side or the other and *somewhat* crooked) or if the rider has a lopsided or unbalanced seat.

Check the condition of the saddle tree with this easy test: With the front of the pommel toward you, braced against your hip or thigh for support, grab the fork (or pommel) with one hand and the cantle with the other and try to bend the opposite ends together. If the saddle hinges or bends, the

tree is broken. A saddle with a broken tree cannot distribute weight evenly along the horse's back because the point of the break will give and dig into the horse's back. Try this in reverse: Hold the fork as steady as possible and try to bend the cantle back away from you. It should still hold steady. Check the bars by placing the saddle on the floor on its side and trying to bend the bars back and forth. They should hold fast.

FINDING THE SWEET SPOT You'll find that at some point along the horse's back the saddle just naturally seems to settle. This "sweet spot" varies from horse to horse. The best way to find it is to repeat this step several times. Some saddlers suggest a firm tug to snap the saddle in place rather than a gentle slide, but either way, when the saddle comes to rest in the same spot over and over again, you've found your horse's "sweet spot" and are ready to proceed.

Another clue is where the girth (or front cinch) falls. Proper saddle placement should allow it to fall in the narrowest part of the rib cage, usually about 3 to 4 inches behind the elbow. The girth will gravitate to that spot anyway, which means your saddle will shift and the cinch will loosen if you don't position it correctly the first time.

The strongest part of a horse's back is between the withers and the last (18th) thoracic vertebra. The most common mistake in saddle placement is setting the saddle too far forward up on the withers. This impedes your horse's range of motion and can make his withers and shoulders very sore. Gaited-horse riders often make the opposite mistake, positioning the saddle too far back in an effort to elicit gait by hollowing out the horse's back under their weight. This tires the horse, causes soreness, and often results in a sway-back.

TIPS FOR CHECKING SADDLE FIT If you find yourself seriously contemplating buying a new saddle, there are some good tools to help you check the fit. It's best to test out any new saddle on your horse. If you can't get the horse and saddle together before you buy, however, there are other options.

Several systems exist to help you measure your horse's back for a custom fit, such as bending a hanger over his back just behind the withers and tracing the shape of it onto paper or cardboard. Take the cutout saddle shopping with you and see how it fits in underneath the gullet of saddles you are considering. This certainly won't guarantee a perfect fit, but it does give a clue as to gullet clearance and back width.

A good commercial product is the EquiMeasure kit, which comes with a flexible pad that can be molded to the horse's back, then taken to the saddle shop or the saddle maker to provide an exact replica of your horse's back. The pad is reusable, so there are many uses over the life of the product.

WARNING SIGNS OF POOR FIT Signs the saddle doesn't fit the horse can be physical or behavioral. Telltale white hairs growing around the withers are a sign that this horse has endured pinching, rubbing, galling, and pain. The same is true when white hairs appear where the girth ring is pulled too tight. Dry patches on the saddle pad can indicate points where either the pressure against the horse's back when saddled is so intense he can't sweat in that spot or where the pad isn't in full contact with his back (bridging).

Many behavioral problems are attributed to the discomfort of poorly fitting tack, but the most obvious is an attempt to avoid the saddle in the first place. If he sidesteps, dances, or rears to dodge being saddled, he is trying to tell you something.

Telltale Hair

It used to be pretty common to see horses with white spots on either side of the withers. This comes from tissue damage to the skin and supporting layers due to rubbing or compression. I first learned about this problem as a kid at the horse auction when I asked one of the horse handlers what those white marks were. "Mean's they're broke," he spat back.

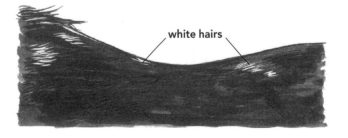
white hairs

White hairs indicate where a saddle has changed the horse and damaged underlying tissues.

How to Check Fit

Figuring out if your saddle fits your horse takes both a thorough visual inspection and using your hands and seat to feel for good fit. Place the saddle on your horse's back with no pad, as explained above, and check the fit first with no rider, then with a rider in place, and finally with the horse moving. What amounts to an unnoticeable problem on an unmounted horse can turn into a gouged sore spot on a moving animal. Here are the steps.

1. Start by stepping back and taking in the overall picture. On all types of saddles, the deepest part of the seat should be level to the ground. If the seat tips one way or the other, it will force pressure on the horse's back and throw your seat off balance. The pommel should never be higher than the cantle; however, in most saddles the cantle should not rise more than 3 inches higher than the pommel. Western styles designed with very high cantles are an exception.

On a deep-seated dressage saddle, the cantle will sit 2 to 3 inches above the height of the pommel, but on hunter or all-purpose English styles the difference may be only an inch. If the pommel and cantle are level, the saddle doesn't fit properly, and the deepest part of the seat will be at an incline, throwing the rider's weight off balance.

2. Next, step up and take a closer look at how the saddle contours to the horse's body. On a Western saddle, the skirts should curve with the horse's body and not stick out to the sides or extend too far forward (impeding the shoulders) or too far back (poking into the hips).

3. Facing the horse from the front, check to see that there is adequate clearance above the withers. You should be able to slide your hand underneath the saddle along the shoulders beneath the withers. This part of the saddle, called the **flare,** is a key aspect of good fit. The saddle should clear the withers completely for comfort and freedom of movement, and the bars or panels should rest behind the shoulders without digging in.

I learned to measure this clearance by sticking my fingers under the pommel (fork) and looking for two to three fingers of air space. This would work fine if we all had the same fingers! So I've estimated here in inches. On brand-new Western saddles, this can be as much as $3\frac{1}{2}$ inches, but since new saddles settle over time, a broke-in saddle needs only about 2 to $2\frac{1}{2}$ inches. On an English saddle, this clearance is closer to $1\frac{1}{2}$ to $2\frac{1}{2}$ inches. With a rider in the saddle, it will settle down more, but there should still be an open channel over the withers. Horses with low, rounded (mutton) withers often have more clearance beneath the pommel. Those with high, narrow withers are harder to fit for clearance.

4. Next check from the back of the saddle to be sure the open channel, or **gullet,** extends all along the horse's spine. This is usually easier to check visually on an English saddle than on a Western saddle due to skirts that extend past the cantle. If you can't easily see it, reach your hand underneath the skirt and feel. Feel the muscles of the horse's back to be sure that the gullet is wide enough to clear the spine and the muscles immediately surrounding it (paraspinal muscles).

The saddle should rest over the center of the horse's back along the much larger *longissimus dorsi* muscles on either side of the horse's spine (see illustration), never coming into direct contact with it. The bars of the tree on a Western saddle or panels of an English one should rest evenly along the back muscles. You should be able to

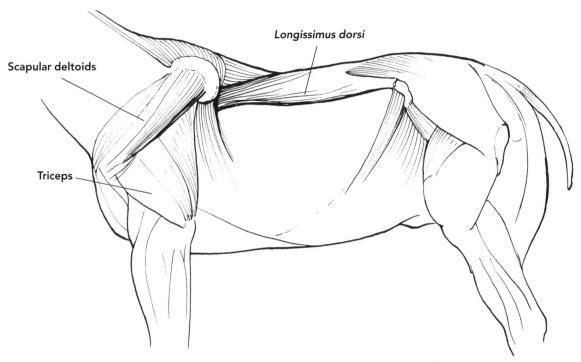

Scapular deltoids

Triceps

Longissimus dorsi

A properly fitting saddle will disperse the weight of the rider along the *longissimus dorsi*, the long muscle along the back, and keep it clear of the deltoid and tricep muscles of the shoulder and humerus.

slide your hand along underneath them and feel light, even contact all the way along each side. With a rider in the seat, this pressure will be much firmer, but pressure should still feel even. Feel for the contact to be somewhat less along the front and back of the saddle, since it should flare enough to allow for free range of motion.

5. Check the length of the saddle to see how far back it sits on the horse's back. Whether due to placement or the length of the saddle itself, be sure the weight-bearing parts of the saddle don't extend past the last rib, because the spine can't bear weight beyond this point. Find the location of the last rib by feeling with your fingers. Decorative skirts can extend somewhat past this point, as long as they are not part of the weight-bearing surface of the saddle.

6. To determine whether the bars or panels have enough contact, grab the saddle at the pommel (swells or fork) and cantle and try to rock it back and forth and from side to side. If the saddle fits, it should remain stable in every direction. It should also stay put when the horse is moving, at any gait. If the saddle rocks, it doesn't fit.

It's important to repeat these steps with a rider in place, because the rider's weight can alter the saddle fit. A saddle on a lopsided horse (or a lopsided saddle on a straight horse) may appear to fit well until the rider's weight causes it to shift or settle differently.

Test the saddle with the horse in motion by watching for spots where the saddle pokes or rubs and by feeling for shifting. After riding for about 15 minutes, dismount and check again.

And finally, make it a habit to check the saddle pad for sweat marks to indicate where the saddle is making contact with the horse. An even pattern of sweat is one more clue in the overall assessment of saddle fit.

The simplest way tell if a saddle is bridging is to run your hand underneath the saddle, feeling for even pressure along the bars (or panels). A gap in contact just behind the withers means the saddle is bridging. Check again with the pad you normally use in place. One cause of bridging is a too-thick (over ¾ inch) saddle pad. The extra stuffing prevents the tree from resting along the natural curve of the horse's back.

Another way to check for bridging is to ride until the horse works up a sweat and then stop, remove the saddle, and examine the padding. If the saddle is bridging, there will be dry spots along the center of the pad. Dry spots suggest that the saddle is not bearing your weight along these areas. (This is not as reliable as testing by feel, however, as dry spots can also signify loss of function of the sweat glands due to tissue damage because of *excessive* pressure. Also, many saddle pads are made of material that wicks away the wetness.)

Sore spots along his back are a dead giveaway. Learn to feel what is going on with your horse's back. With your fingertips and palms, feel along either side of his spine. Look for puffy spots and feel for swelling or heat. Another method is to run a pencil along the muscles on either side of the spine. If your horse flinches, drops his back, turns around and looks at you, or lays his ears back and bares his teeth — depending on his disposition and the severity of the discomfort, he is telling you his back hurts in that spot.

MISFITS Some misfits are easy to spot. If the saddle perches up high on the horse's back, it is too small and the gullet too narrow. It will shift around from lack of contact and will pinch the withers. If it rests too low, the saddle is too big and can cause damage to the vertebrae as the rider's weight bears down on them. Look out for **bridging,** in which the bars make contact in the front and rear but leave a gap along the sides, forcing the rider's weight into four small points rather than along the length of the horse's back.

IF THE SADDLE DOESN'T FIT A poorly fitting saddle doesn't have to keep you off the trails while you shop for a new one, unless the tree itself is too small for the horse. English-saddle fitters can do wonders in restuffing the panels for a custom

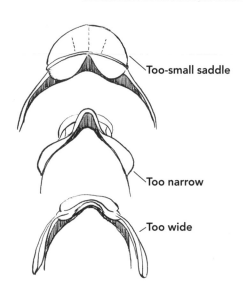

Too-small saddle

Too narrow

Too wide

This saddle is impinging on the shoulders and does not allow enough clearance over the gullet. The result will be uncomfortable, restricted movement for the horse.

fit. This is especially true for horses that are naturally uneven and/or in training so that their shape is continually changing. Realize, though, that the custom fit is only as good as the custom fitter.

Western trees are not adjustable, so special fitting falls to padding and shims. Although extra padding can help a too-wide saddle fit better, it comes at the expense of reducing leg and seat contact with the horse and stability, as it can shift around. Adding padding to a saddle that is already too narrow will only make it even tighter.

Special saddle pads designed to lift the saddle off the withers, or inserts designed to balance out the weight of the saddle across the horse's back, are available and can be a real help for hard-to-fit horses. **Shims,** or bridge pads, help to fill sunken areas in a horse's back due to atrophied muscles or conformational flaws. A "Western" bridge is a larger pad that fills in the midsection of the back in order to keep even bar pressure along this area. A front-lift shim pad is used to raise the front of the saddle, such as for a horse that is built downhill or is sunken behind the withers, while a rear lift raises the level of the back at the rear of the saddle.

STIRRUPS

For trail riding, the stirrups should hang directly below your body to allow your shoulders, elbows, and hips to be aligned in that classic Jineta seat. This allows for the greatest possible balance for the rider in any given situation. The stirrups should be wide enough for support and balance, especially helpful when going up and down hills or posting to the trot. They must be adjusted to a comfortable length, allowing for a little bend in the knees.

On Western saddles, the stirrup leathers must twist so that the stirrups rest at right angles to the leathers. Because the leather resists twisting and wants to go back to its original shape, this creates a torque that can put real strain on your ankles and knees. We used to leave a new saddle on the rack with a weighted broom handle through the stirrups to keep them twisted. This can take months

---

Fitting the Rider

You won't enjoy trail riding much unless your saddle also fits you. Here are some guidelines.

- The saddle shouldn't force you forward (putting pressure on the withers) or back (weighing the back of the saddle).
- The size of the seat is important for both comfort and safety. You should feel comfortable, with enough space for your legs, rear, and tummy, not wedged in or as though you are swimming around in a large, empty space.
- There should be about 4 inches between you and the pommel or swells and a hand's width between you and the top of the cantle. Your fanny should rest against the base of it, not up against the back of it.
- Fenders on Western saddles shouldn't rub or chafe your legs.
- The saddle should position your heel directly beneath your hip (and elbow and shoulder).
- The twist, the narrowest part of the saddle (just behind the fork), needs to fit you. Too narrow and you will be rubbed raw; too wide and you might feel as though you are being stretched out on the rack.

If the saddle doesn't fit you well, there are ways you can adjust it to make it more comfortable, including using fleece seat covers and extra padding. But if your body's alignment is put out of whack by the saddle's basic shape or fit, you'll never find the balance you'll need for your comfort and safety. Another saddle will be worth the investment.

---

to accomplish. Happily, you can now buy specially made stirrups designed to hang at right angles from the end of the stirrup leathers, which eliminates the need for twisting the leather and the resulting stress on ankles and knees.

Stirrup covers (also called **tapaderos** and **stirrup guards**) are another smart idea. They keep a foot from jamming through and getting hung up in a wreck, and therefore make nontraditional types of footwear safer to wear. I used to sling a pair of comfortable shoes over the saddle horn by the tied laces and ride in boots, then switch to the comfy shoes to walk. If I had had tapaderos or stirrup guards, I could have saved myself the trouble.

SADDLE CARE AND MAINTENANCE

Care and maintenance of your saddle are important for both your own and your horse's comfort, as well as for your safety on the trail. The best way to care for your saddle depends, in part, on the material from which it's made. Synthetics are easy care: A wipe or soapy scrub will keep them in their original condition indefinitely. Good leather requires maintenance to stay soft and supple. Wipe off dirt and sweat with a damp cloth after a ride, and soap it with a good saddle soap occasionally. A thorough oiling once a year should suffice.

More important for safety's sake are the parts you don't see when your horse is saddled. The billet(s), the latigo, and the cinch itself must be

A young trail horse in training, decked out in appropriate, comfortable, properly fitted tack.

checked every time you tack up. Before every ride, look for cracks or thin spots in the leather: These are weak points that, given enough wear or a sudden stress, could break. And down will come saddle, rider and all.

Finally, beware of cheap dyed leather; the dye will rub off and create a new look for your jeans or breeches. Black dye is especially unstable. You can try an over-treatment to set the dye, or scrub the saddle repeatedly until the dye stops running. You may find the end result is a blotchy or uneven dye job, often the result of less expensive saddles being made with different types of leather on different parts of the saddle. Different types of leather don't "take" dye evenly.

Saddle Pads and Blankets

Saddle pads are meant to protect your saddle from the sweat and dirt of your horse, not to protect the horse from the saddle, but unfortunately, that's how they tend to be used. In a perfect world, all saddles would fit their horses and there would be no need for the confounding array of saddle pads for improved saddle fit that are now on the market. Just as extra socks won't help the fit of tight shoes,

Dos and Don'ts of Saddle Care

- Do wipe off dirt and sweat after each ride.
- Do occasionally soap a leather saddle with good saddle soap.
- Do treat a saddle with neat's-foot oil once a year.
- Do let a soaked saddle dry out slowly, and then apply a good saddle soap.
- Don't ever throw a saddle.
- Don't set it down with the seat up and the skirts spread on the ground (this stresses the tree and can cause microfractures that could deepen over time).
- Don't allow a saddle to rest on its side for any length of time, because this bends the skirts and fenders (Western) or flaps (English). The result could be an unexpected pinch to you or your horse the next ride out.

extra padding won't make a too-small saddle fit a horse better. Thick pads often are used to compensate for an ill-fitting saddle, but the contact between the saddle and a thick pad is stiffer; the saddle is actually less stable on the horse's back.

Placement of the pad (as well as the saddle on it) affects your horse's comfort and range of motion. Be sure you can fit two fingers (about 1¾ inches) between the horse's withers and the pad.

Your goal should be to have minimal padding for effective protection of the saddle, with the added benefit of shock absorption. I prefer natural fiber saddle pads and blankets, an the fewer pads the better. A folded wool blanket works great as a thin layer of padding, and it's easier to toss in the washer than a thick Western horsehair pad.

Custom pads abound and come with many innovations. Some saddle pad designs have cutouts along the horse's spine to help ventilate the back and keep pressure off the spine. Some are made with a honeycomb pattern to allow for maximum cushion and ventilation at the same time. Some have gel inserts, some space-age polymers, and some special wicking felts. The choices can leave you reeling.

MATERIALS Different materials affect a horse's back in different ways. Wool pads and blankets help retain the horse's body heat while wicking away sweat. They also compress and expand, acting as natural shock absorbers. All of this helps to keep the back muscles from cramping.

If you prefer a pad to a blanket, look for 100 percent-wool pads cut to contour to the horse's back. A comparable, yet superior, fiber that is not yet in use for saddle pads is alpaca. It is finer, softer, and more elastic (depending on the crimp of the fiber); wicks and absorbs moisture; and comes in natural colors right off the critter. Lower grades of alpaca would be ideal for saddle pads and blankets, but the alpaca industry, unlike the Angora goat industry, has not yet recognized horsemen as a viable market for their superior fleeces. Horsehair pads

Keeping Pads Clean

It's important to keep your saddle pad or blanket clean because dirty pads (like dirty cinches) can gall and irritate the skin. Thank goodness caring for them is simple.

Launder wool blankets often or hose off the fleece side of wool pads and place them in the sun to dry. Brush them to break up any mats that could rub against your horse's back. On the trail, be careful never to lay down a pad or blanket where it can pick up debris that will turn into back-grinding pricklies once the pad is on your horse's back.

Rinse off synthetic mats with a hose and let them dry. Don't leave these out in the sun for long, though, as sunlight breaks down the material.

provide pretty much the same benefits as wool, just not quite as well.

Synthetics offer a trade-off of comfort for easy care. Neoprene makes the horse's back sweat more because it does not "breathe." Neoprene pads (as well as cinches) grab onto the surface and allow for no natural "slippage," like natural fibers do. As a result, they tend to pull the hair. This synthetic also tends to deteriorate over time with exposure to the elements. Pads with neoprene filling (for shock absorption) and wool backing should work well, as long as the layers don't create a pad more than an inch thick.

Bridles and Bits

A bridle, with or without a bit, is for communicating with your horse. If either you or your horse is at a stage of schooling that requires a severe bit for control, I certainly don't want to run into you out on the trail. Some of the best trail horses I have ever known have carried their 11- and 12-year-old riders over literally hundreds of miles with nothing more than a halter and lead rope for "control."

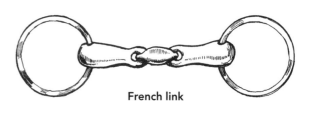

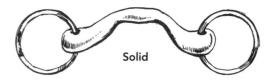

French link

Solid

Different mouthpieces can be used with snaffle bits.

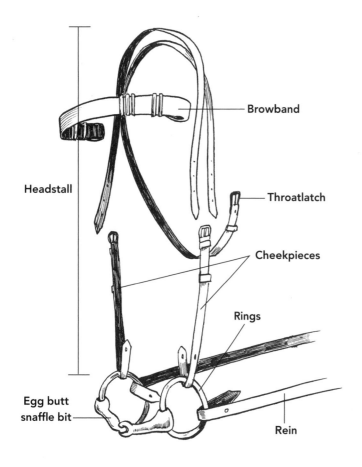

Browband

Headstall

Throatlatch

Cheekpieces

Rings

Egg butt
snaffle bit

Rein

A simple bridle, ideal for trail riding.

BIT BASICS

The best rule of thumb is to ride in the mildest bit in which both you and your horse are comfortable. Most trail riders get along well in mild snaffles or low-port, short-shank curbs, or even hackamores or sidepulls. Special bridles are made with snaps or buckles that let you attach or detach a bit — converting a halter to a bridle and vice versa. These are handy for stopping along the trail for grazing breaks.

Basic types of bits are snaffle, curb, and Pelham, which can be used as either or both a snaffle and/or curb.

Snaffle bits are those with no shanks. With these the degree of pressure exerted on the reins translates directly to the horse's mouth. Snaffle bits consist of a mouthpiece and rings (for rein attachment).

Curb bits differ in that in addition to the mouthpiece, they have **shanks** that extend beneath the mouthpiece and act as leverage to magnify the force felt in the horse's mouth. They also have what is called the **purchase,** or **upper shanks,** which contributes to the degree of poll pressure felt when the bit is engaged.

Pelham bits will create the pressure of either snaffle or curb or both, depending on where on the bit the reins are attached or which reins are in use at any given moment. Reins attached at the mouthpiece rings will convey the effects of a snaffle; reins attached to the rings at the bottom of the shanks create a curb effect.

THE MOUTHPIECE

Mouthpieces come in an amazing array of styles and designs. Jointed mouthpieces are common in snaffle bits, and many people, even people who produce tack catalogs, commonly mistake a jointed mouthpiece for a snaffle, even if the bit has shanks. Any bit can have a jointed mouthpiece.

Things to look for in jointed mouthpieces are smooth joints, without jagged edges to the metal, both in the horse's mouth and at the sides. Poorly jointed rein rings can pinch the horse's sensitive lips. Also, be sure that the roof of your horse's mouth is high enough to accommodate the bit when the reins pull the rings down or back and the joint peaks. French-link mouthpieces are even

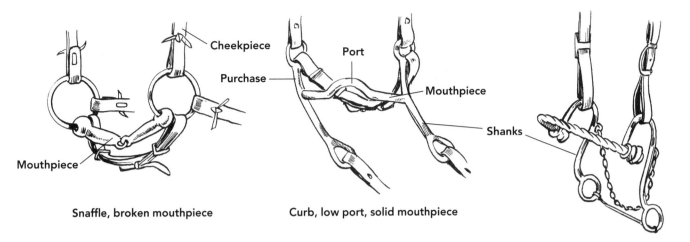

Snaffle, broken mouthpiece

Curb, low port, solid mouthpiece

Bitless, shanked hackamore

Use the mildest bit possible for your horse for trail riding.

milder than the traditional jointed ones because they include a third link that prevents the joint from peaking and jabbing at the horse's upper mouth.

Solid mouthpieces range from a straight bar to a high port. Usually a slight port is preferred, as it provides adequate room for the tongue to lie comfortably beneath the bit. High ports are designed to increase pressure on the horse's tongue and can also poke at the roof of the mouth if the horse's mouth is too small for the bit or if the bit is used harshly. Rollers within ports are meant to keep a nervous or easily bored horse engaged with the bit. Some strange contraptions can be found under the heading "show bits," including mouthpieces made of bicycle chains or thin twisted metal. No horse should ever know such things exist, especially a trail horse.

Some things inherently make a mouthpiece more or less comfortable for the horse. Always check for rough surfaces and file down any that are found. Be sure any joints (mouthpiece or bit rings) operate smoothly and won't catch and pinch tender skin. Cheaper bits often have poorly designed joints, so check carefully before buying.

Generally, the wider the metal of the mouthpiece, the gentler it is on the horse because it provides more surface area to disperse the pressure delivered from the reins. Some bits are coated in rubber, which increases the bit width even more, and while that greatly reduces the pressure on

tender bars and tongues, rubber tastes awful. Stainless steel, sweet iron, and copper are popular choices for bits. Sweet iron and copper tend to increase salivation, which many believe increases the horse's acceptance of the bit. Aluminum bits are cheaper, but also thought to taste bad.

Any mouthpiece must be large enough that the horse's lips clear it easily on either side, but not so large that it will move from side to side as contact is made on the reins. For the average 1,000-pound horse, this means about a 5½-inch-wide mouthpiece.

Bit guards (leather or rubber stoppers attached at either side of the mouthpiece) can be used to prevent the bit from sliding, or use a full-cheek mouthpiece with built-in metal stops to prevent bit slippage.

Curb bits are used with a **curb strap** or **chain.** This provides the fulcrum for the leverage created by the shanks against the horse's mouth. The tighter the curb, the greater the leverage pressure. A curb chain should be loose enough that you can easily place a finger between the chain and the horse's chin.

BRIDLE FIT

Equally as important as saddle fit, the bridle and bit must properly fit the horse (see page 74). An ill-fitting bridle won't function properly and can cause pain and confusion to the horse. If the bit doesn't fit the horse's mouth or isn't held at the proper level in the horse's mouth, it can pinch, gouge, and/or put constant pressure on tender tissues. This discomfort can cause evading the bit,

Fitting a Bridle

The design and fit of the bridle contribute not only to the horse's comfort but also to the clarity of the cues it transmits. Here are some tips.

1. The **headstall** holds the bit in place in the horse's mouth. With the bridle on and the bit in place, check for position by looking for one or two wrinkles at the upper corners of the horse's mouth.

   If the bit is barely crinkling the edges of the lips, it is most likely resting over the **bars** (the toothless portion along the lower jaw) of the mouth — right where you want it.

   If there is a gap between the bit and the edge of the horse's mouth, take off the bridle and shorten the cheekpieces. This will raise the level of the bit in the horse's mouth.

   Conversely, if the bit is stretching the corners of the horse's mouth, possibly even causing the horse to open his mouth to avoid the pressure, lengthen the cheekpieces to lower the bit position. The cheekpieces buckle together and are easy to adjust.

2. If your bridle has a **browband** and/or a **noseband**, check to be sure that neither is too tight or too loose. A too-tight browband can put pressure on the horse's ears, and a tight nosepiece will prevent the horse from opening his mouth and informing you of any discomfort with the bit. Some Western-style bridles are designed to go over one ear, and have neither browband nor noseband.

3. Most bridles have a **throatlatch**, a strap that goes beneath the horse's jaw and buckles in place. Be sure to allow two fingers of air between the throatlatch and the horse in order for him to be able to comfortably flex his neck.

head tossing, stargazing, even clamping down on the bit and running for the hills in an effort to get away from the pain.

BITLESS BRIDLES

Bitless bridles are very popular on the trail because they provide adequate control while staying out of the horse's mouth. Not all bitless bridles, however, are created equal.

Western-style hackamores can be found in bozal and mechanical styles. A **bozal** has a knot at one end that is usually weighted and wrapped with rawhide. Mechanical hackamores can be very severe if they are made with long shanks; the pressure on the bridge of the nose is multiplied from these shanks, just as bit pressure is from bit shanks. Unless your horse tends to be unruly, look for a hackamore with moderate-length shanks.

Sidepulls are similar to reinforced flat halters with reins attached. They are the mildest form of headgear available.

In all of these cases, signals are sent from the reins to the horse's face and poll. Pressure on the reins engages the bozal, nosepiece, or noseband, and at the same time exerts pressure on the poll.

MATERIALS

Although leather is still the most common material for bridles, nylon and new synthetic materials such as Biothane and Beta Biothane are good choices for the trail rider because they are durable and easy-care. As a fun plus, they really expand the choices of colors and styles available. Biothane, a polyurethane-coated, polyester webbing, comes in matte, glossy, or translucent colors.

Like other synthetics, Biothane doesn't absorb sweat and is easy to maintain, cleaning up with just soap and water. Beta Biothane is made from the same material, so it too is easy to clean and care for (you can even toss it in the washing machine), but it is processed to feel more like soft, pliant leather. And all those nifty colors don't fade.

A great addition to the Biothane line, and to any

trail rider's tack trunk, is a bridle made from Glowbelt. This is a type of Biothane that when activated by body heat or exposure to light glows in the dark. (It's a soft white in daylight and lime green in low light.) You can buy the material separately (and no, it's not cheap) and construct or customize your own bridles, halters, and cruppers, or make glow-in-the-dark accessories for both you and your horse to light up the horizon the next time you venture out after dark.

REINS

The reins of a trail horse's bridle should be carefully considered, since styles that work for other activities may not be suitable for the trail. Heavy reins, such as rope reins and fancy, round-braided romel reins, weigh downward on the bit, and over the miles will dull your horse's mouth sensitivity. Lighter reins will preserve a light mouth.

Reins that snap on to the bit are another common annoyance to trail horses. The metal-on-metal contact at the bit, constantly rattling in his mouth, can cause head shaking as the horse tries to evade the clanging vibrations.

Short, looped "roping reins" are another bad choice for the trail, because the instant your horse puts his head down (for example, to watch his footing through rocks or over a bridge), you are either leaning down over his neck to keep hold of the reins or sitting atop your horse with your hands empty. If your reins are too short and you try to "correct" your horse when he puts his head down, his head won't be free to swing with the rhythm of a fast-paced walk or to counterbalance his body going down a steep hill.

Loop reins are a bad choice simply because a loop is easier for you or your horse to get hung up in if there is a wreck. The same goes for tying loose reins together. The end result is a loop that becomes a noose in one bad instant.

It is safest to ride with split reins, even at the risk of dropping one, because they can't catch on your boot or a tree snag. A slick way to avoid a dropped rein is to wrap a short, narrow piece of Velcro around the reins to hold them together. This way you don't risk dropping a rein, but if a sudden move catches you or your horse in the loop, the Velcro will come apart, safely releasing its hold.

Last but not least, don't tie a horse by the reins. If he pulls back, he will hurt his mouth, and very likely break the reins. Always tie him by a lead rope.

Breast Collars, Breeching, and Cruppers

Three additional pieces of tack are of special interest to the trail rider who heads for the hills: breast collars, breeching, and cruppers. All are designed to keep the saddle in place on the horse's back. A breast collar keeps a saddle from slipping backwards, while breeching and/or a crupper keeps it from slipping forward and jamming up against the horse's withers or shoulders (or worse, slipping over them!). Again, the range of styles and materials for these pieces is a little overwhelming, and again, my preferences lean toward traditional leather.

BREAST COLLARS

Leather breast collars with wool flocking are strong, durable, attractive, and comfortable for the horse. Styles that look as if they are made from cinches are also a good choice for strength, style, and comfort, with the added advantages of color choice and washability. Like any other piece of tack, a breast collar will last longer if it is well cared for, and the same standards apply to it as for other pieces made from the materials already discussed. Watch for stickers or burrs that can get caught in the flocking of a fleece-lined breast collar, because these can rub a horse raw in no time as the collar moves and pulls against the horse's chest.

Be particular as to how you fasten a breast collar. It shouldn't ride up along your horse's wind-

A fleece-lined breast collar and crupper are most comfortable for a horse during a long ride.

pipe and cut off his breath just as he is lugging you both up a steep hill, any more than it should sway above his knees. It should ride squarely across the front of his chest, giving him something to pull against in a climb. Proper adjustment is critical to the purpose of the equipment and to your horse's safety and comfort. Horses get tangled up in poorly adjusted tack every day.

BREECHINGS AND CRUPPERS

Breechings and cruppers are blessings to any rider on a barrel-shaped or low-withered horse. A **breeching** works something like a breast collar in reverse, to keep the saddle from slipping forward when a horse is going down a hill. It consists of a strap that goes around the horse's buttocks and attaches to either side of the saddle, with straps that ride over the horse's hips to hold the butt strap at the proper level. Just as for a breast strap, the breeching should neither rub up too high nor sling too low.

A **crupper** is a soft leather (or Biothane) loop that fits around the base of the tail and clips to the back of the saddle. It pulls against the root of the tail to keep the saddle from slipping forward.

Duds and Headwear

Trail-riding apparel should be comfortable and safe. Style is a matter of personal preference. There's not a trail out there that cares if you wear stretch Lycra or faded blue jeans, but some of us have learned the hard way the results that come with different choices. From head to toe, there are choices to be made that can significantly improve your enjoyment on the trail.

Avoid pants with inseams, overalls, or pants with a big fat seam right up the middle of your seat — which may possibly eliminate your favorite pair of jeans. They will bruise and abrade your skin in sensitive places, guaranteed. Elastic waistbands may get you on Blackwell's "Worst Dressed List" but you'll be sitting there in much more comfort than people who place fashion first. Stretch pants can be very comfy, but certain fabrics, such as Spandex and nylon, can leave you slip-slidin' in the saddle.

Here are some more time-tested tips:

✳ Always wear (or at least bring) long sleeves on a trail ride, even if only on a very lightweight shirt. They will protect you (somewhat) from abrasions should you fall and at the very least protect you from sunburn.

✳ Dress in layers even if the weather is warm.

✳ Choose soft, well-worn, or brushed fabrics for maximum comfort.

✳ Don't wear baggy clothes or floppy jewelry; they can catch on your tack, brush, or fence wire.

✳ Ponchos are not practical. They can strangle you or get caught up in your gear.

✳ Cotton is cooler, wool is warmer. But cotton and silk are not great choices if you might get wet, as they will stick to your body and give you chills.

✳ If you ride during hunting season, wear orange or reflective colors.

SAFETY HELMET

Wear a helmet! A fall or a collision with a heavy branch will make you glad your brainbox was protected. Helmets come in an array of styles and designs that are attractive, lightweight, cool, comfortable and, most important, impact-resistant. The visor will help protect your eyes from the glaring sun, too. You can purchase a decent helmet for less than $40.

Don't substitute a bicycle helmet for a riding helmet. The people who design helmets put a lot of work into figuring out how you are most likely to land from either type of fall and the designs differ accordingly.

If you don't have enough sense to ride in a helmet, at least consider the practicalities of a hat. I almost never ride with a hat, and halfway through almost every ride I wish I had one. Western-style ("cowboy") hats keep the sun out of your eyes and shield your face and the back of your neck to some degree, and they can keep the rain off your face as well. Straw is best for summer, felt for winter, and a plastic hat cover for just about anytime in my native Pacific Northwest (or in your area whenever it might rain). Stocking caps keep your ears warm in really cool weather. It's important to remember that a significant amount of body heat is lost through your head, so cold-weather headgear is a must.

FOOTWEAR

The two sometimes conflicting priorities for what you wear on your feet are comfort and safety. Wear sturdy boots with slanted heels (the easier to bail off with) that are comfortable enough to walk in. (You should plan to walk occasionally anyway. This is as good for you as it is for your horse. It helps you work out stiff, sore muscles, and allows your horse to get a breather.)

Boots that pull on are safer than those you have to lace up, because if you ever get stuck in a stirrup, they also pull *off*. Hybrid riding shoes are a good option, and stirrup covers, such as tapederos

and specially designed safety covers, allow you to wear just about any comfy shoe without concern about shoving a foot through the stirrup.

Tapaderos and other enclosed types not only prevent your foot from jamming through the stirrup but also have cozier, more mundane, benefits. They form a neat pocket for handwarmer packets, providing you with toasty toes for hours of comfy cold-weather riding.

OTHER APPAREL

Some riders won't go out without chaps or half-chaps. These can be made of leather or synthetic,

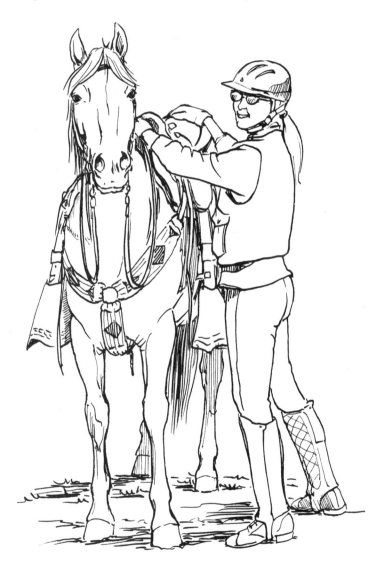

A helmet, sturdy boots, the right tack, and you're good to go.

but as much of a traditionalist as I am, I can see the benefits of lightweight, sturdy nylon chaps. Just like leather, they repel water and brush and help to hold in heat, but they are easier to roll up and stow in very little space when not in use.

Always bring along gloves. Though kid leather is a rare luxury, high-tech substitutes offer some pretty nifty features. Skin-hugging synthetics keep your hands warm while allowing your fingertips to remain free to communicate with your horse's mouth. In colder weather, Gore-Tex and other synthetics are designed to keep your hands warm and dry while still allowing feeling. Even cloth gloves will come in handy if you wind up clearing brush from the trail.

Weather Gear

Mother Nature can have a skewed sense of timing. Try to be as prepared as possible to withstand her whims. Here are some reminders.

If you expect inclement weather, avoid cotton and silk (which cling and chill).

If rain is even a remote possibility, always bring

Private Comforts

——— ❧ ———

Now for the advice mama never told you. Ladies; two words — panty liners. Sweat and moisture can become uncomfortable if not wicked away. Thongs are out; too much shifting in the saddle. Sports bras, as opposed to anything a fancy lingerie shop might offer, are your best friend. On the other hand, the men I've asked claim briefs are more comfortable than boxers on long rides, and I'll take their word for it. 'Tis said boxers ride up. Medicated powder is often recommended to ward off chafing. Oh, and aren't those lamb's wool seat cushions heavenly?

along a waterproof jacket or slicker. Don't wait until you are soaked to get out your rain gear, which can only *repel* water. It can't dry you if you get wet before putting it on. Better to ride for a while overprotected than to listen to your teeth chatter all the way home.

Be sure to practice the art of putting on a slicker while mounted in a safe place. Some horses spook at the rustling sound and the feel of the fabric over their hips. Standing at the crest of a steep trail in the pouring rain is not the time to find out if your horse minds these sensations.

Hot, bright, relentless sun presents different challenges. Cotton and silk are your best bets to stay cool (but should be considered only as the base for other layers). Don't forget sunglasses, and if you wear them (or regular glasses), get a nifty "keeper." This attaches to the earpiece ends of the glasses and fastens behind your head to keep your glasses from falling to the ground. Pretty handy if a horse takes a sudden step to the side.

Remember to protect against skin damage. Sunscreen and lip balm take up so little space for the relief they provide.

And don't forget your horse! If he has any exposed pink skin, he needs sunscreen, too.

Packsaddles, Saddle Packs, and Other Cool Stuff

For horses carrying gear instead of a rider, packsaddles have come a long way. Two standards rule the trails: the sawbuck and the decker. Both normally use a breast collar and breeching to keep the load centered and stable.

Sawbuck saddles are double-rigged and lightweight. **Decker** saddles offer more adjustment options and a built-in board that helps to distribute the weight of the load over the tree. Quarter straps from the breeching to the tree and to the cinch keep the breeching from riding up under the horse's tail. Deckers are single-rigged, and the latigo is passed over this stabilizing board and can be adjusted forwards or backwards. Both styles have exposed parts for tying or hanging pack boxes or bags.

Just as with a riding saddle, the rigging should not be over-tightened because it can badly gall the animal. Packsaddles are often double-padded to provide cushioning from the dead weight bearing down on the horse's back.

Onto the packsaddles are loaded pack boxes (made from bear-proof aluminum or steel), pack bags, or panniers, and top packs, made from leather, canvas, or nylon, that hang from the pack tree. Styrofoam "cooler" inserts can be placed inside the panniers to keep food cold or even frozen for days on a pack trip. But for a short outing, freezing a water bottle overnight and keeping it next to your lunch keeps the water cool and the food fresh.

Outfitters master a range of knots and tricks for balancing and securing packhorse loads. Covers, ropes, and other equipment round out a pack system, or you can purchase complete systems ready to pack and go with built-in side-load and top-load compartments. These are designed with the occasional packer in mind and take the challenge of knot-tying out of packing. What these systems lack in traditional appeal they make up in simple convenience. See page 272 for more on packsaddles.

For day riding, the array of pack equipment is certainly enticing. You can fit a horn pack over your saddle horn, stocked with lip balm, a camera, GPS, and trail mix, and place a cantle pack behind you, complete with a change of clothes and a good book in case you decide to stop and let your horse graze. Throw saddlebags behind the cantle, complete with the real essentials, lunch for you and your horse.

Just don't ever be tempted to carry the basic essentials for survival in anything that isn't directly attached to your body. A fanny pack or a small backpack makes the perfect carryall for a knife, first-aid kit, cell phone, and, of course, a chocolate bar. (See chapter 7 for more on what to take and where to put it.)

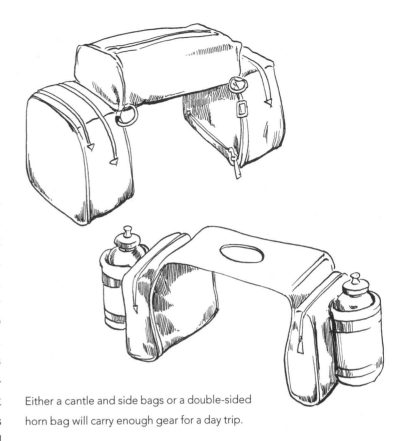

Either a cantle and side bags or a double-sided horn bag will carry enough gear for a day trip.

Bells, Whistles, and ID Tags

Yup, bells and whistles have their place when trail riding. A horse with a small bell attached to his halter is a lot easier to track down if he gets lost than a horse that can sneak through the underbrush unheralded. Another good idea is to get ID tags made for your horse. Pet catalogs and stores offer custom-engraved tags for dogs that fit nicely onto a bridle or halter. Attaching a small reflector to your horse's halter can make all the difference in being able to find him if he wanders loose at night.

The sound of a whistle carries for miles in the wilderness, whereas shouts, hollers, and sobs disperse and die out, deflected by the brush, wind, and humidity. The shrill blast can also be effective in warding off wildlife.

CHAPTER 4

Conditioning the Trail Horse

⊰━◦━⊱

Is your horse ready to hit the trail? This chapter covers how to assess and improve his fitness level. Most of us know better than to jump out of bed one spring morning and run a 10K race after sitting around all winter. Aches, pains, chafing, blisters, irritability, and a firm conviction never to do anything even remotely similar — ever again — are sure to follow. Take the time to evaluate your horse's condition to ensure that this doesn't happen with him. Don't expect a "pasture ornament" to conquer serious trail miles without appropriate conditioning ahead of time.

Assessing Your Horse's Condition

In the days when "horsepower" was *horse* power, horses stayed in condition for their jobs by doing them day in and day out. These days, there is a lot of idle horseflesh standing around. Horses aren't automatically in shape for strenuous activity any more than we are. Stabled horses quickly turn into cream puffs if not exercised on a regular basis. Those that live in a seminatural herd state at least have the benefit of exercising by wandering around. But does wandering around constitute adequate conditioning for a horse to carry himself and his rider over miles of varying terrain?

It depends on the horse, on the rider, and on the trails. Here's a sobering thought: Every year horses die on the trail due to a myriad of causes, not the least of which is overexertion and any number of veterinary emergencies that can arise from that. Perhaps even more sobering is the fact that you are responsible for removing your mount should he expire on the trail. Getting your horse in good condition before you hit the trails is the best way to ensure that he will be packing you out, instead of the other way around.

The better condition your horse is in, the more mental and physical stress he can withstand without developing resistance, resentment, fatigue, or injury. A horse that is out of shape, overweight, or malnourished is prone to sprains, strains, or, at the very least, tiring easily and certainly not enjoying physical exertion.

BODY CONDITION SCORE

The Body Condition Score, developed in 1981 by Don R. Henneke for his Ph.D. dissertation at Texas A&M University, is an excellent starting point for visually assessing a horse's body condition. Henneke's scoring system determines a horse's condition for work or surviving cold. Horses are scored from 1 to 9 based on weight, with 1 representing an emaciated animal (often too far gone to recover) and 9 being a butterball.

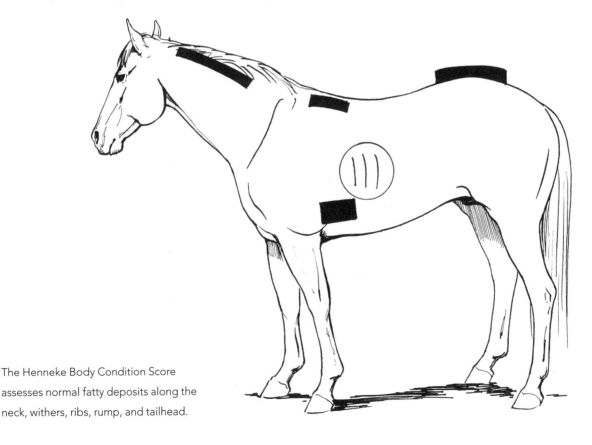

The Henneke Body Condition Score assesses normal fatty deposits along the neck, withers, ribs, rump, and tailhead.

Henneke Body Condition Score

Here are the criteria used to determine body condition score.

1. Poor. Animal extremely emaciated. Spinous processes, ribs, tailhead, and hooks and pins project prominently. Bone structure of withers, shoulders, and neck easily noticeable. No fatty tissue can be detected by feel.

2. Very Thin. Animal emaciated. Slight fat covering base of spinous processes; transverse processes of lumbar vertebrae feel rounded. Spinous processes, ribs, tailhead, and hooks and pins prominent. Withers, shoulders, neck structures faintly discernible.

3. Thin. Fat built up about halfway on spinous processes; transverse processes cannot be felt. Slight fat cover over ribs. Spinous processes and ribs easily discernible. Tailhead prominent, but individual vertebrae cannot be visually identified. Pin bones not distinguishable. Withers, shoulders, and neck accentuated.

4. Moderately Thin. Negative crease along back. Faint outline of ribs discernible. Tailhead prominence depends on conformation; fat can be felt around it. Hook bones not discernible. Withers, shoulders, and neck not obviously thin.

5. Moderate. Back level. Ribs cannot be visually distinguished but can be easily felt. Fat around tailhead beginning to feel spongy. Withers appear rounded over spinous processes. Shoulders and neck blend smoothly into body.

6. Moderate to Fleshy. May have slight crease down back. Fat over ribs feels spongy. Fat round tailhead feels soft. Fat beginning to be deposited along the sides of the withers, behind the shoulders, and along the sides of the neck.

7. Fleshy. May have crease down back. Individual ribs can be felt, but between ribs there is noticeable filling with fat. Fat around tailhead is soft. Fat is deposited along withers, behind shoulders, and along the neck.

8. Fat. Crease down back. Difficult to feel ribs. Fat around tailhead very soft. Area along withers filled with fat. Area behind shoulder filled in flush. Noticeable thickening of neck. Fat deposited along inner buttocks.

9. Extremely Fat. Obvious crease down back. Patchy fat appearing over ribs. Bulging fat around tailhead, along withers, behind shoulders, and along neck. Fat along inner buttocks may rub together. Flank filled in flush.

A thin horse must not start a conditioning program without first putting on weight and building up his reserves. Horses with low scores don't have enough fat reserves, and their bodies must break down muscle to supply them with energy, which in turn further depletes their overall condition. A fat horse can start conditioning, but like any overweight individual should do so gradually, slowly increasing his workload. Fat horses are more likely to suffer from heat stress, colic, and founder.

The optimal score for working horses, including regular trail mounts, is between 5 and 6. Horses that compete in trail-riding sports often score between 4 and 5. In general, it takes about 2 months of feeding or conditioning to raise or lower a horse's body condition score by one point.

VITAL SIGNS

Vital signs reveal important information about your horse's condition. These include temperature, heart rate (pulse), and respiratory rate (collectively referred to as **TPR**), all of which indicate how efficiently his body is working. It's also important to recognize your horse's degree of hydration and gut sounds.

Learn what your horse's individual resting vital signs are and how quickly he returns to them after exertion. A horse in good condition should recover his resting state in 10 to 15 minutes; a horse in poor shape may take up to 45 minutes; a horse in distress, even longer. Recovery rates are an excellent indicator of condition and extremely helpful in deciding when to increase or decrease your horse's level of physical activity.

BODY TEMPERATURE

Body temperature reflects the efficiency with which your horse's body converts stored body energy (that is, fat, glycogen, muscle tissue) into work energy (motion). Converting fat into movement is only about 20 to 25 percent efficient, which means that the remaining 75 to 80 percent converts to heat energy. This heat energy is what increases your horse's body temperature. The dissipation of metabolic heat can present a problem for horses in poor condition.

TAKING A HORSE'S TEMPERATURE Here are the steps in taking your horse's temperature. You'll need a rectal thermometer (digitals are easy to read and dependable), lubricant (this can be petroleum jelly, Chapstick, vegetable oil, or even just spit if you are out on the trail), a piece of string, a clip, and about 1 to 3 minutes.

1 Tie a string to the end of the thermometer. Tie the other end of the string to a clip, and clip it to the horse's tail. This will keep the thermometer from getting lost inside the horse.

2 Lubricate the end of the thermometer.

3 If using a glass thermometer, shake it down before proceeding.

4 Lift the horse's tail and gently insert the thermometer into the horse's anus so that the reading end goes into the rectum about 4 inches.

5 Hold it in place for at least 1 minute. Most digital thermometers will beep when the reading is reached.

6 Be prepared to take a second reading to verify accuracy.

A temperature between 99.8° and 101.3°F is normal for a horse that is resting or working lightly, but hot weather can raise that somewhat. Hard

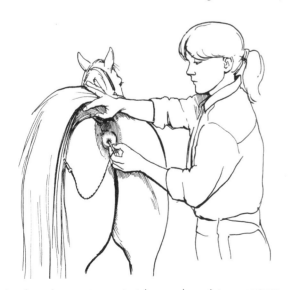

A safe and accurate way to take your horse's temperature

Variable Vital Signs	
Average resting temperature	101.5°F (between 99.8° and 101.3°F)
Pulse:	
Average resting heart rate	Less than 42 beats per minute (bpm)
High fitness resting heart rate	As low as 26 bpm
Working heart rate	From 75 to 105 bpm
Heavy work heart rate	As high as 200 bpm
Average respiration	Between 12 and 16 breaths per minute
Capillary refill time	Less than 2 seconds
Gum color	Light pink

work can raise your horse's temperature by two degrees in mild weather (70°F), and by almost four degrees in hot weather. The closer the air temperature is to the horse's body temperature, the harder it is for the horse's body to dissipate heat. High humidity compromises heat dissipation even further because it severely reduces the cooling that would otherwise occur through sweat evaporation.

In order to know what is normal for your horse, take and record his temperature under a variety of conditions and workloads. Changes in temperature not related to work could indicate illness or heat stress. A sustained temperature above 102° usually indicates disease. Bacterial infections (colds, infected wounds) raise temperatures to between 102.5° and 103.5°, while fevers from 104.5° to 105.5° usually indicate a viral infection. Temperatures due to viral infection sometimes dip below normal in the morning, then rise progressively during the day. It's a good idea to take your horse's temperature throughout the day to monitor changes if you suspect illness. Heat stress is indicated if the horse's rectal temperature remains above 104° after rest (see chapter 10).

PULSE

Heart rate, or pulse, is probably the best way to evaluate how hard your horse is working. Measured in beats per minute **(bpm)**, the pulse tells you the rate and strength of his heartbeat. The time it takes for your horse to recover his resting heart rate after exercise indicates his level of physical conditioning.

The harder your horse works, the higher his heart rate climbs, but as his condition improves, the more work it takes to raise his pulse. The better his condition, the more quickly his heart rate will return to its normal resting rate after it *is* elevated. This makes comparing heart rates through the course of conditioning your best tool in evaluating his progress.

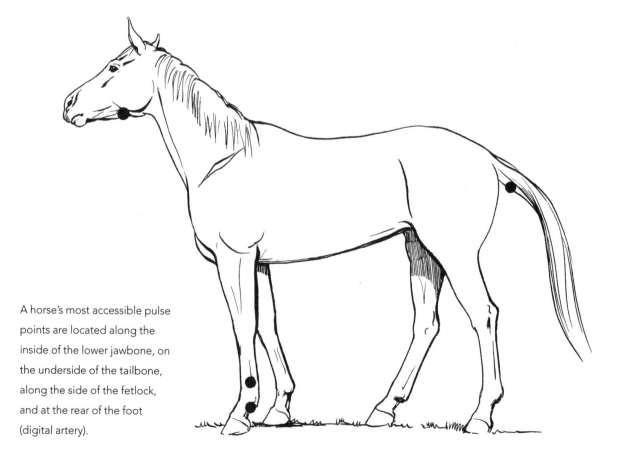

A horse's most accessible pulse points are located along the inside of the lower jawbone, on the underside of the tailbone, along the side of the fetlock, and at the rear of the foot (digital artery).

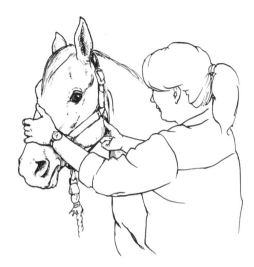

Taking a horse's pulse by hand

There are three reliable ways to measure your horse's heart rate: feeling for a pulse with your finger, listening for heartbeat with a stethoscope, and measuring with an electric heart rate monitor. Since the tool you are most likely to have with you on the trail is a finger, learning to take your horse's pulse by hand is recommended.

Learning to use a stethoscope is valuable, as it can tell you a lot about your horse's health status. A stethoscope also amplifies gut (digestive) sounds and breathing (pulmonary) sounds, and is an easy-to-use, inexpensive, and effective tool for auscultation (listening to the inside of your horse's body).

A heart rate monitor allows you to measure your horse's actual heart rate *during* the peak of physical exertion, as well as before and after exercise. This tool gives a more exact picture of your horse's condition than methods that require the horse to stand still to take his pulse.

MEASURING A HORSE'S PULSE

By hand. Locate one of these pulse points: along the inside of the lower jawbone, on the underside of the tailbone, or along the side of the foot. You can also feel his heart by placing your hand beneath the elbow on the left side of his chest. Feel with your fingertips until you can clearly feel the pulse beating against them, and then apply just

Taking a horse's pulse by stethoscope

enough pressure to be able to distinguish each beat. The best method is to time with a watch for 15 seconds while you count the heartbeats. Multiply the number you get by four to get the beats per minute. Since heart rate drops significantly in the first 30 seconds after a horse stops moving, the best you will get is an average.

Using a stethoscope. Position the diaphragm of the instrument against the horse's left side, along the girth, just behind and a little above the point of the elbow. Let the horse settle for a moment to allow the heart rate to return to normal, then listen for the heartbeat. It will sound like *lub-dub, lub-dub, lub-dub.* Each *lub-dub* counts as one beat. Count for 15 seconds and multiply the number by four for the beats per minute.

Using a heart rate monitor. This instrument works by transmitting an electronic signal from electrodes to a wristwatchlike receiver worn by the rider. Lubricate the electrodes with a special conductive gel, then place the electrodes on the girth and at the withers underneath the tack. To check

Taking a horse's pulse using a heart rate monitor

the horse's heart rate at any point in training, touch a button on the receiver.

Both the rate and strength of your horse's heartbeat are indicators of his condition. A normal heart rate for a healthy horse at rest should be around 38 to 42 bpm. The higher the fitness level of the individual horse, the lower the standing heart rate will be: as low as 26 beats per minute in exceptionally fit equine athletes. A heart rate that stays above 60 in a calm, quiet horse signals trouble; a rate above 80 constitutes an emergency. A pulse between 75 and 105 bpm following moderate work is average; extreme exertion can raise the rate above 200.

CHECKING THE RECOVERY RATE In a healthy horse, the heart rate will fall back down from its peak during exertion to 60 bpm after 10 to 15 minutes of rest; in an out-of-condition horse, recovery may take up to 45 minutes. If the rate falls to 44 to 50 bpm within 15 minutes, that is a good indication your horse is in top shape and can handle even more-intense training. If his pulse doesn't

fall below 72 bpm in that amount of time, he is overexerted. A pulse that is difficult to detect may be weak, indicating possible heart disease, while a vigorous, easy-to-detect pulse is common when a horse has worked hard. Be aware that a strong pulse can also be induced by drugs, poison, or disease: all the more reason to know your horse's normal standing and working heart rates.

When people say a horse has "heart" they probably don't know the half of it. A well-conditioned horse can multiply his heart rate nearly 10 times from a resting state to maximum work output — from around 26 bpm to more than 200. The ideal heart rate during peak exertion for a horse in conditioning training ranges from 120 to 160 bpm. Because a fit horse's heart rate drops rapidly, it should fall back down to the low 60s within 10 minutes after exertion.

To measure and track your horse's recovery rate, take his pulse immediately after training or during regular intervals in your routine. Keep him still for 10 to 15 minutes at each checkpoint and measure the heart rate at 2-, 5-, 10-, and 15-minute intervals. If his heart rate doesn't return to 60 within 15 minutes, the horse is working too hard for his level of condition. The training program should be backed off to a level the horse can recover from properly, then increased gradually as the horse is able to handle it. If he recovers his resting heart rate within 10 minutes, that means the current training level will only maintain his condition, not improve it. To increase fitness, increase his workload.

INTERPRETING THE RESULTS Your horse's heart rate is affected by more than just the work you ask of him. Everything from the weather to the footing to his attitude can add to the load on his heart. A 2-mile trot through the woods can turn into a heart-pounding workout if the trail footing is loose and deep, the temperature and humidity are high, or your horse is overexcited. Excitement or fear can escalate heart rate in seconds.

Elevated heart rate can also indicate pain or illness. If a high heart rate can't be accounted for by work or excitement (or fear), investigate for other signs of illness or injury. Generally, the more pain a horse is feeling, the higher his pulse will rise. Check his temperature, respiration, and gut sounds, as colic is one of the most common reasons for elevated pulse. Also check around his body for heat, swelling, or wounds.

RESPIRATION

There is a correlation between a horse's heart rate and respiration. The heart rate of a healthy horse should be two to three times that of his respiration. **Respiration** is the rate at which your horse breathes in and out. It is the means by which he brings oxygen into his lungs (for distribution throughout his body by his heart) and expels waste products (such as carbon dioxide) from his system. It also plays a role in cooling his body, accounting for about 25 percent of heat dissipation.

Most of the time it is not the amount of oxygen drawn into the lungs that limits a horse's condition or performance, but his ability to convert it to energy. A horse can have compromised lung capacity from illness or congenital defect.

Respiration is measured by counting each complete breath (one breath = one inhale + one exhale) for 15 seconds, then multiplying by four. You can count breaths by watching the horse's nostrils expand and contract, by watching his rib cage rise and fall, or by listening to the sounds of his windpipe. Sometimes it helps to put a stethoscope or your ear to his neck in order to hear each breath. To listen to the lungs, place the diaphragm of the stethoscope between two ribs. It's a good idea to listen to several different spots. It's normal to hear air moving in and out, but sounds of fluid, rattling, or wheezing are trouble signs.

Normal respiration for a healthy horse at rest should be around eight to ten complete breaths per minute. It should take about the same amount of time to inhale as to exhale. Respiration increases as your horse works. Generally at the trot or canter, a horse will complete one breath per stride, and may suddenly breathe much faster as soon as he stops. The respiratory rate usually falls right along with the heart rate as the horse recovers, but a horse that continues to breathe heavily may just be hot. This is one reason why respiration is not considered a reliable indicator of a horse's condition. It is too closely tied to thermoregulation and may represent more of an effort to dissipate heat than to recover spent oxygen or vent waste products.

A horse whose respiration is elevated or does not return to normal may be dealing with more than just being out of shape or out of breath. Elevated respiration is also a common reaction to excitement, pain, fever, and many types of illness. Just as it is for humans, mucus in the windpipe from a simple cold can make it difficult for your horse to breathe.

If you hear a heaving or wheezing sound when the horse breathes out (especially if he appears to be having a hard time exhaling), suspect chronic obstructive pulmonary disease (COPD). This

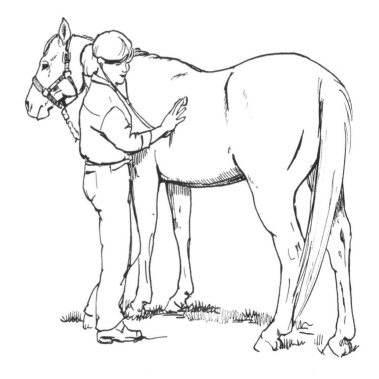

Place the stethoscope between two ribs and listen.

disease, commonly called heaves, broken wind, emphysema, and bronchitis, is similar to asthma in humans. It is most often seen in horses over the age of seven in cold-climate areas where horses are kept indoors through the winter. Affected horses often have little energy and resist exercise. Allergies, funguses, and certain lung parasites also can make exhaling difficult. Other signs of respiratory disease are coughing, nasal discharge, and swollen glands beneath the jaw.

HYDRATION

Hydration is critical to equine metabolism, muscle and organ function, and thermoregulation. About 60 percent of a horse's body weight is water, and a horse relies on sweating to regulate his body temperature when exercising. A dehydrated horse cannot sweat adequately to dissipate excess body heat, has impaired blood circulation, and is at risk for shock, kidney damage, and colic.

Trail horses often get dehydrated by sweating to cool themselves while out on the trail when water may be unavailable (especially on long rides, when carrying a heavy load, when covering challenging

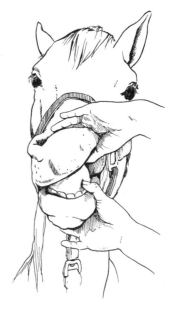

Your horse's gums should be a healthy pink. Check capillary refill time by pressing the gums till they turn white, then releasing. A well-hydrated horse's gums will return to pink in fewer than 2 seconds.

trails, or in hot weather). Dehydration also depletes electrolytes such as sodium, potassium, calcium, and chloride.

Your horse's hydration level can be checked by monitoring **sweat production,** conducting **the skin pinch test,** assessing **gum color,** and testing **capillary refill time.**

A horse that is working should have a characteristic amount of sweat depending on the course of the trail. Sweat production decreases with cooler weather. If a horse stops sweating, he won't be able to cool off and will be at risk for heat stress.

Checking gum color takes only an instant. Gums should be a healthy shade of pink, not too light or too dark. Bluish color or dryness indicates severe dehydration.

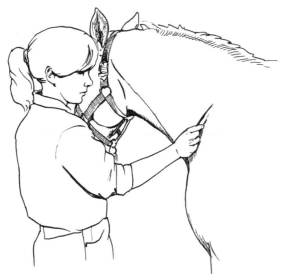

To conduct the skin pinch test, pinch a bit of the loose skin along the horse's neck. It should snap back into place within a second or two. In a mildly dehydrated horse, the skin slowly eases back into place; in more severe cases, the skin "tents" and does not return to normal.

Test capillary refill time by pressing the gums just above (top jaw) or below (lower jaw) the teeth with your thumb until the skin blanches white, then releasing the pressure. If a horse is dehydrated, there will be more than a 2-second delay in capillary refill time. A 10-second delay indicates severe dehydration. Colicky horses and horses in shock also have an increased capillary refill time.

GUT SOUNDS

Gut sounds are the noises that come from your horse's belly. They indicate digestive activity. Some horses are normally more "musical" than others, with normal sounds ranging from gurgles, grumbles, and groans to sloshing, tinkling, and dripping noises.

You can listen simply by pressing your ear to your horse's side or by using a stethoscope. Start with the lower flank area and listen for a full minute. In that amount of time, you should be able to hear a variety of sounds. Listen to both sides of the belly, in various places. Make a habit of listening to your horse's sounds periodically so you know what is normal for him.

Normal sounds should be audible but fairly soft, with three of four gurgling, bubbling noises per minute. A loud growl every 2 to 3 minutes is also normal.

Silence is a bad sign. It usually means digestive activity has stopped (called **hypomotile**), a sign of impaction colic (and severe pain). **This is an emergency situation.** (See Recognizing Distress,

page 233.) However, an excited horse will also have quieter gut sounds than normal, as the autonomic nervous system shuts down digestion in preparation for a "fight-or-flight" response. Dehydration also quiets gut sounds, because a lack of hydration slows the movement of intestinal material. Gut sounds tend to be more audible and distinct when the gut contents contain a lot of water. Pinging or tinkling sounds can indicate distention of the intestines. Constant, loud gurgling noises signal excessive activity (**hypermotile**), indicating digestive distress such as spasmodic colic.

Principles of Conditioning

The better condition your horse is in, the more miles he can cover with the least stress. How well you need to condition your horse depends on how aggressively you plan to trail-ride. Endurance riders and competitive trail riders train their horses like marathon athletes. Pleasure trail riders should condition for slightly more endurance in their horses than they ever expect to tap. If you plan to conquer steep hills, difficult terrain (uncertain footing, stepping over deadfall, crossing rivers, deep footing such as sand or plowed fields), or long miles, plan to condition moderately before ever hitting such demanding trails. Even weekend warriors need to realize that an out-of-shape horse is prone to fatigue or injury — neither of which is any fun on a Sunday-afternoon trail ride — and consider conditioning as part of their regular horse care program.

Conditioning is a process. When you gradually add stress to your horse's routine, his body systems progressively adapt. Called **remodeling,**

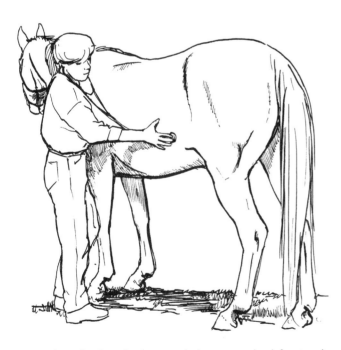

When checking for gut sounds, be sure to check front and back of both sides and to listen for a full minute.

(literally tearing down and rebuilding), this adaptation is his body's reaction to stress that strengthens muscles (including the heart), bone, and (more slowly) tendons and ligaments. During conditioning, each new level of work is maintained until the horse's body adapts (determined by monitoring vital signs) and then the workload is bumped up a notch. Unless you add to his workload, a horse can maintain his current level of fitness but his condition will not improve.

The key to conditioning is to load *enough* stress on your horse's body to cause it to adapt (remodel) without loading *too much* stress (and putting the body in distress).

Never continue to work a horse that is obviously overtired. Doing so risks injury ranging from strains and sprains to "micro injuries" that may go unnoticed but still weaken the horse. When muscle tissue is fatigued, the stress transfers to supporting tendons, ligaments, and bone. Because tendons and ligaments are more flexible and actually stronger than bone, hairline fractures in the bone can result, ultimately leaving the horse lame and leaving you to wonder "when he hurt himself."

AEROBIC OR ANAEROBIC? Conditioning muscles means changing them so that they burn oxygen more efficiently. You will notice most improvement by adding stresses based on the type of work your horse will be doing. If he needs to climb hills, then hill climbing (and the increase in heart rate that goes with it) naturally has to be part of his regimen. If he needs to cover miles fast, with a quick recovery rate (such as for an endurance horse), then his conditioning should focus on speed work. However, the best approach overall is to vary the type of work he does — a few hills, a stretch at a gallop, a 2-mile trot, and so on. Variety helps avoid injuries and prevent problems associated with repetitive use of isolated muscle groups, including shortened muscle fibers and reduced flexibility. These are not the only potential problems, but they are common.

A comprehensive conditioning program for your horse should include both aerobic and anaerobic exercise. During aerobic exercise; the body delivers oxygen to muscle tissue for the breakdown and metabolism of glucose into energy. By gradually increasing the level of activity, more and more oxygen is drawn into the muscle, and lactic acid (a by-product of anaerobic exercise; see below) is metabolized. But in anaerobic exercise the muscles actually function for a short time "without oxygen." This happens in short bursts of extreme effort. When the effort outpaces the available oxygen, lactic acid forms, and can build up into hard deposits in the muscle tissue. Lactic acid interferes with muscle contraction and causes muscle fatigue and soreness. Anaerobic work builds the horse's endurance by increasing his threshold of muscle fatigue. The more efficiently his body burns oxygen, the longer it takes to begin producing lactic acid and the faster it can metabolize what is produced.

It is important to understand that a horse's body systems remodel themselves at different rates. The first changes are the rate of oxygen consumption, blood plasma volume, and the sweating response. These systems will all show improvement after a week or two of conditioning training. You'll know you're making progress when your horse sweats earlier in the workout but smells better. It takes about 2 to 4 months to see an increase

Trail Trivia

More than 40 percent of body weight is muscle tissue.

When muscle tissue is fatigued, the stress transfers to supporting tendons and bone.

in red blood cells and hemoglobin (necessary for oxygen delivery to the muscles); the number of new muscle capillaries can be detected in from 3 to 6 months.

Heart muscle (like other muscles) actually enlarges in as soon as 10 to 12 weeks. A big heart is a good thing in more ways than one. A larger heart muscle lowers heart rate by pumping more blood with each contraction. Larger hearts don't have to work as hard to supply the body with oxygen, and your horse recovers faster following exercise.

If you keep up with your horse during this conditioning phase, you'll reap all the same benefits, to one extent or another, including improved utilization of fuel — translation: fat burning. Four to 6 months of conditioning will increase your horse's aerobic enzymes, which he uses to "burn" blood sugars for energy. Anaerobic enzymes will increase in about the same time frame.

Most studies agree that tendons and ligaments are among the last to improve in conditioning, taking as long as a year or two to reach their maximum strength; bone density can take even longer — up to three years, although some bone-density improvement comes within four or five months. To improve bone density requires training at high speeds with high impact — for example, galloping for short bursts. Remodeling hard tissues requires more intensive conditioning than remodeling soft tissues. These are goals for the serious trail-riding competitor more than the relaxed rider, but the better your horse's condition, the better he can carry you anywhere you choose.

With improved condition, your horse's thermoregulatory system (ability to cool himself) also becomes more efficient. About 70 percent of a horse's body heat is lost through sweating. Because sweat is mostly water, your horse's body robs the fluid in and between cells, from the gut, and even from his blood to sweat. This is why skin texture changes, gut sounds quiet, and his blood actually thickens as a horse dehydrates.

All Systems Go

Conditioning improves:

- Cardiovascular system by increasing capacity to deliver oxygen to muscles
- Muscular system by increasing oxygen and fuel-"burning" efficiency
- Supporting structures by increasing size and strength of bone, tendons, and ligaments
- Thermoregulatory system by increasing the body's ability to dissipate heat
- Nervous system by increasing coordination

Improved condition changes the sweating response. The horse actually begins to sweat earlier in his workout (with less exertion) and sweats more, in order to keep his body temperature under control. Extra water is essential for a sweating horse.

The remaining 30 percent or so of body heat is dissipated through exhaling and by the expansion of blood vessels near the skin surface, which cools the blood (provided the air temperature is lower than the blood temperature). The increase in blood plasma over the first couple of weeks of conditioning provides increased blood flow to the skin.

High heat and humidity also challenge your horse's thermoregulatory system. Be sure to bring your horse up gradually if you move from an area of moderate temperature/humidity to one that resembles a hot, damp sponge. While it takes only a week to build up blood plasma in such areas, the sweating response is slower to change under hot, moist conditions, since it is virtually rendered ineffective. (The body isn't cooled by sweat that doesn't evaporate.)

BEFORE YOU BEGIN

The first step in launching a conditioning program for your horse is to assess his current condition.

Establish his baseline heart rate and heart rate recovery time. You'll use this information to track his progress and to know when to increase his workload. Also take into account his age, general health and soundness, and the level of work he currently performs. Your horse's sweat can tell you about his degree of condition. Smelly, sticky sweat that works into a lather quickly is a sign that your horse is sweating out more electrolytes and protein than he should. This is common with out-of-shape horses. Horses in good condition tend to have watery, clear, less stinky sweat.

Inactive horses are the slowest to progress and need more time to reach each new level of condition than more active horses. If you have an event such as a competitive trail ride or group outing to prepare for, be sure to begin early and give your horse plenty of time to get in shape.

There is a bit of a debate about the age at which a horse can begin serious training for endurance or competitive trail riding. The prevailing wisdom holds that since a young horse's body is not mature before the age of five, horses younger than this should not be worked hard for fear of permanently damaging those structures that don't fully develop until that age, most notably the spine. However, evidence strongly suggests that younger horses have a greater capacity to remodel in response to conditioning. This is apparently especially true of tendons, which don't respond much at all in older horses but show the greatest change in horses around the age of two years. And not surprisingly, older horses, especially those past the age of 20, don't tolerate exercise as well as their younger counterparts.

Don't forget to take environmental factors into account. High humidity makes it harder for your horse to cool his body, as the sweat evaporation can drop by as much as 90 percent (which also increases his water requirements by 90 percent). On average, it takes between 10 and 14 days for a horse to begin to acclimate to high humidity and/or high temperatures. Note that a horse doesn't acclimate to work in high heat and humidity just by *being* there; he needs to train in those conditions. Of course, heat and humidity are relative to what the horse is used to, but temperatures or humidity above 90 are very stressful on equine body systems. See page 237 for a thorough explanation of the heat index — the measurement used to determine a horse's threshold.

Horses actually vary quite a bit in their individual response to the stresses of conditioning training. Some horses show marked improvement in a few weeks, others seem to take forever to adjust, so be patient and stay within your horse's ability to adapt to the workload. Remember, overstressing can lead to decline rather than improvement in your horse's condition.

It's easy to get carried away with pushing your horse to be in the best condition possible, but he only needs to be in sufficient condition to carry out the work you intend to do. So before you jump into a conditioning regimen, it's smart to take stock of just how conditioned your horse already is and where he realistically needs to be. He may need a lot of conditioning to bring him up to par before you start riding, or he may already be fit enough to handle what you expect of him.

To find out, take your horse for an hourlong outing, similar to what you would ask of him on a regular ride. If you only take easy rides, then let him saunter along; if you plan to push the limits of equine endurance, then let him work hard for an hour. After an hour, dismount and immediately take your horse's pulse. Keep checking every 2 to 5 minutes until it goes down to no more than 64 bpm. If it still hasn't dropped to that level in 30 minutes, he's in no shape to start at the level of work you intend to do and needs to begin with a conditioning program instead. If however, he drops to this rate, or lower, within 10 minutes, he's already in decent shape for the work you expect of him and may need no further conditioning other than hitting the trails with you a couple of times per week.

Especially during conditioning training, make it a practice to "pre-flight" your horse. Conduct a pre-ride test by checking his vital signs, hydration, and gut sounds and visually sweeping his body for any signs of injury. It's a good idea to feel his back and legs for any heat, filling, hardness, or pain reactions. Follow this with a warm-up period to prepare your horse for the workout ahead and to complete your mental picture as to how he is feeling.

WARMING UP

Begin by walking, then trotting (or slowly gaiting), in large circles in both directions for 5 to 10 minutes. Start a little more slowly and allow a little more time to warm up in cold weather, and consider rubbing down older horses to jump-start their circulation before working on conditioning. As you ride, check for stiffness, off gait, resistance, or lameness. Some people prefer to longe a horse for warm-up, as it allows them to further visually inspect the horse's way of going; others prefer to warm up in the saddle.

Warming up benefits your horse in several ways. It raises your horse's body temperature and increases blood flow to the muscles by diverting it from the major organs. This physically loosens muscles and tendons, which helps to avoid pulling or straining during work. Warming up gradually helps your horse's thermoregulatory system kick in so that he can dissipate heat more efficiently during the more demanding parts of his workout. And making a habit of warming up before heading out puts your horse in "work mode" mentally.

AEROBIC CONDITIONING

Regardless of your horse's age, cardiac capacity, or environmental influences, the best way to begin a committed conditioning program is with low speeds over long distances. Long, slow distance training, or LSD for short (also called legging up), is aerobic conditioning that builds endurance by improving cardiac capacity, muscle efficiency, and thermoregulatory ability. It is ideal for trail horses.

It's also the best way to bring horses that have been idle for a while back up to their previous level of fitness, and a great minimum-stress start for youngsters for which the goal is to make slow progress.

LSD STEP-BY-STEP Start LSD training by walking your horse for about 20 to 30 minutes the first day and then adding 10 minutes a day until he is working an hour a day, or covering about 5 miles. Plan to ride 3 to 5 days a week, making sure your horse gets a day off at least every 3 or 4 days. Working more days a week is not recommended, as your horse's body needs time between workouts to rebuild tissues. Overworking a horse, even at slow speeds over long distances, can lead to fatigue, lameness, injury, and even depressed immunity. After he can cover this distance without tiring (and returns to his resting vital signs within 10 to 15 minutes), add trotting (or gaiting) to his routine in 2-minute bouts, walking in between. After 2 or 3 weeks of this, increase the distance you cover until your horse is working for 2 or 3 hours per ride, walking most of the time, with intermittent periods of trotting (or gaiting). When he can cover 15 to 20 miles at an average speed of 8 to 10 miles per hour, he will be in great shape!

Warming up puts your horse in the right frame of mind to work

Be sure to keep tabs on his heart rate and recovery throughout your horse's conditioning program. He will reap the most benefit by working in a "target zone" of 135 to 155 bpm (about 60–80 percent of maximum heart rate). Unfortunately, it's difficult to catch a heart rate greater than 120 if you have to stop, dismount, and take a pulse. For "at work" readings, you will need an electronic heart rate monitor.

When your horse can cover the same distance at the same speed with a lower heart rate (or quicker recovery time) than when he started, it's time to step up the program, by increasing either the distance or the speed he works, but not both. Adding only one variable at a time to your horse's conditioning program is the best way to increase his stamina without overstressing his system, and allows you to monitor his progress clearly. Keep an eye on his vital signs and let his heart be your guide.

Since most people don't have time in their schedules to ride 4 hours a day 3 or 4 days a week, the most common way to build up condition after the first few weeks is to add speed to the routine. The goal of LSD training is to get your horse to where he can work for about an hour at a walk, trot (or gait), and slow canter and return to his resting heart rate within 10 minutes. When he has reached this point, your individual riding goals will determine whether you advance to more strenuous levels of training or maintain his current condition. It all depends on the type of riding you intend to do.

Most pleasure trail horses won't need further conditioning, provided they are trail-ridden regularly, but endurance prospects are only just beginning their conditioning and need to advance to a more demanding program that will prepare them for covering more miles at higher speeds.

ANAEROBIC CONDITIONING

Anaerobic conditioning, also called interval training, is especially useful for trail horses that have to cover ground fast, climb steep hills, or face other such exertion on the trail. Since it employs extreme stress, anaerobic conditioning should not be started until your horse has completed at least 2 months of more gradual conditioning. The goal is to build up your horse's work capacity before he begins to fatigue.

When your horse is ready to move to this level of conditioning, begin by asking for a sudden burst of speed. For as little as 30 seconds to a minute, urge him to gallop all out, then pull him back down to a slow trot or gait. If he is wearing a heart rate monitor, pull him back down as soon as his heart rate reaches 180 to 200 bpm, but don't let him exceed 2 minutes of extreme exertion. Let him

jog, gait or walk until his heart rate drops below 100 bpm, then ask for a second burst of speed and check him as before after a minute or two.

The idea is to gradually add more short spurts of intense exercise to his established slow routine, so that over time, his recovery time decreases. Alternate intense workouts with long, slow rides to help the horse's body eliminate the build up of lactic acid produced by his anaerobic effort. It takes from 48 to 72 hours to replace the sugar (glycogen) depleted from cells during just one anaerobic burst. So allow at least 2 or 3 days between them — giving your horse perhaps 1 day off and a day or two of slower work.

Be sure to make allowances for hot or humid weather, keeping a close watch on your horse's heart rate.

POST-RIDE CHECK AND COOLING OUT

Anytime your horse works up a sweat, he needs and deserves an appropriate cooling-out period to avoid stiff muscles and/or cramps. High-intensity workouts in particular should be followed by a post-ride check, including a final check on heart rate to determine ultimate recovery rate. If your horse's heart rate doesn't return below to 72 after 10 minutes, he is working too hard and needs to step back his training. If it returns to normal (38–42 bpm) within 10 minutes, then you can add another 2-minute, high-intensity workout per session. It's also important to feel the legs and back for signs of heating or swelling, as it is much easier to injure a horse during a mad dash than on a mile-long walk.

High-intensity workouts also require a cooling-out period to bring his temperature and other vital signs back down to normal. To cool him, keep your horse working but at a much slower level, until his heart rate returns to normal. A good way to do it is like a warm-up in reverse. Slow down to a trot for 5 minutes, then walk. If you are riding away from home, walking back the last mile or so is a good way to let him cool off mentally as well, and will avoid him developing the habit of rushing home (see chapter 8.) Once home, let your horse stand for a few minutes before turning him out. If he is still hot, be sure not to let him drink more than a few swallows at a time until he is completely cooled down. And if necessary, consider hosing him off to help cool him.

Cooling down your horse helps prevent him from being stiff and sore the next day by aerobically removing lactic acid from his muscles. Since lactic acid can crystallize and form sore spots within your horse's muscles, you may also want to consider a good rubdown after a strenuous workout. Massage manually breaks up lactic acid deposits and stimulates blood flow to carry them away, into to the lymph system to be eliminated through the kidneys. It also allows blood flow to redirect from the demands of work (to the heart and limbs) back to the major organs of the body.

Cooling out is necessary to avoid stiff muscles and cramps.

ADDING CHALLENGES

By varying the terrain over which your horse works, you will stimulate his mind and his body. Working on hills increases heart rate without having to increase speed, which takes some of the load off his bones, tendons, and ligaments. Walking, trotting, or gaiting up and down progressively steeper hills will not only develop his muscle strength, lungs, and heart, but also improve his coordination. Galloping uphill provides an intense cardiovascular workout. Working in sand or plowed fields (or other soft footing) greatly increases the "drag" on a horse's limbs, thereby working (and stressing) all of his body systems harder. Along with working in bursts of speed, they are a useful addition to interval training.

However, some "challenges" are best avoided. Even though the object of conditioning is to expand your horse's limits, avoid unnecessary stresses that can fatigue or injure your horse, such as pushing beyond the limits of his natural conformation, poor riding, and mismatching a small or refined horse with an overly heavy rider, or any

number of similar disadvantages. A rider who rides with an unbalanced seat can throw the horse off, forcing him to constantly compensate for the rider, which not only butchers the quality of the gait, but also tires the horse needlessly. Likewise, a tense rider who bounces around in the saddle, constantly pounding on his back, will tire a horse more quickly than a relaxed rider.

DAYS OFF — AFTER A LAPSE

Once your horse is in condition, he will retain his basic degree of fitness for 6 to 8 weeks with no further training. Horses that have been in condition but were laid off will come back more rapidly than first-timers. However, horses laid off due to injury or for longer periods should be brought back slowly, using LSD techniques.

It's always better to err on the side of your horse's physical well-being, so if your horse has been off duty for a while, begin with a slow pace and carefully monitor his progress before adding more distance or speed to his workload. It's better to take a little longer for him to get into shape than to risk hurting him and losing even more riding time.

Horses that have been laid off for 4 to 5 weeks, especially if they were in good condition prior to the layoff, generally don't lose cardiac or muscle fitness in this amount of time. After a layoff of 4 to 8 weeks, some loss is evident, but the horse should still be ready to hit all but very challenging trails. Longer layoffs will lead to a decline in the condition of all body systems, including bone density, the slowest to rebuild. A rule of thumb is that each month of lay up after the first month or two requires a month of reconditioning. Because horses really do respond at their own individual pace, be sure to use your horse's heart rate as his individual guideline.

If you don't trail-ride much during the off-season (too hot or too cold), you can keep your horse in shape by giving him a good cardiovascular workout twice a week. A warm-up, followed by galloping around a track or arena until his heart rate rises to his working level, and then cooling down will keep your horse in relatively good shape until he can go back to his regular work schedule.

Because wide fluctuations in fitness can lead to long-term unsoundness or health problems, just as for humans, it's much better to keep your horse as fit as possible, rather than to bring him up to good condition only to let him slide for the winter and then start all over again next spring. The older your horse, the more important this is, as older horses need progressively more time to rebuild body tissues.

STRETCHING

Just as for the human half of a trail-riding team, stretching is a great way to warm up the body, induce suppleness and flexibility, and prevent muscle strains. But since horses are built a little differently than we are, teaching a horse to stretch and bend is a little more complicated than asking him to bend over and touch his toes.

Neck stretches are an easy way to start. They benefit the horse by encouraging flexibility in the neck, the horse's main "counterbalance" against his hind end. They can also be used to stretch the topline, thus strengthening the back. Tell your horse to "stand" or "wait" and gently pull his head

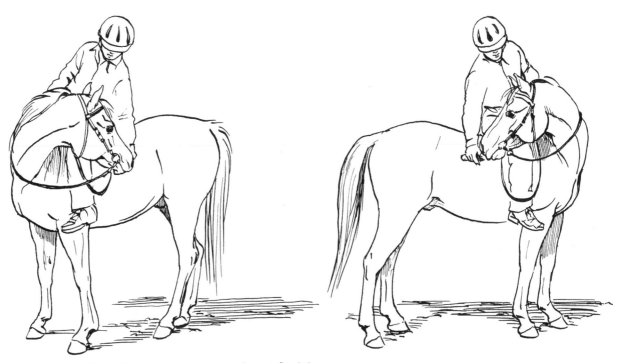

Neck stretches, up and down and from side to side, improve your horse's flexibility.

toward one side. Don't ask him to bend any farther than he is obviously comfortable with because bending and stretching too far can pull muscles.

Encourage him to reach for a treat to get him to reach to his limit. If he tries to move his feet, try to be quicker than he is and stop him. Gradually, over a period of several days, ask him to stretch a little farther each time until he can touch his nose to his side in either direction (one side will probably be more flexible than the other). Once your horse has learned to reach for a treat, you can add stretching forward, downward, and (with the help of a stepladder) even upward to his repertoire.

You can transfer neck-stretching exercises to the saddle by gently pulling his head around toward the stirrup. Begin when standing still and then progress to asking for the bend while moving along at a walk. Be sure to stretch both sides. Don't let him rush or lag, but keep his forward motion controlled as you ask for the bend. Be ready with leg aids in case you need them to keep his body straight.

Another way to encourage stretching and balance in your horse is to work him in circles. The smaller the circle, the more he will have to bend, but try to keep him relaxed. Small, fast circles can be frustrating to a horse, as well as hard on his legs, so don't overdo them. Be sure to work in both directions, in a variety of gaits and speeds, and strive toward getting him to bend his entire body along the path of the circle.

GAITERS VS. TROTTERS

Listen to the "party line" of a lot of the gaited-horse associations and you'll be told that the horses can go all day in gait providing smooth comfort to the rider with no adverse effects to the horse. That's one of the great selling points of gaited horses. It would be even better if it were true.

There are several things wrong with this idea. For one, any animal — human, hamster, or horse — must be in physical condition to "go all day"

doing anything. A sedentary horse that hits the trail for an all-day ride will be just as achy and cramped from gaiting as from trotting. Second, the quality of gait, and thus its effect on the horse and rider, varies from individual to individual. Just as the speed, stride, and stretch of the gallop varies from racehorse to racehorse, so too does the comfort and caliber of any of the multiple saddle gaits from horse to horse. Finally, due to the nature of the horse's carriage in certain gaits, some gaits are just hard on the horse — period. Horses that are ridden relentlessly in certain gaits are almost guaranteed to break down over time because of the constant stress to back muscles and supporting structures.

Before any gaited horse should be conditioned in gait, he should be "legged up" with long, slow distance training at the walk for at least 8 weeks and should be in good overall condition. Horses with strong, well-conditioned muscles are much less likely to tire and break gait once they begin gaiting under saddle. Conditioning improves gait training as much as gait training improves condition.

Pushing a horse too much in gait can have immediate effects as well. If a young, inexperienced, poorly trained or tired horse is pushed too far in gait, the quality of the gait will quickly deteriorate as the horse searches for the least stressful way to carry his body. He may pace, trot, or mix up gaits that you can't even recognize. Nobody chooses to ride a gaited horse for a rough ride, but over-conditioning in gait can lead to a horse that learns to carry himself improperly.

That doesn't mean you can't condition a gaited horse to cover miles of ground in superior comfort to both of you. Remember that most gaited horses can do more than just the gait their particular breed is known for and that some gaits are harder on the horse's body than others. So even though your gaited horse may offer you only one gait today, you can improve his condition tremendously by encouraging other gaits and teaching him to respond on cue with the gait of your choice so that you can alternate gaits during conditioning, as well as while on the trail. This allows one group of muscles to rest while alternative muscles take the strain of motion, which many believe gives well-trained, well-conditioned gaited horses a definite edge in trail endurance.

Because working in gait can be demanding on a horse's body, those truly knowledgeable in gaited horses recommend not training hard in gait until a horse has fully matured, roughly until the age of five to five and a half years. Until then, it is advised to work young gaited horses in varying degrees of the walk (dog walk, flat walk, fox walk). Advance to gait work a few minutes at a time, gradually building up until the horse can sustain his gaits for longer periods. I know this flies in the face of what you will see in the show world, but your horse's long-term soundness is a pretty fair trade-off for the rushed, "time-is-money" approach that dominates that scene.

Conditioning in gait builds "muscle memory," which can eventually make the execution of each gait a nearly automatic response.

Some gaits shouldn't be executed for long regardless of the degree of conditioning. The rack family of gaits and the stepping pace (and related gaits; see chapter 2), which place the horse's body in a reversed flexed — ventroflexed, or hollow — posture, should be limited. Because the horse has always one or two feet on the ground, the rack is extremely comfortable to the rider. However, that moment of single-leg support is very hard on the horse's body — from the hoof, lower limb, upper limb, shoulder/hip, and spine — as that one hoof bears all the weight/force/impact of the horse and rider. Because of the support sequence and pick-up/set-down pattern of the feet, the rack requires more energy from the horse and is more tiring to maintain than most other saddle gaits. **Pacey** (lateral) gaits put even more strain on the horse's body, as not only is the back hollow, but the

muscles along each side of the back work independently, alternately shortening and lengthening from one side to the next. This is an inefficient form of motion that is tiring to the horse and stressful to his spine. All this also puts incredible strain on the muscles supporting the back and belly and over time can lead to excessive soreness and swayback. As a rule, it is detrimental to the horse's body to maintain these gaits under saddle for more than 15 minutes at a stretch. On a level trail, that should cover anywhere from 1 to 4 miles, depending on the gait and the speed.

The saddle gaits easiest on a horse's body are the fox trot and walking gaits, including the running walk. I'm referring not to extreme show-ring versions of these gaits, but to the natural way of going born to gaited horses (before they are "improved" with training). In the fox trot, the horse can round his back and keep his body loose. Since he always has two or three feet on the ground, he works with minimal stress on his body, and if in good condition can cover long distances in this gait. Remember, this is an uneven, four-beat gait, which means there will be some movement to the rider. Some might consider a little more rider motion to be a trade-off for better back health and comfort for the horse, but a fox trot is still incredibly smooth compared to any regular trot.

The running walk — one of the smoothest of the saddle gaits in terms of rider comfort — also allows for some, though not much, rounding of the back and is also a two/three support gait, naturally performed with a loose, relaxed body. Since the back can at least maintain a neutral frame (neither rounded nor hollow), the horse can maintain the gait for quite some time before experiencing soreness or fatigue, making it another excellent choice for eating up trail miles.

Just as for a non-gaited horse, start your conditioning program with lots of walking, beginning with 20 to 30 minutes, and then progress to an hour or more several times per week. With gaited horses, this has the added benefit of enforcing the balance and timing of the walk (the basis of all saddle gaits). Be sure your horse is sufficiently "legged up" with lots of long slow miles at the walk before introducing gait into the conditioning program. Give him at least a month or two to allow for remodeling of heart and leg muscles before pushing for much work in gait.

When he is ready, the best way to condition (and trail-ride) a gaited horse is to use a variety of gaits. Keep gaiting to a minimum while you condition your horse's body to the stresses it requires, and build up gradually. Start with no more than 2 minutes at a time in gait and build up to no more than 15 minutes for the rack or stepping pace, and as much as an hour or more for the fox trot or running walk. Just as for non-gaited horses, be sure to vary the pace and check your horse's vital signs to evaluate his stress load and progress.

TRICKS OF THE TRADE There are a few tricks to encouraging and maintaining gait, which not only help improve your horse's overall condition, but also help to lock in the gaits themselves. They can't be considered "training" the gaits (since the horse does them naturally anyway) so much as reinforcing your horse's response to your cues.

As you ride up and down a gradual slope at a walk, push for more speed but check the horse if he breaks into a trot or pace. This encourages him to engage his hindquarters. Another strategy is to ride through plowed fields, sand, boggy soil, or even tall grass, for this encourages the horse to break up uneven footfall timing. Pacey horses tend to break up their gaits toward a more even four-beat tempo on uphill climbs and over rough ground, as do trotty horses on downhill slopes. Remember to initiate any changes slowly and build up the distance or speed gradually.

Don't forget that, just as for a non-gaited horse, there are factors that can affect the horse's quality of gait, and thus his ability to hold one for any length of time. These factors include his age/ development, any conformational defects (see

> ## Gaiting Guidelines
>
> A gaited horse in good condition should be able to maintain the following:
>
> **Fox trot.** 15 minutes, three times per hour, walking between, to an hour of steady fox trotting, in a loose frame at slow to moderate speed
>
> **Running walk.** 10 to 15 minutes, three times per hour, walking between, to an hour of run walking, in a loose frame at slow to moderate speed
>
> **Rack.** 5 to 15 minutes, three times per hour, walking between
>
> **Stepping pace.** 5 to 10 minutes, three times per hour, walking between

chapter 2), discomfort from tack, and the rider. A too-heavy rider, perched above his kidneys, can wear out a racking horse in no time, even though that is precisely the madness behind a common show-ring method to "improve" the gait. He will drag his back legs up underneath himself desperately to keep his footing and put on a spectacular show — for a little while. Another problem is a tense or stiff rider, which usually translates to a stiff horse that hollows his back in an effort to avoid contact (translation: bouncing) from the rider. This not only ruins the horse's gait, but it tires his back out all the more quickly as well.

SWIMMING

Even if there are no rivers to ford on your trail map, you can still find exceptional benefits for your horse in the water. And it's always better to master such a specialized skill before you need it.

Swimming isn't just for rehab. It's a phenomenal way to condition a horse and improve his cardiac capacity with minimal impact on limbs and back. Equine swim centers estimate that (for those with access to facilities) up to 60 percent of a conditioning program can be replaced with a swimming program, which, they are quick to point out

Swimming is a superb conditioning exercise for a horse, allowing him to improve his cardiac capacity without stress to his limbs and back. It's fun, too!

equals a 60 percent drop the chance of injury.

A typical program starts with the horse swimming for about 200 yards and increasing that up to 1,500 yards in 15 to 60 days. Each session is broken into short swims, similar to interval training, where the horse is rested between bursts of energy.

It takes a horse only 500 yards of swimming to equal the exertion of galloping for a full mile. It takes only four or five sessions in the pool for a horse to show improvement in his fitness level.

Swimming works muscle groups differently than groundwork, especially the hindquarters, chest, and shoulders. By combining it with LSD or ground interval training, you can build up a horse's maximum fitness level much more quickly.

CHAPTER 5

Trail Training

⊱─◈─⊰

YOU'LL NEVER APPRECIATE SOLID TRAINING MORE than when you are miles out on the trail. From your horse's earliest memories to step-by-step lessons in negotiating obstacles, countless experiences contribute to his training. This chapter aims to help you understand when, why, and how horses learn and what they retain. This is important because a trail horse needs many varied skills and has to be absolutely reliable in his responses. A horse that backs up beautifully in the arena but won't step backwards if caught in a bad spot on a narrow trail can be lethal. Training counts only when you can count on it.

Early Learning

If you are lucky enough to share the birth and/or early life of your future trail partner, there are some sensible, simple things you can do to ensure smooth trails ahead. Handling a foal can have tremendous long-term effects. Whether those lasting effects are good or bad depends on how that early handling goes.

EXPOSING A FOAL TO STIMULI

Research into how early experience affects later behavior reveals that the younger the animal, the more dramatic the influence and the less reversible the impact. In other words, if a foal is exposed to lots of new sensations followed by a reward, those things will become associated with positive reinforcement and be perceived as "good" to the young horse. Gradually increasing those stimuli expands the youngster's acceptance of new situations. The effects are set in more deeply, and will be harder to change later in life, than those same experiences at a later age. The earlier you expose your prospective trail mount to varied stimuli with a positive result (reward/reinforcement), therefore, the more easily he will accept strange new sights and sounds for the rest of his life.

Unfortunately, the same applies if a foal is distressed. Mishandling at a young age that hurts, frightens, or frustrates a horse can cause him to avoid the associated stimulus — a horse trailer, a saddle, the trail, or a rider. Therefore, even though the goal is to expose a young horse to "a lot," how much depends entirely on the individual and his reaction. It's crucial not to overwhelm a youngster.

You can teach a foal to accept sounds, sights, and tactile stimulation even before he rises to his feet. You can introduce "training" — developing a learned response to a stimulus or cue — within hours of birth. You can begin the basics of equine education — yielding to pressure; forward, backward and lateral movement; and accepting restraint — when the foal is just a few days old. So

handling a foal is recommended, as long as you are calm, competent, and careful. Rush things now, and you can create a problem for life.

HALTER TRAINING

Halter training can begin within days of birth, provided you don't use force. Take your youngster on walks to show him the strange sights and sounds of the world. If Mama is quiet and dependable, start when Baby is still at her side. What the mother accepts, the baby will not question. Make the walks short and fun. Be sure when halter training that you never drag or force. If a foal balks on the lead, try gently pulling to the side to put him off balance, then reward any step taken.

A **butt rope** is often used (in combination with a lead rope) to annoy a foal to move forward. This is a long cotton rope or lariat looped around the foal's hindquarters, with the free end held by the handler. If the foal balks, gently pull on the rope to tighten the loop around his rump. As soon as the foal takes a step forward, release all pressure from both the lead rope and the butt rope. Reward those first few precious steps profusely, first by instantly releasing all pressure, then by praising and

Loop a butt rope around a foal's hindquarters. Ease him forward with a gentle tug and release as soon as he takes a step.

stroking. If a foal learns early on to appreciate praise as a reward, it makes future training so much easier.

There are lots of good references to early handling and halter training (see appendix), but the most important things to know are to be gentle and consistent and to stop asking when the foal does as you wish. Even though foals are cute, be smart about not rewarding inappropriate behavior. It's a lot easier to train a 100-pound foal not to step on you than it is to train a 1,000-pound horse! Be consistent, firm, but gentle with foals when enforcing ground manners.

WORKING WITH WEANLINGS

From weanling to breaking age there are countless ways you can improve your young horse's future trail reliability. Many of these lessons take very little time or effort on your part. Simply leaving strange (but safe!) items in the baby's paddock or pasture for him to investigate on his own allows him to conquer his fears and satisfy his curiosity at his own pace. A tarp, sheet of plywood, kiddy pool, plastic bag of cans, scarecrow, squawking radio: anything you can think of to stimulate investigation can make a great lesson.

As the baby becomes desensitized to each new thing in his territory, he unconsciously learns that strange new things in unaccustomed places are no big deal. Many are the frustrated trail riders whose horse has balked or shied on a familiar stretch of trail, simply because of a glinting soda can left along the trail's edge. Early foal exposure would have helped.

Just be sure to monitor Baby carefully while the new items are within his reach. Anything he can reach has the potential to be dangerous; foals have even been known to ingest and choke on bits of tarp. This risk is magnified when an item such as a dirt bike or scarecrow has toxic or removable parts that a foal might nibble. Supervision — even if from the other side of the fence — is the key to a safe encounter.

Early Foal Handling

The first few hours in the life of a new foal can be critical in forming his attitude toward human handling. A foal's first encounter with human handling can occur even before he rises to his feet for the first time. Spend some time to introduce him to some of the stimuli he will face in the future.

- DO gently rub the foal all over.
- DO breathe in his nostrils.
- DO gently handle mouth, ears, genitals, and anus (in that order!), and keep your fingers in place until the foal stops struggling or objecting. If a foal wins an argument at this stage, he will be set up for a lifetime of challenging human handling.

Throughout his early handling and into his young adulthood, bear a few caveats in mind.

- DON'T allow anything to frighten or hurt the foal.
- DON'T force anything on the foal that he is not physically able to accommodate.
- DON'T drag a foal by the halter. A foal's cervical vertebrae are the last to develop and are extremely fragile. A single frantic reaction can result in permanent injury.

Early, appropriate handling helps ensure a willing and capable trail partner later in life.

Walk with your weanling through various types of terrain, near obstacles, through water, and around other horses, ATVs, and traffic, with reward breaks along the way (not just at the end) to keep him looking forward to outings. A reward break can be as simple as a pause to nibble grass or a handful of grain, a moment to stroke and praise, or a few minutes for a good scratchin'. The idea is not so much to reward any specific behavior, but to create a feeling of positive anticipation in the foal toward your outings together.

Keep early walks short and avoid extremes such as very deep mud, fast-moving water, and severe slopes. At this stage you want to build strength and confidence slowly. One frightening or hurtful encounter can risk undoing all the good work you have done up to that point.

As he matures and develops strength and condition, continue his education by leading him from another horse (called **ponying**). The comfort of other horses will reinforce his acceptance of new and strange experiences as business as usual.

Simple Truths for Effective Training

When your colt is mature enough for saddle training, keep the following tips in mind as you prepare him for his future role as a trail horse. Whenever you interact with your horse, whatever his age, is a training session. Your bad day is his bad lesson, and one bad day can take weeks to work past. So plan ahead before you launch into any training program. Clear your mind before you begin, have a plan as to what you want to cover, and proceed with confidence and enough flexibility to alter the plan according to your horse's progress on that day.

Probably the most difficult part of teaching a horse anything is keeping your mind in the moment. Your horse has no idea that you ultimately envision him rocking back on his haunches, planting a hind foot in the dirt as a pivot point, and spinning around until you're both dizzy. He's just trying to figure out what you want *now*. Visualize what you want your horse to do now, today, not what you hope for 6 months down the road. You and your young horse will train together better when you are reaching for each short-term goal. It's easier to be patient through many steps when your eye is on the next small goal rather than on something so far off.

ACCEPTING YOUR LEADERSHIP

When training your horse for trail (or when going back to the basics), you have to understand how his mind works. A horse's brain, culture, and language are the results of millions of years of evolution, and luckily, they are understandable, malleable, and exploitable.

You probably know that horses are prey animals and prone to react to what they perceive as threats with a flight-or-fight response. They evolved in the best possible way to survive as members of migratory herds on vast open grasslands. Survival depended upon eating, not getting eaten, and reproducing, so not surprisingly, those are the things that occupy a horse's mind.

Your horse spends much of his time eating or engaging in food-seeking behavior (for example, chewing on trees or fences or munching bedding). If distressed, either physically or mentally, horses often refuse food, so your horse's eating habits can tell you a lot about his state of mind or health. Unfortunately, since eating grass doesn't require hunting skills, horses never bothered with developing a lot of unnecessary cognitive thinking.

Because horses still think they may get eaten, they are ever watchful for threats, even though the last saber-toothed tiger left the neighborhood eons ago. New things, strange sounds, and sudden movements instinctively arouse suspicion. Horses watch their "leader" (alpha female, dominant herd member, or you) for cues regarding how to react. If you are nervous or lack confidence, that puts your horse on notice to be ready to flee the scene.

If you are angry or upset, your horse can only conclude that you are about to attack. If you are afraid, your horse can only "reason" that there must be imminent danger. Check your negative emotions at the gate.

Reproductive urges are part of dealing with a live animal. If you own a mare, expect hormone fluctuations to affect her about once a month. Some mares never raise much fuss; others get extremely emotional or cranky. Most geldings bypass hormonal changes, which is why they are so popular as trail mounts. They are generally more predictable and steady than stallions and mares.

Life on the open plain required only enough cooperation to coexist, so horses developed a rudimentary, primarily nonverbal, communication system with emphasis on distinguishing subtle cues, such as head and ear position. This stems from the fact that survival and evolution favor those that don't take unnecessary risks. It's much less risky to learn to avoid laid-back ears than the kick that follows. Thus horses have evolved to be masters at picking up on and differentiating among physical cues such as body position, leg and seat movements, slight shifts of a bit, and so on.

SIXTEEN SIMPLE RULES FOR WORKING WITH A HORSE

There are a handful of basic truths to keep in mind when working with horses. Here are 16 fundamentals.

1 Think like a horse. Know your horse's basic nature and needs, such as to stay with the safety of the herd, maintain his place in the herd hierarchy (and benefit from his association with higher-ups, including you), flee in the face of danger, resist restraint, and avoid being thrown off balance. You have to understand how and why a horse reacts in order to mold those reactions.

2 Start with trust. Take the time to bond with your horse and gain his trust. You'll get a lot more

Signs That Your Horse Is Cooperating

In addition to his performing perfectly whatever maneuver you asked for, there are some other clear signs that your horse is paying attention and accepting your leadership. Look for:

Head carriage. A calm horse is a learning/listening horse. He holds his head at normal height, roughly level with his withers. A tense horse holds his head high, possibly using that great vision to look for a way to escape.

A respectful posture. During groundwork, a horse that is paying attention to you and ready to do as you ask will face you. A disrespectful, unhappy, or frightened horse will turn away.

Licking and chewing. A tense horse is not listening or learning. Tension in the jaws is a sure sign that a horse is upset. When he relaxes emotionally enough to relax the muscles in his jaw, he will lick his lips and chew. This probably goes back to the laws of survival on the plains: When all is well, we can relax and eat; when danger is near, we stop eating and prepare to flee.

from a horse that knows you are safe and fair than from a horse that is wary of you. Touch is a great way to build trust. Just spending time grooming your horse will build the bond between you. And keep your cool. Even a horse knows you can't trust a leader that flies off the handle. Confidence is contagious.

3 Have a plan. Have a plan with a specific goal or purpose for each lesson. For instance, if you are working over ground poles to teach your horse to pick up his feet, and he watches where he places each hoof and sails over the poles without touching a single one on the first try, reward (especially a young horse) right away and move on to something else or end the session. Once the horse has accomplished the day's goal, don't drill for the correct response over and over. At best this makes the horse think he is not doing what you want, and at worst it creates frustration, confusion, boredom, and resistance.

4 Understand pressure and release. Whatever cue you use, start with so little pressure that it seems you are only *thinking* about cueing your horse. Horses are so sensitive to body language that they can actually pick up on cues that you are not even aware you are giving. Increase the pressure you use to ask for any given response until the horse does as you ask. ALWAYS release the pressure the instant your horse does what you ask. Release of pressure is the quickest, surest reward, and failing to do so confuses and frustrates the horse. Repeat, gradually reducing the pressure you apply to get a response over many repetitions, until the response is given with the least pressure possible.

5 Use positive and negative reinforcement. You'll achieve better results, faster and more clearly, if you reward the behavior you do want and adequately respond to the behavior you don't want. That's basic behavioral conditioning, and it is consistent with the real-life experiences your horse has already had. Other horses kick or bite when a herd member misbehaves or challenges them for dominance. Whether you call it negative reinforcement, punishment, discipline, or correction, your response should be just as quick, clear, and effective as a reward.

The major caveat is that you should never punish a horse out of anger. This can be a double-edged sword, since many of the things that deserve punishment can also really tick you off, and you don't want to jeopardize your horse's training by waiting until you are back in your "happy place" to deal with it. Whack him if he deserves it (steps on your toes or bucks) but don't allow your emotions to rule you. Be sure the punishment fits the crime.

A good scratch can be a simple, effective reward.

6 Reward effectively. Rewards communicate to your horse that you will take care of him, that you like and appreciate him, and that he is doing what you want — yet another way you reinforce your position as leader. Make rewards worth working for by learning what your horse enjoys. Praise, a stroke on the neck, a scratch on his chest or under his jaw, or a quick treat will teach your horse that something good awaits when he does as you ask. And remember, the most important reward when a horse has done what you ask is to quit asking!

7 Set yourself up for success. Be as sure as possible that your horse is physically and emotionally ready for each new step in your training program. Don't skip a step "to see what will happen." Follow the rule of TV attorney Perry Mason: Never ask a question to which you don't already know the answer. Also, take advantage of natural tendencies. Wait until after your horse has "worked the kinks out" before introducing a new obstacle.

Put him at the back of a group to get him to slow down or to follow other horses past an obstacle that frightens him.

8 Build cooperation. Begin each lesson by asking your horse to do things that you know he or she will do willingly and well. Each time your horse obeys you, he reinforces his own opinion of your status as "herd leader." In addition, building up cooperation at the beginning of a lesson sets the stage for a positive training session. Ask for one thing at a time until he complies, then step up different easy requests to build up to the day's lesson. For instance, when training a horse to back out of a trailer, ask first for a few steps backwards on the ground, then over a plank, then across a sheet of plywood or over a tarp, and only when he has mastered these begin working with the trailer.

9 Introduce new things in small steps. Expect to teach new maneuvers in steps or stages. Break down each new lesson into the smallest possible components, then ask your horse to master these one step at a time. Once your horse learns that the faster he masters the lesson, the faster he gets your approval, a rest, or a reward, the faster he will learn to learn.

10 Keep lessons short. Especially with young horses, you will see much more improvement in several 10- to 20-minute lessons a day than in a 2- to 3-hour marathon training session. The equine attention span is short, especially at the beginning of training, but can be built up over time.

11 Don't rush! Be sure your horse is comfortable with each stage of each lesson before moving on. Resist the urge to "get on with it." Rushing often leads to frustration and not learning.

12 Master good timing. A horse's mind can connect a reward or discipline with a deed only if

Treats as Rewards

Bite-sized, hand-held treats, such as a "horse cookie" and "horse candy," work best during training sessions. They are quick for you to deliver and for the horse to finish. A treat a horse can devour in one bite is best because he will not be distracted by hunting for a feed bucket or chewing for so long he forgets what he did to earn it.

Some caution, however, is advised in using treats as a reward. Horses learn quickly about human candy dispensers, and some can become aggressive in seeking out the goodies. Here are some tips for success:

- Handle the horse firmly but gently from the start.
- Insist on proper respect: Don't allow the horse to step on you, crowd you, or sniff around for a treat.
- Give the treat ONLY right after the horse has earned it — not when he asks for it or as a bribe to get him to do something.
- A brief rest before you ask for the next maneuver allows the horse to remember his actions and their consequences and to connect the dots.

it follows said deed within about 3 seconds. Timing really is everything! Be aware that if a reward follows too long after a job well done, your horse won't realize what he did to earn it, and if you discipline him too long after he misbehaves, he will not connect the punishment with the action. Always try to think ahead of your horse and make sure you time your reinforcements so they can do their job.

13 Assert your leadership. Everything you do — from your posture to your voice to your touch — should express confidence and leadership. Body language is especially effective for this. Direct his movements by walking in front of your horse's shoulder to make him step back away from you, behind his shoulder to make him step forward away from you, toward his flank to make him swing his hip away and turn his head toward you, straight behind his tail to move him straight forward, or in front of his head to make him step backwards.

14 Get physical. Teach your horse to move away from pressure. He should respond predictably, depending on where you apply pressure. He should move his front end away (to the side) from pressure ahead of the girth, his hind end away laterally from pressure behind the girth, his whole body laterally with pressure at the girth on one side, and his whole body forward with pressure at the girth on both sides. This starts with early ground training and continues under saddle.

15 Remember, horses never forget. Elephants don't have the memory market cornered. Good or bad, whatever your horse learns is indelibly imprinted in his brain. This is why it is so important to avoid negative learning experiences and to capitalize on the positive.

16 Always quit on a good note. You will proceed much faster in each new lesson if you always end on a positive note. Go back to something your horse does well if you encounter a roadblock and reward him when he succeeds.

Equine Learning: The Basics

Horses have amazing memories. If the same result occurs two or three times (for example, if you release leg pressure when he takes a step sideways), your horse most likely will already have

made the connection. Using trial and error, on the other hand, your horse can only guess at what it is you want until a clear cue/response path is established. In this case, if he learned early in life to move away from pressure, making the connection to step sideways may not be too much of a stretch. However, since horses usually instinctively move *toward* pressure, a horse that never learned this lesson early will be much less likely to respond by moving away from pressure.

The more your horse learns, the more he builds his confidence and his ability to learn even more. Horses can learn to give a series of responses to a single cue, and to master new responses in a single try.

For example, watch a horse trained to spin or pivot. A single cue sets him into a sequence of motions that was actually learned in small increments over time: First he took one step, then another, building up the number of steps and the momentum over time until eventually he spins so fast you can hardly see what his feet are doing.

Additionally, the more educated a horse is, the easier it becomes for him to learn new behaviors. Throughout their evolution, horses that learned the quickest survived the longest. Thus horses are capable of understanding and learning a new response the first time they experience the stimulus — if it works for them.

A great example is rattling a feed bucket. How many horses have to be shown twice what's inside before they learn to come running? Your understanding and use of positive feedback will guide your horse toward the desired response each time.

DESENSITIZING

The world we live in, and expect our trail horses to work in, is a far cry from the vast, open grasslands of their ancestors. A horse won't believe you when you insist it's a safe world. As a prey animal, he is programmed to think, "If it's strange, run first and ask questions later, because it just might eat me." Persuading him to accept strange things takes a little planning, a little work, and a lot of patience. But just as Rome wasn't built in a day, neither can you expect to turn a hypersensitive migrating grass hunter into a bold and curious trail partner overnight.

Equine learning is based almost entirely upon repetition. If a reward consistently follows a response to a cue, then that response becomes learned. The same learned response occurs when

things don't happen. If a loud noise (train whistle, car motor, vacuum cleaner, motorcycle engine, siren) doesn't hurt the horse, he learns in time to ignore it. If a tarp, flag, streamer, or pair of long johns flapping in the breeze never attacks him, he learns to ignore that as well in order to conserve energy and keep an eye elsewhere for legitimate threats. Such is the benefit of desensitization. The more exposure a horse has to something that doesn't hurt it, the less frightening that something becomes. By association, the more things a horse learns not to fear, the less likely he is to fear new things he encounters.

Studies have noted that multiple exposures in a short time period — say a train passing by the same spot in the pasture every day for 2 months — are much more effective at desensitizing a horse

Common scary things

Garbage can

Paper bag in road

Barking dog

Tractor starting up

Kid with ball

Rabbit crossing path

Mountain biker

than the same number of exposures drawn out over a longer time period. If an alien spacecraft lands in his pasture only once every month, it will spook the bejeebers out of him each time, but if the ship lands every day and leaves him alone, he'll learn to ignore it.

Lots of things can be used to build up your horse's confidence. Tarps, road flares, firecrackers, goats, barking dogs, motors, air compressors, vacuum cleaners: anything that won't actually touch or hurt the horse will teach him, through multiple uneventful exposures, to accept all manner of strange human inventions. I use a heavy-duty air blower designed for grooming cattle to groom my horses. The blast of air takes some getting used to, but it doesn't hurt, and, in fact, once they get past the noise and the sensation of warm air on their skin, all my horses have come to accept this. Not only is this just one more way to desensitize a horse from overreacting to strange new things, but it is also a great quick way to blow off dust, dander, and dead hair.

As your horse learns to accept new experiences, no matter how frivolous, he is taking a step toward becoming a braver, bolder, better trail horse. The best results come from introducing him to bizarre sights and sounds in a safe environment where you control the outcome — because sooner or later, you won't. Later in this chapter, after your horse has some trail skills under his girth, I'll offer options for helping your horse handle trail "monsters" with ease.

Desensitization is really a process of getting your horse to ignore some stimuli (startling distractions) and focus on others (your cues) instead. It is also a process that teaches your horse to trust in your judgment and respect your courage. After all, you aren't afraid of the "bogey" and you were right, it didn't eat him!

The old "cowboy" way of desensitizing was called **sacking out.** It involved forcefully flapping a sack or slicker all over the horse, often while he was snubbed so tightly to a post that he could barely move, until he stopped struggling. Whether from exhaustion or acceptance didn't matter. Our approach is both more humane and more effective than this obsolete method.

LOWERING THE HEAD

Lowering the head is hardly a challenging new skill for your horse; he does it every time he takes a bite of grass. It is easy to overlook as a valuable skill for your horse to master, even before you saddle him up for the first time.

The benefits are varied. It's a lot easier to halter or bridle a horse that will lower his head on cue. Lowering the head lengthens the neck and spine and is helpful in stretching and building or maintaining flexibility. But an even more valuable effect of a horse lowering his head is the biophysical reaction it elicits in his body and mind.

Consider all those thousands of years of evolution as a plains-roaming, grass-munching critter of prey. While the wily grass blade didn't require the ancestors of our current trail companions to strategize in order to hunt and eat, other hunter's skills did come into play. From the way his ears swivel to let him catch the sound of wolves approaching from all directions, to the position of his large eyes to allow for glimpsing a stalking tiger in a nearly 360-degree range, to that long neck that lets him raise those eyes and ears to the highest possible vantage point, equine evolution has made detecting danger a top priority. In fact, about the only time a horse is vulnerable to sneak attack is when his head is down in the grass.

Even now, when predators with a taste for horseflesh are few (outside of France and Japan), a horse still has an ingrained need to be darn sure it is safe before he risks his life by lowering his head to graze. Under stress, involuntary biological responses within the horse's body shut down his appetite and make eating (or digesting food) difficult to impossible. The result is that a horse must be calm and confident to lower his head and eat,

A good introduction to desensitizing involves some treats, such as carrot sticks and apple pieces, and a plastic grocery store bag. Most horses find the crinkly crackling of those plastic bags disturbing. This exercise is best done with your horse at liberty so he accepts the strange stimulus on his own terms.

1. Approach with the plastic bag in hand and hold it out for him to sniff and investigate on his own (see drawing). If he approaches close enough, reward with praise in a soothing voice and a piece of the treat from the plastic bag.

2. Repeat and increase the "crinkling" as you move the bag with your hands. If he wants to stick his nose inside to grab a treat, let him.

3. Proceed slowly, and don't worry if you have to come back to the exercise over the course of a few days.

4. When he allows it, rub his neck with the plastic bag in your hand, praising him as you do so, and giving a treat now and then during the process. Your goal is for the horse eventually to allow you to rub the plastic bag all over his body while he stands unconcerned.

5. Gradually decrease the frequency of the treats. This principle of behavioral conditioning, called a **diminishing schedule of reinforcement,** is a powerful training tool, as it teaches a horse to perform for fewer and fewer rewards. It is considered the most effective reinforcement schedule, since the behaviors continue well past the reward phase of training.

6. Repeat the process with other objects, such as a tarp, rain slicker, or a gunnysack full of rattling tin cans. Always take your time to allow the horse to accept your crazy idea — the stimulus.

7. When your horse has accepted a few such challenges at liberty, halter and tie him and offer another challenge. Instead of deciding on his own to accept the stimulus, he must now become mindful of your restrictions of the halter and rope, whether you hold the rope or he is tied. Standing quietly under these circumstances is an important responsibility for the horse, and the switch from desensitization at liberty to desensitization under your control is an important milestone. The first phase builds his confidence in you and in himself, the second builds his obedience: all critical components of a good trail horse.

Hold out a plastic bag for your horse to sniff (step 1).

and most interesting and useful to you, the inverse is also true. A horse that lowers his head (as if to eat) experiences involuntary biophysical responses that help to calm him. It is the discovery, acceptance, and exploitation of such instinctive behavior that makes horse training possible, and at times almost magical.

STARTING FROM "BROKE"

A "broke" horse that is ready to begin trail training needs a specific set of skills that you can utterly count on. If he hasn't already mastered the following skills, brush up on the basics in a confined area before heading out on the open trail. Wait until he is qualified to advance to the next phase of training. If you rush a horse that doesn't understand the basics into any type of specialized training, it will only build resistance and frustration in both horse and rider.

A broke horse . . .

✳ Leads properly. Doesn't crowd you or step on you. Stops when you stop and waits for your cue to move.

✳ Ties up. Stands quietly (for hours if necessary) without pawing, neighing, or pulling back.

✳ Stands quietly to be groomed, shod, haltered, bridled, saddled, and mounted. Does not employ evasive maneuvers.

✳ Moves away from pressure at a rate corresponding to the pressure. A gentle pressure elicits a mild response; a firm or sudden pressure tells him to MOVE!

✳ Moves forward freely when asked.

✳ Stops upon request, not six steps later.

✳ Executes a half halt.

✳ Yields to the bit or gives to a nosepiece.

✳ Transitions between gaits on cue; walk, trot (or saddle gait such as tolt, running walk), and canter.

✳ **Rates his speed** (speeds up or slows down upon request) in each gait.

✳ Backs on cue while yielding to bit or nosepiece.

✳ Turns (changes direction) on cue.

And though not necessary to be broke, it helps tremendously if the horse also loads and rides quietly in a horse trailer.

If your horse doesn't qualify in any of the above,

STEP-BY-STEP TECHNIQUES	Lowering the Head

This exercise stretches muscles along the horse's back, helps him keep his cool, and reminds him who's boss: three good things for the price of one.

1. To teach a horse to lower his head on command, use a gentle downward pressure on the lead. Most likely, he will at first respond by resisting, maybe even pulling his head up.

2. Keep the downward pressure firm until he gives in by lowering his head, even just the tiniest bit, then instantly release the pressure.

3. Give a word of praise and a pat and repeat.

After the horse has yielded to the pressure a few times, add a treat to the reward.

4. After he has lowered his head a few inches, offer the treat at that level or lower.

5. Eventually, ask him to hold his head lower and lower, until he has it between his knees, then continue to build the exercise by asking him to hold the position for increasing lengths of time, up to a minute or two.

Ultimately you can ask for this response as your horse is walking along.

go back to the drawing board until he does. A horse that flips out when tied, sidesteps and whirls when you attempt to mount, or stops 3 feet *after* he steps in quicksand can bring dire consequences to both of you out on the trail!

Advanced Maneuvers for the Trail

At first, some of the following exercises may seem to belong more naturally in the dressage ring or reining pattern than on the trail. Maneuvers such as the leg yield (or two-track), turn on the forehand, pivot, side pass, or neck reining might not be necessary on every trail ride, but they have two benefits on the trail. One is that they add up to a well-trained horse with a balanced education, a benefit to any equine discipline. The other advantage is the extra maneuverability that may come in handy in an emergency. No one gets stuck on the trail on purpose.

Five skills that every trail horse should master, above and beyond the basics for broke, are:

✳ Collection (though this could also be included as a requirement for "broke")
✳ Standing
✳ Neck reining
✳ Lateral movements (including leg yields and side passing)
✳ Taking a single step when asked

Additional skills will be broken down later in this chapter under the headings Obstacles and Special Skills. In training these new skills, ride with the mildest bit your horse responds to (or without a bit in a sidepull or hackamore), and be sure all tack is well fitted and comfortable. Annoying or painful distractions keep your horse from focusing on what you are trying to teach.

COLLECTION

A commonly misunderstood concept, **collection** is too often associated with a curved neck and "headset" than with the actual components of this

Collection and Gaited Horses

Trotting horses are most easily taught to collect at the trot, but for most gaited horses it is next to impossible to achieve much collection past a walk. Part of this is because traditional training practices impede collection. In general, the execution of saddle gaits requires more flexibility of the lumbosacral junction of the spine than does a walk, trot, or canter. This translates into dropping the back into a hollow position in which the spine dips toward the center. Prolonged periods of this type of carriage weaken the horse's back and eventually lead to breakdown.

Unfortunately, many gaited-horse riders misinterpret a forced headset, short steps, and a hollow back as collection and persist on riding in gait with such posture for prolonged periods. The good news is that since collection, hollowness, and gait are all matters of degree, even gaited horses can achieve some collection in some gaits. The fox trot is the easiest to collect, followed by the running walk (called the paso llano in the Peruvian Paso breed). The least likely gaits to collect are the racking gaits (including the Icelandic tolt and the Paso Fino fino and corto) and pacey gaits such as the stepped pace.

classic equine carriage. The actual purpose of collection is for the horse to use his hindquarters underneath himself in order to balance both his weight and that of his rider more on his haunches than forward over his shoulders. A collected horse rounds his back, lowers his haunches, takes short steps, increases the flexion in the joints of his hind legs (as they come up more beneath his center of gravity), lifts his neck, and flexes at the poll.

The benefits of working off the haunches with the back rounded (and therefore *not* hollowed or stressed) can make all the difference in controlling your descent down a steep hill. Being able to shorten and precisely guide your horse's steps comes in quite handy in tricky footing, such as on rocks or ice. Collection is a necessary component to every well-schooled trail horse's repertoire. It can also help your horse remain sound well into old age.

Most horses tend to drop the back away from the weight and travel in a somewhat hollow position when first learning to balance a rider's weight. Teaching collection (and allowing the horse's body to adjust to it) will help him to first pull up his back into a more neutral (neither rounded nor hollow) position and then to begin to develop the muscles and balance necessary to round his back.

STEP-BY-STEP TECHNIQUES	**Collection**

Ultimately, your horse should be able to collect at a walk, trot (or certain saddle gaits), and canter, to maneuver precisely in collection, and to control his balance on the flat and up and down hills.

1. Riding at a walk or trot, encourage your horse to step lively. With one hand on each rein, establish contact with his mouth. This does not mean pulling back or balancing your weight on the reins. If you've taught him to yield to rein pressure, you'll feel him soften his jaw.

2. Urge him forward with your legs and seat while continually lightly giving and taking with the reins as you ask him to shorten his strides and maintain forward momentum. He should begin to take shorter steps but maintain about the same speed in response to your collecting aids.

3. You may be able to feel his hind end drop and his back round up, and his neck should rise slightly (see drawing). Once he does this, keep him moving forward for a few steps, then relax your hands and legs until he returns to his normal walk.

4. Repeat the exercise a few times per lesson over a period of weeks until you are able to achieve noticeably shorter steps for an increasing duration. To keep the horse focused on engaging his hindquarters, it helps to stop whenever he begins to shift his weight onto the forehand and back a few steps in order to get the horse settled over his haunches.

Since collection causes the horse to use different muscles in different ways, be sure to alternate collection work with work in a looser, more extended frame. Otherwise, muscles can get sore or cramp and make the exercise uncomfortable.

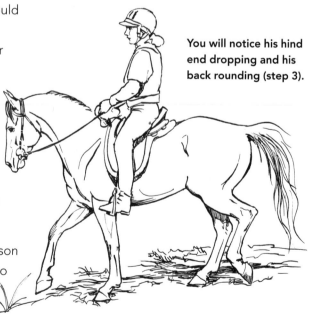

You will notice his hind end dropping and his back rounding (step 3).

STANDING

Standing, or **ground tying,** is something every horse should know yet no rider should trust further than he or she can reach.

Your horse should be trained to stand quietly for grooming, hoof care, and mounting. Horses trained to stand do not run off if the rider should fall.

Understand that horses move around, fidget, or

STEP-BY-STEP TECHNIQUES	Standing

Before you begin training your horse to stand, choose clear cues for "stand still" and stick to them. I like the word *wait* better than *stand* because the w sounds like *whoa* — which your horse should already know. (If he doesn't, reinforce that first.) Be sure you use a clear, commanding tone of voice and don't talk unnecessarily, as you want his focus on the command "wait." I also combine the verbal cue with a hand signal, holding my open palm at the horse's eye level.

1. In a secure area with your horse on lead or on the longe line, work him a few minutes, then give the command WHOA. If you need to tug on the line to get him to stop, continue working on "whoa" until he will stop in response to the verbal command and your body position (stepping slightly toward his head). When he stops on a loose line, you are ready to proceed to "stand."

2. As soon as he stops, take up most of the slack in the line so that if he moves, you will not have to haul in the line before you can correct him. Give the verbal command WAIT (and give the hand signal if you choose to use one).

3. If he holds still for as little as 5 seconds, reward him profusely with praise, petting, and even a treat (see drawing). Make sure he knows he's a genius for "waiting." Lead him off.

4. If, however, your horse moves even one foot before the allotted time is up, correct him with a tug on the line. As quickly as possible, move him back to his exact prior position and repeat the command WAIT. Repeat several times. Gradually increase by a few seconds for each repetition the length of time you expect him to stand still.

5. After a few lessons, add distractions, such as your moving around at the end of the line, until you can walk a full circle around him and stop to tie your shoes while he stands obediently in place. Then lead him out around other horses, dogs, and kids. Make sure nothing harms or frightens him as he is learning to be brave and independently responsible, or you will undo your good work in a flash.

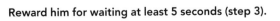

Reward him for waiting at least 5 seconds (step 3).

bolt for reasons that range from inexperience and impatience to anticipation, discomfort, and outright fear. The best-case scenario for trainers is a young or inexperienced horse that gets antsy and just doesn't know any better than to move around. A more difficult situation arises from a horse that has been hurt repeatedly while being mounted, groomed, harnessed, and so on; he just *knows* he had better get out of there.

There are three simple keys to teaching your horse to stand still. First, understand that "stop" and "stand" are two distinct concepts and train them separately. Second, make sure that you are not *causing* your horse to move off. And third, repeat the lesson often in a variety of conditions, from the quiet of your paddock to the chaos of a parade. You want your horse to stand where *you* want him to stand.

Once your horse has mastered ground tying when you have control of him with a rope, longe line, or reins, put the finishing touches on this skill with a length of super-heavy-duty fishing line. He can't feel it or see it, so when he feels a correction from your tug on the line, he can only connect the sensation to your command. While the line won't hold him back if he makes a mad dash, his discovery that you can correct him from a distance makes quite a mental impression.

Loop the line through the bit rings, then tie it back onto itself. Give yourself about 20 feet of line, and tie the other end to a piece of leather or rope for a handhold. Once he is standing well on cue, dismount, cue to *WAIT*, then move away. If he so much as moves a foot to take a step, snap the line and repeat *WAIT*.

Gradually increase the distance between you and him, and the length of time he must wait. Having already gone through these steps with a longe line, he will probably snore through it.

STANDING FOR MOUNTING

Every horse should learn to stand for mounting. It's potentially hazardous to climb aboard a moving target. If you have a horse that turns inside out in an effort to get away from you as you mount, take a good look at the signals you are sending him before you correct him.

Often when a horse avoids mounting, the rider unconsciously tightens the reins, inadvertently jerking the horse's mouth and/or pulling his head around and causing him to swing his hips away. The rider also may jab her toes into the horse's side and/or drag herself up the horse's side (which tips the saddle and digs the bars into the horse's back).

Use a mounting block to avoid tipping the saddle and leave some slack in the reins, then place one hand on the withers for balance and swing as smoothly as possible over and into the saddle, settling your weight gently. Reward your horse for standing still.

Make sure you don't instantly cue the horse to move off as soon as your fanny touches down, whether by inadvertently shifting your weight or digging in your heels or by intentional cues to move forward. If you are cueing or hurting your horse when you mount, his moving off is your problem. Likewise, confusion or discomfort to the horse once you are in the saddle (due to ill-fitting saddle [see chapter 3], poor riding, or stressed training) will also inspire your horse to try to make a quick getaway.

Transferring the "stand" lesson to mounting is easiest if you break it down into steps. Even if it seems to be slow going, don't rush. Proceed to the next level only when your horse is solidly standing still at the stage you are in, and don't be surprised if you don't get to mount the first day.

Once your horse will stand for mounting, get on and just sit there. Bend down and tie your boot strings, put on a saddlebag, tie your coat to the back of the saddle, turn and talk to a friend. These routine movements will make your horse more and more reliable in time.

I make it a habit to mount, sit a few seconds, and then ask for "back up" or a turn on the haunches — anything but forward motion — to prevent my horse from anticipating my cue to move forward. Anticipation is the number one reason most horses move forward during mounting. Isn't that always what comes next? Make sure it isn't always.

When out on the trail, disarm his desire to go "home" or back to the trailhead by facing him in the opposite direction before you mount.

EMERGENCY DISMOUNT

Once your horse stands for mounting, you can take him one step further by training him to stop, then to stand for dismounting, even when the dismount is a bit rough and unintentional on your part. This is a skill best taught by those who do not bruise easily.

As you ride along at the walk, suddenly (because most falls *are* sudden) pull both your feet from the

---

Standing for Mounting

Horses that have learned to expect discomfort when a rider mounts may suffer a setback of the *STAND* command when saddled and then approached by a rider. If so, go back to the steps he is already comfortable with, even if that means working on the longe line under saddle.

1. When he will stand saddled and bridled and let you move around and do all the things you could do prior to saddling him, ask your horse to stand while you are at his side, then turn and face the saddle as if to mount but remain standing.

2. The instant he moves, correct him and put his feet back where they were; reward him if he stays put.

3. Ask him to stand, turn to face his side, and put your foot in the stirrup (toe pointing toward his head, not into his side). Correct or reward for immobility, and repeat.

4. Put some weight in the stirrup. Correct or reward; step back down and repeat.

5. Spring from your foot or a mounting block and balance at his side, standing in the stirrup

for a few seconds while he waits (see drawing). Correct and reward; step down and repeat.

6. Mount and settle in the saddle. This is a great time for a horse treat if he responds with stillness! It changes his mind-set from worrying about getting jabbed or yanked to expecting a reward.

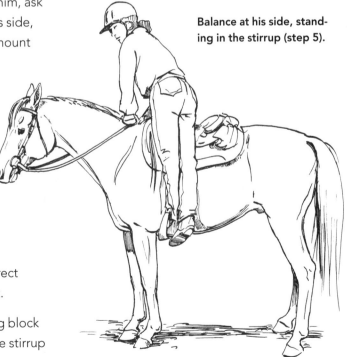

Balance at his side, standing in the stirrup (step 5).

stirrups, shove off with both hands at the withers, and bail off to the side of the horse. This emergency dismount is a valuable skill for you to master anyway, for that unavoidable occasion when parting company with your saddle is your best available option. Learn to pick your landing and try to land on your feet or your shoulder with a rolling motion to absorb as much of the impact as possible.

NECK REINING

Neck reining has two advantages over direct reining. It leaves one hand free and it can be employed quickly without changing your grip on the reins. It's a lot easier (and safer) to munch a snack, lift a branch out of the way, or snap a photo when it takes only one hand to guide your mount.

Any horse that can relax and walk forward on a loose rein is ready to learn to neck-rein. Think of

---

STEP-BY-STEP TECHNIQUES	**Emergency Dismount**

Mastering the emergency dismount is one thing, but teaching your horse how to react to it is another.

1. Tie a knot in the reins and leave them over the horse's withers so they don't come off when you do. Attach a separate long line to the bit (or halter beneath the bridle), fold it up, and hold the bulk of it in your right hand.

2. Pull both feet from the stirrups, shove off with both hands at the withers, and push yourself off the horse (see drawing).

3. The instant you hit the ground (landing on your feet if possible), tug at the line and command *WHOA*. It is likely your horse will be startled enough to stop automatically.

4. Verbally praise and follow with the command *WAIT*. Don't move for a few seconds (unless to correct him he should not stand still), then praise, reward, and treat lavishly.

5. Sorry to say . . . repeat.

If ever you are separated from the saddle on the trail, the best you can rely on is your horse's instant expectation of a treat. It probably won't be enough to take his mind off a rampaging bear, but it may keep him still long enough for you to remount in the face of less drastic distractions.

Shove off with both hands (step 2).

neck-rein training as asking for an already established response to a new set of cues, some of which can be eliminated after the horse learns what you want.

The cues are rein, seat, and leg, and, if desired, whip. Begin with very exaggerated cues and gradually tone them down as your horse gets the idea.

After a lesson or two turning in one direction, reverse the cues to turn in the opposite direction and practice in that direction alone for a lesson or two. After that, work on turns in both directions. Vary the degree of the turns. It helps to impress on your horse the cue for a sharp turn by planning the turn so that a tree, fence, or barn wall makes it necessary for him to make the turn sharply.

Some tips for teaching neck reining can help speed your progress and avoid miscuing your horse.

STEP-BY-STEP TECHNIQUES	Neck Reining

Ride at a walk, with both hands on slack reins about 4 inches above the saddle horn or pommel. Decide in advance where you want your horse to turn: for example, to the left. In quick sequence, so that the cues almost flow together:

1. Shift your weight to the left (push with your left leg behind the girth and lean a little into the turn).

2. Place your right leg on, or just in front of, the girth and press to suggest your horse move his front end away from the pressure.

3. Lift the right rein and place it against the horse's neck about halfway up so that your hand crosses over the center of his neck (he will quickly notice the feel of the rein this way and be more likely to realize that you are cueing for something), and squeeze on the direct (left) rein (see drawing).

4. After many repetitions, your horse will anticipate the sequence of events and turn before you pull on the direct rein. Reward him well when he first makes the connection.

5. An optional cue is to tap the horse's neck with a riding whip opposite the direction you want him to turn (for a left-hand turn, tap the right side of his neck) just prior to giving the neck-rein cue. Follow with a direct rein if necessary.

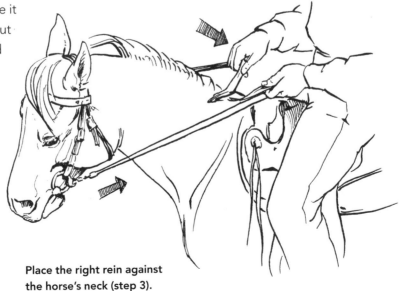

Place the right rein against the horse's neck (step 3).

Be clear, even exaggerated, in what you ask. Here are the steps in sequence:

1 Shift your weight decidedly before you cue to turn. (Odds are your horse will at least take a step or two to the side just to recover his balance. Take advantage of that beginning!)

2 Lay the reins higher up on his neck than you would on a finished neck-reining horse to be sure he is aware that this is a cue.

3 Tap his neck strongly with a whip, if necessary, to draw his attention to the neck cue.

4 Direct-rein with give-and-take tugs to cue a full turn, not just a gradual change of direction. Be careful not to pull back or up on the neck rein, as this cross-cues the horse and can be confusing or frustrating, especially for horses ridden in a curb bit (a bit with shanks). Pulling on the neck rein can tip the horse's head away from the direction in which he is traveling.

Avoid training gimmicks such as crossing the reins under the horse's neck as a shortcut to training him to neck-rein. This is not as effective as the clear, distinct cues recommended here, and it is not safe if the horse should suddenly bolt. You'll have no way to guide his direction or bend his neck around to the side for an emergency stop.

Practice turning around trees, stumps, cars, fence posts, buckets, and anything else your horse can bend his body around. Weave in and out and repeat the same patterns at first to encourage your horse to anticipate the turns and respond before you have to apply the direct rein. Use your legs to help him bend. Don't drill relentlessly on one turn; make circles, serpentines, and sudden changes to keep the horse from getting bored.

Eventually you will no longer need the direct rein. At this point, you can carry both reins in one hand. It is conventional to use the left hand. Until you are certain your horse understands the new cues to turn, it helps to keep your fingers between the reins. This subtly adds a bit of a direct rein to a neck-rein cue, if needed, by tipping your hand to one side or the other. At this stage, you can work on neck reining at a trot and/or saddle gait and a canter. Your goal is a horse that turns to the degree you request, at any gait, with a slight weight shift, a leg cue at the girth, and a barely perceptible shift of the reins along the lower half of his neck.

LATERAL MOVEMENTS

Lateral movements are those in which your horse moves sideways to some degree. They include maneuvers such as leg yield or two-track, turn on the forehand, turn on the haunches, and side passing. Sounds fancy, but what they really boil down to is controlling your horse's body, one end at a time. The ability to keep your horse straight, or to move one end or the other (or both!) where you want, can be critical on a steep, narrow, rocky, crowded, overgrown, or otherwise challenging stretch of trail.

TWO-TRACK OR LEG YIELD In the two-track, the horse moves with his front feet on a different plane than his rear feet, creating two sepa-

Is Your Horse a Lefty?

————— ✧ —————

Horses are either left- or right-"handed" — stronger on one side but more flexible on the other. You can expect work in one direction to proceed more easily than in the other, and take advantage of this by starting to teach new concepts in the direction that is easier for your horse. Most horses are "left-handed." They turn more easily toward the left because their right side is more developed, or stronger. You can actually see the difference in development from one side to the other if you get up on a stool or stump and look down your horse's spine.

rate sets of tracks. He moves forward and somewhat sideways at the same time, with his head bent away from the line of travel. This comes in handy on the trail when a horse doesn't want to approach something headfirst, or when he needs to be aware of something alongside his path, such as when riding beside traffic. It is also a practical starting point for teaching all other lateral movements. As an exercise in its own right, it loosens up the horse's shoulders and strengthens his hindquarters.

TURN ON THE FOREHAND In a full turn on the forehand, the horse makes a big circle around his own front end with his hind end. Mastering this skill allows you to move the horse's rear to one side or the other while keeping his front end stationary or while moving in a straight line.

STEP-BY-STEP TECHNIQUES	Two-Track

It's easiest to train the two-track in an arena with soft footing because you can use the rail to guide your horse and see for yourself the tracks in the footing, but this is an exercise that can be taught by "feel" anywhere. Here's how to do it.

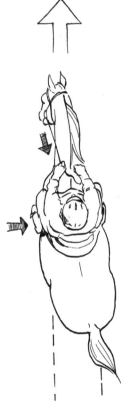

Squeeze with the left rein and apply pressure with your left leg (steps 1 and 2).

1. Riding in a straight line, with your hips and shoulders in line with the direction of travel, take up contact on one rein (left, for example) and squeeze (don't pull) and release so that your horse begins to turn his head toward the left. Keep the right rein taut enough to prevent him from following his head and changing directions (see drawing).

2. At the same time, shift your weight to the left and apply pressure with your left leg on the horse's side, just behind the girth. Your right leg should be "silent," or at most mildly in touch with the horse's right side, just ahead of the girth. Your horse should swing his hips away from his head (toward the right).

3. Let up on all cues as soon as he does and reward him so he understands that he has done what you wanted.

4. Repeat the lesson and work in both directions, until he will freely move his head to one side, his hind end to the other, while continuing straight forward, traveling in "two tracks" for about 100 feet.

That's barely a starting point for dressage training, but it will lay a good foundation for a flexible and maneuverable trail mount.

TURN ON THE HAUNCHES The turn on the haunches is the opposite of the turn on the forehand, with the horse making a circle around his hindquarters with his front legs. It's not the speedy pivot of a reining horse, but a quiet, controlled turn around, with the hind legs remaining in roughly the same spot, not with one pivot foot seemingly bolted to the ground. Being able to control exactly where a horse positions his front end will guarantee you the best spot at the berry bush and make him more maneuverable in general.

STEP-BY-STEP TECHNIQUES	Turn on the Forehand

This turning maneuver comes in very handy on the trail when covering difficult terrain or steep descents in which a horse often tends to let his hind end "drift" to one side or the other of the trail. Keeping your horse straight will help to keep more weight on the haunches, making descents more controlled and safer.

1. Begin to teach this maneuver from the ground by standing at your horse's side and pressing on his ribs, just behind the girth line, as you tilt his head toward you.

2. Reward him as soon as his hind end takes a step away from you.

3. Repeat, then switch to the opposite side. (Never forget that horses often have to learn things all over again when you switch sides. Usually they learn the same lesson faster on the second side.)

4. Once he will shift his hindquarters away from you easily, keeping his front end relatively still, with a minimal cue, transfer the lesson to the saddle (see drawing). Cue with your leg in the same spot and reward with

release if he gets it. Sometimes it helps to have someone on the ground to "remind" your horse of what he already knows about pressure on his side.

5. Practice moving his rump to one side, then the other (this is fun because it looks like your horse is dancing). Practice swinging his hind end over as you keep him walking forward.

Cue with your leg and reward with release (step 4).

SIDEPASS Nothing beats a sidepass for getting closer to a buddy to whisper a secret (or away from someone whose secrets you don't want to hear), easing your horse away from the edge of a steep drop-off, or closing a gate without having to dismount. Once your horse has learned to neck-rein, turn on the forehand, and turn on the haunches, the sidepass is easy to teach by combining the cues for all three. If your horse has also mastered the Single Step (see below), your control over his movements will be that much more precise.

It helps to start the lesson under saddle, with your horse facing a fence or wall to prevent him from moving forward in an attempt to guess what the heck you want.

By now your horse should understand when you are trying to teach him a new concept and be willing to work for you. Be sure not to rush or let him get frustrated with the combined cues. If he

does, go back to the established turn on the haunches, or the turn on the forehand, and reassure him that he does know what you are asking. You might find it easier to get the point across from the ground, by parking your horse in front of a fence, standing beside him, and nudging his side with your knuckle. Most horses will learn to sidepass away from a light fingertip touch, once they understand the concept.

> *Horses learn one side at a time, so expect to teach lessons anew when you switch sides. Usually they learn the lesson faster on the second side.*

A SINGLE STEP

A Single Step can save your life on the trail, just as a single misstep can end it. Drastic, but true. For that reason alone, it is smart to teach your horse

---

STEP-BY-STEP TECHNIQUES	**Turn on the Haunches**

Again, start this lesson on the ground. It helps to have your horse saddled and bitted with one long rein running through a ring on the off side. This way you can cue the horse to move his front end away from you without having to reach around.

1. Give a firm cue on the off rein at the same time you press against his near side, just ahead of the girth. The idea is to shift his front end away from you with the rein, applying pressure away at the same time. It may take a few tries for him to understand what you want (see drawing).

2. Ignore it if he backs or sidesteps, but as soon as he curves his front away while keeping his rear relatively stationary, reward him as if he just invented chocolate.

3. Once he will take a few steps away from you with his front end, mount and transfer the lesson to the saddle.

Cue the off rein and simultaneously press his near side in front of the girth.

the simple command *STEP*. You can ask for this with a verbal command or a physical cue, as long as the horse understands that *STEP* — forward, backward, or to the side — means one step only.

To teach a Single Step, your horse must first lead properly. This means following slightly behind you to your right. He should stop when you do, with his head and nose about even with your shoulder. A lot of trail riders prefer that their mounts walk several feet directly behind them. This comes in handy when the trail is too narrow for the two of you to walk side-by-side. But in most circumstances, it is safest for your horse not to be directly behind you in case he spooks and leaps forward. You don't want to be the most convenient landing pad. A good trail horse learns when you want him to lead slightly behind and off to the side and when you want him to follow at a safe distance behind you.

CRUISE CONTROL

Cruise control frees you from a horse that constantly needs to be hounded to stay in gait. Never forget that the pace your horse sets is your choice, not his. Ask for a walk, gait, or trot and regulate the gait steadily as long as you ask your horse to hold it. Depending on the horse, you may have to prod or hold him back.

Alone on the trail, his pace may be constant, but often, when other horses are around, a horse will try to keep up with the pack. Some horses just naturally like to take the lead, while others prefer to hang back. When riding with friends, there is a simple exercise that can help all types of horses to keep their focus and learn to accept whatever pace, or place, you set for them. Play leapfrog.

With all riders moving out together, take turns having one horse trot (or gait) ahead of the other horses for a short distance (10 or 20 yards) and

---

STEP-BY-STEP TECHNIQUES	Sidepass

Be prepared to start from scratch when teaching this maneuver in the opposite direction. One mare I trained would practically fly to the right but would only grudgingly stumble a step or two to the left. Be patient, and make the rewards worth the work.

1. Keeping light contact with his mouth (to signal that you do not want him to step forward), cue with your leg just behind the girth to ask him to step over with his hind end.

2. Apply neck-rein pressure to ask him to move his front over in the same direction (see drawing).

3. If he manages to get both ends moved over a step or two to the side, release all cues and reward him.

4. Repeat the lesson and gradually time the cues closer together until you are applying the neck-rein and the leg cue simultaneously.

Apply rein and leg cues separately at first (steps 1 and 2).

A Single Step

Teaching the Single Step is merely a matter of slowing down your horse and asking him to think about each step as an individual act.

1. Standing at your horse's head, give the command *STEP* and give one gentle tug on the lead.

2. As soon as he moves one hoof forward, lean toward him and be ready to stop his forward motion with the lead if necessary, then reward him (see drawing). (At this point your horse is bound to be thinking, "Dang! This is too easy. My owner must have forgotten that I already know how to lead!")

3. Repeat until your horse will move just one hoof at a time and hold it in place for increasingly long periods (from seconds up to a minute or more) until you reinforce with a reward.

4. Providing different things for your horse to step over will help reinforce his concept of Single Step. Begin with something obvious to the horse, such as a ground pole, rather than an insubstantial line or rope. Ask him to *STEP*, stop him as soon as one hoof steps over the obstacle, and reward him. Repeat this exercise, and build on it over the course of a few days by asking him take one step and stop, then a second step and stop, then a third step and stop, each time holding his position after he stops. The classic test (and common obstacle in trail classes) for this skill is to step into the center of individual tires positioned on the ground at one-step (about 18 to 24 inches) intervals.

5. The next lesson is to ask your horse to step *onto* something like a sheet of plywood, a difference of footing (such as where blacktop meets grass or gravel), a tarp, or a mock bridge. Repeat the phases of asking for one step at a time and holding his stance.

6. Transferring this lesson to the saddle works best if you have a helper on the ground who can watch where the horse places his feet. Go back through the phases of stopping on the flat, stopping when stepping over a pole, and finally stopping at different points while walking onto an obstacle. By continually challenging your horse to take a Single Step over or onto a variety of surfaces, you will build his confidence and teach him to think about where and how he places his feet.

Add a potentially life-saving aspect to this lesson by loosely wrapping a soft rope around your horse's legs, then asking him to step and stop. One of the most dangerous things a horse can do is to freak out when his feet become entangled (in brush, vines, wire, or rope). His confidence that together you can work out of a tangle may never be required — or it just might pay off.

Stop him after one step and reward him (step 2).

then slow that horse back down to a walk. Next have another horse advance past the group, catching up to the horse in front, and return to a walk. By regularly alternating which horse has the lead and which horses move out alone, the concept of "leader" becomes muddled and each horse learns to work independently. When all horses in the group are comfortable passing and being passed at a slow speed, you can step up the pace.

Other tricks to get your horse to keep his mind on you rather than other horses include turning around and heading back up the trail (leaving the group to go on without you), stopping and waiting until other horses are out of sight (and sound) before proceeding (with the other riders waiting for you just out of sight), and stopping for brief periods before proceeding. A horse that fights being separated from other horses needs more practice than one that accepts it.

Obstacles

The phrase *trail obstacle* is not easy to define because an obstacle for one horse isn't necessarily an obstacle for the next. I've found the most practical definition on the trail is anything your horse won't readily proceed through or past.

So how do you prepare your horse in advance to face such fierce and frightening obstacles as crumpled bits of paper, revving dirt bikes, mud, and bridges over noisy, sparkling, swiftly flowing water? What about those obstacles that physically bar your path, such as deadfall and a closed gate? You can never prepare your horse (or yourself!) for *every* possible "obstacle," but you can build enormous confidence and a repertoire of skills from which each of you can draw when confronted with something on the trail that makes you think about turning around.

Schooling over and through obstacles in your horse's own familiar paddock or pasture — before you ever ask him to attempt them on the trail — will build both his confidence and yours. It's a process that can really stretch your imagination, offer some great "funniest home video" moments, and, best of all, be fun. Even though the possibilities of what might be an obstacle for your horse are literally limitless, I've broken them down into six types: Scary Things, Things to Step Over, Things to Step On, Things to Jump, Gates, and Steep Climbs.

As you ask your horse to overcome his inborn, natural fears, keep the list of Simple Rules in mind (see page 105). They will help you in every situation. Whenever possible, take a young or inexperienced horse out with more experienced trail horses. Never allow a horse to bluff his way out of something he can do.

PLAN OF ATTACK

Although the details of the desensitizing plan will be different for each obstacle, the underlying strategies are always the same:

Simplify getting past the obstacle. This may mean breaking it down into steps, approaching only one part of it at a time, or setting it up to be much easier to navigate in the beginning, then progressively tougher. An example is widely spacing ground poles to back through at first, then gradually bringing them closer together.

Proceed positively. Read your horse and don't ask him to do something when he is upset. Keep sessions cool, calm, and relaxed and rely on reward, not punishment, when asking for new things or approaching something scary.

Step back. If your horse is flustered or not comprehending a particular phase of an obstacle, go back to something that he has already mastered.

Reinforce. Repeat, reward, repeat, reward, and rest. Four seems to be the magic number for repetitions. Fewer and the horse may still be unsure or anxious; more and he may begin to get bored, resentful, or confused that maybe he really *isn't* doing what you want.

Build up. Add challenges gradually. Add extra poles to the Step Over, make the jump broader, add smoke and noise to the Scary Thing, place a log under the plywood "bridge" so that it moves . . . the more creative you become in training at home, the more crazy things your horse will accept as a matter of course.

Save riding for last. By making sure your horse is mentally prepared for the obstacle before you add the physical demands of carrying a rider over or through it, you give both of you a little more insurance that he will succeed.

SCARY THINGS

Scary things come in many forms that may not be obviously scary to you but are blatantly so to your horse. They can be:

* visual, such as a strange object on the trail that wasn't there before;
* visual and animated, such as flags fluttering in the breeze, spinning plastic pinwheels, bobbing birthday balloons tied to a mailbox, or an umbrella that suddenly opens;
* visual and tactile, such as deep brush (or show-ring obstacles that resemble it) in which your horse is touched by branches, or 6 inches of cold, smushy snow where the previous afternoon there had been hard ground;
* auditory (noisy), such as firecrackers, a loud radio, running vacuum cleaner, or dogs barking behind a fence;
* visual and auditory, such as kids riding bikes toward you on the road, hollering back and forth at each other as their tires whir;
* olfactory (smelly), such as the strange scents of predators or rutting deer;
* visual and olfactory, such as smoke bombs, or your perfumed aunt visiting after church;
* visual, auditory, and tactile, such as the wooden bridge over rushing water that makes a weird hollow clomping sound and shudders slightly when your horse steps on it;
* visual, auditory, and olfactory, such as the traffic whizzing past, with motors humming, horns honking, and exhaust pipes spewing;
* or any other combination of scary sensory threats.

In teaching your horse not to fear such a list, where do you even begin?

The easiest way to start to desensitize your horse to Scary Things is to let him do it himself. Find whatever you can that your horse might perceive as Scary. Use your imagination — old furniture, a bicycle, a tarp, a sheet of plywood (which will come in useful later for training your horse to Step On Things or cross a bridge), a flag, a giant-sized blow-up Easter Bunny.

Leave the Scary Thing near — not in — his paddock or pasture, so he can maintain a barrier between himself and it. Distance is a great comfort to a prey species. Horses, just like humans, have a comfort zone that is interwoven with the familiar things in their lives. By introducing Scary Things within sight of his familiar surroundings, you leave your horse a way to deal with it and still remain in his own personal comfort zone, even if that means hanging out at the opposite side of the paddock and snorting at the Scary Thing.

In time, especially if you leave his hay or a bucket of grain nearby, your horse will venture nearer the Scary Thing to investigate. If he panics, move the Scary Thing farther away until he behaves normally, then bring it closer, a few feet (or inches) at a time, until he accepts it.

Don't rush a horse toward an obstacle, especially in the early phases of training. Your goal is for him to develop more confidence on his own. The more repetitions you can set up, the faster he will work past his fears. You are forging new paths through some very old and established territory — equine instinct.

You can leave certain items in the paddock with your horse, such as a sheet of plywood, a bridge, or a tarp, but just make certain the situation is as safe as possible and that you keep a close eye on them both. Horses will often paw at things and can get tangled in a tarp in no time, so think like a horse when you ask him to share his space with a Scary Thing. The more curious your horse is, the faster he will learn to accept something new in his space. Each new thing that your horse learns to accept will build his confidence for the next. Time and repetition are on your side.

Once your horse has accepted a few Scary Things on his own, work with him on a longe line (you may need the extra length of line for safety's sake or to bring your horse back under control should he bolt). Longe him past Scary Things, then practice leading safely, with your horse off to the right-hand side with his head level with your shoulder. Walk past some of the old Scary Things, then around the paddock, coming closer to each Scary Thing every time you pass. Place a few new "ringers" in among the more familiar objects. Ignore them. Don't approach them, just pass by. Don't forget to include Scary Things from all sensory categories, such as a running vacuum cleaner, a tethered goat or dog, a loud radio, a flag flapping in the wind, streamers, kids on skateboards nearby, and a bouquet of helium-filled balloons.

It can help to have an experienced horse and a helper on hand to broach these Scary Things at first. Horses read and trust other horses readily, whereas your signals might not be as clear or as credible.

Only after your horse passes near Scary Things without incident should you try to approach them, and even then it isn't really necessary. On the trail, the best way past a Scary Thing is to focus at least 20 feet ahead of it, with both your eyes and your mind. Your unconscious attitude and balance in the saddle will transfer to your horse that the Thing is not important, and to keep his own mind up the trail.

Still, having your horse approach and investigate Scary Things is a great confidence builder. If he finds a treat in a scarecrow's pocket, he'll be much more likely to approach the next one. Allow your horse to step as near as he is comfortable to the object and do not press for more. Odds are he will get closer on each encounter. Some horses are just naturally curious and will sniff and nibble at strange things. Others are content to stand back a little and look. Your

Your goal is for your horse to approach the Scary Thing on his own.

goal is to have a trail mount that will not spook at odd sights, sounds, smells, or surfaces, not a circus act where he will pick the pockets of the clown. Be content with what you need.

Ideally, your horse should come to trust your judgment over his own. You are his leader and therefore his salvation, and he should believe that. By taking time to expose him to many new and Scary Things, in which each encounter results in no harm (even better, in rewards), you will reap the benefits of your horse's trust.

THINGS TO STEP OVER

Things to Step Over are present on even the best-kept bridle trails, and luckily are easy to train for at home. The handiest props to have on hand for training are ground poles or **cavelletti,** with cinder blocks or buckets to hold up the poles at varying heights.

Begin the lesson by setting out just one pole on the ground. Most horses will walk over it without a second thought. Add a pole or two, placing them about 2 feet apart, or equal to the distance of your horse's stride. Lead your horse over them in both directions, adding poles until he walks over six to eight poles coming and going without bumping any. Alter the distance of the poles from each other, place three or four poles farther apart (about 3 feet) and three or four closer together (about a foot apart) and practice again.

Next prop up one end of one or two poles so that if your horse doesn't watch where he places his feet, he will bump the poles. Don't punish him if he bumps a pole or two in the beginning, but if he persists, be prepared to jiggle the lead, tap him with a riding whip, or tug upwards on the reins the instant he does to let him know he needs to pay attention. Vary the distance between the poles, the height, and the width (by placing two poles close together).

Practice asking your horse for a Single Step (see page 125) to reinforce focusing his attention on watching where he places his feet. Over the course

Finding a carrot in a scarecrow's pocket will build your horse's confidence.

of as many lessons as it takes, lead, longe, or ride over the obstacles, varying your pattern and speed until your horse can step over them without bumping a single pole.

Next, add different obstacles to step over (being sure to avoid anything that might hurt or frighten your horse). Again, the list here is limited only by your imagination and what you have on hand. Some suggestions are tires, straw bales, rolls of paper towels, a rolled-up sleeping bag, logs, branches with leaves or needles, stuffed animals, and pillows.

This category can get really tricky when you add backing and sidepassing. Ask your horse to step partway over a log, then sidepass off one side or the other. Have him walk between two ground poles, then back out. Such "obstacles" are common in trail classes at shows (see chapter 11).

When schooling with man-made obstacles, be sure to make them as easy as possible at first, then gradually add challenges. When training a horse to enter a box of poles on the ground — an L shape made of poles or any other such obstacle — start out with the poles as far apart as it takes for the

Allow him to step over the obstacle at his own pace.

horse to begin successfully, then as he gets more practice, bring them closer together, a few inches at a time, until he can walk, back, sidepass, and turn in a small space.

THINGS TO STEP ON (OR IN)

Things to Step On (or In) can be more challenging than merely stepping over an obstacle because, once he takes that step, your horse is on (or in) the obstacle and still has to deal with it. Common examples are strange or difficult footing, bridges, mud, and water.

One old trick to accustom a horse to mud is to soak the ground around his watering trough thoroughly. Wet ground turns to mud pretty quickly as horses walk through it. Keeping the ground muddy around his water supply desensitizes your horse to mud (teaching him that where there's mud, there's water), and as a bonus if your area is arid, a regular mud bath helps to keep his hooves hydrated and healthy.

Caution: Be sure your horse has dry land to stand on as well. Constantly standing in mud or wet ground softens a horse's feet and makes them susceptible to stone bruises or **graveling** (in

which small pieces of gravel work their way through the sole and into the hoof, where they either abscess or continue to migrate through the hoof until they emerge near the coronary band).

Your best asset at this stage of training is your horse's trust, which you have earned through desensitization training up until this point. Nothing threatens a horse more than losing his footing. In his mind, loss of footing equals falling and falling equals becoming dinner. So when you ask him to step onto uncertain footing, he thinks you are asking him to place his life in your hands.

Approach any new surface as though you expect your horse to cross with no fuss. At this stage, your "bluff" may pay off; your horse is reading you for clues. Don't tense up at the thought of how your horse might react, and don't fight or force a horse over or onto any strange surface. He must be able to think about where he is placing his feet, not how fast he can get them out of there. First lessons should be very calm and quiet; they will make the most lasting impression for how your horse will approach new surfaces in the future. They also have to be successful or your horse will decide right off the bat that he doesn't really *have* to step on something just because you ask him.

Never bribe your horse onto a surface. Remember, treats are for rewards, and rewards are for *after* he does what you ask.

THINGS TO JUMP

Things to Jump turn up when you least expect them. Any good trail horse should be able to clear a low or narrow jump if that is the only way past the obstacle. Things you might have to jump on the trail are logs barring the path and washouts too big to step over. It's best to practice jumps before your way home depends on one.

Even though babies can leap and cavort in the pasture, don't ask your horse to try jumping with your weight on his back until he is mature enough to handle it, usually around the age of four or five.

For low jumps, approaching at a walk or trot

Stepping on Things

A mud puddle, sheet of plywood, gravel pile, and a tarp are all great tools for training your horse to Step on Things. If possible, place one of these obstacles along a fence or wall so that he can't swerve and avoid the surface by going around it. One trick is to pull your horse trailer alongside a choice mud puddle; another is to set heavy-duty fence panels on either side of an obstacle so the horse can't evade it. Work on only one obstacle at a time until he calmly steps where you ask him, then proceed to something else.

Give your horse time to sniff and investigate, but don't overdo it. Some horses will paw, sniff, snort, anything but actually step on the surface. At some point he *has* to step on it to learn that stepping on it is no big deal. The more fuss he makes in advance, the more you have to overcome. Keep a businesslike attitude.

1. Start by leading your horse on the longe line and stride confidently across the tarp, plywood, or puddle (see drawing). (When you work with a puddle, be sure you are wearing your boots. If you tiptoe across, your horse will figure he should avoid it.)

2. Your horse may follow your lead (literally) and go where you go. If so, praise and reward. If he tries to skip off to the side, slow down and ask for one step at a time. Be sure both you and your horse keep your cool.

3. If he is very resistant, ask him to step over the very corner of the plywood or puddle, or roll or fold the tarp up so that he can step over it.

4. Repeat stepping over several times, gradually asking him to move closer to the center of the obstacle until he inadvertently steps on it, and then praise, reward, and quit for a while.

5. Once your horse is crossing over the obstacle, whether on lead or on the longe line, ask him to stop and stand for just a few seconds at first, working up to a longer wait. This teaches him not to rush over strange surfaces and reinforces his faith in your judgment.

By now you have a bag of tricks from which to draw if a horse is particularly challenging. Try to back him onto the surface and reward him if he lands just one hoof on it. Or ask for a turn on the haunches to move his hind end onto the surface. It also helps to have another, experienced horse walk over the surface to show your horse that he won't get swallowed up by it.

You can also set up the obstacle where you longe your horse. Start with a large circle and longe him closer and closer until he has no choice but to step on it. The first few attempts may seem wildly uncontrolled, but be persistent.

Confidently lead your horse onto the obstacle (step 1).

will allow your horse enough momentum to collect himself, launch, and clear the jump. Gaited horses *can* clear a jump in gait. However, because of how they must hold their bodies in order to perform saddle gaits, it is a real challenge for them to go from hollow (or neutral at best) to a rounded back with their hind legs under them enough to push off for a jump. It's best to teach your gaited horse a slow, controlled, collected canter and to approach jumps in that gait under saddle. And, of course, a collected canter is also great for non-gaited horses to use in approach to a jump.

You'll most likely notice that the first few times your horse clears a 2-foot-high jump he has about 6 feet to spare. Horses generally overestimate at first, but with practice will sail over obstacles much more closely. Once he is clearing jumps comfortably, and this could take 10 minutes or 10 days, transfer the lesson to the saddle. The first

---

Jumping

The easiest way to start your horse over jumps is to use your ground poles, a familiar tool to your horse. Start with two poles, each one raised at one end and positioned so that they cross with the center being the lowest part of the jump. This arrangement helps the horse focus on jumping obstacles at the center.

1. Lead your horse up to the jump and let him look it over.

2. Go back and lead at a trot up to the obstacle and hop over it (see drawing). Your horse should *follow* you right over. Keep a safe distance ahead of him so he doesn't calculate you to be a landing site.

3. Reward, repeat in both directions, and then move onto something else. Jumping should be fun, and too much practice can stress muscles as well as get your horse overly excited, so don't overdo it.

An alternative that is probably safer and won't wear you out as fast is to set up a single jump in your horse's regular longeing area. Longe him over it a few times in each direction. Reward and move on. You can add more jumps to his path and increase the difficulty as he progresses.

Hop over the obstacle, leading your horse after you (step 2).

few hops may be awkward as he learns to rebalance, but be patient, have fun, and keep the sessions calm and low key. If your horse refuses any jump, go back to a simpler jump and practice and reward. Build up the degree of difficulty a little bit at a time.

Over time, increase the height and/or width of the jumps and vary their position. You can increase the width by placing two or three pole jumps side-by-side. Bear in mind that jumping height is one thing and jumping width another, but jumping both high and wide is a serious challenge, both mentally and physically, for your horse. Build up very gradually.

GATES

Opening Gates from horseback is an excellent excuse to use the skills of backing, turning on the forehand, turning on the haunches, and sidepassing in one maneuver. You'll find that you'll have to practice gates that swing open from the left and right, or that swing in or out, separately. Once your horse understands this, he will anticipate and try to maneuver the entire process of opening and closing the gate as one set of moves. I've had horses become very flustered just because I pulled the gate toward me when they expected it to swing out.

Before attempting to manipulate the gate, you must be able to ride right up to it so that your horse is almost touching it and lean over (somewhat) in the saddle without your horse moving. Practice first riding straight up to the gate, then turn and continue. Then ride up to the gate and stop, back up, and ride away. Ride up to the gate, stop, and stand. The idea is for the horse not to get antsy trying to anticipate what you want. The close quarters of the fence/gate often makes horses uneasy. Once you can ride straight up to the gate, begin to move over to it laterally. Ride alongside the gate and stop with your horse's body parallel to it, half halt, then ride on. Ride alongside and stop, then back up. Ride alongside and stop and stand.

Again, the idea is to reinforce the cues your horse already knows, forward, back, and sideways, without letting your handling of the gate interfere with his responses.

When your horse is comfortable maneuvering around the gate, position him parallel to it, ask him to stand, and lean over slightly. If he remains stationary, reach for the latch, chain, or whatever holds the gate closed. If he moves away, be patient and reposition him, then ask him to stand again. The leaning, close proximity, and sound of the latch or chain make a lot of horses nervous or at least nosy, so be prepared to repeat this phase of the training until he settles.

The good news about a gate is that even if you can't get it open from horseback, it's never a true obstacle. You can always get off and open it.

STEEP CLIMBS

Steep Climbs separate the horses from the good trail horses and the riders from the trail riders. How you handle hills is as much a reflection of your own skills and savvy as it is of your horse's.

Training for steep grades should begin on the flat with work in collection (see page 114). Once your horse knows the cue to pull his hindquarters beneath himself and redistribute his weight, he is on his way to being able to negotiate hills.

Progress to a gentle slope. Walk up the hill slowly. Even a slight hill requires your horse to use his rear-end muscles more than walking over flat ground. Sit forward in the saddle and lean forward *slightly* to help take the weight off his hindquarters when you ride uphill. Don't allow him to charge the hill. Some horses will try to trot or canter and wear themselves out quickly.

Let him catch his breath at the top, then turn around for the descent. On the way down, cue your horse to collect slightly so that he works off his rear. Sit squarely, but lean back *slightly* to take the weight off his forehand. As he walks down, use your leg aids (turn on the forehand, turn on the haunches) to keep his hind end straight with his line of travel. Do not let him trot or hurry downhill. Work on a gradual hill over a period of several weeks to build up his muscles and condition before you head out to more challenging terrain. Weakness and inexperience are the leading reasons for accidents on hills, and both are avoidable.

Once your horse is mature enough, trained enough, and conditioned enough, you are ready to hit the hills. How much is "enough" varies from horse to horse, but if he is at least four years old

---

| STEP-BY-STEP TECHNIQUES | **Opening and Closing a Gate** |

The best way to open a gate on the trail is to keep control of it. This is especially important if there are animals on the other side of it! The instructions that follow are for one way to open a gate that opens away from you. You may want to experiment with a different sequence of maneuvers with your horse.

1. With your horse parallel to the gate and facing the end that opens, undo the latch.

2. Keeping one hand on the top rail of the gate, cue your horse to back a few steps. Keep his hind end straight by maintaining a little pressure behind the girth with the leg on the side opposite the gate.

3. When his head can clear the opening, push the gate away from you and your horse a few inches, being careful not to lean far enough to lose balance.

4. Cue one step sideways toward the gate. Push the gate a little farther out and cue another step until the gate is open enough for your horse to walk through it.

5. Once his hind end clears the opening, cue him to turn on the forehand, moving his hips through the gate and around until he is facing the opposite direction, on the opposite side of the gate, from where you started (see drawing).

6. Back a few steps, keeping his body straight by maintaining a little pressure behind the girth on the side opposite the gate.

7. Stop when your body is parallel to the latch and secure the gate. Stand for a moment while you reward your horse.

If your horse is calm, you may get through all of this on the first try, but if he gets ruffled at any point in the sequence, stop and have him stand for a moment until he calms down. If he gets too flustered, dismount and walk him through it, or go back to reinforcing simpler aspects of the maneuver, such as backing alongside the gate and sidepassing up to it.

Once his hind end has cleared the opening, have him turn on the forehand (step 5).

and sound, has mastered all of the training we have talked about here, and has had at least four to six weeks of conditioning, he can surely conquer a few hills. The only way to really practice steep hills is to go out and ride them (see chapter 9.)

Special Skills

If your horse has passed all the tests to this point and mastered all the skills we have covered thus far, congratulations! You already have a trail partner worth his weight in gold. (If you don't believe it, just try and *buy* a horse with this level of natural ability and training!) There are a few more specialized skills that can add to your horse's usefulness on the trail, or anywhere else.

Special skills set good trail horses apart from the rest. These skills include working off lead or from verbal cues and performing a number of practical tasks. Teaching your horse to work "off lead" sounds a lot harder than it really is. You can train your horse to come when called and to lead at liberty, either of which can be a tremendous relief in the right circumstances. Almost any established skill can be made all the handier when your horse can perform it on a verbal command. Other special skills are tying to a highline, hobbling, lowering the head, kneeling, pulling (or dragging), packing, and riding double.

COMING WHEN CALLED

Coming when called may sound more like something to teach your dog than your horse, and the process can be much the same. It is most welcome when you are in the worst possible fix — on foot.

Training your horse to come when called is simple. Every day at feeding time, call him to you and reward him with praise, a pat, and his supper. Use a happy tone of voice or a distinct tone of whistle. Over just a few weeks you will rack up dozens of positively reinforced repetitions. Never call a horse to you in order to punish him. He will learn to associate the punishment with coming to you.

You can work at reinforcing the come-when-called response on a longe line by first asking him to stand, then walking to the end of the line and calling him to you. A tug on the line to encourage a quick response and a reward when he reaches you will quickly deepen his understanding. Replace the longe line with a length of high-tensile-strength deep-sea fishing line (with a handhold tied to one end) and then have your horse stand. When he feels himself being tugged toward you, even though he can't see a lead he will just naturally assume that you have the power to make him come to you.

LEADING AT LIBERTY

Leading at liberty is the same as "heeling" for a dog. It means your horse will follow along in the same way as he does with a lead rope, without the lead rope. He'll stop when you stop and proceed when you do. You may never need this skill, but it helps to deepen your horse's level of obedience and is very useful if you ever have your hands full walking home. (It can happen.)

Practice leading your horse around the paddock, pasture, or yard, gradually minimizing the cues you give through the lead. You will find that your horse picks up on other cues readily, such as your posture and your attitude. Switch to a lighter lead and continue to practice simple leading skills a few minutes at a time every day.

When you are ready, it's best to proceed in an enclosed area, such as a round pen or paddock if you have it available. (If your horse does bolt, or even just wanders off, all you will lose is progress.) Attach a lightweight twine or heavyweight fishing line to your horse's halter before you place the halter on the horse so that he doesn't notice the attached line. Cue to move out, and if at any time he doesn't instantly react as if he still had a full-fledge lead rope, give him a serious tug on the line. Working in an enclosed area sets up your horse for success and repetition reinforces his response to follow you.

"Here, Red!"

One glorious fall day in 1975 my friend Laurie Saint and I were riding down some long-forgotten logging roads just north of Adna, Washington. Her horse, Red, was a small, scrappy Morgan gelding that, at first glance, didn't rate much admiration. Oddly enough, I can't remember which horse I was riding. I was too impressed, by the end of the day, with Red.

Riding through a clear-cut (harvested timberland), Laurie and I decided to practice our trail-jumping skills (translation: goofing off/showing off) over some logs that were lying about helter-skelter. My horse cleared the jumps with ease, but Red's landing was a little rough and Laurie plunked to the ground. In those days, the only thing that could ruin a day riding was to break a bone or lose a horse. After we figured she hadn't broken anything, we looked around and realized we had lost a horse. Red was nowhere in sight.

We were a few miles from home and I didn't know if my horse would tolerate riding double. I was expecting a long trip back when a shrill whistle pierced the air. Laurie just grinned at me, her circled fingers still touching her lips.

A gallumping sound came pounding through the overgrown brush and suddenly there was Red. He galloped within a few feet of Laurie, then stopped and walked over to her. He rubbed his head into her chest, just soaking up the praise she gave him. After a few minutes, she mounted up and we went on our way, but 30 years later, I still put Red up there with the best trail horses I have ever known.

ROUND PEN BASICS Many trainers prefer working in a round pen to teach leading at liberty as a basic part of their curriculum because it impresses your leadership on the horse, with the result that he chooses to "follow the leader" on his own. There are many books and videos on round pen work, but in essence, the round pen is a tool that allows you to impress your horse with your right to dominate him. By using nothing more than the confined space of the pen, your body posture, and a working knowledge of equine reaction, you can make astonishing headway in a short period of time precisely because the foundation of the training is taking and enforcing your role as leader.

Round pen work is not about sending your horse in endless circles to wear him out; it's about establishing and refining your control over his body and mind. You keep the horse moving by changing your body position relative to his body.

By standing at an angle behind him, you drive the horse forward; you can turn him on a dime by stepping toward his head. If the horse turns his fanny to you, you send him forward with a stomp or hand-clap. All this quickly teaches the horse that you can make him dance to your tune.

When he begins to make eye contact with you, begin to think about leading at liberty. Stop the horse by moving toward his shoulder. If he moves forward, follow his motion with your own body and stop him again. Once you can stop him and hold him in place, approach, pet, praise, and reward, then take a step back. Most horses will take at least a step or two with you on the first try. Continue to work on controlling your horse's movement around the pen, then stop and repeat the backing-away exercise. Back farther with each lesson and offer a reward after he has followed you a respectable distance.

Following behind you is a submissive act by your horse. Doing so means he is voluntarily acknowledging you as his leader. Be sure to keep an eye on your rank, and don't allow the horse to pass or crowd you; if he does, take a tip from the alpha mare and send him away. Send him around the pen, turn him, stop him, and make him back or side pass in response to your body position. Round penning is a great way to jump-start your training, and of course has many applications beyond leading at liberty, but this brief overview should give you an idea of at least one way you can use this method in your horse's overall education.

RECOGNIZING VERBAL COMMANDS

Verbal command recognition is a real asset in any horse. If ever there is a time when you cannot physically execute a cue, it's sure nice when your voice can get the job done. Training a horse to respond to verbal cues is easy. Just add a verbal cue to your training regimen, or if your horse already knows a specific skill to which you would like to add a verbal cue, offer the verbal cue prior to any other cue and exaggerate the other cues as you did in training. A classic example is *WHOA*.

A lot of horses will stop most impressively before the rider ever so much as twitches the reins. First, most riders instinctively shift their weight in preparation for a stop, and that alone cues a good horse that a change in momentum is about to be requested. The next step is to say *WHOA*. By the time you can actually lift the reins, your horse is already on his haunches. The same goes for any skill: Simply incorporate a verbal cue prior to any other cues in the training phase, such as *STEP, WAIT, GEE* (go to the right), *HAW* (go to the left), *OVER GEE* (side pass right), *OVER HAW* (side pass left), *WHOA*, and *BACK*. A horse that recognizes and obeys just these few commands is an incredible asset, on the trail or off.

> **GEE** and **HAW** *are old-time verbal commands for "go right" and "go left," respectively. Some team drivers and dog sledders still use these commands today.*

Approach quietly and confidently. Reading your horse's body language will tell you how he feels.

TYING TO A HIGHLINE

Tying to a highline is an extension of the basic requirement for a broke horse to stand tied quietly. You'll find highlines extending from tree to tree at a level above the horse's head in horse camps all over the world. Sometimes the bobbing of the line (caused by things such as another horse down the line shaking his head at flies) upsets a horse. To be a good candidate for highlining, a horse must have solid training in standing tied, and he must not pitch a fit and fling himself about or try to pull away. It's good insurance to practice having your horse stand tied in familiar territory.

The worst thing that can happen when a horse pulls back on a highline is that he hurts himself or he breaks free. Set your horse up for success by using only good-quality, buckle-type halters and 1-inch-thick cotton lead ropes (nylon can slip when tied). For proofing (see Proofing discussion on page 146), equip your horse with two separate halters and two separate lead ropes tied so that they are about the same length.

If you feel you might need added insurance, tie a small loop in the end of a 30-foot length of half-inch-thick rope, run the rope through the loop to form a large loop, and place the loop over the horse's hindquarters. Run the other end of the rope through the tie ring of the halter and tie it to the same post as the lead ropes, with less slack than the lead ropes. This "butt rope" will tighten and encourage your horse not to set back on the rope should he pull back.

Avoid anything that can really frighten or hurt your horse, but do tempt his resolve to stand tied. Proof with distractions such as waving a tarp, setting off a firecracker, or suddenly revving up your car motor. Ride by on another horse at speed, turn other horses loose in the distance to run and romp,

This knot is quick to tie and even quicker to release, but will hold your horse safely in the meantime. To undo the knot, just pull on the free end of the rope; it will release in an instant.

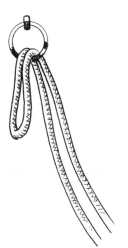  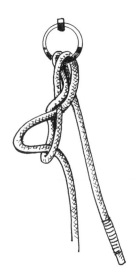 

1. Make a loop about 8 inches long, leaving 6 inches of the end of the rope free. Pass the loop through the tie ring.

2. Twist the rope a couple of times, leaving an opening at the end.

3. Make a short loop in the rope that goes back to your horse and pass it through the opening at the end of the twist.

4. Make a fold in the free end of the rope and pass it through the second (horse-end) loop. Pull on the horse-end of the rope and draw the knot snug.

A butt rope will keep the horse from pulling back.

clang together pots and pans, shake out a blanket: anything you can think of that might occur in a trail camping situation and rile a tied horse.

Once he stands tied for up to 3 or 4 hours at a time, rig a mock highline, with the line above the horse's eye level, or about 7 feet high, between two trees (see chapter 12 for more information). Attach your horse to it with a lead rope tied in a quick-release knot to a carabiner and repeat the "proofing." A horse that has learned that Scary Things won't hurt him is a lot less likely to get startled by a bump in the night when tied out on the trail. One that has learned the futility of pulling back when tied is less likely to bother.

HOBBLING

Hobbling helps to keep your horse close to camp, but unlike most other skills your horse can master, it's not necessarily in your best interest for him to get good at being hobbled. Some horses can move out very quickly when hobbled. Never assume that hobbles will prevent your horse from wandering away: The best they can do is slow him down.

Hobbles are restraints that connect to your horse's front **pasterns** (ankles) like shackles to prevent him from being able to walk around easily. Some horses panic when first hobbled because no horse likes to have his flight response impaired. But once they get used to hobbles, most horses take them in stride — literally. I've heard stories of

horse campers being a little too trusting and leaving their horses hobbled overnight so that the animals could graze and relax, only to find themselves horseless in the morning.

Train for hobbles in the familiarity of your horse's paddock, or round pen if you have one, preferably in a spot with deep, soft footing, just in case your horse does resist and goes down. The idea is to get your horse to accept the restraints, but also to understand that they mean to hold still, or at least to move as little as possible.

KNEELING

Kneeling might seem like a circus trick to some, but for those who manage to get past a low-hanging obstacle with no way over or around or who cannot mount a horse at full height, having a horse trained to kneel can save the day. Just think of RC (see chapter 2).

Kneeling is also considered an extremely submissive position by the horse. He will not accept this stance before any but the most dominant herd member. In the wild, horses bite at their rivals' forelegs in a violent effort to drive them to their knees. The term for assuming a stance of submission is **obeisance,** defined as a position that signifies supreme submission, similar to the human position for prayer.

Because of its extreme significance, many feel that kneeling is a skill best taught at liberty, with the horse confined only by a stall or round pen. The horse will not go down until he is absolutely certain of what he is doing, and truly accepts and processes the lesson, more so than if restrained with ropes. Alternatively, finding a quiet spot to work with your horse on a lead also works, provided you are patient and give your horse the time he needs to progress. Of course, you *can* force a horse down, and fight him for the right of supreme leadership, just as his counterparts in the wild (and old-time cowboys) would do. Maybe it's just me, but I try not to pick fights with anybody who outweighs me by 900 pounds. I like my way better.

PULLING A LOAD

Pulling (or dragging) is just another way to harness your horse's strength and usefulness. A horse that will confidently pull a load can drag logs (or whatever necessary) out of the path (of other, less educated trail horses), pull a travois with an injured friend, or bring home a Christmas tree.

Start by allowing your horse to sniff and look over whatever it is you are about to ask him to drag. A fence post or short section of log is a good

---

STEP-BY-STEP TECHNIQUES	Hobbling

Using a thick, soft rope (cotton, at least 1 inch thick), work with the rope around his front feet until your horse ignores the feel of the rope.

1. Loop the rope around his pasterns and tug gently, asking your horse to "give" to the pressure.

2. Once he gets the idea that something on his ankles won't hurt him but will affect his ability to move around, have him "stand." Attach the (long cotton) rope to his halter.

3. Attach the right-side hobble first. (This way, if he does try to jump, you won't be slapped in the face by the hobbles.) Praise him quietly and reinforce the *STAND* command. It may take him a few minutes to get used to the feel of the fastened right-side hobble. (Another way to introduce hobbles is to fasten the hobble above the knee loose enough so that you can slide it down in place.)

4. Attach the left-side hobble and tell him to stand, then move off to the end of the lead rope and ask him to move (see drawing). The point is for him to test the hobbles and realize that they can stop him.

5. As soon as he tries to move and realizes he can't, tell him *WHOA* and *STAND* and reward him.

6. Let him test the hobbles two or three times (over a period of no more than a few minutes) during the first lesson, each time telling him *WHOA* and *WAIT* and rewarding him for standing still.

Repeat the lesson over the next week or two, asking him to stand for a few more moments each time he tests the hobbles. Eventually you will have a tough time getting him to test the hobbles, and he will have made a mental association that it's just plain easier to stand still while wearing those darned things, but they really aren't all that bad.

Have him test the hobbles (step 4).

For the first lessons, it is essential to have a quiet spot, with deep, soft footing and limited escape options (a stall is great). Soft footing is important because you don't want it to hurt your horse when he does what you ask, and his first attempts might cause him to lose balance and go down harder than intended.

Like most maneuvers, this is actually a set of skills that are gradually combined into one exercise. You will have the fastest progress by breaking down the kneel into several steps: raising a foot, lowering the head, going down on one knee, going down on two knees, holding the stance, and, if you so choose, moving forward on his knees.

1. Reach down, press on the tendon behind the cannon bone, lift up, and command *FOOT*. Most horses understand this in a few repetitions. Reward each effort and gradually extend the period of time he holds up each hoof, picking it out and drumming along the inside. Switch sides and establish the same response. (Do the same on the hind feet just for the sake of handling his feet.)

2. Stand at his head and using a stick or dressage whip, tap his cannon bone and command *FOOT*. As soon as he even shifts weight from that foot, praise and give him a break from the tapping. Repeat, extending the time he holds up his foot before he gets his reward, until he will stand on three legs for up to a minute. (This is a great confidence and balance builder.) Switch sides and start over.

3. Ask him to lower his head slightly while holding up one foot (see drawing). Reward, switch sides, and repeat. Encourage him to bring his head lower and lower while holding up one foot, until (perhaps over several

lessons) he relaxes and drops to one knee. Reward him with stroking, praise, and a treat as soon as his knee touches down. Give him time to get used to balancing on the way down. Sometimes it helps to pat him on the belly to get him to loosen his back. (Eventually, your horse can learn to associate the pat on the belly as a cue to drop.)

4. Gradually increase the time you ask him to stay on one knee. Switch sides until he can balance on either side. The transition to both knees requires just a little tug on the lead, a treat in front of his nose at ground level, or gently pulling his head to the side of the down knee.

5. Once your horse will go down and hold the pose, ask him to move forward while on his knees. Reward him for any forward progress with praise and by letting him get up. He will soon learn that sometimes the only way up is to move forward. Practice this under a raised pole until he will clear it on command.

Ask him to lower his head while holding up one foot (step 3).

You never know when pulling "a load" might come in handy.

not downright humor). Ride or lead your horse forward in a familiar open area, and if possible have a helper drag the log in front of him, around him in circles, and behind him. (If you can't find a helper, start by leading the horse and dragging the log yourself, just a few feet at a time, stopping often to reward.)

Once your horse accepts the sound of the log dragging close to him, tie the rope with a quick-release knot to the horn on a Western saddle, or loop a length of soft cotton rope around his chest to give him something to pull against, with a quick-release knot where you can instantly reach it in case of trouble. Lead him forward just a few steps until he can feel the pull of the deadweight and hear the log chasing him. Reward him and let him stand a few moments to let the new lesson of the drag sink in. Repeat, gradually increasing the number of steps you ask for before rewarding. Once he is all but ignoring the weight, shift the lesson to the saddle. Again, ask for just a few steps in a straight line until your horse is fully confident with the lesson, and then gradually ask for turns.

thing to start with. By this point, he should look at any new thing you show him with minimal skepticism and possibly a bit of curious expectation (if

Using Shafts

Teaching your horse to accept shafts along his side is a basic part of harness training and is useful on its own for teaching your horse to accept restriction of his movement. It will also come in handy if your horse ever needs to pull something out of the trail that he can't drag or that can't balance on his back. You can fabricate mock shafts with black ABS pipe (about 1¼ to 1½ inches diameter), which is lightweight and inexpensive (and a bit stouter and less distracting than white PVC pipe). Thin wooden poles work well, too.

Cross one end of each shaft over the other and tie together, then tie the opposite ends together with about 3 feet of slack in the rope

or twine. Rest the crossed end over the front of the saddle (another time saddle horns come in handy). Ask for just a few steps forward, rest and reward, and gradually ask for turns. Expect your horse to notice the difference in his mobility, but be patient and reward his progress accordingly. Eventually, you can ask for circles and a turn on the forehand or haunches and your horse will accommodate the poles.

Weight the makeshift travois. Transfer the lesson to the saddle and again practice turning, circles, and serpentines until your horse is comfortable dragging anything anywhere.

PONYING

Leading another horse, or **ponying,** is a useful skill, whether you use it to get a less confident trail companion past an obstacle, to leg up a colt, or to lead a packhorse. The lead horse has to learn to ignore another horse crowding, as well as the feel of the rope across his croup or flank or, worse, caught underneath his tail. An old-time solution to the latter is to place a short section of broom handle or doweling under a horse's tail while he stands tied or in a stall or corral. Most horses instinctively clamp down their tails over this intrusion at first, but as soon as they relax their tail muscles, the offending bit of broomstick falls right out. Once a horse has learned to release his grip on something stuck beneath his tail, he is ready to resume pony horse training.

Be careful in how you handle the lead of another horse. Wear gloves in case the ponied horse pulls back, and use a long (12 foot or better) 1-inch cotton lead rope. If possible, start out in an enclosed place such as a round pen or arena. Practice at the walk, stopping, turning, even backing up. Proceed to a trot and build up to a canter only after the two horses have become accustomed to working together.

If you ride a Western saddle, never tie the lead to the saddle horn, except to take a single dally for a little leverage. This comes in handy if the ponied horse balks or lags. While he'd probably have little trouble outpulling your arm, the force of the lead horse should keep him moving forward. A few lessons with the lead dallied should eliminate the need for it. The safest way to lead another horse

Ponying is a handy skill for both the lead horse and the led horse.

from your saddle horse is to hold the lead in your free hand so you can maneuver the ponied horse or drop it if necessary to prevent a wreck.

Practice and attention are the best tools to develop a reliable pony horse. Most horses appreciate the company of another horse, and because the pony horse is in the lead, he enjoys the position of herd dominance between the two. Check your horse if he rushes or in any way fusses with the horse behind him. Some horses instinctively object to another horse following too closely and take a lot more time to adjust than others. If the horse being ponied crowds or is unruly, pop him with a dressage or driving whip to remind him of his responsibilities.

It's important not to let go of the line just because the pony horse balks or your saddle horse develops an attitude. That just rewards bad behavior. However, knowing when to let go is just as important here as in parenting. If you encounter a bees' nest and both horses panic, if one horse falls,

if either horse reacts with such force that he could pull you out of the saddle — it's best to let go of the line and recover it later.

PACKING

Packing is a specialized skill that any good trail horse can easily master. Not only does it add to a horse's overall usefulness to be able to pull pack-horse duty, but also it is not unheard of to run into something (or someone) on the trail that needs to be packed out. For this reason, your horse should accept anything you place on his back as his personal responsibility. All it requires is cooperating, following a leader, balancing under a load, and watching where he steps, including not getting too close to trees or other obstacles.

Since your horse is already broke to ride, accepting weight is not the challenge here, but accepting strange things that perhaps smell funny, wiggle, or slide around, all while following you or the horse ahead of him, certainly can be.

A trained packhorse accepts just about any load as his personal responsibility. You never know what you might have to pack out!

Begin practicing at home by asking your horse to stand while you load something into the saddle. That something can be a bag of potatoes, a dog, a rattling bag of tin cans, a sheep, anything you have available that might challenge your horse's composure. Practice leading him from the ground, around trees and cars, and in between tight spaces, then practice leading him from another horse. A trick mule packers use is to turn the mule loose (either in his pasture or to follow a pack string) with a 6-foot beam strapped crossways to his packsaddle. So encumbered, any critter that values staying on his feet quickly learns to avoid walking too close to trees and other obstacles. Anytime he does, the beam slams into it, rudely knocking him off balance.

Any horse that will accept weight, pony behind another horse, and has enough confidence to set out on the trail is ready to begin packhorse training. Until he has his "pack legs" and/or until a horse is fully mature, don't ask him to carry a full load (up to 20 percent of his body weight). Start out with a light, secure load and advance to more challenging ones over time or if the need arises.

RIDING DOUBLE: NOT RECOMMENDED

Riding double is asking for trouble. The second rider has no control, compromised balance, and all of the risk. A second rider to the rear puts weight on the least supported part of your horse's spinal structure, and by her mere position is more likely to dangle her feet into the horse's flank, irritating or at least distracting the horse. Backseat riders are also notorious for dragging the front rider off the horse if the horse suddenly lunges or bucks, because they all too often lock arms around the only thing they can grab on to — the front rider. A rider in this position is also more likely to fall off the back of the horse should he spook and then is vulnerable to getting kicked. A second rider in front (such as a small child) is vulnerable to falling forward or getting compressed between the main rider and the saddle or the horse's neck if trouble

arises. So in short, I don't advocate it.

However, just because anything can happen on the trail and does every day (it's just a matter of *which* day is *your* day), it's not a bad idea to teach your horse to accept whatever you place on his back, including a second rider.

To teach your horse to ignore a second rider in front of you, start with a dog, piglet, small goat, or other luggable animal, and a helper. Ask your helper to hold the hapless creature in place as you lead your horse around. The idea is for your horse to accept a noisy, squirming, thrashing creature on his back. You can hope that any toddlers you allow to ride your horse would be better behaved, but this way, your horse will welcome almost any child by comparison. Reward, and when he seems ready, mount up and have your helper hand you the second "rider." Ride around with the critter up front until your horse is at ease with it. Some horses take only a few seconds to adjust, others several lessons. It's much better to find how your horse will respond out in your front yard or arena with a dog than out on the trail with your neighbor's kid.

To teach your horse to accept a second rider behind you, find a heavy dummy. A 20-pound bag of potatoes is a classic, because even though it is deadweight, it tends to flop around. Loosely tie down the deadweight to the back of the saddle and ride around. Execute maneuvers, take a short trail ride, walk, trot, and canter. Do all the things you might normally do when alone in the saddle. One trick is to tie a shoe to either end of a 6-foot piece of twine and drape this under the deadweight. The shoes will dangle into your horse's sides. One of the toughest things for horses to learn is which "cues" to instantly obey and which to ignore. Second riders unwittingly cue a horse. Next, up the odds with a heavier weight, such as a 50-pound bad of feed. Using extra twine or rope, tie the larger, heavier second "rider" in place and again go through your routines.

Only when you are willing to risk the lives of yourself and a friend or family member should you allow a second rider on your horse with you. Ride in an enclosed space, such as a paddock or round corral. Be sure someone besides the two of you knows what you are up to in case of accident. Give your horse his head and let him move about freely while he gets his bearings and balance. Gradually ask him for a few moves. Collect him; turn; work circles, serpentines, a turn on the haunches; ask for a slow trot or gait; talk to your passenger, ask him to move around a little, until it is clear your horse is okay with the extra rider. Spread this out over several lessons and never ask your horse to carry double riders for more than about 10 to 15 minutes. If you are faced with a situation on the trail where he has to carry out a second rider, rotate riding double with riding single and walking.

Demand Proof

How can you know how your horse will respond in any given situation, including a stray dog running up to sniff and bark at him? The same way good dog trainers do — proof.

After your horse is stone-cold reliable in any given exercise, add distractions, first in the background, then bringing them nearer to the horse.

For example, on a ground-tie, first leave your horse and walk away and shake a rustling slicker or clanging bag of tin cans. On the next lesson, pick up the slicker or bag and approach the horse with it. On a future lesson, put the noisy thing in the saddle or mount while carrying it. Break down proofs into "doable" components and then build, build, build.

Thinking up challenges is limited only by your imagination. Traffic, other horses, goats, llamas (exotic animals, because they smell unfamiliar, are often a big challenge to horses), and busy neighborhoods offer limitless opportunities to practice a known skill with the added challenge of distractions. Horse shows are a great proofing ground because they come tailor-made with loudspeakers, flapping banners, strange sights and sounds, and other excited horses.

By building each proofing session on previous ones, you will be reasonably sure that your horse can easily conquer each new step. It is the building of small steps that leads you and your horse to the heights of training, trust, and communication. Just be sure to keep the situations safe and positive, and to make rewards for each new challenge worth the effort for your horse.

CHAPTER 6

Traffic School

RIDING DOWN THE ROAD IS NOT WHAT MOST OF US consider a "trail ride," but often it is the only way to reach the trails. And of all the ways a person can get maimed or killed on a horse, riding in traffic is probably the surest bet. The sounds and sensations of giant metal monsters rushing toward them not only unsettle many horses, but they can also make riders equally, if not more, tense. A tense rider will make the horse nervous, even if he was fine on his own. Since many motorists don't have a clue about driving near a horse, the problem can quickly become dangerous.

Rules of the Road

Road riding demands attention, common sense, and, on any given day, luck. Remember the scene from the movie *The Horse Whisperer,* in which a car strikes a girl and her horse? Horrible accidents happen, and they happen too quickly to do anything about them once they begin to unfold. Drivers don't expect to suddenly encounter a horse on the road. You have the best chance of avoiding an accident if *you* are aware of, and prepared for, the possibilities.

Before you even think about riding in or near traffic, be sure all is in order with your horse and gear. A quick inspection is a good idea anytime you ride, but it is critical before putting yourself in the path of motor vehicles. Be sure all equipment is in safe, comfortable working condition. Check for weak spots in the girth, stirrup leathers, and reins especially. Losing physical control of your horse around traffic can lead to no good.

As a nonmotorized "vehicle," you are expected to follow the rules of the road. Cross at crosswalks, yield the right-of-way, and stop at traffic lights and stop signs. Obey the speed limit and signal when you turn. In some areas, you are also expected to pick up after your horse.

WHICH SIDE OF THE ROAD?

Since individual states and Canadian provinces have varying laws about horses on public roadways, be sure to contact local authorities as to the rules of the road before you ride. Above all, use common sense: Always put your safety first, based on the individual situation.

In areas where horses are considered vehicles, the rules of the road say to ride with traffic: that is, on the right side of the road. This places your horse in the same lane as traffic coming up from behind you. However, Colorado State Statute 42-4-109 stipulates the opposite: "Persons riding or leading animals on or along any highway shall ride or lead such animals on the left side of said high-

way, facing approaching traffic." Riding against traffic gives you advantages of having a little more space between you and an oncoming vehicle and being able to see what's coming in time to react.

Developing Street Smarts

As in all trail situations, when riding near traffic think of your own safety first and courtesy toward "the other guy" second. Don't let anything distract you near traffic. Don't worry about how you look or about anything anybody says or does. People can holler some incredibly stupid comments to horseback riders, honk, wolf-whistle, and screech their tires. Pay close attention to everything drivers do while ignoring 90 percent of it.

Not that all motorists are morons. Odds are you can always tell a fellow horseman in traffic. He's the guy who slows down, possibly moves over to the other lane, or will even shut off his engine and wait for you to pass if you are on a fractious horse.

Because hitting the trails often means first pounding the pavement, both you and your horse should develop some street smarts. The responsibility for a safe crossing is mostly yours.

Here are some tips:

- Investigate in advance the traffic rules and conditions of the area where you'll be riding.
- Learn and use hand signals.
- Familiarize your horse with motor vehicles ahead of time in a controlled situation.
- Inspect your tack before every ride to be sure it's safe.
- Wear a safety helmet.

SCOPE OUT THE AREA AHEAD OF TIME

Before riding down an unfamiliar stretch of road, scope it out in advance if at all possible. Take a drive and make mental notes of narrow or drop-off shoulders, intersections, sight distances around curves and over hills (so you'll know where motorists won't be able to see you), obstacles, driveways, and escape routes should you need to get off the road quickly. As you'll see later in this chapter, it's also a good idea to find out about local bus or garbage truck schedules. Large, noisy trucks can spook horses that never give ordinary cars a second glance.

LEARN HAND SIGNALS

It helps to use hand signals to convey your intentions to drivers. When you check with your local authorities as to the rules regulating horses on roadways, ask if there are specific requirements for hand signals.

Desensitizing to Traffic

Living proof that a horse of sound mind and body can be effectively desensitized to traffic can be seen on the streets of major cities every day. New York, Houston, Boston, Detroit, and Memphis, among others, have mounted patrol units, and these

TO SIGNAL A RIGHT TURN, extend your right arm out parallel to the ground. (Most people no longer learn the old bicycle signals that required all signals to be made with the left hand, and this is simply clearer.)

NEVER, EVER, STOP IN TRAFFIC if you can help it. If you have no other choice, give the hand signal with your left arm extended down at about a 45-degree angle, with your palm flat facing backwards to warn traffic behind you.

TO SIGNAL A LEFT TURN, extend your left arm out level with with the road. It's not an official part of the signal, but pointing with your finger seems to make your intentions clearer.

TO SLOW OR STOP ONCOMING TRAFFIC ahead of you, raise your hand up high, palm extended toward the vehicles.

Traffic Tips

- Stay to the right side of the road, unless unsafe to do so or the rules say otherwise.
- Keep your eyes busy. Scan ahead and to the side for cars merging onto the road, kids on bikes, loose dogs, and other potential spooky things.
- Remember to sit tall and balanced in the saddle. Not only will you look more confident to passersby, but you'll also be in the best position should your horse react to something.
- Always look both ways twice before crossing the road to be sure there are no oncoming cars.
- Offer a hand signal to traffic when changing lanes or turning. Avoid stopping in traffic.
- Ride in single file alongside the road when in a group.
- Keep nervous, fractious, or inexperienced horses toward the center of the lineup. They will be less likely to spook from ahead or behind if they have more stable horses nearby for comfort.
- Ride as far from the lanes of traffic as possible, but keep your eyes peeled for trash, debris, and especially broken glass on the shoulder or in roadside ditches. Keeping to the shoulder not only keeps you farther from traffic, but it also spares your horse's legs and spine from the jarring impact of the road surface.
- Never ride faster than a walk on pavement.

Crossing the Road

- If you ride with a group on a road with much traffic, it's better to cross the road all at once than to string out crossing single file.
- Cross at a right angle to make the shortest crossing possible. This puts horses on the roadway for the briefest possible amount of time.
- If possible, appoint a crossing guard to stop traffic, either on foot or on horseback, and have that person stay in position until all horses have completely crossed the road.
- Be sure that young or inexperienced riders "buddy up" with more-experienced riders when crossing the road.

horses see (and hear and smell) it all. Keep these icons of traffic reliability in mind as you work your horse through his vehicular jitters. (It can be done. It can be done. It can be done . . . .) Unfortunately, teaching your horse how to behave near traffic means getting out there with the cars, motorcycles, and semitrucks.

Once your horse is fairly comfortable around cars, the next step is to condition him to accept traffic moving close by. It's best (though not always feasible) to practice this in a controlled environment where you have helpers driving the cars. As always, be sure to pick the most controllable, or at least unpredictable, environment in which to introduce new things to your horse.

How you accomplish this depends on your circumstances. It's best to work in a familiar environment if at all possible so the only new thing your horse has to contend with is the motion of cars. If you board at a barn with other horses, ask other boarders to drive around the parking area for a few minutes. If you live in or near a neighborhood with quiet streets, take your horse for short, quiet walks or rides along a predictably quiet route. If you are out in the sticks, you may have to ride or trailer your horse to an area where there is traffic.

One idea is to organize a traffic desensitization clinic with fellow horsemen. Look for an area where there is no regular traffic, such as a track, empty parking lot, or a deserted stretch of farm road. The goal is to have as many uneventful vehicle encounters per horse as possible. Ride your horse while a designated driver slowly passes back and forth, and remember to keep the rewards coming. When your horse is thoroughly bored with the cars, ask the driver to speed up. Introduce the horn by having your helper honk first when far from the horse and gradually honking closer with each pass. Then take your turn in the driver's seat while another person rides.

The best way to desensitize a horse to traffic is to expose him to it on a regular basis during his training phase. You have to get him out there.

Because there is no way to know what kind of traffic you might encounter, even on a normally quiet country road, it's best to condition your horse to accept anything on wheels. Once he has learned to disregard it, he can return to traffic months after his last exposure to it and still be pretty darned uninterested.

BUILD UP GRADUALLY

If traffic is scarce or, worse, scary near your home or barn, consider trailering your horse to the home of a friend in the suburbs and letting him see how the other half lives. Riding first where traffic is slow and infrequent, then moving up to more bustling roads (if necessary), will help acclimate your horse gradually rather than overwhelm him all at once. By allowing a horse to desensitize gradually, you can help keep him from forming negative associations with traffic. And never forget the benefits of bringing an already confident horse along for the ride.

Cars may be scary to some horses, but even more terrifying are semitrucks, logging trucks, custom vehicles, motorcycles, and parade floats.

STEP-BY-STEP TECHNIQUES	Getting Used to Cars

Some horses believe that cars are monsters with very large mouths, just waiting to consume them in one quick bite, but most just get a little snorty because a close-up view of a car is something new. The idea of this exercise is to desensitize your horse first to the sight of a still car, then to the smell and sound of its engine and its motion.

1. Park two or three cars in a row. Ride your horse around and through them, letting him stop and sniff if he is so inclined. It may take days just to get to this step, or he may loosen up in a few minutes.

2. Start one of the cars and let it idle as you ride around and past. Alternate which car is running. Do this for several days.

3. When your horse accepts the above, have someone sit inside and rev the engine of one car or honk the horn.

4. Eventually, have a friend slowly drive the car around until your horse gets bored; then in progressive lessons, ask her to pick up speed, peel out, honk, stop, and slam the door.

Calmly riding near or between parked cars (step 1) is a good way to desensitize your horse to their looks, smells, and sounds.

Horses notice the difference in sound and smell between a gasoline-powered engine and a diesel. The whine of small motors seems to disturb some horses. Desensitizing your horse to traffic means exposing him to more than just your mother's Oldsmobile.

BICYCLES

Bicycles present a special challenge, because they bear down on your horse almost silently, both on the road and out on the trail. Taking the time to desensitize your horse to bicycles is just smart. Start by propping a bike near where the horse can see it, then progressively let him come closer to investigate. Because bikes look very different in different positions, let your horse watch you move it around, climb on, pedal, and lay it on its side.

Once he is comfortable with the bike close up and stationary, have a friend ride it at a distance while you sit your horse in a deep, relaxed seat. Speak reassuringly and reward him with a treat if he notices the bike but doesn't spook. Meanwhile, your friend should gradually ride closer and closer until she can ride right past your horse, slowly, at close quarters. Have her speak to your horse so he knows that this thing is actually part human, and even have her offer your horse a treat as she comes to a stop. Gradually step up the pace and occasion-ally invite her back to ride by quickly, skid to a stop, jump (catch some air!), and do some of the other things your horse might see a mountain biker do on the trail or an urban cyclist do on the road. The more exposure and the more varied, the less likely a biker is to catch you or your horse off guard.

Surviving to Tell the Story

It seems that no one likes to read about safety, but given the number of people seriously injured or killed riding along America's roadways, the fact is that you can't take your safety for granted. Here are some basic recommendations to reduce your chances of an accident.

HELMETS: A NO-BRAINER

Even if you never wear a helmet, because you're old and set in your ways or because you believe you can defy gravity in a nanosecond should a horse wreck happen, wear one when you ride on the road. A head with a helmet on it looks better and is infinitely more comfortable (not to mention useful) than one without, after impact with the blacktop. Head-impact accidents happen in horse wrecks every day, and wearing a helmet is your best insurance for living to tell the story. Regardless of your skill level, wear a helmet when you

---

TRAIL TALE — *Life by the Fast Lane*

An easy way to accustom a horse to traffic is to pasture him near a busy street. For us, the ideal answer to traffic desensitization came when we wound up — literally — on Easy Street. Our little 3-acre paradise was on a corner lot, so cars zipped and crept by all day long. Whenever we rode in the neighbor-hood we could count on passing at least three or four cars. Fortunately, they were neighbors who knew us and either didn't want us to get killed or knew we'd report them if we survived, so there was never any monkey business.

This is how LadyHawke was desensitized to traffic, and she always took it as part of the regular rhythm of life.

Experienced riders wear a helmet and reflective gear on roads likely to have traffic.

ride on the road and through rocky trails. It's cheap insurance.

TIMING IS EVERYTHING

Timing your ride might also help to cut your odds of competing with traffic. Try to avoid peak driving hours. A study of horse/car accidents by the Ohio Department of Public Safety (related to horse-drawn Amish vehicles) pinpointed high concentrations of accidents occurring early in the morning (5 A.M. to 7 A.M.), midday (1 P.M. to 3 P.M.), and early evening (5 P.M. to 7 P.M.). How much of this relates to rush-hour commuter traffic and how much to low lighting conditions is tough to confirm.

If you must ride on the road in low light or after dark, deck out yourself and your horse in reflective gear first. Reflective vests, leg wraps for your horse, and stirrup, saddle, and/or saddle pad reflectors will help to increase visibility in low light. Some areas require horses to wear reflectors or lighting any time they are on a public road between dusk and dawn. Carry glow sticks and fasten one to the back of the saddle (or crupper if you ride with one) and one to the browband of the bridle to alert motorists that something is off the roadway. They won't be able to tell what you are, but they'll at least have a heads-up that you are there.

PAVEMENT AND YOUR HORSE

Be careful when riding on pavement. It is very easy for a horse to slip, especially a horse whose shoes have a little wear. Smooth steel and smooth pavement don't provide much friction for traction. Don't ride faster than a walk over pavement if you can help it, and never run a horse down a paved road.

Trotting or galloping on pavement or blacktop (or other hard-packed surfaces) creates tremendous concussion on a horse's legs and back, especially when the horse is shod with metal shoes. Working in a saddle gait creates somewhat less concussion, but has the same effect. It takes remarkably little work at speed on pavement to road-founder a horse.

SHOES FOR THE ROAD Pavement, especially when wet, adds the danger of being slippery. Even though a barefoot horse has better traction (in a lot of situations) than does a horse shod with ordinary shoes, traveling on pavement or gravel with the extra weight of a rider and gear will quickly wear away the hoof wall unless it is protected. For brief stints across roadways or rocks, riding your horse barefoot may work fine for your horse. You may want to consider carrying removable hoof boots for occasional longer stretches of road.

Discuss your riding habits with your local farrier, and he or she will likely have plenty of suggestions, often including alternate trails! One farrier adds corks to regular shoes for added traction

Riding along the road can be safe and pleasant.

polyurethane tread, with steel studs in the toe and borium-enhanced steel shoes on the hinds. Several alternative shoe companies hawk products especially designed for traction on pavement. Be sure to include shoe life (wear) and traction on other surfaces, especially grass, in your discussion.

See page 214 for information on special traction enhancers for snow.

SIGN UP FOR SAFETY

The main reason horse/traffic accidents occur is not because a horse panics, acts up, or slips on a slick road; they're due to the element of surprise. Motorists don't expect to be suddenly confronted with 1,000 pounds of moving roadblock. If our roads were clogged with horses on a daily basis — good horses, bad horses, fractious horses — motorists would adapt.

One way you can help alert drivers to your presence, or just the possibility of it, is to ask your local

on pavement, but it wears away quickly. Police horses often work in steel shoes with borium added at the heels and toes. Police horses in Oakland, California, wear front shoes that are a composite of

---

TRAIL TALE | *Molly's Triumph*

Molly was a timid Thoroughbred filly with a terror of traffic. Even if I couldn't see it, I could feel a car coming up the road from a half-mile away because Molly would positively quake in her shoes. She would break into a sweat and try to dodge off the road before I could even hear a car. At first I rode her off to the side and let her stand until the car passed by, but she only got worse. I realized I was confirming her fear that cars were scary and something to avoid. Unfortunately, cars were few and far between, so she wasn't getting enough exposure to desensitize her to them. We needed more cars.

Not far from our house was an intersection with the two-lane highway. There was just

enough room to stand out of the way on a nervous horse and watch the traffic rumble, rattle, and roar by. The plan was to stand for a while quietly watching the traffic and gradually to move closer as Molly progressed. The first day the closest we could get was well off the road, knee deep in blackberry briars. We stood for about 40 minutes while I soothed Molly's nerves as she watched the traffic. Eventually she got bored. So day after day, we rode down to the highway and stood waiting for nothing to happen, each time a little closer to the road.

Gradually, Molly came to accept the noise, motion, and smell, and could ride along the edge of the highway ignoring traffic.

road department to post WATCH FOR HORSES warning signs near where you ride. If for some reason you meet with opposition at the official level, take your request to the grass roots. Ask local landowners if you can post signs along their rights-of-way on frequently traveled roads. Getting approval for such signs is usually easy, especially if you foot the bill for decent-looking signs, and exponentially so if children ride in the area.

Legal Issues on the Road

At the time of this writing, the state of New York had the most comprehensive and current set of

No Jumping off the Bridge!

Most states have something on the books regarding the obligations of motor vehicle drivers who share the road with horses. Most are not new laws and unfortunately tend to sound silly these days, but the rationale behind them was to make the person with the least risk (the automobile driver) more accountable for the safety of the situation.

If you ride your horse on the road in Indiana, for instance, it is illegal for motorists to pass you. The same sort of law applies in New Jersey for buggies and other horsedrawn vehicles. In Pennsylvania, the law once stated, "In the event that a horse refuses to pass a car on the road, the owner must take his car apart and conceal the parts in the bushes." Louisiana dispenses with the problem by forbidding anyone to ride a horse on asphalt-treated highways, and New Mexico has outlawed riding after dark.

Other laws regarding the responsibilities of operating your horse as a "vehicle" on the public roadway address a variety of practicalities. Several states, including Oklahoma, New Jersey, Pennsylvania, and Rhode Island, have rules against "horsing around" or riding too fast, especially over bridges. Mississippi imposes a $5 fine for jumping on or off a bridge. Public highways and interstates are off-limits to horses in most states. In Alabama it's illegal to graze your horse along the right-of-way, and New Hampshire and New York prohibit tying horses to trees or shrubs or otherwise damaging roadside flora.

Of course local ordinances can vary, too, and aren't always so practical. It's illegal to ride an ugly horse in Wilbur, Washington, and Hartsville, Illinois. A 1907 Cumberland County, Tennessee, statute established a speed limit, sort of, in that "Speed while on horseback upon county roads will be limited to three miles an hour, unless the rider sees a bailiff who does not appear to have had a drink in thirty days, then the horseman will be permitted to make what he can." Bluff, Utah, even relegates riding to church on Sunday to be a crime, stating, "Women who happen to be single, widowed or divorced are banned from riding to church on Sunday. Unattached females who take part in such outlandish activities can be arrested and put in jail."

But the clincher warning about the hazards of accidents on the road has to be this Hortonville, New York, law that admonishes, "The rider of any horse involved in an accident resulting in death shall immediately dismount and give his name and address to the person killed." You can see why it's important to know the local laws where you ride.

horse/traffic laws of any state. Article 34-B, under the state Vehicle and Traffic Code, addresses riding on the right-hand side (with traffic) of the road, riding single file, and not carrying anything that could prevent the rider from controlling the horse. The law also bans night riding and requires riders under 14 years of age to wear a helmet.

In the California State Code, meanwhile, Vehicle Code Division Section 11, Chapter 3, Article 3 states: "The driver of any vehicle approaching any horse-drawn vehicle, any ridden animal, or any livestock shall exercise proper control of his vehicle and shall reduce speed or stop as may appear necessary or as may be signaled or otherwise requested by any person driving, riding or in charge of the animal or livestock in order to avoid frightening and to safeguard the animal or livestock and to insure the safety of any person driving or riding the animal or in charge of the livestock."

It is common for state statutes to require drivers to exercise special care when encountering a horse on a public road to avoid frightening the horse, to the point of stopping if necessary. In all other cases, automobile drivers have an obligation to exercise what is described as "due or ordinary care." This doesn't sound like much, but it amounts to legal liability if they fail to drive responsibly. Drivers should give horses adequate leeway, watch for signals, be prepared to stop, and in general expect horses to act like horses. They can face penalty of law, criminal charges, and civil action for endangering riders, especially when children are present, by honking, reckless driving (driving too fast), "peeling out," weaving through horses, or just failing to exercise *ordinary care* — not watching the road, failing to signal, or talking on a cell phone.

LIABILITY IN A TRAFFIC ACCIDENT

Legal precedents abound for who is and is not liable when horses meet up with traffic. That duty to exercise ordinary care is common. Don't expect more than that. In the case of Parsons vs. Crown Disposal Co., 1997 WL 230026, in Burbank, California, one Darrell Parsons was thrown and injured when his horse spooked on a bridle path that was near a roadway on which a garbage-truck just happened to be making its rounds. Even though the garbage truck driver knew the trail was there, and knew that the noise and motion were likely to frighten a horse, the Supreme Court found that "no duty of care was breached."

So what about your legal responsibility while riding on the road? Again, case law depends on the circumstances. A rider who loses control of a horse that then veers into traffic is liable, as opposed to a car that frightens a horse and then strikes it.

In all cases, it's best to know your rights and responsibilities ahead of time to avoid a problem in the first place. As mentioned, find out what your state laws are before you hit the open road.

CHAPTER 7

Pleasure Trail Riding

⤐⟐⤖

BY FAR, THE MOST COMMON USE FOR THE AVERAGE American trail horse is as a pleasure horse. Whether you ride from home or commute to faraway trails, alone or with a large group, there are countless little ways you can improve your, and your horse's, trail-riding experience. From finding great trails and riding partners to getting there and back efficiently, this chapter will guide you in making the most of your ride. While safety should always come first, comfort, awe of nature, and fun are also important; otherwise, you might as well stay home and watch TV in a recliner.

Prepare to Enjoy the Ride

Good horsemanship revolves around understanding the nature and needs of your mount. It takes some imagination to realize the vast potential for hazard when working with horses. In fact, if we thought of everything that could go wrong, we might never go near our horses again. But the most basic aspects of horsemanship depend upon anticipating and preventing problems. Being watchful and thoughtful equals being safe. More advanced concepts in horsemanship involve training to improve communication with your mount and your relationship with each other (see chapter 5).

These are the things that make trail riding on a horse more worthwhile to us than hiking or mountain biking. There is another living, breathing, feeling individual there, sharing the experience with us. Good horsemanship means you both thoroughly enjoy the ride.

12 HABITS OF GOOD HORSEMANSHIP

Here are some basic guidelines for maximizing your and your horse's enjoyment and well-being on the trail.

✳ Feed your horse before you leave for a ride so he's not tempted to snack.
✳ Water your horse before you ride and at any reasonable opportunity on the trail.
✳ Keep an eye out for rocks, roots, bottles, holes, and anything else that could trip up your horse.
✳ Leave plenty of room between you and every other horse on the ride, in front of you, behind you, and to the side.
✳ Don't tie other horses' lead ropes to your saddle horn. You could get hung up if your horse shies or bucks.
✳ Wear gloves if you ever have to lead a horse, and use a thick cotton lead rope. Avoid nylon.
✳ If you carry a lariat, keep it in a bag or wrap it to prevent it catching on something or unwinding.

✳ If your horse is winded, stop and let him breathe.
✳ Check vitals whenever you deem it necessary, even if it means getting left behind (see chapter 4). Realize, though, that staying back can upset your horse, and vitals will be elevated as a result.
✳ Tie your horse high, short, and to a live tree or other sturdy upright by the lead rope — never by the reins.
✳ Periodically check your cinch for snugness, your saddle for slippage, and your gear for any brush or debris that might have gotten snagged or could irritate your horse.
✳ Periodically check your horse for burrs, injuries, swelling, heat, and loose shoes.

WATER

Be sure to bring plenty of water with you to the trailhead. Don't rely on a water source, especially at undeveloped trails. Five-gallon plastic jugs (the kind water-cooler water is sold in) are perfect, provided you can find or improvise a cap. One-gallon milk jugs work too, and you can freeze them in advance and get double duty out of them as coolers. You'll need from five to ten of them to supply your horse's water requirements for just 1 day of moderate riding if no other water is available.

Ideal water temperature is between 45 and 65 degrees F. Horses are less likely to drink their fill if the water is too cold or too warm, and they need the hydration when working on the trails. Stow water under the trailer or in the shade if it is hot out, or inside the truck if it is cold.

Some riders recommend burying water jugs at camp or near your trailer at a trailhead, since the earth will keep it at a cool temperature. Just remember to fill in the holes and tamp them solid before you depart.

Even if water is available at the trailhead, a lot of horses hesitate at the unfamiliar tastes or smells of strange water. Mixing it with water brought from home might help. Some folks add salt to grain (2 tablespoons) to make the horse thirsty enough to overcome his aversion. Getting your horse used to flavored water at home is a great way to ensure that he'll accept water anywhere. Peppermint, licorice, or other flavoring in the water will mask strange tastes. It takes about ¼ teaspoon to flavor a gallon of water. Offer him flavored water from time to time at home so that he is used to it before you strike out on a 2-week trail ride, lest it turn out to be something he has an aversion to.

Electrolytes are an important supplement for horses that work hard on the trail, and easily lost as the horse sweats, which can lead to dehydration problems (see chapter 10). You can purchase these essential salts through feed stores or horsemen's catalogs. Pack electrolytes and a separate bucket for mixing electrolyte solutions.

Riding Alone

This is where I'm supposed to tell you never to ride alone. For me, that's right up there with "Never eat chocolate." *Fuggedaboutit.*

I have ridden more miles with only the company of a good horse (and often a good dog) than I have ever put behind me with human companionship. High on my list of reasons to ride are peace and quiet. The silence sings. Worries are replaced by sunlight on my face or rain in my hair. Thoughts are replaced by feelings. Senses live to their fullest. Alone on the trail is never lonely. Life is good.

So instead of recommending the safest thing to do, I can only in good conscience recommend the sanest alternatives. Always understand that riding alone is potentially dangerous — not as dangerous as crossing the street in most cities — but fraught with risk nonetheless. But it's not as if those risks are totally unforeseeable or beyond your control. The trail you ride, your horse, and your level of skill are all critical elements in how much risk you are taking.

File a flight plan. Always let someone know when, where, and for how long you plan to ride.

Leave a note at home, taped or tacked where someone in your family is sure to see it. If you board your horse, check in — and out — with your barn manager, and again, leave a note tacked to the front of your horse's empty stall. If you live all alone in the middle of nowhere, keep your horse at home, and have no family or friends, call *someone* and let her know you're going riding down to the pond and expect to be back in 2 hours.

That said, **ride where you say you will.** If you make a last-minute detour (and isn't that what life is all about?) mark the trail so that searchers can find you in the event of emergency. During their expedition across the vast, uncharted American West, Meriwether Lewis and William Clark often separated and left notes for each other as to their plans. If they can find a note on a tree somewhere between Missouri and Oregon over a two-year trek, you can manage to leave clues where your friends can find them if you're not home by dark.

Always carry ID, a waterproof jacket or coat, water, a halter and lead rope, a knife (in a boot scabbard, on your belt, or in your Just-in-Case kit), a hoof pick, and, if you have one and it works where you ride, your cell phone.

You can put together a personal Just-in-Case kit, stash it in a resealable plastic bag, and keep it where you will always remember to grab it when you head out for a ride. (The hollow beneath the saddle horn of a Western saddle is a good place.) When you ride alone, make sure this kit is on your person, not strapped to a saddle that could take off without you. (Likewise your cell phone!) A fanny pack is perfect for this. Items for a Just-in-Case kit should be those few things that will be most appreciated should you run into unexpected trouble on the trail. The ones suggested here require little space for the good they will do if you ever need them. Items vary by time of year (you won't care about mosquito repellent in the snow) and by your own priorities, so feel free to customize your own kit. Incidentally, Just-in-Case kits make perfect gifts for the other trail riders in your life.

What to Carry Where

Certain items belong on your person during a trail ride, and others can be tied to your saddle. At right is a checklist to help you pack.

helmet

smile

vest with pockets for essentials

JUST-IN-CASE KIT

breeches

Western endurance saddle

saddlebag

breast collar

tapaderos

JUST-IN-CASE KIT

Keep this kit in a backpack or fanny pack on your person. Heaven forbid you should be separated from your horse, but if so, at least you will have some basic essentials with you. All of these items will roll together and fit in a gallon-sized clear plastic zip-close bag. Bring a spare plastic bag along with you.

❑ ID card with address and phone number; emergency contact numbers; vet's number; and any pertinent medical information such as allergies to medication and organ donor information

❑ Water purification tablets

❑ Teabags (for bee stings or a pick-me-up)

❑ Aspirin

❑ Antihistamine (in case of bee sting or an allergic reaction)

❑ Bute or banamine (horse aspirin)

❑ Waterproof matches, paper, and firestarter (lint, shavings, dry moss)

❑ A large bandanna

❑ Baling twine

❑ 2 large plastic garbage bags (for a tent, bed liner, sling, raincoat)

❑ Toilet paper

❑ Mirror (for signaling or fire starting)

❑ Paper and red waterproof felt-tip pen (Sharpies mark on anything)

❑ Energy bar

❑ Bandages or gauze

❑ Antibiotic ointment

❑ A roll of brightly colored Vet Wrap (for bandaging or to mark the trail)

❑ 3 or 4 horse treats that your horse appreciates (for treats, rewards, or to help catch him)

❑ About 2 feet of aluminum foil (to boil water in)

❑ About 50 feet of nylon twine

❑ Individually packaged wet wipes

❑ Duct tape

❑ Reflectors or reflective tape

❑ Leatherman-type all-purpose tool

❑ Survival or "space" blanket

❑ Insect-repellent wipes

❑ Sting dabbers

❑ Lip moisturizer or small canister of petroleum jelly or Bag Balm

❑ Handwarmer packets

❑ Sunscreen

❑ Comb

❑ Whistle (to call for help or to scare off wildlife)

❑ Firecrackers (ditto)

❑ Fishing line

❑ Wire saw

❑ Needle and heavy-duty thread

❑ Plastic zipper pouch

IN YOUR SADDLEBAG

For longer or more challenging rides, tie a second kit to the cantle of your saddle so that you can reach it easily. (Rig it so that it doesn't protrude above the cantle. That way, if you need to bail off, it won't hinder your escape.) Bring this kit on longer rides or any time your little voice warns you to be cautious. It can include:

❑ Small folding saw

❑ Gloves

❑ Hat

❑ Dry socks and spare clothes (for you)

❑ Wool blanket

❑ Slip-on temporary horse boots

❑ Stethoscope

❑ Equine first-aid kit

❑ Human first-aid kit

❑ Roll of toilet paper

❑ Plastic collapsible water bucket

❑ Glow sticks

❑ Flashlight with *working* batteries

❑ Disposable camera

❑ Extra horse treats

❑ Additional food

❑ Book

❑ Deck of cards or crossword puzzles with pencil

No law says getting stranded overnight has to be scary or boring.

ON YOUR PERSON

Items to keep in your pockets are your car keys (if you drove to the barn or trailered your horse to the trail), glasses in a hard case, a compass if you are riding unfamiliar trails, any regularly necessary medication, a watch (for monitoring vital signs), a can of pepper spray and, if it functions where you ride, your cell phone.

Riding in a Group

Whereas riding alone poses the risk that there will be no one around if you happen to get into trouble, riding with a group means that there will always be someone around to get you *into* trouble.

You ride with a group for fun and companionship, but what the experience really tests is your awareness, wariness, and good manners. Ride your own horse but watch out for the other guy.

THE YIN AND YANG OF RIDING IN A GROUP

You'll notice a pattern to the following tips. Know the right thing to do, but assume the other guy does not.

● Never start off before everyone is mounted, and then do so only at a walk, unless another gait has been agreed upon by the group. If you take off at a gallop, someone's liable to get dumped or run away with.

Riders should wait at the bottom or top of a hill until the others arrive, allowing enough space for their arrival.

○ Be prepared for some idiot to take off at a gallop while you are mounting with one foot in the stirrup.

● Don't crowd. Some horses become very nervous, bite, or kick.

○ Be wary of people who crowd. Tie a red ribbon to your horse's tail if he kicks, or if you want people who crowd to think he does.

● Don't allow your horse to nip or kick at other horses.

○ Look out for horses that nip or kick at your horse.

● When you are in the lead, walk or ask the group what gait they prefer. Don't suddenly stop on the trail. Take turns leading. Be sure no one falls behind.

○ Be prepared for the leader to leave without you, hog the lead all day, or stop without warning.

● Don't run up behind other horses.

○ Be prepared for other horses to run up behind you when you least expect it.

● If your horse is fractious, ride **drag** (at the end of the group). A restless horse can upset other horses and will benefit from the example set by more-experienced horses in front of him.

○ Watch out for fractious horses in the lead, right behind you, or next to you.

● Wait at the top or bottom of hills until everyone arrives, so the last horses don't rush. Allow space for their arrival. Don't rush, crowd, or stop without warning on a hill.

○ Be prepared for other riders to take off while you are halfway down the hill, to trot the entire hill, to crowd or bump into you, or to stop dead in their tracks right in front of you.

● If you lead or ride toward the front of the group, warn others if there is a challenge ahead such as a hole, a swarm of bees, or oncoming traffic.

○ Be prepared to encounter a hole, bees, or oncoming traffic without warning.

● Avoid alcohol, and don't smoke on the trail. One sets a bad example and impairs your horsemanship; the other is also a fire hazard.

Things to Check Before and After You Ride

Whenever pilots prepare for takeoff, they go over a checklist, even if they've done it 1,000 times. Develop the same mindset with your horse and gear, and run through this checklist before you head out. These tips will make your ride safer and more pleasant for you, for your horse, and for anyone along for the ride.

WHAT TO CHECK FOR YOURSELF

Starting at the top of your head, check yourself and the gear on your person. Check:

- ❏ Helmet
- ❏ Hat (stocking for cold weather, shady for hot)
- ❏ Glasses, hearing aid
- ❏ Water bottle or canteen
- ❏ Clothes in layers: breathable fabrics, wool, and silk
- ❏ Waterproof jacket
- ❏ Wool socks
- ❏ Pull-on boots with slanted heels, comfortable enough to walk in
- ❏ Just-in-Case kit in a fanny pack (see page 161)
- ❏ Personal items or medication
- ❏ Personal identification
- ❏ Hoof pick
- ❏ Knife (a folding type with a blade that locks in place when open)
- ❏ Compass
- ❏ Cell phone

WHAT TO CHECK ON YOUR HORSE

Before you mount, go over your horse and his gear. Check:

- ❏ Halter and 10-foot lead rope under bridle (or a continuous rope and halter ensemble)

- ❏ Bridle for bit fit, loose connections, ID tag, buckle, rein attachments
- ❏ Breast collar for snug fit
- ❏ Saddle pad for any protrusions that could gouge or rub your horse
- ❏ Saddle for fit, pinching at the withers, bridging, trapped mane hairs, loose fittings or screws
- ❏ Latigo and cinch, or billets and girth, for wear, thin spots, and cracks
- ❏ Girth or cinch for appropriate snugness (you don't have to squeeze the air out of your horse, but the saddle shouldn't move around either)
- ❏ Back cinch if your saddle has one, tightened so it touches your horse's belly
- ❏ Support boots if your horse wears them
- ❏ Fronts of hooves for missing nails
- ❏ Underside of hooves for loose shoes

(See chapter 3 for more information on appropriate gear and how to pack.)

POST-RIDE CHECK

Don't pull the saddle immediately. A rider's weight compresses the skin and blood vessels in the horse's back. By pulling the saddle off as soon as you dismount, blood rushes in to refill compressed capillaries, which can cause blood vessel ruptures, tissue damage, blood congestion within the tissue, and, ultimately, a sore back. Leave the saddle on for a cool-down period, walking the last half-mile home or longeing for 15 minutes after your return. Upon pulling the saddle, visually check over your horse's body, and feel his back and legs with your fingertips and palms for any heat or swelling. Check the soles of his feet for stones and debris. Brush or rinse him off as needed and consider a 10-minute rubdown/massage as a final bit of cooling down.

O Watch out for intoxicated riders and keep an eye open for anyone flicking cigarette butts. Resist the urge to flick theirs right back, but do be sure their cigarettes are completely out, even if that means stopping, dismounting, and picking them up.

● Stop if there is an accident.

O Be prepared to handle the situation if an accident leaves you stranded, without your companions.

● If you pack it in, pack it out.

O Be prepared to pick up other people's trash.

● Leave your dog at home or in camp. Some horses are just naturally flighty around dogs.

O Watch out for dogs.

● Be aware of how you push branches out of the way. If you grab one and let it go, it could swat the next rider right in the face. If she's right behind you, it's better to duck and gently move the branch around your body, or at least holler LIMB!

O When riding through brush or woods, stay well behind the horse directly in front of you or you might receive a limb in the face.

● If you are riding a mare in season or a stallion, ride well away from other horses.

O Watch out for mares in season and stallions.

Group rides usually have a fairly diverse mix of people and horses. You will surely learn from riders with more experience or new ideas, but at the same time you are an example for those with less experience (or few ideas). Expect to share the trail with people you might avoid in the grocery store checkout line. Exercise tolerance and good manners, and if anyone annoys you, try not to return the favor. Ride on your best behavior. Be sure your horsemanship sets a good example, but don't forget to relax and have fun. If there are children or inexperienced riders in the group, be sure that the group leader knows this. Such riders will have a much better time if they "buddy up" with an old hand, even if they don't realize it. Having someone keep an eye out for the kids and greenhorns is just good horse sense.

OTHER HORSES' HEALTH

Another thing to be cautious about when riding with other horses is their state of health. The list of diseases horses can catch from each other (some of which they can pass on to you!) is daunting. Although no one should knowingly bring a sick horse on a trail ride, sometimes symptoms are not obvious, sometimes symptoms don't develop until well after the contagious phase of a disease has begun, and sometimes people just don't know any better or care. Your own best insurance is to keep your horses vaccinated, especially against any diseases known to have surfaced in your area, and to keep your distance from strange horses or any that don't appear to be in perfect health. Watch for nasal or ocular (eye) discharge, lethargy, bare patches of skin (mange), and swollen glands along the neck (see page 88).

Because parasites are spread through manure, don't allow your horses to eat from the ground near the trailhead. You have no way to know who was there before you or how they care for their animals, and some parasites and disease organisms can remain viable in or on soil for a long time.

GROUP HORSEMANSHIP

Expect to see a lot of mediocre (or worse) horsemanship. After one group trail ride, a horse that had been tied very long and low to his trailer predictably got hung up in the rope. The owner was quickly notified as a crowd of us hollered in unison, and he jumped right up to untangle his horse. Good. Then he retied him just as long in the same spot. Setting a good example doesn't matter much if people don't know the difference. I never say anything to other riders about their horsemanship; nobody likes a know-it-all or a tattletale, *unless* there is imminent danger or if a child is in harm's way.

See page 287 for how to tie your horse correctly.

PRIZES AND INCENTIVES

Some group rides offer awards and incentives, even calling on the community to donate prizes, then collecting money to benefit a charity. Poker rides are a fun way to test your "hand" on the trail, and add a little friendly intrigue to a friendly outing. Riders pick up a playing card at one of several checkpoints, and at some point are usually allowed to exchange cards (just as one would in a game of poker). The rider who has cleared all the checkpoints with the best "hand" of cards wins first prize. Second-best hand wins the next prize, and so forth.

One way to improve horsemanship on group rides, and to make them safer, less frustrating, and more beneficial to all, is to offer a horsemanship prize at the end of the ride. One person, a panel, or all the riders can vote on the award. By adding a contest to the picture, most people will at least realize that their horsemanship is being noticed. This also gives the ride organizers an excuse to make brief fliers available that specify what is being judged (complete with suggestions), and gives the riders an incentive to read it. Improving your horsemanship is something that should happen every time you ride; getting a prize for it just makes it more fun.

Riding Near Home

When you ride from home, it's easy to be careless. It's just a casual jaunt, after all, out of your own backyard. But every ride deserves your full attention, and riding close to home has its own unique concerns. The same warning applies when hacking out of your familiar boarding barn.

Let someone know where you will be and when you expect to be back every time you ride from home alone, even if you are just riding out on your own back 40. If no one is home, call a friend or leave a note detailing where you plan to ride.

Consider your neighbors. Some are delighted to see horses passing by and some even allow you

---

to traverse their land; while others seem to be in a perpetual panic that, heaven forbid, your horse will poop on their lawn. (Don't bother trying to educate them as to the botanical benefits of horse manure.) Be very respectful of your neighbors, even the ones you don't like; they vote and may have input into what trails are kept open to horses or even whether it remains legal to ride in your neighborhood.

VARY THE ROUTINE

Horses may become barn sour or herd-bound (bored with regular trails and routines), as can you. Try not to ride in the same direction every time you leave home. Horses are quick to anticipate. Vary your routine, your route, and your gait, and do exercises (such as collection or extension at the walk, leg yields, bending, and half halts) along the way to stay sharp and keep your horse's attention. This helps to prevent barn sourness as well as boredom.

A great responsibility-builder for your horse is for you to stop and yak with a neighbor while insisting that your horse stand still. If he dances around or paws, give him a sharp *NO!* (combined with a smack if warranted) and demand he stay put until he calms down, stands quietly and, ideally, starts licking or chewing.

Don't overdo it at first. Reward him after a few minutes of standing quietly, by letting him move forward, but extend the time of each visit until you can stop and go at will.

When you head home, stop short of your driveway, ride past it, speed up gait as you ride past it, or back past. These are precautions against your

Vary your routine by riding past your driveway instead of turning into it.

horse getting barn sour and heading home before you say so. You'd be surprised how many otherwise obedient and reliable horses resist passing the driveway when they *know* they are going home.

See chapter 8 for more tips on dealing with a barn-sour or herd-bound horse.

BRINGING YOUR DOG

Whether or not you bring along a canine companion when you ride out your driveway depends on the trail and the dog. A lot of public areas do not allow dogs or require them to be on a leash. While you *can* control a dog on a leash from horseback, it's an art form all its own that requires significant training and practice on the part of all concerned. Special electronic dog-training collars are as good as, or better than, a physical leash and allow you maximum control without getting tangled up. Any competent, compassionate dog owner can learn to use one appropriately, and most have different settings that range from a buzz or "alert," to a minor zing, to a downright painful zap. If your dog isn't responsive enough to obey without being harshly shocked, leave him home. (See chapter 10 for more about dogs on the trail.)

If riding with dogs sounds like something you'd

like to try, check out chapter 11 for the sport of field trialing — the ultimate dog-and-pony show.

Riding Far from Home

Discovering and exploring new trails is one of the genuine thrills of trail riding. Anticipation runs high in both you and your horse. Take time to plan and prepare, to help keep that excitement from turning to distress.

A well-mannered dog can be a great trail companion.

FINDING TRAILS

It can be tricky to find out which trails are currently open to horses, but the Internet has become a great tool for exploration. Pull up a search engine, type in "horseback riding trails," and be prepared to spend some time surfing the World Wide Web. Specify the state where you want to ride to narrow down your search.

It's also a good idea to contact the local representatives of the various agencies that oversee trails. State and federal parks departments, conservation and wildlife departments, the Forest Service, and the Bureau of Land Management should have information and maps available for free or a small fee. Hunters, bird-watchers, hikers, dirt bikers, snowmobilers — in short, those other trail users — can also be great resources for trail information.

One of the best ways to find trails is to invest in some of the wonderful equine trail guides finding their way onto the market. More often than not, these are firsthand reports of trails on which the authors have put many miles in the saddle to share with you. Area-specific guides for all over the country are available either through bookstores,

Top 50 Trails

Check the resources section, beginning on page 300, to find my lists of the 50 Best Trails and 50+ Top Outfitters and Organized Trail Rides

over the Internet, or through businesses like Bonnie's Two Horse Enterprises. The benefit of using a service like Bonnie's, a longtime, well-known trail-riding advocate, is that you have assurance from someone other than the author that the guides are useful and correct.

Public trails are not the only trails. Timber companies own a lot of land, as do railroad companies, school districts, colleges and universities, corporate investors, land developers, and private individuals. You can find out who owns any tract of land in your county by visiting your county courthouse and talking with the tax assessor. It's public information.

Once you identify the property owner, contact whoever it is by mail and introduce yourself. Ask

| TRAIL TALE | *My Advance Guard* | |

Why bother to bring a dog at all? A well-trained, trustworthy companion dog that doesn't need a leash can be a godsend on the trail. Keep a leash with you, or detach a rein to use in case of emergency.

Minnie was a mutt that resembled a miniature yellow Lab and was the sweetest soul ever to pant over a sunlit trail. Too small to be kept in by our gate, she felt it was her personal duty to accompany me every time I rode through it. She usually trotted about 50 feet ahead and cleared the way for me.

Any time other dogs approached my horse, there was Minnie, smiling her doggie smile, wagging her bent tail, and defusing any crisis before it occurred. Kids on bikes would stop to pet her. Cars would slow down for her. She ran interference for me for more than 10 years, until we moved near an unfamiliar highway and passing cars didn't act the same way they did in our old subdivision.

Remember, above all, that highways and dogs don't mix.

permission to use his land and offer to sign a liability waiver (one of the main reasons private land holders are not willing to allow any type of use on their land is the fear of being sued). Guarantee you will not smoke on his land and will watch for fire, pick up litter, shoo off unauthorized users, and just generally police his property for him, all for the privilege of riding there.

Sometimes it helps to hint at the good public relations it would be for a company to support your trail-riding group, schoolchildren, cancer survivors, an arts group, or handicapped riders — whoever will actually be benefiting from the owner's gracious decision to grant use rights. If looking for a trail for yourself turns into an opportunity to help others in your community, everyone gains!

Above all, no matter whose land you ride, treat it as though it were your own (especially since public land is!). This means being a caretaker of all terrain you cross. Ride with an attitude of gratitude and all your trails will be happy ones.

PLANNING AND PACKING

Leaving behind the comforts and conveniences of home can be a little traumatic, but all you really need to concentrate on are the essentials for safety, convenience, comfort, and fun.

For extended trips, pack brushes, a bucket and horse sponge, fly repellents and/or masks, a sweat scraper, horse blanket, and other grooming and comfort items. It's never a bad idea to take a spare halter and lead rope, saddle pad, and bridle. You don't want to have to stop if something gets broken or your saddle pad gets filthy or loaded with burrs.

Bring a shovel (for cleanup), trash bags, and, if you will be staying out overnight, a rake for cleaning up your area.

See chapter 12 for information on camping with horses.

Riding Strange Trails

When in unfamiliar territory, your two biggest concerns are:

1. Not getting lost.
2. Watching for hazards.

Bring a map and a compass and don't be embarrassed to mark your way. If you do this by bending back branches that hang in the trail, no one will be the wiser. Surveyor's tape is lightweight to carry and easy to spot, but be sure to take it down on your way back. Note (in writing if possible) each turn in the trail, and keep an eye out for landmarks.

Try to find out in advance what to watch out for on new trails, from either trail management or other users. Predators, rock slides, washouts, water crossings, and other potential dangers are easiest to deal with when you are forewarned.

Always keep your attention first on your own horse, second on the trail ahead, and third on the trail stretching behind you.

Trailering and Traveling

When trail riding away from home, the first order of business is getting there. Hauling a horse involves special equipment and special skills. If you rent, borrow, or share equipment, be very cautious. Don't assume the owner has maintained it. Be sure to inspect each piece of equipment well before your planned departure. Nothing ruins a trail ride faster than transportation that breaks down on the way to the trail.

Obviously, owning your own truck and trailer gives you ultimate control over their condition and maintenance. It also allows you to move your horse anywhere and anytime, to evacuate in a fire or other emergency, to transport him to the veterinarian, and to go to shows, trail rides, and other equestrian events. Here's a prime example of why it's true that the purchase price is the cheapest part of owning a horse.

CHOOSING A TRAILER

Horse trailers come with more bells and whistles than a convention of gym teachers in a church tower. While living quarters or expansive tack rooms can be very handy, they don't get your horse there any faster or more safely. Extras aside, there are some things to look for and some things to look out for.

Studies show that horses exhibit fewer signs of stress when traveling in slant-load trailers than in front-load trailers. Behaviorists theorize that this is related to horses' natural tendency to put their rumps toward a threat or discomfort. Think of how they stand in a storm, heads down, backs hunched, and rumps to the wind. Slant-load trailers without fixed partitions are also safer when loading and unloading horses. Countless horses have gotten hung up in immovable partitions. Swinging partitions are good for keeping horses from fussing with one another, but a horse can get hung up on any type of partition if he tries hard enough. Statistically, open stock trailers are safest.

Trailers can be step-up or ramp-load, and neither is inherently better than the other; plenty of horses have managed to hurt themselves on both types. I prefer a step-load trailer with individual doors because I can close them. Ramps can be heavy, dirty, and awkward when you are loading and unloading all by yourself.

In horse trailers, newer really is better. Older models are not as well designed, more hazardous, heavier, less aerodynamic, and, in short, not as safe, convenient, or user-friendly as newer models. We made good use of 1960s and '70s horse trailers when they were all we had, but we don't use them now.

RATING Be sure that the towing rig is rated for the weight of the trailer. Most three-quarter-ton pickups fitted with a towing package can safely pull a two- or three-horse trailer. Larger stock trailers (especially full of horses) need more horsepower up front.

Trailering Tip

Line the inside of your trailer with particleboard or trailer mats to prevent horses from kicking or pawing holes in the metal, which can then slice their feet.

MAINTENANCE

Trailer maintenance is a serious commitment. Among the things that require regular attention are the tires (rotate, replace, keep them inflated), wheel bearings (repack), axles (grease), brakes (check, adjust as needed, and check and replace if necessary the breakaway battery), and the physical structure of the trailer, including the sides and the floorboards.

LOADING YOUR HORSE

Be sure your horse is trained to load and ride in a trailer ahead of time. Wrangling a reluctant horse into a strange metal box and then dragging him along for hours will not put him in the best frame of mind for a fun outing.

If you have a long drive ahead of you, be sure your horse is fed and watered before you go. The wisdom of feeding in a trailer is debatable. It does make the environment seem friendlier for the horse, and it is convenient, but often it also proves to be unsafe. Horses can climb into front-end feeders, and hanging hay feeders can tangle up a horse or get untied, fall, and wind up at your horse's feet.

How you balance the load in the trailer is important because of how roads are constructed. Paved roads, including highways, are built with a convex curve across the surface to allow for water runoff. The center of the road is higher than the edges. This makes the right side of your horse trailer imperceptibly lower than the left. If you use a straight load two-horse trailer and load only one horse, put him on the left side. (This also gives the driver the benefit of being able to look back along

Predeparture Inspection

Inspect your trailer a week or so before the first haul of the season, just in case you need to make repairs. Don't assume you'll "get by" if you wait until the last minute.

A visual inspection takes only a few moments and is time well spent. The little things can be critical.

Hitch the trailer to the rig to complete your inspection.

❑ Be sure the hitch is secure. There should be a cotter pin or other final securing device: Be sure it is intact.

❑ Cross and fasten safety chains.

❑ Plug in the electrical cord and check the trailer signals (both left and right), exterior lights (just because you don't plan to drive after dark doesn't mean you won't wind up doing just that), and brake lights.

❑ Be sure the jack is wound all the way up.

❑ If you will be driving in snow, carry tire chains.

❑ Check the engine oil, transmission oil, and antifreeze/coolant levels in the towing rig and top up as necessary.

❑ Adjust the side-view mirrors.

❑ Take a test drive up the road or around the block, with the trailer empty, to be sure your towing rig can handle the load and to familiarize yourself with the different feel of the weight behind you, the different stopping distances, and the slower acceleration.

HITCH. Check the hitch for wear. Be sure it fits the ball of the towing rig. Check that the electrical cord (for the trailer lights and breaks) is wired to fit the towing rig, as well, and that safety chains are present and show no sign of wear between links.

FINAL CHECK

• **Just before your departure,** double-check the oil, transmission oil, and antifreeze/coolant levels in the towing rig. Be sure windows and mirrors are clean and that nothing will block your view.

• Take a walk around to be sure there is nothing under the tires, that all doors are securely latched, that nothing is hanging out of the trailer, and that you haven't left your sunglasses sitting on the fender.

TIRES. Check the trailer tires for air pressure and adequate tread, and be sure the lug nuts on the wheels are tight.

TRAILER DOORS. Be sure all trailer doors latch securely and that you can operate the latches.

FLOOR. Look to be sure that floorboards are fully intact. Since they are wood, they are susceptible to rot. Rubber mats help to make the floors easier on your horse's joints and body if he has to stand for prolonged periods, but they can hide problems underneath. Be sure to pull them out entirely and inspect the floorboards at least once every riding season. Replace any boards that are split or rotten.

SHARP THINGS. Look and feel around the inside of the trailer for loose bolts, sharp edges, protrusions, anything a horse could find to hurt himself on.

the horse side of the trailer through the left side mirror.) If you load two horses in such a trailer, put the heavier of the two on the left. Slant-load trailers place the horse's head and forehand to the left, thereby balancing up to 70 percent of each horse's weight to that side.

Speaking of balance, some horses balance better in a moving trailer than others. Some rarely move, whereas others step around to keep on their feet. Shipping boots or heavy leg wraps will help keep such horses from hurting themselves. This is especially important for horses that are shod with studs for traction. Be sure the wraps cover the heels and coronary bands, as these are most vulnerable to injury. Bell boots are great for extra protection of these sensitive areas.

If you are hauling a long distance, stop every 2 hours for 15 or 20 minutes to let the horses rest. Balancing in a moving box is work, and muscles can get tense and sore before you ever get to the trail. It's not necessary and (unless you can stop in a secure area away from traffic) not safe to unload. A horse can rest in a stationary trailer.

HIT THE ROAD — GENTLY

No matter how you normally drive, when you are towing horses, drive as if you have a load full of eggs. When you are ready to head out, accelerate slowly and smoothly. Drive with your lights on.

On the road, leave extra space between you and the vehicle in front of you, and when (not if) someone passes you and squeezes into that extra space, back off to re-create that buffer zone.

Brake early, gradually, and smoothly. Hit the brakes before speed bumps or potholes and release as you go over them so that the tires roll through smoothly. If you are on a long downhill stretch, try to find a spot to pull off and let your brakes cool. Downshifting works too, but stresses your transmission.

On the highway, keep an eye out for slow-downs ahead. Make lane changes early. On back roads, watch for potholes and rough stretches.

Bring along a horse blanket when trailering. In cool weather, the rush of wind through the open areas of a horse trailer can chill a horse, and in warmer weather, a blanket will help prevent a chill after the ride if the horse is still sweaty on the journey home.

AT THE TRAILHEAD

When you arrive at the campsite or trailhead, scout out a good parking site. You want a spot as level as possible, away from other rigs, with little brush, and with water nearby. (A restroom is a nice plus.) It doesn't matter if you have to ride a half-mile to the trailhead. You came to ride!

Block the trailer wheels before you unload.

If you have been traveling for hours, give your horse a chance to look around and stretch when you unload. Walk him for 10 minutes or so to let him get his bearings and work out kinky muscles and stiff joints. Allow him to drink, eat grass hay, or graze, but save the alfalfa or grain for an hour or so later.

Tying to the trailer itself is fine, as long as there are no sharp edges and nothing for your horse to get hung up on. Tie only to a trailer that is still hooked to the towing rig, and be sure the tires are blocked to keep it stationary.

Use a quick-release knot (see page 318) high up on the trailer to keep your horse from getting hung up. If you are traveling with more than one horse, tie them to opposite sides of the trailer so they can't fuss with each other.

Be sure hay bags are tied high and feed or water containers are fixed securely to the trailer so your horse can't knock them loose. Police the area around the trailer for trash, broken glass, rocks, and other hazards.

Be sure to lock up before you ride off, and stash spare keys somewhere on or under the rig in case you lose the main set on the trail. When the ride is over and you are ready to head back home, be sure to check beneath the trailer and to inspect the hitch and door latches all over again.

TRAILERING OUT OF STATE

Traveling out of state means your horse must have his affairs in order.

Federal law now requires that horses pass a Coggins test with negative results before they can be transported across state lines. The Coggins test, named for Dr. Leroy Coggins (who developed it in 1970), detects **equine infectious anemia** (EIA) also known as swamp fever, a deadly virus transmitted through mosquito and other bug bites. (Positive results require quarantine and, often, putting the horse down.) The test must be repeated every year to be current. A Coggins test requires a veterinarian to draw blood and document which horse is tested. Some veterinarians can do the testing in-house; others send blood samples out to an approved lab, which means you will have to plan ahead in order to receive your results back in time.

Legally, you are also required to have a health certificate, acquired after your veterinarian gives your horse a "physical," and a brand inspection certificate. Health certificates are typically valid for only 30 days, but a brand inspection is good for as long as you own the horse.

Preserving the Right to Ride

The most challenging thing about the horseback-riding trails in some areas is finding them. It's not that the trails are hidden away, but in more and more areas across the United States and Canada, fewer and fewer trails are open to equine access. It's a trend with no end in sight.

PUBLIC LANDS: ACCESS AND MULTIPLE USES

The reasons for the dwindling availability of trail miles are many and diverse, and the worst thing is that some of these are our own fault, especially on public trails. Horses are hard on trails. Shod hooves tear up and compact soil both on the trail and where riders veer off the beaten path. Irreversible environmental damage happens, one hoofprint at a time.

Conflicts (even just perceived conflicts) with other users make multiple-use trails harder to share. Hikers can seem unjustifiably fussy when those $200 sneakers step in a pile of manure or tip-toe through a stretch of trail churned deep and muddy by industrious hooves. Garbage along the trail, messy camps, degraded trails, slides, short-cuts across switchbacks, damage to riverbanks, conflicts with other trail users, and countless other problems are easy to avoid with a little fore-thought and consideration. Yet these are the very types of things that inspire authorities to limit — or eliminate — equine access to trails. After all, we are the minority in a democratic process in which the majority rules. If other users don't want us on the trail, we're out.

But take heart. Trail riding is not just your passion and mine; it is an American birthright. Just ask U.S. Rep. George Radanovich, chairman of the National Parks, Recreation, and Public Lands Subcommittee. On September 21, 2004, Congress passed the Right-to-Ride Livestock on Federal Lands Act (H.R. 2966), proposed by Radanovich. This bill refers to the long-standing tradition of horseback riding throughout our history.

The law states, "The Secretary of the Interior shall provide for the management of National Park System lands to preserve and facilitate the continued use and access of pack and saddle stock animals on such lands, including wilderness areas, national monuments, and other specifically designated areas, where there is a historical tradition of such use. As a general rule, all trails, routes, and areas used by pack and saddle stock shall remain open and accessible for such use." It goes on to conclude, "The Secretary shall provide for the management of public lands to preserve and facilitate the continued use and access of pack and saddle stock animals on such lands, including wilderness areas, national monuments, and other specifically designated areas, where there is a historical tradition of

Loading into a Trailer

Loading shouldn't be a traumatic experience for your horse or for you. Teaching to load on cue in advance is not hard; it just takes a little time and a little planning. Trying to force an untrained horse to load on the spot, when you are probably in a hurry to leave, is a lousy start to a trail ride. Follow these steps and you'll have a horse that loads up faster than you do.

1. Secure the trailer to the truck and block the tires. With a "step-up" trailer, it is helpful during the first lessons to back the trailer up to a curb or slight incline to minimize the "vertical ascent."

2. Lead your horse around for a few minutes; ask for stop, back up, step over to build up cooperation.

3. Lead near, past, and around the trailer for a minute or two.

4. Lead up to the trailer and ask the horse to stop, then back. Then walk away.

5. Finally, walk up to the trailer as close as your horse will get before he seems uncomfortable. Let him look and sniff, then lead him away.

6. Repeat until you can walk right up to the trailer and walk in yourself. Don't ask the horse to follow you the first time, just let him watch you. Stand inside the trailer until your horse gets bored. For some horses, this alone will inspire them to step into the trailer unasked. They get bored or insecure and want to be closer to you. If this happens, reward him profusely. Handfuls of grain (stashed in the trailer in advance), treats, lots of "Good boys" and stroking will tell him he did something wonderful all on his own.

7. If the trailer is large enough to allow him to turn around, carefully let him do so and stop him for a second before he exits. Knowing he can get out goes a long way toward defusing your horse's fear of the box.

8. If the horse must back out of the trailer, ask him to back one step at a time, and pause after each step to praise and comfort him. Often a horse will just fly backwards as soon as his first hind foot touches down. It's better if he comes out calmly, but don't fuss over him if he hurries the first

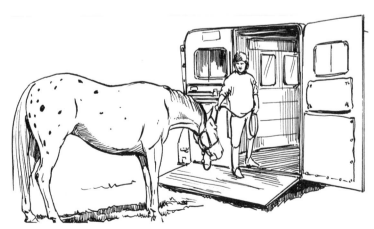

Let your horse look at and sniff the trailer, then lead him away (step 5).

few times. Keep your cool and he'll soon realize that he doesn't have to make a quick "escape."

9. After a few tries, ask him to slow down, and offer a treat as soon as his hind foot reaches for the ground or the ramp. Ask him to stand, for just a few seconds, with his front feet in the trailer and his hinds on the ground (or on the ramp). Reward him with praise and a few bites of grain from a bucket (this keeps him still while getting, and continuing to earn, his reward). With practice, you should be able to stop him at any point as he loads or unloads and he will stand quietly until asked to proceed.

10. If he doesn't load the first time, ask him to stretch his neck forward or place a foot in the trailer. *After* he makes any progress, reward and back off. Then return later and ask for a bit more. It can take as little as 20 minutes to introduce a horse to a trailer and establish a positive connection in his mind, but I've seen people drag, force, bribe, or try to beat a horse into a trailer for an hour or more before they resort to a different plan, or a different horse.

11. Every time he makes progress, reward him and have him stand. Never try to bribe a horse into a trailer. This is a lesson he has to learn as a response to your cues, not a choice to make if he is hungry enough.

12. Once your horse will load willingly and unload quietly, tie him to the front of the trailer and walk out, calmly reassuring him as you secure the butt bar or trailer door.

13. Reenter, untie, and unload. This lets him know that even if he is tied, he won't be stuck there forever.

TAKE A TRIAL RIDE

1. On the next lesson, load, tie, exit, and close the door. **Don't ride in the trailer with your horse.**

2. Make the first ride brief, slow, and easy. Come to a stop and walk back to the trailer talking to your horse. Offer him a special treat, talk to him, then get back in and drive home. Unload as if nothing special has happened.

3. Repeat, expanding the length of the ride, driving cautiously and with consideration for the live cargo in the back. Periodic rewards for loading, riding, and calmly unloading will keep your horse's outlook on the experience positive.

For more information on trailering, see the appendix.

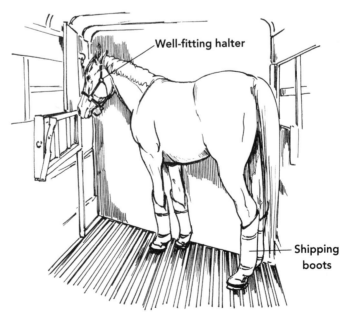

Well-fitting halter

Shipping boots

This horse is ready to roll (step 12).

such use. As a general rule, all trails, routes, and areas used by pack and saddle stock shall remain open and accessible for such use."

AMERICANS WITH DISABILITIES ACT

Another law that has been broached with respect to the right of Americans to access public lands on horseback is the Americans with Disabilities Act (Public Law 101-336, enacted July 26, 1990), which prohibits discrimination on the basis of disability. The rationale is that if the disabled (defined by the act as anyone with a physical or mental impairment that substantially limits one or more of the major life activities of an individual) are denied the right to use their horses to access public lands, this constitutes a violation of the act. And how can missing a sunset over the Sierras or the sound of hoofbeats through an old-growth, moss-enshrouded misty forest not be counted as a substantial limitation of one of life's major activities?

> *". . . all trails, routes, and areas used by pack and saddle stock shall remain open and accessible . . ."*
> — the Right-to-Ride Livestock on Federal Lands Act

PRIVATE LAND: TRESPASSING AND LIABILITY

Private property doesn't have to be posted for you to be guilty of trespass. Anytime unauthorized people enter land that belongs to someone else without consent, they are trespassing. As such, landowners in most states have no duty to make their land safe for you, and you are liable for any damage you cause. However, since liability in this day and age is a major concern for all landowners, finding out that people are using their property without permission is enough to upset and anger many that might not have minded had they been asked properly in the first place.

In a court case in Idaho in 1997, a rider fell off her horse when chased by the landowner's dog, and she sued the landowner, who had no idea she was riding on his land because she was trespassing at the time. A jury entered a judgment against the trespasser, but the Idaho Supreme Court reversed the ruling because the jury had not been instructed on the duty of a property owner to a trespasser in that state. In some states, landowners are liable for anything that happens on their land, whether or not they contributed to it or even knew about it.

The bottom line is this: If trespassers can hold property owners liable for their own lack of consideration and any consequences, then landowners are going to be increasingly unwilling to allow trail riders on their land.

PERSONAL LIABILITY ON THE TRAIL

The worst word in the equine enthusiast's vocabulary is *liability*. Take the "L" word seriously. It has cost many a horseman a pretty penny.

As with traffic accidents (see pages 155–156), most states have instituted equine-activity statutes that make it harder to sue a facility or landowner if a rider gets hurt in the normal course of equine events. But the ability of these laws to protect the individual horseman has yet to be well tested in court. What if your horse kicks another horse on the trail, steps on someone's foot, or kicks someone's dog as it snaps at his heels? As in any legal case, much depends on the circumstances, but often you can be held financially liable, or at least inconvenienced by the time, trouble, and expense of a lawsuit. That said, ride defensively.

Along these lines, be very cautious in lending or borrowing horses or equipment. A horse that is as good as gold for you may not react the same way for a different rider. People's expectations and riding styles vary so much that riding an unfamiliar horse can invite disaster should any serious challenge arise on the trail. Court cases abound in which horse owners get sued for unhappy (or even tragic) results of their well-meaning generosity in sharing their horses or equipment.

Join a trail-riding group and (literally) expand your horizons.

If you do offer to lend or ask to borrow, seriously consider the condition, training, and temperament of the horse to be sure it is compatible with the rider, and the condition of any equipment to be certain it is as safe as possible. Don't be shy to ask a borrower to sign a waiver absolving you from liability. Because a good waiver must anticipate all aspects of liability, it's a smart idea to pay a lawyer for an hour of his or her time and have one drafted especially for your circumstances.

LIMITATION OF LIABILITY Finally, riding facilities and events are being afforded some degree of protection under the law by equine-activity statutes that limit their liability, based on the assertion that equine activities bear a certain amount of inherent risk. These laws protect equine facilities, event organizers, landowners, and others from frivolous lawsuits and limit their liability should the worst happen. At the time of

this writing, only Alaska, California, Maryland, Nevada, New York, and Pennsylvania did not have such laws on the books.

The benefit of these laws to trail riders may not be obvious at first glance, but what they say is that as a group, horsemen are willing to take responsibility for our choice to be involved with horses, and that we realize and accept the risks involved. From the point of view of the general public, including landowners, this says we won't try to stick them with the bill if we have a problem.

JOIN UP

Joining a riding group is a great way to meet people with common interests, learn about trails, share advice on farriers, veterinarians, and hay suppliers, and add weight to your cause. Most regions have groups, and some of these have national affiliations such as the Backcountry Horsemen of America. To see if there is already a club in your area, check with your local tack store or veterinarian, or post a notice in those places asking for input.

As a group, you will have more influence with government agencies that control access to the trails. The old adage "There is strength in numbers" is as true here as anywhere. Groups can raise funds for trail maintenance, repair trails, organize rides, utilize local media, and keep the authorities accurately informed on the need for equine access to public trails.

Groups can also make others aware that when trails are degraded by horses, the fault may lie with the design and construction of the trail itself rather than with the users. As one trail conservancy source put it, "Abuse is designed into the trail." A geology study in Colorado involving the National Park Service concluded that "intensity of use is not the controlling factor in trail stability" and that "stock use was not the single dominant process active on trails." The lay of the land, geographic composition, and climate all play a role in how well a trail can stand up to use. Design and construction must take all these factors into account in order for trails to hold up to the uses for which they are intended.

There is a frustrating "catch 22" even here: *Lack of deterioration* often misleads authorities regarding the degree of use the trail is getting. Those who ride conscientiously leave no evidence of ever having been on the trail. Consequently, the lack of evidence of trail use leads agencies to conclude that the trails aren't being used by horses, and therefore no longer need to be maintained or left open. Bonnie Davis, of Two Horse Enterprises (see appendix), has devised a users' report card. By filling out and mailing to authorities a report card every time you use a public trail, you not only let them know of any problems on the trail, but you also make them aware that even though you left it as pristine as you found it, the trail has been in use.

In an age when funding for these activities is declining, your trail-riding group can work with authorities to improve and maintain horseback trails by researching proper design improvements, installing water access away from main bodies of water, clearing brush and deadfall after the winter, and improving campsites, and can make countless other contributions as well.

Aside from using the trails and helping those in charge maintain them, one of the most important things you can do to preserve equine access to trails is to communicate with federal, state, and local agencies as to the very need for horse access to public trails. Local park and public land supervisors often have little or no say in how trails are managed, so fish upstream. Vote for people who understand that public land is public land. When timber companies get priority to access parkland over someone who just wants to ride through it, thank a politician.

We trail riders must consider and contain our own liability: to ourselves, to others, and to the environment. Whenever horses leave damage, their hoofprints leave behind proof of the culprit. We can run, but we can't hide.

The good news is that there is plenty we can do about securing our rights to public trails. By practicing what basically amounts to good manners (and good public relations), horsemen can do more good than harm. Be aware and respectful of the environment and other users. Set a good example for other riders to practice good horsemanship. Make it a habit to carry everything out that you carry in, as well as any other litter you come across on the trail, whether it comes from horsemen or four-wheeler riders.

All of these things help to upgrade the image of horsemen on public trails. The single most important thing you can do, however, is to join your local horsemen's association — and if there isn't one, start one.

CHAPTER 8

Trail Vices

⊱—◦—⊰

IF YOUR HORSE DEVELOPS NASTY HABITS ON THE TRAIL, take responsibility and take action. You can rehabilitate almost any bad behavior with a good plan and a steady hand.

A horse, though, is a notorious tattletale. He stores away every mistake you make in one of the most unrelentingly accurate file systems on earth — the equine brain. Then, when you assume that he has long since forgotten "that incident at the mud hole," it all comes back to him. And you. He will remind you that you tried to whip him through it last time, and that, given the right amount of lift and torque, you can be abruptly dislodged precisely mid–mud hole.

The Nature of Vices

Trail vices are those bad habits that some horses act out on the trail. The origins of these "bad behaviors" are almost always in the horse's natural survival instincts. They don't think about how to be bad, they just react to any given situation in the way that nature has prepared them to. It's how *we* react to and shape their instinctive behavior that matters. The funny thing about "trail vices" is that they are most often trained-in behaviors. Before you shake your head in doubt that anyone would train a horse to shy, stumble, balk, or toss his head, remember that every session with a horse is a training session. The question is who is teaching what to whom?

Horses, like people, pick up odd little habits that, while they may seem just incidental, are actually intentional behaviors serving some end. If your horse has bad trail habits, such as **jigging** (that infuriating habit of picking up a choppy trot when you want him to walk), shying, and **balking** (refusing to move forward), he has picked these up because they serve some purpose, and because his rider has allowed them.

"Oh, no, no, no, not I," you say. "I smack him with the whip every time he shies at that mud hole." If that is your experience, this chapter should be a valuable one for you. For the most part, punishing a horse that shies or refuses to execute a command only reinforces his idea that something awful will happen if he steps in that mud hole. This is a classic example of how we inadvertently "train in" trail vices.

CHALLENGING DOMINANCE

On the other hand, another way we teach a horse to do something annoying is that we let him do it without effectively or consistently correcting the behavior. What we perceive as bad behavior may be the perfectly natural equine tendency to challenge dominance. Take, for instance, the horse that stops whenever he feels like it to munch grass.

One day, his rider is fine with it, as she is in a lackadaisical mood herself, but the next time she rides, she's in a hurry and finds it frustrating, thus jerks the reins or lays on the whip. The horse knows only that he wants the grass and that the rider unfairly doesn't want him to have it, so any time he *does* get away with a mouthful, he feels vindicated as the rightful leader of the team. In short, more than satisfying his hunger, he's showing you who's boss, and it ain't you.

Step into your horse's shoes for a moment and you'll see that as equines evolved, they developed behaviors that established and maintained their places in the herd hierarchy. Since full-fledged fighting could maim or kill, often as not opponents would settle for a dirty look or a threatening posture, and often it worked. Horses are masters of the bluff. It's just another method to get their way or, again, assert their dominance.

Many riders are intimidated by their horse, believing he will panic, fight, hurt himself, and so on. In fact, that horse has made a series of small discoveries about the ineffectiveness of his rider and developed a habit that asserts his own power over the rider. He has his rider buffaloed.

DON'T MAKE IT A HABIT

So does this mean you should knock the tar out of your horse the next time he daydreams and stumbles on the trail? That's not the sort of thing a leader worth following would do. This chapter is about relating to problems before they become habits.

The truth is, if you blame the horse for something that you have allowed to become a habit, you lose the chance to correct it. When a horse goofs up the first time, it could just be an accident, or he really is just having an off day, or is tired or sore, or any of a number of other things that can account for some of the more common trail vices. But if you allow a behavior to continue until it becomes a habit — a conditioned response — then the credit is all yours.

Among the most annoying and potentially dangerous habits that a horse can pick up on the trail are shying (whirling, bolting, bucking, or rearing), head tossing, stumbling, avoidance of being saddled or mounted, stopping, refusals, jigging, and nipping at foliage along the trail. Even minor vices can cause major vexation. The worst thing about head tossing, stumbling, jigging, and nipping at foliage is that those habits divert the horse's attention from the trail (a serious danger on steep trails or unstable footing) and from the rider. Inattentive horses trip, bump into other horses, rub their riders into trees, and commit countless other irritations. Their riders must constantly keep after them to pay attention, which cuts down on the enjoyment of the ride.

THREE EXPLANATIONS

If your horse doesn't do what you ask of him — or chooses to do something else instead — consider why before you react. There are only three reasons a horse doesn't cooperate.

1 He doesn't understand what you want.

2 He does understand, but he can't do what you ask. For instance, he may not be physically able.

3 He understands, but he doesn't want to do it.

This last reason doesn't instantly translate into a lack of respect for you as his leader. It could also signal fear, anticipation of discomfort, fatigue, or other valid reason to resist. And never underestimate your horse's innate ability to assess the natural world. If he smells cougar and you insist he move toward it, his senses will argue with your sense*less*ness.

It's up to you to figure out what is going on when a horse doesn't respond as you ask, and to act accordingly. Punishing a horse for your own lack of communication may eventually elicit the response you want, but it makes you less of a leader

A Vice Can Arise from . . .

- Insufficient training/inexperience
- Physical problems
- Lack of confidence
- Inattention
- A dominance challenge
- Bluffing

in his eyes. In addition, ignoring his superior senses could have dire consequences for you both.

The first thing to resolve is whether your horse's behavior could stem from a physical problem. A horse could stumble because of a conformational flaw such as long toes or he could have tender feet after a fresh shoeing job with a close trim. Lameness, illness, or a sore back could inspire him to stop and be reluctant to proceed. Something gouging him under the saddle could cause him to jig in an effort to escape the discomfort. Poor technique (see chapter 5) could be cueing him to move away when you mount. Flies buzzing relentlessly around his head could make him toss his head in frustration. Be a responsible partner and make sure your horse is not trying to tell you that something is wrong before you assume he needs to be corrected.

Despite all of these possibilities, the number one reason for bad behavior on the trail is simply a lack of proper training. The good news is that some of the best training your horse will get is out on the trail and you can correct bad behavior as you ride along. Just be sure your horse is "broke" to the basics mentioned in chapter 5. A horse that doesn't understand when or how to stop, go forward, or turn will be a lot harder to control out on the trail than in the arena. It's a lot safer, smarter, and more effective to train your horse in the basics at home before you hit the trail. He will know how to handle himself, have a more confident attitude, and not be rattled by every little distraction.

Shying

Shying can be as mild as a sudden snort or as drastic as a sudden bolt for the hinterlands. A horse that puts on a dramatic ballet when he shies can be a real challenge to stay on top of, especially if the rider was daydreaming, too. Shying often arises from inattention; the horse suddenly notices something in his field of vision and because he suddenly noticed it, in his mind it just *suddenly appeared* and jumped right out there. (Of course, if you've ever flushed a grouse or pheasant on the trail, it sometimes does happen just that way.)

WHAT'S GOING ON?

When something startles your horse, his first involuntary reflex is to stop. The autonomic nervous system shuts down all movement — even breathing — to focus the senses on the potential threat. While it may take only a heartbeat, the impulse to whirl, bolt, buck, rear, or stand and watch further is a semiconscious one. Your challenge is to intervene in that split second between *STOP* and *GO!*

The decision to take off (**flight response**) is an instinct shaped by what the horse has learned. Smack him for bolting and he'll know to run faster next time. Try this the next time he bolts: Stop him, move him away from the source of his panic, allow him to stand at a comfortable distance and observe, then reward him for his bravery. Next time he just might want a closer look at that spook. Reshaping instinctive behaviors means you have to be calm, fair, and, above all, clear and consistent.

If your horse is prone to shying, you must stay alert in the saddle. This may not seem like the best frame of mind for a relaxing trail ride, but it can be therapeutic. If you are forced to keep your mind on your horse, your eyes and ears on the trail ahead, and your butt firmly in the saddle, you are a lot less likely to worry about taxes, step-kids, or last night's failed meat loaf. Focus can be a very good thing.

THINGS TO CHECK

How a horse shies is just as important as *when* he shies. A confident horse will hold his ground, snort, collect his thoughts, and possibly investigate. An equine scaredy-cat may leave you in a heap and vanish over the horizon. Shying usually subsides with experience, as the horse gains confidence both in himself and in his rider's ability to guide him safely through the perils of the trail. But if it persists as a habit, odds are your horse is more interested in dislodging a load than in fleeing from imminent peril.

Vision problems can contribute to shying. "Floaters" are visible in the eye of the horse. They can cause unclear images that seem to suddenly appear out of nowhere and startle the horse. Who can blame him when mysterious shapes float past, suddenly appear and disappear, or when part of the field of vision suddenly blacks out? Another vision "problem" is that a horse with eyes set more to the sides of his head has limited forward, binocular vision. His brain is processing two images at once,

Allow your horse to look carefully at whatever it is that terrifies him.

and he may not get a good look at something until he changes his perspective, sometimes suddenly.

Good vision is a must for a trail horse, although people have enjoyed trail riding on a one-eyed horse. Any trail horse with limited vision must have exceptional confidence and trust in his rider.

PREVENTIVE TREATMENT

The best way to deal with shying is to desensitize the horse ahead of time with progressive, controlled challenges. Build up his confidence by setting up spooky obstacles in the pasture, paddock, or barnyard that he can approach on his own terms (see Scary Things in chapter 5). When out riding, don't focus on the spook; keep your attention about 20 feet ahead of it. Reward your horse for bravery and ignore cowardice.

A common mistake is to punish a horse when he shows fear. Nothing says "See, I was right, that tarp *is* dangerous!" to a horse more than getting clobbered for trying to run away from it. As he learns to accept that there are weird things in your world, you can work your way up to confronting obstacles more directly. Let him sniff or nuzzle

---

| TRAIL TALE | *Spooking in Place* |

A few years ago I brought home what I thought was a "green-broke," part-Arabian mare we called Daisy. She was just so pretty that I couldn't wait to ride her around the neighborhood, especially since two of our neighbors raised Arabians and I wanted to show her off. I saddled her up for her first jaunt around the neighborhood.

Heading out the driveway, Daisy shied at the gate, then at the spot where the gravel driveway met the blacktop road, then at each and every crack in the road, at the ditch, and — I kid you not — at her shadow. To say I was "alert" is an understatement. Every quiver in her body, every flick of her ears, every snuffle, snort, and sigh kept me on the edge of my seat. Cracks in the blacktop that had been filled in with tar were especially suspect. Apparently, to Daisy they looked like seams just waiting to open up and swallow us whole.

Later, I found out that "green broke" didn't mean she had been actually *ridden*. Not realizing that this was her under-saddle debut, I was simply relieved that each spook alarmed her less than the previous one, and that in about an hour we made it all the way around the block without being swallowed.

The positive side of Daisy's spooking was that she had enough presence of mind to **spook in place:** In other words, when frightened, she never tried to whirl, run, or buck. She would just make a sudden stop, shudder, and snort. If a horse *has* to shy, that's the best you can expect.

Lack of experience and confidence is a common reason why horses shy in the first place. Daisy's spookiness was due to the fact that she had been thrust into a strange new environment without fair preparation. Had I known the true extent of her training, I would have started much differently.

All along the streets of my neighborhood I used to tell Daisy that I was the bravest of the brave and as long as she was with me she had nothing to fear. Tell your horse he can trust you. Say it out loud. Say it proud. The neighbors may laugh, but your horse just might buy it.

Herd Dynamics

Herd dynamics can have a strong effect on how a horse reacts to a perceived threat. A dominant mare is always on guard for predators, even in a 5-acre white-board-fenced pasture, with a herd of one or two other horses and a goat. That is her station in life as it has been for thousands of generations of horses. The same goes for a stallion. His purpose in life, aside from procreating, is to protect his herd.

Horses that fall lower in the pecking order must rely on other, more dominant, herd members. It is infinitely easier to persuade a less dominant animal (such as Daisy) to trust your judgment than it is a more dominant one (such as May, page 187). Less dominant individuals are already programmed to accept another's protection and authority. It takes more time and firmness with a horse that questions your authority, but the rewards are worth it. Once you assert yourself as leader to a dominant horse, you have an outstanding trail-riding partner.

things if he wants. Pet, praise, and reward him the instant he succeeds. It doesn't hurt to reinforce his courage with a treat. His thinking will be diverted from "fear" to "food."

DEALING WITH SHYING

Knowing how to react when your horse shies means knowing your horse and understanding his motivation. A horse will tell you he is frightened with wide eyes, flaring nostrils, and rapid breathing. Never punish a horse for reacting out of fear or you will only reinforce the fear. A stubborn horse, one who has learned to shy because it serves his purpose, will have a hard look in his eye. He knows exactly what he's doing. The seasoned trail horse that goofs very often, on the other hand, will look embarrassed or apologetic. Horses that enjoy their work have a sense of pride in what they do.

When your horse does shy on the trail, the most important thing you can do is stay mounted. Try to

relax. If you "stay on" by throwing the reins in the air, bear-hugging his neck, and clamping your legs with your heels in his flanks, you have a new set of problems.

If you are thrown, your options are limited by whether or not you are injured and how easy your horse is to catch. Do not turn around and go home; that sends a very clear message to the horse — rider off, ride over. If you can get back on and continue, try to do so in a relaxed manner and chalk it up to experience. If you are hurt, be sensible and keep your own well-being as a top priority (see chapter 10).

Assuming you manage to stay seated, how you proceed depends on the horse. If he is a seasoned trail horse and was just momentarily inattentive, let him know he blew it. A verbal reprimand in a disapproving tone of voice and possibly an open hand against his neck will tell him you didn't appreciate his reaction. (You'll need excellent timing to correct him in mid-spook.)

If the horse is inexperienced and truly afraid, remain as calm as you can. Lie to him if you must. Act, talk, or sing as though the spook was no big deal. Don't try to force your horse near something that frightens him, but do give him ample opportunity to look, sniff, and get as comfortable with it as possible. Let him stop and stare if he is so inclined, but do not allow him to whirl, bolt, or pitch a fit. Be ready for his reaction and act accordingly.

CHANGE HIS FOCUS You may have to employ some creative horsemanship to get past the spook, now that it has revealed itself. Remember, your goal is to ride *past* it, not up to it. Keep your focus, physically and mentally, on the trail ahead and your horse's focus on you.

To get his attention back on you, ride away from the spook and ask for three or four different maneuvers, one after the other, and praise him for each successful execution. Ask him to back and turn on the haunches. You'll never get a more enthusiastic turn on the haunches than when a horse wants to get away from something that spooked him. Take advantage of the incentive and ask for the turn *away* from the spook, not toward it. Circle and collect going away from the spook, then stop him far away from the spook so that he is still reasonably calm and ask for the head down. Praise him well, and once he is calm (he may start licking or chewing, or his breathing noticeably slows), ask him to move forward, toward the dreaded spook.

You may get only two steps closer to the spook, but take what he offers and then ask for some other maneuvers again, culminating with the head down. You may be able to get entirely past the spook in this way, which is preferable since it reinforces not only your dominance, but also your horse's opinion that you really can keep him safe. For all he knows, it was that perfect sidepass that saved you both! It might take you an hour to ride past a shiny tin can in the grass, but it will be an hour well spent, asking for — and receiving — obedience and trust from your horse, even if it is literally one step at a time.

LEAD HIM PAST THE PROBLEM Getting off and leading your horse past a spook is always an option. Horses generally lead past scary things more easily than they pass them under saddle. Just seeing you go first and not get eaten may be all the proof your horse needs that he can pass safely . It also reinforces your herd-leader status, as the lead mare would be the one to guide the herd safely past danger in a natural herd situation.

The downside is that once you are off your horse, you're on the ground. He can step on you. If he shies and tries to get away, you are at the mercy of your grip on the lead or, worse, the reins, which seem awfully short when trying to lead a nervous horse. (It's always a good idea to carry a length of rope on a trail ride. See chapter 7 for other essential items to bring along.)

If you do opt for leading your horse past a spook, go forth with an air of confidence. Your goal is to wrest your horse's attention back onto you and to proceed past the spook in a calm, controlled fashion. Lead him away first, ask him to back and turn on the haunches, and finally ask for a head down, rewarding him each time he complies with a soothing word and a stroke on the neck.

OTHER SOLUTIONS If for whatever reason you really can't get him past the spook by riding him through it, there are other options. If you are riding with other horses, let a calmer horse take the lead and your horse may follow him. If your horse is really freaked out or stubborn, you may have to **snub** him (tie his head tight to the saddle of the other rider) to a larger, stronger, calmer horse and actually pull him down the trail. This is not as traumatic as it sounds, because his attention will be diverted to the other horse and to keeping his feet under him. Once he is past the spook, ask for a few maneuvers to get his focus back on you, reward, and continue on your way.

Lead him past the scary object.

Other tactics to try are:

* backing your horse past;
* riding in a two-track so that his head is away from the spook;
* blindfolding your horse (something I have never tried);
* smearing a dab of mentholated jelly under his nostrils to disguise an olfactory spook (something that smells bad).

Regardless of how you do it, once you are past "the spook," reward your horse with praise and a stroke on his neck as you continue to move forward up the trail. If you don't make a big deal of it, chances are he won't either.

Finally, some horses make a habit of shying because they have learned that by shying they get out of work. Show them the opposite. If a horse shies at something as a matter of habit, ride him past it over and over and over again, until he is sweaty and noticeably tired. Make him trot, canter, collect, back; drill him hard. Sternly admonish him when he acts silly. Reward him only when he passes the spook without incident; praise him and allow him to finally move on up the trail. Most horses will quickly figure out that obedience allows him to simply walk along, whereas acting just the least bit dramatic will cost him serious effort.

Shying can be caused by inexperience, attitude, or even vision problems.

Bolting, Whirling, Bucking, Rearing

When a horse shies, he may spook in place, lock up, snort, and stare, the way Daisy did (see page 183), or he may react more dramatically, as May did (see page 187). Bolting, whirling, bucking, and rearing are not always initiated by the horse shying and are worthy of more explanation.

There are some important things to keep in mind with such potentially dangerous behavior.

Even though only 20 percent of equine-related fatal accidents result from bucking or rearing, such shenanigans should not be allowed to persist. However, only good, experienced horsemen should attempt to reschool a horse that bolts, whirls, bucks, or rears out of habit. Not only is it dangerous, but it also calls for a level of experience and skill that you can't get from any book. You will need an excellent seat (so you don't get dumped), superb timing (so you can correct at just the right moment), physical strength (again, just to stay on and execute any necessary corrections), a confident attitude, appropriate knowledge, and a strong heart.

WHAT'S GOING ON?

Just as for shying, it helps to know why your horse reacts as he does in order to be able to effectively correct the behavior. Several factors play a role in his decision to bolt, whirl, buck, or rear: your horse's age/maturity, level of training, natural degree of nervousness or level of confidence, and his trust in and respect for you. A onetime incident, while requiring all the same attributes listed above, can be nipped in the bud and considered a positive learning experience, whereas a *habit* requires planning and expert reactions.

To a frightened horse, bolting, whirling, bucking, and rearing are all perfectly legitimate responses to a death threat. They can also be considered progressive reactions. Bolting and whirling can be a direct expression of the "flight instinct" or they can be established habits that the horse has learned will unseat the rider and reward him by ending the ride. Bucking and rearing are instinctive reactions to a sudden attack by a predator leaping onto the horse's back. If first attempts reward the horse by unseating the rider, bucking and/or rearing can become a habit, taught and reinforced by poor handling.

In the old days, horses were saddled and "bucked out" as part of the breaking process. They bucked, reared, and ran around desperately trying to unload the "threat" on their back until they were exhausted. That method worked for the time and place in which it was used, and the experienced cowboy had little trouble sticking to the saddle. The horse learned two things from it: how to buck and rear and that bucking and rearing didn't

get the desired results. Horses that buck and/or rear as a matter of habit have learned a very different second lesson.

If you pay attention and know how to read your horse, he will give you fair warning before he bolts, whirls, bucks, or rears. His ears will prick forward,

---

TRAIL TALE *Buffaloed*

Be aware that some factors can *influence* (not cause) shying: how the horse is feeling, his condition, and his rank in the herd hierarchy, and for mares, their cycles.

May, a show horse, didn't have much confidence in Shaun, her young owner, outside of the show ring. Professionally trained in an indoor arena, she was secure in that environment but questioned every decision Shaun made on the trail.

On one ride to their regular practice area, down a lane about a mile from home, she spied a scrap of paper in the grass. Just prior to that she had walked past a large brush pile next to the lane without even seeming to notice, but when the breeze barely rustled that piece of paper in a horrifically terrifying manner, she managed a pirouette fit for a prima ballerina. May wasn't one to spook in place. If she was going to do something, she did it with flair. She was also very athletic. She had the unique talent, so sought by rodeo stock contractors, to simultaneously leap, twist, gain altitude, and relocate yards away from the point of liftoff.

They landed well past the frightening paper, luckily with Shaun still attached, then proceeded down the lane, out through the pasture as though nothing spooky had happened at all, and went through their routine

of walk, jog, lope, collect, extend, change leads, and flying changes. Finally Shaun couldn't think of anything else to work on and resigned to head back down the lane toward the danger that lurked in the grass.

Around the bend, they both saw it at the same time. The neighbor who lived on the lane had lit that pile of brush and had a splendid bonfire going that all but blocked the way out. May's head went up, she sniffed the air, but she never missed a step and calmly proceeded to walk within inches of roaring flames while bits of paper and ash floated heavenward and sparks crackled.

Why did the paper freak her out but the fire did not? Consider the horse's point of view. On the way out, May knew they were heading to their "workplace." She was fresh from the pasture and feeling pretty spunky. She was also a show horse, which meant she was full of good grain. Horses on good feed have high spirits. An undernourished, calm horse may have a completely different demeanor when well fed. On the way home, May was heading where she wanted to go, had the kinks worked out, and was tired.

The real problem, though, was that May had Shaun buffaloed. She had more confidence in herself than in her owner, and so did Shaun.

he will look intently in the direction of whatever is bothering him, his muscles will tense, his steps become stiff and/or exaggerated, he will sidestep, snort, or otherwise tell you, "Look! A horse-eating monster! What are we going to do?" If you don't give him an acceptable answer pronto, he may decide for both of you to make a hasty exit, or he may decide he can make a quicker getaway without you along for the ride.

BOLTING

Running away, or **bolting,** is scary because the horse takes off at top speed and you have no control, but it is the easiest to stay on of the four evasive maneuvers. A horse that bolts through dense woods or on a steep, narrow, or otherwise difficult trail is either scared out of his wits or wise to what he is doing. You have to know which in order to deal with it. Bolting into traffic is especially dangerous. Try to stay calm and recover control of the horse if it is safe to do so. But be aware that there are times when an emergency dismount is the best option.

When your horse bolts, you have only a split second to react. Your first instinct should be to get him back under control before he builds up speed. Do not pull back steadily on the reins; at this point he will push back against the pressure. Instead, pull back and forth on one side, then the other, giving and taking, as this doesn't give your horse anything to lean against. Try to get him to circle as you pull and release one rein, as any response to your cues will help to bring him back under control.

If there is a hill nearby, try to get the horse to head up it to wear him out faster. I've heard of one gal driving a runaway smack into a river to slow her down.

A popular technique is the "one-rein stop," which in essence pulls your horse's head around and disengages (throws off balance) the horse's hindquarters. Be aware that if the hindquarters are not disengaged, the horse can continue to run full blast, straight ahead, even with his head yanked clean to your boot, with the added danger of not being able to see where he is going.

An old cowboy cure for runaways was to ride it out. Once the horse began to tire, he was whipped, spurred, and urged forward at top speed, sometimes literally until the horse dropped. Most horses never tried it a second time. One problem with this solution these days is that a bolting horse can cover 2 or 3 miles before he lets up, and most of us just don't have that much uncluttered space in which to ride.

PREVENTIVE TREATMENT If a horse has a habit of bolting, work with him extensively in an arena before you venture onto the open trails. Concentrate on transitions from slow to increasingly faster gaits, until he will stop every time, precisely when you ask, even at a dead gallop. A runaway horse often develops the habit from being ridden with too much pressure on the reins. As soon as you let up pressure on the reins, he takes it as a cue to take off. Work the horse as you normally would, and then when he is somewhat tired, ask him to walk on a loose rein. Any time he speeds up, take up contact again, but as soon as he cooperates, slacken the reins. When the lightbulb comes on as to what you are asking of the horse, you will see a real change in his attitude.

WHIRLING

When the horse rocks back on his haunches and executes a sudden, impromptu pivot on the hindquarters, it is known as **whirling**. (Even in the heat of the moment you may find yourself thinking, "Gee, I wish he'd do it this well on cue.") This alone is enough to unseat you because it suddenly throws you off balance, but since a bolt for parts unknown often follows, it's best to try and get control of the horse before he can really get going.

Take advantage of his momentum and try to keep him turning in that direction. Circling a horse is a good way to bring him back under control while letting him know he did wrong. Push with your legs, pop him with the whip on the rump, and cue on the inside rein.

Settle for five or six circles and don't overdo it, as tight circles are very hard on a horse's joints and tendons, and can mentally frustrate the horse. If you can get him under control by circling, break out of the circle at the point of your choice, ride forward a few yards, then circle him again, in the opposite direction. Then switch directions again. Your best bet to discourage whirling is for your horse to connect it in his mind with lots more whirling, circling, and hard work.

If you can't get him back under control quickly, the next step in his repertoire is most likely to bolt. See text at left.

STEP-BY-STEP TECHNIQUES | **The One-Rein Stop**

To be effective the horse has to learn the one-rein stop *before* there is an emergency!

1. Begin by sitting on your horse at a stop and pulling his head toward your knee with one rein (see drawing). He will likely move his hind end away from the direction of the rein pressure.

2. Sit straight, give no leg cues, wait for the horse to stop moving, and reward as soon as he does by releasing the rein pressure and praising. Do this several times on both sides.

3. Repeat the lesson until he stops moving every time you pull his head around. Then progress to asking for the one-rein stop at the walk and eventually at faster speeds. The faster he is going, the less bend you should have to ask for to get him to disengage the hindquarters and stop.

Pull your horse's head toward your knee with one rein (step 1).

BUCKING

Bucking early in training is a direct result of the horse running out of options. When a horse bucks early in training it is because he is nervous and confused, usually because he has been pushed with more than he can mentally handle. His tension signals a danger warning to his brain and instinct takes over. On the flip side, a lot of horses buck because they feel good! Healthy, well-fed horses that are confined, then suddenly saddled up, often need a chance to "work out the kinks " beforehand. Turnout time is the best, as the horses can run and buck at liberty. Bucking on the longe line is still misbehaving, but the horse can be worked out of it. Bucking under saddle should never be tolerated.

Horses that buck out of habit have learned that this behavior gets them out of work or relieves either physical or mental pain. Horses quickly figure out that if bucking ends the ride, it will also end back pain due to a poorly fitting saddle, or foot or leg pain from carrying the weight of the rider, or even mouth pain due to poor hands on the bit or teeth that need floating. If bucking ends the ride, that's also an end to being yanked around, pushed, overfaced, frustrated, or worked into the ground. Be sure you do not make bucking your horse's best option.

Because a horse gives a lot of warning signs before he bucks, you have a pretty fair shot at preventing it. Before a horse bucks, he clamps down his tail, hunches up his back, throws his weight forward, and puts his head down. He may do so in one violent thrust (especially if he's an old pro at it) or he may sneak his head down or even politely ask first.

The best way to prevent your horse from bucking is to keep his head up and keep him moving forward. Divert his attention with a change of gait and direction at the first hint of a buck (usually tensing up and "hunching" the back). Try either to keep him moving forward or to rock his weight onto his haunches. A horse can't buck when he is off the forehand. Ask for a trot to the left, a rein back, or a turn on the haunches. Don't stop or get off; these are rewards to the horse. Keep his head up; he has to get it down to buck, but don't yank up violently or you could divert him right into rearing. Keep him working if you can, and if he does buck, pop him hard on the rump and holler "No!" in your most disapproving voice. When he moves out, praise him and ask for something he does well so you can fully reward him. Another trick is to pony a horse that is prone to bucking so that the pony horse can keep him moving forward if he threatens to buck.

It's best if you can prevent a horse from bucking altogether by discouraging "pre-buck" behavior. Sometimes this works, sometimes it doesn't. There are times when you have to let the horse buck in order to make the point that he had better not do that again.

Like all other training sessions, teaching your horse not to buck should be set up to your best advantage. To work with a bucking horse, find a place with soft footing. This is not just to make

Warning signs of an imminent buck: head down, weight on forehand, back tense and hunched.

your landing softer, but it can also wear out the horse so that you might not even *need* it as a landing site. Deep sand, snow, or even water can help to wear down a horse that thinks bucking will get you off his back. Work your horse as usual, but try to pick something you know he doesn't like. Unfortunately, getting him in the mood to buck may not seem fair, but lots of horses tolerate unskilled hands, working in circles, and repetitive requests, without resorting to a bucking fit. If you know what pushes your horse's "buttons," push. Then reward when he performs or correct when he retaliates.

Most horses that buck now and then aren't really that good at it. They crow-hop — stiffening their legs, dropping their heads, and pushing up and off with their hind legs. A good rider can keep her balance and correct the horse, then move on to the work at hand. Few and far between are the hardcore bucking horses that will buck with any rider, any time, anywhere, until they unburden themselves. But even they can make good trail horses.

REARING

Rearing may be the most dangerous thing a young horse can do because he doesn't have the physical development or equilibrium to balance on his hind feet. The rider's reaction can contribute to the loss of balance and result in the horse actually going over backwards. When rearing is a habit, the horse has learned to keep his balance and probably knows just the right moment to rear in order to lose a rider or avoid something on the ground.

THINGS TO CHECK If your horse has a rearing problem, first check the bit. Be sure it doesn't pinch, have sharp edges, or bump into teeth. If you use a curb chain, be sure you can insert two fingers between it and the horse's jaw and that it lies flat

---

TRAIL TALE *Extreme Measures*

Shaker is a Quarter Horse gelding that came to my brother, Brian, as a hardcore bucker, destined for the killer pens. The owner had been the victim of an unscrupulous horse trader, and after suffering a broken arm just wanted the horse gone. Extreme problems call for extreme measures, and considering that the horse's next stop was the glue factory, Brian figured that extreme measures were called for.

He took the horse into a round corral and started to "tease" and intentionally frustrate the horse. It didn't take long before Shaker blew a fuse and did what he knew best. He rocketed, pitched, twisted, and leapt. Brian stayed put, while applying corrections appropriate to the level of the behavior. In his own words, he "crucified that horse." He spurred and whipped the horse every time he bucked and then egged him on to do more. When the dust cleared, Shaker was bleeding, trembling, exhausted, and seriously rethinking what his bucking had accomplished.

The point of this story is one often overlooked in modern horse-training manuals: Sometimes you have to do what it takes to solve the problem. I didn't learn of Shaker's reputation as a rodeo prospect until the end of a very pleasant trail ride, throughout which he was my ideal trail mount. One experience can change a horse's life and, as in this case, literally save it.

with no twist. If the horse is being ridden with a long-shanked curb, be aware that this alone in the wrong hands can cause the horse significant pain. For correcting a horse after rearing, a snaffle bit works best, because you are going to use it to pull the horse's head around, and a shank bit makes that more difficult as the leverage of the shank twists the bit in the horse's mouth if you pull from the side.

RETRAINING A REARER Breaking a confirmed rearer is potentially more dangerous than breaking a horse from bucking because the horse is already off balance when he's misbehaving. If you (or your trainer) are going to attempt it, make it count the first time and you may never have to repeat it.

As with bucking, if the horse has made a habit of rearing, he does so because it works for him. To break him of the habit you have to allow (or incite) the problem in order to correct it. Again, only a very experienced rider should even attempt to punish this kind of bad behavior. Riding out a rearing horse requires exceptional confidence and balance. For a chronic offender, follow the suggestions above, but carry a riding whip or 2-foot section of dowel in one hand. When your horse begins to rear, you'll feel his weight shift to his hind feet. As soon as his front feet clear the ground and you have your balance, clobber him — hard — right between the ears.

Your goal is to connect with enough force to make him believe he has hit the unseen ceiling of the world, to knock him off balance (forward), and to make him think twice about doing it again. You have to be forceful, but not brutal. It's unlikely you can actually hurt the horse with a riding whip or small stick given the difficulty in bracing in order to deliver an effective whack at this angle in the instant you will have to do it. But if you are afraid of really doing damage, a "bat" (wide leather type of riding whip designed to make a loud *crack!* when slapped against the horse's hide) is a plausible substitute. It doesn't have the sting of a whip or the impact of a dowel, but the loud noise may be enough to dissuade further attempts. Choose your aids according to the severity of the problem, as it's better to enjoy the benefits of one effective correction than to have to do it again.

Balking

Although the causes can vary greatly, the signs of balking are easy to recognize. The horse simply stops and refuses to move.

WHAT'S GOING ON?

Stopping can be caused by confusion, distress, fatigue (especially with a young or inexperienced horse), inattention, laziness, or a bald-faced vote of no confidence.

THINGS TO CHECK

Refusing to move forward can be sign that a young horse has been pushed past his physical and/or mental limitations. All the cajoling, cueing, and punishment in the world won't budge the poor animal if this is the case. Being out of condition, such as in the spring after spending a winter off duty, can also contribute. If you are riding a young horse that suddenly stops, give him a few

Handle with Care

Incompetent handling is the major cause of any bad behavior with a horse. Very often you simply can't expect a trainer to fix the problem because she won't experience the problem. The trainer knows what she is doing and communicates (by her attitude and technique) that she knows what she is doing. Have someone knowledgeable explain bluntly what you are doing wrong, so you can learn a better way of doing things.

moments to catch his breath and his thoughts. Don't ask for anything for a few minutes, then cue him to move forward. If he still will not proceed, check for signs of physical distress (see chapter 4).

DEALING WITH BALKING

A horse that stops due to inattentiveness is the easiest to move forward. A quick pop of a riding whip or rein or a nudge with the spur will remind him that stopping is not the most comfortable thing he can do. The best way to discourage a lazy horse from stopping whenever he feels like it is to make stopping more work than going. Allow him to come to a stop, but every time he does, forcibly cue him into a trot (or gait) and make several circles in each direction, ending back at the point where he stopped. This actually makes more of an impression than constantly urging a lazy horse forward.

Another reason a horse balks is because he just doesn't want to go where you point him. This is called a **refusal.** Common refusals are mud and water. Refer back to chapter 5 for ideas to persuade your horse to step on something (for example, backing, leg yielding, being ponied by another horse). If all else fails, climb off and lead. But be sure you proceed in the direction of *your* choice.

Head Tossing

A horse that tosses his head can ruin your ride. Flip, shake, flop: restlessly tossing his head in the air, over and over again. You grit your teeth.

STEP-BY-STEP TECHNIQUES	Teaching a Horse Not to Rear

When a horse rears up with you, here's what to do.

1. Keep your balance forward (see drawing).

2. Don't yank back on the reins — that will only help to pull you both over backwards.

3. Do grab a handful of mane, stand in the stirrups, and lean forward alongside the horse's neck as far as possible while you shout "NO!" in an angry (not terrified) voice.

4. As soon as the horse touches down, force him forward.

5. Don't let him stop. Stopping is the first thing a horse has to do to rear up. Forward momentum prevents upward momentum.

6. With your hands low, direct him around by the bit into a circle. The idea is to enforce forward momentum while controlling the direction. Circle him as fast and hard as he'll go. This is punishment for a serious offense.

NO!

Keep your balance and your cool (step 1).

Riding down the trail, he shakes his head for the umpteenth time and jerks a rein out of your hand. As you lean over his neck and grab it, he steps on the end of the loose rein. His head is pulled back between his knees as the momentum of his stride carries him forward. He jolts his head back up, snaps the rein in two, and smashes the back of his head into your nose just as you are in perfect position to grasp the dangling rein. These are the moments that challenge your imagination to come up with a better story explaining why you are riding home with a bloody nose.

WHAT'S GOING ON?

Most often the "cure" for head tossing is a matter of figuring out why your horse is doing it. It may be a direct result of discomfort, which he is doing his utmost to communicate to you, or it could be the equivalent of an obsessive/compulsive habit. Sometimes just the memory of pain is enough to ingrain the habit; at other times a horse tosses his head because it gets him something he wants, most likely a break in the work.

THINGS TO CHECK

First, run through the following checklist to be sure he doesn't have a legitimate problem with discomfort.

Check the bridle. Be sure the browband isn't riding up into his ears or pinching his ears. Be sure his forelock is braided or secured under the browband, as it can blow back into a horse's ears and tickle.

Check the bit. If it is too narrow, it will pinch the corners of his mouth and your horse will toss his head in an effort to get away from the pain.

Check for bugs. Flying insects can drive horses to distraction in hot weather. Be sure he is protected with a good insecticide or a fly mask. Small midges that lodge in the ears and feed on blood can cause extreme sensitivity. You can spare your horse a lot of misery by carefully cleaning his ears, treating him with a product that kills as well as repels flies, and fitting him with a fly mask with ear covers or using the ends of nylon stockings over his ears (tied together between the ears, and then to the halter, or together under his jaw).

Check his teeth. Be sure the bit is not banging into teeth, and that your horse is not suffering from painful wolf teeth.

Check the reins. Avoid heavy reins that can put constant (confusing) downward pressure on the bit. Don't use reins that snap to the bit. Sometimes just the constant rattling against his teeth is enough to drive a horse batty. Use lightweight reins that buckle to the bit.

Check the reins, again. Probably the most common cause of head tossing is a rider who keeps

---

TRAIL TALE | *Snickers-Style*

Some horses balk with style. Snickers, a Quarter Horse gelding belonging to Lynne Pomeranz, of Corrales, New Mexico, shifts into reverse rather than just stop and refuse to move. Lynne believes he isn't afraid; he is asserting himself as leader by dictating in which direction they travel.

Lynne's solution is to ride him through it and when he is finished backing, she makes him back more, and more, and more. The habit is rare these days with Snickers, because he knows that his rider will decide which way they will go, for how long, and at what speed.

nagging pressure on the reins, so that the horse is in a constant battle for his head. Give your horse enough slack in the reins to move out.

Check his eyes. Vision problems, including floaters, can make the horse think he is dodging something aimed at his eyes.

Check the saddle and pad. If the saddle is pinching at the withers, your horse may toss his head in an effort to free himself from the constriction. Look and feel along the saddle pad for any foreign objects that might be sticking him in the back.

Check other gear such as a breast collar and noseband for bad fit, rubbing, or sticking.

Consider allergies. Does your horse toss his head more on a clear day with a light breeze than in overcast weather?

DEALING WITH HEAD TOSSING

Often the original cause of head tossing gets lost, and it then becomes a compulsive habit. It is tiring for the rider to correct each and every toss of the head, but that is exactly what it takes to make it stop. A tug on the reins, a snap on the neck with the reins or riding whip, and a sharp "No!" with each head toss will eventually make the habit uncomfortable enough for him to stop. Some folks find that switching to a slightly harsher bit while breaking the habit pays off in that the tug on the reins draws.

One old trick is to feed the ends of the reins through the rings of a snaffle bit and leave it floating on the reins under the horse's neck. As soon as his head flips up, the bit sails along the length of the reins and automatically smacks into the horse's jaw at the exact moment his head goes up. He quickly learns that "toss" equals "ouch!"

Stumbling

It's not unusual for a horse to stumble — occasionally — on the first few rides of the season, which can be enough to rattle an otherwise pleasant trail ride. But after a few rides most horses

Thread the reins through the rings of a snaffle bit under his head. When he tosses his head, it will smack him.

savvy up, and their condition and coordination improve with the exercise so that the problem self-corrects. Often a horse will handle a ride well until the last mile or so, or until the terrain gets more challenging, and then suddenly missteps several times in a short distance.

Fatigue catches up with all of us a lot more quickly when we are out of condition. Give your horse a break. Loosen the cinch (or girth) and let him stand and breathe for 10 or 20 minutes. Over time and with proper conditioning, he'll be able to cover more ground before he tires.

WHAT'S GOING ON?

A horse that stumbles loses control of his feet, if only temporarily. This could be due to how he is ridden, inattentiveness, conformation, inexperience, fatigue, lack of condition, laziness, illness, poor vision, sore feet, or improper shoeing or trimming. Regardless of the root cause, stumbling almost always catches the rider off guard and throws both horse and rider off balance, which can cause the horse to fall, especially on steep trails or in difficult footing. Give me a horse that knows where his feet are any day.

Young or inexperienced horses are more prone to stumble because they often lack the physical condition, coordination, and mental alertness of a more experienced trail horse. They get tired, they misjudge the trail, or they look off in the distance and not where they are placing their feet. This type of stumbling will correct itself over time with additional conditioning and practice on the trail.

Don't push a young or out-of-condition horse too hard for the first few rides of the season.

A lot of horses stumble because they just haven't learned to pick up their feet very well. This is most common in horses raised in stalls or level paddocks and horses that have spent their lives just standing around. A horse that hasn't physically experienced dips, bumps, and inclines in the trail has no way to know they exist until he does. You can help your horse realize that it is important to watch where he places his feet and to master precise control over them by setting up ground poles or other obstacles as discussed in chapter 5.

THINGS TO CHECK

As always, check first that you are not somehow causing the problem. Be sure you are not throwing your horse off balance or allowing him to do it himself. An unbalanced rider makes for an unbalanced horse, especially on steep hills and difficult footing (see chapter 9). Horses that tend to be heavy on the forehand (lean most of their weight onto their front end) from either habit or conformation (see chapter 2) are good candidates for stumbling even on a flat trail if there are dips, roots, or bumps in the path.

An unfortunately common cause of stumbling is improper hoof care. Improper trimming in which the flare of the hoof is not removed can leave the horse's feet too big and cause him to stumble. A horse with long toes (and usually correspondingly low heels) will often catch the end of his toe as his hoof breaks over if he doesn't lift his hoof high enough (which is extra effort and will tire him all the more quickly on the trail). This is one of the few "downsides" to trail-riding show horses, especially types that are kept in extreme shoes, such Park horses, Fine Harness horses, and the "performance" horses of the gaited world. Shoes devised to exact extreme lift or breakover have no place on any but the most placid and well-groomed trails.

Of course a horse can have long toes and/or low heels simply due to inadequate or infrequent trimming. A trail horse needs to be kept trimmed and (depending on the terrain) shod on a regular schedule of every 6 to 8 weeks. Otherwise, horn growth in the hoof gradually alters the impact of his hoof, which strains supporting muscles, tendons, ligaments, and bones of the hoof, legs, shoulders, hips, and back.

Any horse that tends to break over too late in his stride, such as an older horse, or one with arthritis or limb soreness, is a candidate for stumbling. Sometimes conditioning helps, other times simply rolling (rounding off) or rocking (angling) the toes when shoeing helps the hoof to break over sooner.

A stumbling horse may be telling you that his feet hurt. This happens easily with barefoot horses ridden over hard, rocky, or gravelly terrain, as the soles are easily bruised. It happens when a horse is trimmed too closely (the hoof wall is filed too close to the sensitive white line tissue of the hoof, or the sole is dug out too deeply) or if a shoe nail is "quicked" (driven into the white line). Sore feet can also be an early warning sign of road founder or laminitis. Sore feet can be helped with pads, but be aware that pads cost traction, as they eliminate the natural cup of the horse's sole. Always use rim shoes with pads — they allow dirt to pack in over the pad, offering better traction than rubber (or synthetic) pads alone.

Other sources of pain, such as back and leg pain, may cause a horse to stumble, as can certain types of illness. If a horse stumbles routinely, be sure to have your veterinarian check him over thoroughly.

DEALING WITH STUMBLING

A lazy or inattentive horse, or one who has learned he can make you get off if he stumbles, is a different matter. If your horse just hasn't figured out that where he puts his feet is his responsibility, or worse he has figured out that he can get out of working by bungling a few steps, he needs to learn that it's easier to watch his step. Work him over the ground poles at home and when he taps an obstacle, pop him with a dressage whip with enough pressure to let him know he goofed. At the same time, tell him "No!" in your "you-blew-it" voice. If you are coordinated enough to pop him on the leg that stumbled, some trainers feel this is a quicker way to relay your displeasure, but most horses will put together the verbal reprimand and the whip correction fairly quickly wherever they feel it.

Avoid the almost universal reaction of yanking up on the reins when a horse stumbles. You want him in the habit of carrying his head low enough to watch his footing.

Jigging

I once had an Appaloosa mare that jigged so much, I actually wound up teaching her a second bad habit (which was easier to break) to get her over the first one. I'm not sure if that's creative horse training or just desperation.

WHAT'S GOING ON?

Jigging — or more accurately jig-g-g-g-g-g-ing — is the most annoying habit of half-walking/half-trotting in short, choppy steps when you want the blasted horse to walk. (Gaited horses do the same thing, only with slightly less jarring.) It can arise from several causes but often seems to become an end in itself. The horse just gets used to doing it.

The most common causes of jigging are poor training and poor riding. A horse that is pushed too hard in early training or is given inconsistent aids in a rushed or inappropriate attempt to teach "collection" often develops nervous habits, including jigging. A heavy-handed rider or a bit that is too severe for the horse can also lead to frustration for the horse as he is cued to hurry up and slow down at the same time. A nervous rider who constantly hangs on the reins will inevitably teach the horse to ignore or push back against the pressure.

A tense horse makes the situation all the more stressful, and the horse virtually can't contain himself. With tension his head goes up, his back hollows out, and he takes short, choppy, often higher-than-normal steps. This posture is strenuous to the horse's body and can fatigue and strain muscles; it doesn't do your muscles any good either. A horse that constantly jigs is exhausting to ride.

THINGS TO CHECK

Sometimes a poorly fitting saddle is to blame. A saddle that pinches at the withers and bars that dig into his back — common with a too-small saddle — can irritate the horse to the point where he does whatever he can to get away from it. Saddles, like ladies' swimwear, must fit properly in order to do their job well. (See chapter 3.)

DEALING WITH JIGGING

The best way to cure a horse of jigging is to prevent it from becoming a habit in the first place. But if you are faced with a horse that already has the habit, after ruling out any physical discomfort your objective is to demand obedience in your choice of gaits. Avoid cantering a "jiggy" horse at first, as the added rush of excitement can be counterproductive, but do give clear signals for a walk or trot and insist that he follow them.

Sometimes just letting a horse trot out (or gait) for a while helps to burn off excess anxiety (and energy). Bring him down to a walk for a few strides, then cue him back to a trot. As he tires, he will see the opportunity to walk as a reward. Any time he starts to jig again, instantly cue him to trot (or gait). Work on extending and collecting the faster gait, then bring him back down to a walk again for as long as he will maintain the gait. Some horses *love* to trot and will last longer than you will. For them, try the opposite approach.

Each and every time the horse jigs, stop him in his tracks and ask for three steps backwards, then stop him again and have him stand. Allow him to go forward only on your cue. He will fight you. He will fuss, fidget, and possibly even pitch a fit. This was Mariah, my Appy mare.

Mariah was fine to ride around the pasture, but around the neighborhood trails she was a basket case. She would get so worked up that I was constantly on guard, and she would jig so roughly that my spine hurts just thinking about it. She could trot for 75 miles straight (give or take), so stopping her on command was my best option. Then she would prance in place, toss her head, snort, and just generally show her impatience to get on with it. I worked with her and tried everything. After a dozen or so rides, I finally had her to where she would stop, back, and stand until cued to move forward, but inevitably she would be jigging again within a few steps. It was exasperating and uncomfortable, and I had just about run out of ideas when I happened to stop her in a lovely green clump of grass.

We stood for several minutes, until she finally noticed and plunked down her head. A few minutes later I cued her forward, but then stopped her in the next green clump about 15 feet away. Within 10 minutes she was stopping of her own accord at every inviting patch of grass. Her attention was diverted from jigging to "pigging" (out). After several days of this (and feeling really silly), I started to correct her for stopping on her own. A mild nudge was all it took and she would walk a few more steps to the next clump. After another week, she hardly dropped her head at all, and the next week she was sold.

Snacking

You might be thinking, "Hey, I enjoy a nice snack on the trail myself. What's the big deal?" For the most part, this particular habit may not seem all that bad, it's just a horse doing what a horse does naturally, and in the case above, it actually came in handy. But nipping at grass, stems, foliage, and buds along the trail is a habit that should be nipped in the bud.

WHAT'S GOING ON?

When a horse sneaks a snack on the trail his attention is not on you or the trail. It's on his stomach. Horses often keep walking while they snake their heads up, around, or off to the side for a choice morsel and can easily lose their balance. One horse I rode literally tripped over his own head when he put his head down to eat and kept walking. That's another bloody nose that was embarrassing to explain.

Another reason to quash any unauthorized munching is diet control. Not every lush green leaf on the trail is good for your horse, but in his zeal to grab *something* he won't be as discriminating as he normally would be. Toxic plants along roadsides and trails are common in many areas (see chapter 9 and appendix).

Really, though, the only reason you should never allow your horse to eat when he is working is that it is a blatant, albeit seemingly insignificant, defiance of your authority.

THINGS TO CHECK

How you counter this habit depends somewhat on your horse. It helps if you know that your horse isn't hungry in the first place. Feed him before you ride. A hungry horse is bound to try to eat.

DEALING WITH SNACKING

The best deterrent for a lazy horse is a sharp cue to move out every time he reaches for a self-designated treat. Stay alert and warn any riding companions of your plan ahead of time. Your horse will quickly realize that his snacking is costing him calories.

An alternative is to devote a training session to eliminating the vice. Carry a dressage (long-handled) whip and pop him on the nose whenever he grabs a mouthful, then quickly reach down and remove the foliage from his mouth. Keep your balance. If he is dropping his head to reach for a snack, you are in the added peril of being caught off guard and sailing over his withers if your momentum doesn't stop at the same time his does.

Drape the reins over the saddle horn, or tie his head up by a lead rope so that he has enough freedom to walk along on a loose rein, but not enough slack to reach the grass with his mouth. Any time he starts to drop his head, correct him with voice, whip, and a *slight* tug up on the reins. Let him know in clear terms to pull his head back up where it belongs and keep his attention moving forward down the trail.

Calling Out

A horse that neighs at every other horse within earshot can be a real headache. From shrill whinnies to gutsy neighs, horses' voices carry very well, and not every rider wants her approach heralded around every bend.

WHAT'S GOING ON?

This is yet another bad little habit that boils down to the horse's attention not being on you. It is often a problem with young or insecure horses, or with "herd-leader" types that feel they need to let every horse in the vicinity know of their reigning status. Such a horse needs to learn that proper horse etiquette calls for keeping one's whinnies to oneself.

A young or nervous horse will usually settle down after a few rides, but many horses have never been taught not to whinny or call out to other horses.

DEALING WITH CALLING OUT

The best way to discourage your horse from neighing at other horses is to hush him every time he does it. You must be clear and consistent. Since he is in "verbal mode," verbalize your displeasure loudly and correct him physically. Pop him with a whip or spurs and keep his attention and movement forward. Pulling him into a tight spin every time he gets verbal will discourage him. Other horses, he should learn, are none of his concern.

Barn Sour/Herd-Bound

A horse that is **barn sour** or **herd-bound** is one that is reluctant to leave the comforts of home or his herd mates, or both. It is important to realize that this is about as basic an instinct in horses as eating, and at times, just as tough to discourage.

WHAT'S GOING ON?

Horses are deeply ingrained with the need to stay with the herd. Straying off alone could result in getting eaten, their all-consuming fear. So if your horse resists leaving other horses, he isn't trying to misbehave; his need is real. Likewise, horses resist leaving home because of the combination of their sense of security at home and their fear of the unknown. Again, this is understandable from an equine evolutionary standpoint, but a horse with that attitude is no fun to ride.

Unfortunately, horses that are barn sour or herd-bound will also employ many of the previously mentioned "trail vices," from balking and calling out to rearing, whirling, and bolting. Correcting the problem calls for a methodical approach to avoid those extremes and win your horse's confidence and respect, even if it's one step at a time.

DEALING WITH BARN-SOURNESS

As with overcoming any "vice," begin your training session with something your horse does well. Rack up compliances and build up his cooperation. Here are some suggestions.

* Reward him for each well-done maneuver, and then gradually ease him away from his comfort zone.
* Ride out just a little farther each lap around the barn or yard, and pay attention to his demeanor.
* Turn toward home at your discretion, not his.
* Watch for any early warning signs of tension.
* Encourage just a few extra steps out with each lesson as he expands his comfort zone.

How long it will take to get him to walk confidently away from home depends on the horse. But the idea at the beginning stage is to gain his compliance and to prove to him that you won't let anything outside of his comfort zone eat him.

After you have managed to enlarge the area in which he feels comfortable, place a reward about 20 to 50 feet outside of his normal range, before your next outing. His familiar feed bucket with about 2 cups of sweet feed makes a welcome treat,

---

STEP-BY-STEP TECHNIQUES

Curing Barn-Sourness

This technique, called an **intermittent reward,** is one of the most powerful motivators known to behavioral science.

1. Fill the grain bucket, then ride out and let him discover somewhere new. Repeat. Usually by the third repetition, the horse heads straight for the bucket.

2. On the next lesson, move the bucket farther away from his old comfort zone for three or four repetitions, then farther on the next lesson and farther yet on the next.

3. After about a week of always placing the grain bucket farther and farther away from the barn, take it away completely on the second or third repetition. Ride out and allow him to discover his reward as before, but on the next repetition (same lesson) leave the bucket empty and praise and stroke the horse as reward instead. (See drawing.)

4. Take him home and repeat, this time with the bucket refilled.

5. Over the week or two, place the bucket farther and farther away from home, sometimes with grain, sometimes without, gradually cutting down the number of times there is grain.

6. By the end of 2 weeks, plan on placing a bucket of grain out for your horse only once in a great while to reinforce his confidence and trust in you.

After a week, leave the bucket empty and reward him with a good scratch instead (step 3).

and odds are he will make a beeline for it as soon as he sees it. As you work in gradually larger circles and patterns, let him "discover" his reward, and give him ample time to relish it. As soon as he finishes, return to the barn and let him stand tied for a while to ponder his discovery.

LEADING INSTEAD OF WALKING Some horses can be led away from the barn, but not ridden. If this is the case, try leading your horse on increasingly long walks away from the barn, with or without treats along the way. Stash some horse cookies in your pocket so that you can offer a quick incentive any time you sense your horse needs some inspiration. Just be very sure that you are safely able to control your horse on the ground if he is nervous about leaving home.

A less severe form of barn-sourness is when a horse leaves with little or no fuss, but prances, jigs, or bolts on the way home. Anticipation is your enemy here and a horse can best be dissuaded from hurrying home if there is no reward in doing so. Enforce the gait of your choice, even if that means backing home. Ride past your driveway or lane (and be prepared for the balking and whirling that might accompany this) back and forth several times. It helps to start out the ride by riding out the driveway, then back and forth past it, rewarding the horse with a treat only after he is away from home. Whatever you do, don't hurry home, don't reward the horse with feeding or turnout as

soon as you get back, and don't allow him to turn into the driveway of his own volition. Turn him on the haunches away from the driveway, back him away, side pass . . . whatever it takes for you to maintain control of your direction of travel.

Always make homecoming as undramatic as possible. A lot of people make the seemingly harmless mistake of allowing a horse to rush home or of feeding a horse as soon as he gets home. These signal to the horse that it is better to be home and thus contribute to barn-sourness. Instead, leave your horse tied for 10 or 20 minutes after you ride back to the barn, or bring him back and work him hard. He'll soon stop wanting to rush home.

Separation Anxiety

When it comes to curing your horse of separation anxiety from other horses on the trail, the trick is to make it as gradual and uneventful as possible. If you ride with other horses, rotate who leads and who follows and occasionally stop your horse when he is behind until the other horses are out of sight. Arrange with your riding partners that when you are out of sight, they are to stop and allow you to catch up, and then do the same drill for them. Gradually increase how far away you expect your horse to work from his companions and for how long.

CHAPTER 9

The Nature of the Trail

⊱⊶⊙⊷⊰

PART OF WHAT MAKES TRAIL RIDING OUR SPORT OF choice is the opportunity to commune with Mother Nature. Sometimes, however, her bag of tricks can make trail riding miserable. If you don't occasionally come home wet, muddy, dehydrated, bruised, or battered, consider yourself lucky.

The conditioning and training you undertook in chapters 4 and 5 will serve you well in challenging situations, as will the close partnership you are developing with your horse. There are additional strategies to prepare for and cope with weather extremes and nasty surprises. Here's how to be ready for whatever the ol' gal can dish out.

Trail Conditions

Different types of trails present different types of challenges, and they can change with the season. Having a game plan will increase your confidence, which tells your horse he is in good hands. Consider these tips for conquering the lay of the land, whatever it might be.

WET AND WILD

Water, mud, and bogs all have the ability to swallow your horse, and he knows it. Teaching your horse to cross water at home will help, even if you teach him to cross a puddle and then meet a river on the trail. His positive memories of the experience should help you ease him through a bigger, faster-moving "puddle."

RIVERS, CREEKS, AND STREAMS The nice thing about finding water on the trail is that it gives your horse a chance to drink and stay hydrated. A thirsty horse will more eagerly approach water. See the box on the next page for some guidelines for handling rivers, streams, and other water systems that cross your path.

Often, getting your horse into the water is the tough part. Once they realize it isn't going to devour them, most horses relax pretty quickly. It helps tremendously to have other, water-savvy horses lead the way. If worse comes to worst, you may have to pony a horse across (see page 143). Crossing a river alone on a green horse is not advisable unless your life insurance is paid up.

Leg wraps or support boots can protect your horse's legs if you must ride where slippery rocks are a hazard (such as rocky-bottomed creeks).

GREEN HORSES AND OTHER CHALLENGES You may have to ride along as close to the water as your horse will go and then stop and stand long enough for him to settle down before you ask him to move closer. After a series of stopping and moving closer (and wishing you had

brought something to read), eventually you'll reach the water's edge.

Once there, allow your horse to stand and watch the water for a while. When he seems at ease, ask him to move forward with gentle but firm cues. Ask him to put his head down so he can sniff or, better yet, drink. Don't rush him into the water, as he could slip. River bottoms can be made of anything from sharp, loose rocks, to soft sand to sucking mud. As he approaches and enters the water, let him have his head so he can navigate his feet.

A different problem is a horse that has learned that if he balks at water, no one will call his bluff. It's important to know your horse. If he is spoiled and refusing because it earns him what he wants, make sure it doesn't. Spurs or a pop of the whip can make the water seem much more inviting.

A more experienced horse can successfully lead one that has never crossed a river.

If he paws, push him forward quickly. I found out the hard way one hot August day that a horse that paws the water is *not* merely splashing for the fun of it. He has something else in mind. He's thinking, "Gee, this stuff is nice and cool, and my back is hot and itchy. I think I'll just roll around in it for a while and see how good it feels."

MUD Mud sucks. It pulls at your horse's shoes, drags at his muscles, bones, and ligaments, and

Crossing Rivers on Horseback

Your horse will hear and smell water long before you perceive it. You'll be one step ahead of him, therefore, if you have familiarized yourself with a map of your route well before the trip.

APPROACHING WATER

- Choose water crossings carefully. If you are fording a stream or river, find a shallow edge with a gradual approach. Horses are bound to become anxious about the crossing if they have to slide 50 feet to reach it.
- Don't let your horse rush down the bank. A controlled descent is safer for both of you, and more environmentally responsible, than a headlong dash.
- Find the widest spot of the river to cross, as wider areas are generally smoother on the bottom and have slower-moving water.
- If the current seems swift, begin crossing several yards, or more, upstream from where you want to come out of the water. The current will push your horse downstream, making it almost impossible for him to walk straight across.
- If the water is more than 2 feet deep, remove any tie-downs, martingales, draw reins, and other gear before you cross. **Never attempt to cross deep water with a tie-down on your horse.** If his head goes under, he won't be able to pull his head up out of the water. Extraneous gear can get tangled up with your horse if he falls.

GETTING ACROSS

If you're traveling in a group, the most experienced riders (and horses) should go first and last, with the others in the middle. And if the water is deep or fast moving, think twice about just how much you need to get to the other side.

- As you cross, keep your eyes fixed on where you want to come out. Not only does this help your horse focus, but it also keeps you from staring at the water, which gives a lot of people vertigo.
- Keep a centered seat and do not move around unnecessarily. Your keeping your balance helps your horse to keep his.
- Leave plenty of room between your horse and the one ahead of you. Crowding excites horses and interferes with their watching their footing.
- If there are large rock slabs on the river bottom, steer your horse toward the center of each rock slab, which is less likely to cause a wobble.
- Expect that your horse will slip, and be ready to soothe him when he does. If you aren't surprised by a minor slip, you'll both handle it better.
- Finally, be ready, God forbid, should your horse go down. Keep your feet loose in the stirrups in case you have to bail off, and try to go off his rump if you do. If you go off the "upstream" side, the current could pull you beneath your horse.

generally feels to the horse as if it wants to draw him into the very bowels of the earth. It is little wonder that so many horses try so hard to avoid it. Horses that willingly cross clear water will balk, shy, or otherwise refuse to set hoof in the dark, pulling abyss of a mud hole.

Sometimes you can find a way around a muddy patch of trail, but often other horses trying to skirt the rim have already tramped even the very edges of the trail. Besides, as any conservationist will tell you, it's better to stick to the main trail.

Try to approach a muddy spot in the trail calmly to avoid exciting your horse. The calmer he is as he approaches and enters, the less likely he is to panic or hurt himself when he feels the pull of the mud. Some people don't mind trotting or cantering through shallow mud, but the faster they go, the more of it they carry home with (or on) them.

Since it's easier for your horse to slip at higher speeds, common sense says it's better to walk through mud. If your horse refuses, try backing him into the mud and asking him to stand for a few moments before turning him and walking out. As always, if more-seasoned horses are with you, let them lead the way, or pony a reluctant horse through the mud.

BOGS Bogs can be particularly unpredictable and should be avoided if at all possible, and entered only with extreme caution. Horses sometimes get stuck and you should be ready to bail off. Approach calmly, and consider tying your horse at a safe distance so that you can check boggy spots on foot before attempting to cross.

BRIDGES

Bridges may seem like the perfect way to avoid water, mud, or bogs, but they can turn out to be obstacles themselves.

Bridges on the trail can be frighteningly flimsy affairs. Before crossing any unknown bridge, dismount and walk up to check it out. Better an

---

| TRAIL TALE | *Man-made Dangers* |

A man-made reservoir can be a death trap. One day, Danielle Poe was riding her horse, Blue, near her home above Lake Coeur d'Alene in north Idaho. They rode a little farther from home than usual and came across a man-made pond. Blue wasn't one to shy away from a little water; in fact, he loved it. So when Danielle gave him his head to reach down for a drink, he plunked right in, rider and all.

The water was deep, and Blue couldn't touch down. With Danielle in the water next to him, Blue started swimming around the edges, looking for a foothold to climb out, but the pond had been dug out by machinery and the edge was a straight drop. Danielle quickly realized there was no way to get her horse out of the water, and she stayed with him for an hour that must have seemed like an eternity, eventually having to pull his head out of the water with the reins to keep him from slipping under.

Then something truly amazing happened. A farmer on a tractor appeared over a rise. He hadn't seen the near tragedy in the water, but had just happened along. With his help, Danielle was able to pull Blue out of the water. Both survived; they were incredibly lucky.

intentional water crossing now than a surprise one later. Look for missing planks, holes, and loose, missing, or rotten support beams. Be sure there are no gaps between boards wide enough to allow a hoof to slip through.

Walk across by yourself to be sure the bridge feels stable at least with your weight. This has the added benefit of allowing your horse to see you cross the bridge. Remount and approach the bridge as though you expect your horse to walk right across; allow him to put his head down and watch his feet. Never rush over a bridge, because the extra force could rattle the structure. Be especially careful when crossing a wet or icy bridge to avoid causing your horse to slip.

Bridges on the roadway can be a challenge, as you have the added concern of traffic (see chapter 6). Try to gauge traffic so that you are not crossing the bridge along with any cars. The hollow sound under his hooves may be enough to startle your horse without the distraction of traffic noise.

Never rush across a bridge on horseback.

Cross at a walk or controlled jog. Be ready to dismount and lead if you don't feel safe in the saddle.

If you are riding with another horse that is more traffic-savvy than yours, ask your riding buddy to take the lead to the inside of traffic. Ride with your horse's head about even with the lead horse's stirrup, which puts the other horse between your horse and traffic.

GATES

Gates on the trail are usually there for one reason: to keep livestock on one side or the other. If a gate is left open, it is probably intentional. It might be that there is stock in a lower pasture that has access to water only in an upper pasture, or it might be that some ninny ahead of you on the trail left it open. The best thing you can do is leave the gate as you found it; if riding over private land, especially if you see signs of livestock, notify the landowner of your concern. Provided you had permission to ride there in the first place, most landowners are happy to know that someone is looking out for their interests. If possible, ask in advance if there are any gates or other things to be aware of when riding on private property.

Opening gates can be done from horseback, as described in chapter 5 (page 133), or on foot. It all depends on the situation when you get there.

ROCKS

Rocks, rough footing, and hard surfaces can injure your horse, often in ways you can't see until the next day or later. Working a horse on hard surfaces can strain muscles in his legs and back. Never run a horse on a paved or blacktop road. The concussion can damage his joints.

The best way to handle riding over rocks is to avoid them, even if it means making a detour around a stretch of trail. If you can't bypass a rocky area, and you know in advance that you will have to go that way, consider protective shoes for your horse (see page 214). Pads under your horse's shoes help protect him from sole bruising.

Keep your horse at a walk through rocks and rough footing and give him his head to pick his way through.

MOUNTAIN TRAILS

Mountain riding combines several challenges at once, including steep hills, narrow trails, switchbacks, high altitudes, and the potential for snow and ice. Any one of these can challenge and tire your horse, but put them together and they make for a serious test of his training and conditioning. Practice on gradually increasing slopes, and by the time you hit a steep hill in the mountains, you both should have the knowledge, skill, and coordination to handle it.

Your most important task on hills, up and down, is maintaining control of your horse's speed. Never let your horse rush up or down a hill; keep his speed in check. When riding with other horses, be sure everyone knows to wait for other riders at both the top and bottom of each pull, or else the other horses may rush to catch up.

Keep your weight forward when riding uphill.

GOING UP When riding uphill, give your horse's back a break by standing in the stirrups and leaning forward slightly. It's easy for a lazy, tired, or insecure rider to settle back against the cantle. Don't be that rider. Your horse will appreciate your keeping your weight forward. Some hills are simply too steep to ride safely, so don't rule out leading your horse up. Make sure your horse knows how to lead by following at a distance or off to the side, or he could step on you. Another alternative is **tailing,** whereby the rider, now on foot, holds on to the horse's tail and the horse actually helps pull her up the hill. Again, this is a skill you want to practice at home. Huffing up a steep hill is not the time you want to learn that your horse kicks if you pull his tail. If the hill is both long and steep, find a spot (or two) along the way to stop and let your horse blow. Turn him sideways so that he can balance his body and fill his lungs.

GOING DOWN Riding down steep hills requires caution and balance. Lean back just enough that your body is parallel to tree trunks (perpendicular to the ground) and keep your weight in the stirrups. Often, especially with youngsters, a horse will get increasingly disjointed going downhill until he breaks into a clumsy trot. This is a sign that he is putting all his weight on the forehand and stringing out his hind end as if it was just accidentally following him along. Slow him and shorten his strides by asking for a little collection on the way down, then give him his head. Half halt at various points if he gets ahead of himself again. He needs to keep his hind end beneath himself in order to balance his and your combined weight.

While you should give him enough rein to be able to move his neck as a counterbalance, don't let him pull his head down. Don't allow him to go downhill with his head up and/or his back hollowed, either. This causes undue stress on his body and forces him out of balance.

NARROW, STEEP TRAILS Narrow, steep trails and drop-offs are scary and potentially dangerous. If your horse gets fussy when he's in a spot like this, it's better to follow behind him (using a long lead line for control) or to pony him from another horse.

Try not to pass anyone on a narrow steep trail. Use common sense: Whoever is closer to a safer, wider spot on the trail should backtrack to that spot if passing is necessary. In the event you must go backwards, it's easier for a horse to turn in a tight spot than you might think. Just be sure to turn him with his head toward the downhill side so he can see where to keep his feet. It's scarier but safer than turning him into the hill.

Lean back only slightly when riding downhill.

SWITCHBACKS Switchbacks are "those zigzag trails that loop around the trails that go straight up and down mountains." Or at least that is how some people seem to perceive them. Switchbacks are built not only to ease the grade at which users have to climb or descend, but also to help preserve the integrity of the trail itself. Switchbacks spare your horse the stress of a long, steep climb or a perilous descent, but the trade-off is more steps to get up or down the mountain.

Always use the switchbacks instead of cutting corners, for your horse's sake and that of the trail itself.

HIGH ALTITUDES High altitudes are nothing to sniff at. Altitudes above 6,000 feet can make some people and horses accustomed to lower elevations feel weak, and altitudes above 8,000 feet can cause altitude sickness. Especially if you plan to ride away from home, know the elevation of the trails you've chosen. If you will be tackling the heights, here are some guidelines.

✴ Be sure that both you and your horse are in excellent physical condition.

✴ Allow yourself (and your horse) from 1 to 3 days to acclimate to the altitude before any hard trail riding.

✴ Be sure that both you and your horse drink plenty of water, but forgo alcohol (yes, your horse, too), as the effects are intensified at high elevations. The same advice goes for tobacco products and any other mood-altering substances.

✴ Eat a high-carbohydrate diet (your horse is all set here), wear a hat to negate the effects of the mountain sun, and bring along ibuprofen for you and phenylbutazone ("bute") for your horse.

✴ At the first signs of altitude sickness — weakness, disorientation, dizziness, nausea — or if your horse shivers, stumbles, or appears over-tired or confused, head downhill.

INTO THE WOODS

Riding in the woods, at any elevation, has its own roster of possible surprises. Here are some conditions you might encounter.

BRUSHY UNDERGROWTH Brush and thick woods can be tough to pick your way through. The main things are to take it easy and to keep a close eye on your feet and gear. A horse that tries to rub you off on trees can be dissuaded with a few good boots (or spurs) in the barrel should he get too close for comfort. Watch your boots and be ready to move a foot out of the way before your horse wedges it between himself and a tree. It's easier to discipline a horse when your foot isn't twisted and throbbing in pain.

Low, prickly brush can rake your horse's legs. Protective gear, such as splint boots, is a good idea if you have to ride through much of it.

One of my weirdest memories as a young rider was getting caught in an alder grove. The narrow-trunked trees grew within inches of one another and the farther into the grove we rode, the harder it was to find a way among the tree trunks.

Finally, I had to stop. We couldn't even turn around. Frightened and frustrated, I dismounted and tried to bend back the smallest trees , but once I was off my horse, she started weaving her own way through the trees. I let my horse lead the way and we were out of the woods in no time.

Watch the trail ahead and don't feel as though you have to plunge straight ahead. Even though the rules say to keep to the main trail, always let your common sense be your guide. Even familiar trails can become overgrown if it's a long time between rides.

BLOWDOWNS AND DEADFALL Blowdowns (downed trees) are common in wooded and logged-off areas. A horse that has already been taught to step over things and to jump (see chapter 5) will know how to carry you both over safely, but bear in mind that this is hard work for him. If

Dismount Where Footing Is Precarious

Be extremely cautious if riding downhill on unstable footing. Exposed mountain hillsides can be little more than glorified rock slides. If you have to stop on a steep hill and there are riders behind you, give them ample warning before you put on the brakes. There is no shame in walking where the footing threatens your safety. It's much easier for your horse to keep his own footing when he doesn't have your shifting weight to balance every time he slips.

If you decide to dismount and lead your horse downhill, keep him off to your right side, even if he is well behind you. Gravity is not always your friend, and if he should slip or trip, you don't want to be the first thing to break his fall. Or let him lead you, as you follow along with a long lead rope (or longe line) behind him.

Be sure to dismount, and remount, from the uphill side. This will put less stress on your horse's back. It really helps to have a horse that will tolerate you mounting from either side. Be sure to practice this at home; it feels awkward to mount from the right side when you are used to the left.

you have to transverse much deadfall, be sure to rest your horse periodically to avoid strains and muscle pulls.

DESERT RIDING

Deserts offer some unique challenges to both horse and rider, with the most obvious the need for constant hydration. Hot weather will evaporate your horse's sweat so fast you may not be aware how much he is sweating. Rest in shade where possible and offer water frequently.

Encourage your horse to drink well before you leave for the ride and again upon your return. If staying out for an extended ride or overnight, scout out water sources before ride day or plan to pack in water. Since each horse will drink 10 gallons — 80 pounds — or more per day, packing in enough water for an extended stay can be a challenge. If safe, natural water is not available along your route, consider dropping off a water cache (5-gallon plastic water bottles work well) at regular intervals. Some regular desert riders bury water stashes for their desert escapes.

Sandy footing is also stressful on your horse's limbs and can contribute quickly to fatigue. Take it easy in deep footing and monitor his attitude, degree of sweating, and temperature. Heat stress is another possibility. See chapter 10 for ways to recognize, and protect your horse from, this and other trail emergencies.

Finally, never underestimate hypothermia. Desert temperatures can plummet in the evening. Wear layers or bring along extra clothing in case you are caught out later than intended.

BEACH RIDING

Beach riding offers the same challenges to footing as desert riding does, but the biggest concern here is accessibility. Very few beaches are open to horses these days because of the public perception that horsemen are too hard on the delicate environment.

When granted access, ride on the beach as though you were on display. Every time you ride in a multiuse environment such as this, you represent all horsemen.

✴ Use exceptional manners and good horsemanship to maintain a good impression.

✴ Check out the rules of any individual beach in advance. You may need to avoid turtle nests or clam beds or the nesting grounds of rare birds.

✴ Carry out anything you carry in, and be prepared (with a shovel and a plastic bag) to bury or pack out manure.

The most obvious challenges you will face on the beach are other beach users, from kite flyers and ATV users to kids, dogs, and all manner of tourist activities. Horses eventually learn to ignore background silliness if it doesn't "get" them, but be prepared for anything.

For some horses, the sound and motion of the surf is disturbing. Don't push. Let him walk along as close as he is comfortable, and in time you will be able to ride closer and closer as the waves repeatedly fail to consume him.

Other challenges are indigenous to the beach environment. Check the tides before your ride to be sure you can ride where you want to when you want. Because wind is common along beaches, bring sunglasses or a scarf to keep the wind from your eyes and don't ride directly into the wind (usually coming in straight off the ocean).

When riding on a sunny beach, be sure to wear sunscreen and apply it to any white skin areas on your horse, especially around his muzzle and eyes. (Don't put sunscreen directly on his upper eyelids, however; it can run into his eyes.)

Ride on the beach as though you are on display.

Weather or Not to Ride

Lousy weather won't stop intrepid trail riders from meeting most of the challenges of the open trail, but if they have any sense, it will inspire them to prepare well and, in some cases, to reconsider.

RIDING IN THE HEAT

Hot, dry conditions present much the same challenges that desert riding does, even if you are riding only a few miles from home in Minnesota. The most serious consideration is your horse's need for water. (See Desert Riding, above.)

Something else to watch out for in dry weather, especially in the summer or fall following a damp spring, is dry grass. Standard keg shoes become skids on dead, dry grass, especially on trails where the grass has already been knocked flat by other horses. Never run your horse on slick grass, and be cautious walking down even a slight incline.

Even more than hot, dry weather, hot, humid weather creates deadly conditions for a hardworking trail horse. Hot air prevents work-generated body heat from dissipating efficiently; humidity can impede thermoregulation by as much as 90 percent at a time when it is most needed. While a horse's body can sweat to expel heat in dry air, in high humidity, when sweat evaporation is so compromised, he relies more on his lungs to help with heat expulsion. Dehydration is a serious threat in hot, humid weather, even though the air is saturated with water; heat exhaustion is another concern. Horses need much more water in hot, humid conditions than in more moderate temperatures.

Pay close attention to your horse's degree of hydration, respiration, and heart rate (see chapter 4). Don't force an exhausted horse to keep working. Try to rest in a shady spot, and if possible, sponge the horse's head and the underside of his neck with cool water. Bring along a sponge on a string, so you can drop it into a pool or stream. If you don't have a sponge, a wadded-up T-shirt will work.

RIDING IN THE WIND

Wind makes most horses nervous, to say the least. There are perfectly good reasons why your horse acts nutty, and understanding them might help you feel less like clobbering him and more like helping him overcome his natural fears. Or you may decide to wait for a calmer day instead.

Wind fouls a horse's early warning systems. It whips up strange and confounding smells, drowns out normal sounds, rushes against his skin, and makes things that normally sit still — leaves on trees, grass, debris on the trail floor, his rider's clothing — cavort deviously.

Proceed just a little more slowly than normal. Warm up your horse before hitting the trail, and odds are good he will cope.

Some horses stay on high alert as long as the wind blows. They are much more reactive than they would be normally. Others settle down as they get used to the distractions. Use discretion. Riding on a breezy day is one thing, but wind often heralds worse things to come, such as thunderstorms.

RIDING IN THE RAIN

Rain isn't much of a problem for most horses. I grew up right smack dab between Seattle, Washington, and Portland, Oregon. If I didn't ride in the rain, I might never have learned to ride at all.

The biggest problem for your horse is slick footing. Barefoot horses do well in damp areas, but it all depends on the quality of your horse's hoof and the terrain over which you ride. Blacktop gets horribly slick in the rain, as do rocks, bridges, and deadfall. (See Pavement and Your Horse, page 153.)

The biggest problem for you is keeping warm. This is a simple matter of dressing in layers, the outside of which should be waterproof, which brings us to one important consideration for wet-weather riding.

Desensitize your horse to rain gear. Practice untying, shaking out, and donning your slicker before you are out on the trail so it doesn't rattle your horse right out from under you. Because you must turn in the saddle, and your hands are full, it's easy to get unseated when putting on (or taking off) a raincoat, and darned if a slicker doesn't seem just like a scary tarp that suddenly pounces on your horse from out of nowhere.

Personally, I don't like poncho-style slickers. They are too easy to get tangled up in. I prefer a raincoat with sleeves.

Finally, be sure your horse is thoroughly cooled down after a ride in the rain. If he gets overheated

Accustom your horse to the idea that you may need to put on rain gear while sitting on his back.

and is not cooled and/or dry before you turn him out, he can suffer from chills and muscle cramps.

RIDING IN SNOW AND ICE

Snow and ice, whether in the high country or down the block, pose a real threat to your horse's traction. It's easier to maintain traction in snow than on ice, but snow can ball up under your horse's feet and turn him into a four-legged toboggan.

If you ride only irregularly, you can grease the underside of your horse's feet to prevent snow-balling. People report success with cooking sprays, shortening, silicon sprays (which have the disadvantage of acting as a hoof "sealant," preventing the sole from "breathing"), and petroleum jelly.

Many people prefer to ride their horses barefoot in snow. There is less chance of snow balling up under the hooves, and the snow itself provides some cushioning against normal wear and tear from the trail surface. Traction is certainly better than with normal shoes. But others prefer specialty shoes to keep their horses from crashing through the snow (see box on next page).

Even with traction devices, however, ice is treacherous footing. Avoid it if possible. When crossing ice, proceed with extreme caution, or dismount and let your horse pick his way without your added weight. Since ice tends to form in shaded or shallow areas where water collects, think ahead and avoid it. Ice and deep snow are least likely along the tops of ridges.

Frozen ground has essentially the same effect on your horse's body that hard-packed surfaces do, so ride accordingly. Beware especially cautious of refrozen snow. You yourself might be able to walk on its surface, but your horse will break through and the hard crust can actually cut through his skin. If you have to ride through it, consider leg wraps or support boots for your horse's legs.

Riding in the cold carries the risk of hypothermia or, at the very least, cold hands and feet for the rider. Be sure to dress in layers (long underwear is a plus) and to wear good-quality wool socks and gloves. Avoid cotton, as it clings and gets cold when wet. Small, chemically activated hand-warmer packets are wonderful. Slip one in each boot and each glove and enjoy a warmer ride. Insulated stirrup covers are also now available to keep your tootsies toasty.

CARE AFTER A COLD RIDE Proper cooling out is critical after riding in snow. A horse wet from sweat and melted snow (or cold rain) should be toweled and brushed off before being put up or trailered home, especially if he has a thick winter hair coat.

If you are trailering home after a snowy ride, pick out your horse's feet and add some wood shavings to the trailer floor to keep him from slipping on wet mats on the way home. Throw a blanket (made of breathable fabric) on him to prevent him from getting chilled.

Once home, make sure your horse is dry, then brush him out. Disturbing the hair adds air between the fibers and this insulates him from the cold. Feed grass hay to help warm him from the inside as he digests the fiber, and, of course, make water always available.

Store your tack in a warm, dry, well-ventilated place to keep mold from growing on it, and keep it away from direct heat or sunlight, which can make leather dry, crack, and curl. Don't allow latigos and girths to dry in a bent position. Consider keeping at least your bridle in a warm spot. Cold bits are a nasty surprise to your horse.

STORMY WEATHER

Thunder and lightning storms are not the time to be out riding. Lightning can be deadly and is certainly traumatic. In some areas, a sudden storm can bring on torrents of rain, leading to flash floods, trail washouts, mud slides, or at the very least a slippery ride home over wet rock or slogging through mud-choked trails. Having a section of trail drop out from you and your horse can be catastrophic.

Shoeing for Traction

There are many different traction enhancers and hoof grips on the market. Here is a brief overview.

- One traction aid is similar to studs on snow tires. Special horseshoe nails called **ice nails** extend beyond the flat undersurface of the shoe to provide added grip in snow or on ice. **Ice nails** are made of the same steel as regular shoe nails, but have a specially shaped head that works like a cleat on a sports shoe.
- **Dura-Tec nails** have a drop of ultra-hard tungsten or carbide steel at the nail head to bite into the surface. They are longer-lived than ice nails, but the head surface is much smaller, and they don't grip as well.
- **Screw-in studs** can be manually added before a ride in the snow. The farrier makes holes in the heels of the shoes and the studs are simply screwed in whenever you want to ride. You can select from a variety of sizes to fit your situation. Just remember to remove the studs when you're done riding. They alter the balance of the hoof, and your horse could easily hurt himself on the sharp edges.
- **Drive-in studs** work the same way, but are smaller than the removable types because they are meant to be left on all the time.
- **Borium** (tungsten carbide in brass) is a favorite among farriers and cold-weather riders alike because it will bite into any surface, from concrete to ice, thus providing traction. Your farrier can add as much borium as necessary to shoes to increase traction or combine it with pads to add protection from snow balling up inside the cup of your horse's hoof.
- Hoof grips are popular for those who ride through lots of hard-packed snow. They are added to the horseshoes as partial pads that go between the shoe and your horse's foot and work with the pumping action of the frog to push snow out of the hoof.

Other types of traction enhancers are built into the shoes. Talk them over with your farrier.

The main disadvantage of traction enhancers is the unnatural stress they put on your horse's legs because there is no natural give. The feet grip instantly. Beware of the "more-is-better" mentality. Too much borium on the shoes, for instance, can prevent the foot from rotating naturally after the hoof lands and the horse's body weight begins to move over it. This displaces the twisting force of the action farther up the limb, causing pain and lameness.

Regular snowball pads cover the entire bottom of the horse's foot and work best in dry snow that isn't prone to forming balls. These pads are most often used along with borium for added traction. Snowball pads are thicker and tougher than hoof grips and can be attached directly to the shoe. The main disadvantage is that they don't allow the hoof to breathe normally, and thrush may be a concern due to moisture buildup. Rim pads can help to prevent balling without covering the entire sole.

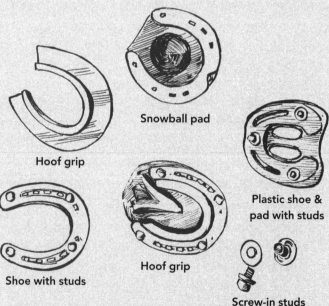

Snowball pad

Hoof grip

Shoe with studs

Hoof grip

Plastic shoe & pad with studs

Screw-in studs

Special snow shoes for horses are designed to expel snow and give your horse more traction.

While thunder spooks some horses and lightning can send them into a panic, most horses seem to take a storm in stride better than we do. After all, unless a horse is new to a storm-prone area, odds are he has lived through storms before and has been somewhat desensitized. If you remain calm about the noise and bright flashes, odds are your horse will, too. Your goal is to get yourself to cover and reduce the risk to your horse.

If caught in a storm, get off your horse and pull his gear. Metal attracts lightning; remove as much of it as possible. Since he is taller than you, stay away from your horse. Here is one time when it would be handy to have a horse taught to kneel! Don't tie him to anything taller than himself, unless he is in a grove of trees of uniform height.

If lightning seems imminent, don't lie down. Crouch with your feet together and your body in a fetal position with your hands over your ears. This gives the electrical current of a lightning bolt the smallest possible route of travel through your body. According to a *Back Country Horsemen* publication, if you so much as put your feet apart, "lightning can travel up one leg, across your chest and down the other leg." The idea is to have the smallest possible surface area of your body in contact with the earth.

RIDING IN THE DARK

Darkness is not nearly as scary for your horse as it is for you, since he can see quite well in low light. Use common sense, however, and don't gallop through unknown territory after nightfall.

If you feel that you need more light, consider desensitizing your horse to a flashlight (at home, before a ride) and carrying one with you. Glow sticks are another way to light up your path, and have the added benefit of making your horse visible in the dark. Snap the sticks to activate them and fasten (with twine or duct tape) one or two to the saddle or breast collar, and you will put on a healthy glow. Reflector tape on the back of your jacket and/or around your horse's legs or used as

Lightning Safety

If you hear thunder, lightning can't be far away. While you are exposed to the elements is not the time to try and outmaneuver a storm. Here are the basic rules every trail rider should memorize:

- If you are in high country, ride for lower ground, since lightning strikes the highest point.
- If you are in an open space, seek shelter in clumps of brush or trees, a ditch (unless filled with water), or even a dip in the landscape.
- Stay away from such potential lightning rods as tall, isolated trees; rises; water; tall objects and rock outcroppings; and other riders.
- Never seek shelter underneath rock ledges or in caves. Electricity can travel through mineral deposits.

a tail wrap will also make him more visible and could save your life if you ride along a road after dark. And don't forget those nifty glow-in-the-dark Glowbelt Biothane bridles and accessories.

Realize that it gets dark earlier in the woods, or along the east side of hills, than in open country, and keep an eye on your watch. Since anything can happen on the trail (or otherwise), it's quite easy to get caught out later than you intended. Good planning will help but can't guarantee everything will go as you may have hoped. If you intend to ride more than 2 miles within three hours of darkness, carry emergency overnight supplies with you. (See chapter 10.)

Poisonous Plants

Enjoying the flora is part of the trail-riding experience. Spotting trillium in the woods on an early-spring ride is a primal thrill for many of us. The beauty of summer wildflowers touches the heart of all who pass by. And fall colors can put even the most glorious summer floral display to shame. But unfortunately, some of those wonderful wildflowers are noxious weeds, just waiting to make your horse sick.

It depends on how long you ride as to whether or not your horse will need to eat anything on the trail. A well-fed horse will do just fine on a day ride without having to stop at all, although he will most certainly appreciate a snack along the way and the boost of energy that goes with it.

The easiest way to avoid accidental poisoning is not to let your horse eat anything on the trail that you haven't packed in for him. If you do let him graze, make sure all he eats is grass, and keep him away from unfamiliar plants. It's best to know the plants in your area, and if you are riding in a new place, ask about any plants that could harm your horse.

If you let him graze, make sure he eats only grass.

Different areas have different types of toxic plants, although some are all-pervasive. To learn about what toxic plants grow in your area, contact your county Extension agent, weed board, or local veterinarian. If you don't know what you might encounter, carry an illustrated field guide with you. Or you can photocopy the Guide to Trailside Toxic Plants in the appendix and stick it in your saddlebag.

Toxic plants that horses tend to nibble include bracken fern, buttercup, sweet pea, lupine, red clover, locoweed, and even some tree leaves. An occasional mouthful of these won't hurt most horses, but the consumption of significant quantities can cause distress. Horses not used to rich pasture can founder on an afternoon of grazing in a clover patch.

Not even all grasses are safe. The seeds of certain types of grasses (squirrel grass, foxtail) can become embedded in the horse's mouth or face and lead to painful abscesses. One type of fescue can contain nematodes (tiny parasitic worms) in the seed, making both the seed and the grass toxic, and another can be infested with endophyte (the fungus *Acremonium coenophialum*), which can cause poisoning. Unless you are competent to identify these plants' toxic stage, it's best to make it a rule *not* to let your horse graze on them on the trail.

Some tree leaves, including oak, red maple, black locust, and horse chestnut, are toxic to horses. Beware of tying a horse to a black locust tree, because horses have been poisoned just from chewing on the bark. Yew is especially toxic and horses have been known to collapse immediately. As little as ¼ pound, a mere mouthful, can be lethal.

Most poisonous plants taste bad, but a treacherous few are actually sought out by horses. Normally, most horses won't touch toxic plants like nightshade, milkweed, skunk cabbage, foxglove, larkspur, death camas, jimsonweed, oleander, spurge, St.-John's-wort, and tansy ragwort because these plants taste so awful — although there can be exceptions. For example, poison hemlock, one of the most lethal plants to horses (and other mammals), has a light, ferny texture that a lot of horses seem to enjoy and seek out, and most horses relish locoweed (and other types of vetch), which if consumed in quantity are toxic. They are most likely to grab these things when nipping foliage along the trail. If you train your horse not to sneak snacks, this will keep him from grabbing something that might harm him (see chapter 8).

When grazing horses on lengthy rides or overnight (or longer) pack trips, check with trail officials for rules as to whether or not grazing is allowed and/or whether you need to pack in feed. (See chapter 12.) On a longer ride it's even more important to bring along an illustrated field guide to plants, and to keep an eye on your horse whenever he is grazing.

Beware the Wild

Sharing the trail with wildlife is both a thrill and a responsibility. It can also be a hazard. Watching a shy doe melt into the forest, glimpsing a bunny darting into the brush, and gasping as an eagle circles your camp are just some of the wondrous rewards trail riders enjoy.

It's amazing how much closer to wildlife you can get on horseback than when just hiking. Some-thing about the smell and appearance of a horse, even with that ungainly lump on its back, reassures wild things that it's just another critter. Seeing wildlife is also a matter of timing. Deer are common in many areas and most active early in the morning and toward dusk. Coyotes are often all around you, but they are crafty enough to stay out of sight; again, they are more active in low light hours. Small animals, such as rabbits, skunks, and squirrels, may rustle brush and catch your horse's attention, but rarely do most horses give them a second glance.

It used to be that if you wanted to see wildlife, you kept quiet, and if you were riding in an area with large predators, you kept up some chatter. The idea was that noise warns animals that you are in the vicinity so that *they* can avoid *you*. These

Animals don't fear a person on horseback as much as they do a person on foot.

days, though, it all depends on where the trails are. Increasingly, wildlife has become remarkably adapted to our presence and will ignore you even if you have a boom box blasting rap music strapped to your packsaddle.

Even harmless creatures can startle your horse until he is thoroughly seasoned (and sometimes even then). Pheasants, grouse, and quail have the amusing (to them) habit of hunkering down so you can't see them, waiting until the fraction of second before a hoof is planted on their heads, and then flying up in a flapping, squawking sputter of feathers. When a grouse or pheasant suddenly flaps up from underhoof, a deer bounds away, or a snake darts across the path, your horse might spook. If you have built up his trust and confidence in you at home, he'll be more likely to accept whatever he encounters on the trail. Just try to keep your cool, and your seat, through his learning curve and reassure him that these critters are just part of the scenery.

ENCOUNTERING LARGE PREDATORS

Larger animals, such as bear, deserve your undivided attention and respect. Do not venture anywhere near a bear, large cat, or other predator. They are private citizens that prefer to keep to themselves. If you are in an area known for bears, especially likely along rivers and streambeds, make plenty of noise so that you don't inadvertently sneak up and surprise one. Running water makes it harder for a critter to hear you coming, so periodic bursts of song might be a good idea.

Wildlife has become increasingly adapted to the presence of horseback riders (and humans in general) on public land such as parks and other multiuse trail areas. Some animals learn that people are mobile treat dispensers and can actually become aggressive in seeking out goodies. This is obviously scarier with bears than it is with squirrels, but it can be a strange experience either way. Don't feed any wildlife when you are out on the trail.

You must exercise more caution when riding through areas with large predators. Know the species that inhabit the area where you intend to ride. Bears and cougars (mountain lions, pumas) have been known to attack horseback riders. Often just their scent will put a horse on edge. If you are riding in an area known to harbor large predators and your normally quiet trail horse suddenly begins to fret or act fearful, take his word for it and exit posthaste.

It's smart to carry a gun in predator country (carry the registration papers with you) because just the noise can scare off a predator. Keeping firecrackers and a lighter in your gear may also do the trick, and though I wouldn't want to be the one who tested the product, manufacturers claim that pepper spray (with capsaicin) will ward off a grizzly bear.

MEETING A BEAR If you happen to see a bear, you might be lucky enough that it doesn't see you. Bears have poor eyesight. If it is in the distance, remain as still as possible (motion will draw his attention) and it may go on its way without ever knowing you are there. If you can, stay downwind. If a bear does see you, it may stand up to get a better look. Don't look back. Never look a bear in the eyes, as that is a direct challenge and it could charge at you.

Black bears can achieve speeds of up to 30 miles per hour. The question isn't whether your horse can outrun a bear (most can if they get a head start) but whether *you* can (in case your horse gets a head start without you). And you can't.

Once it figures out what you are, most bears will leave, but if yours doesn't, your best bet is to pretend to ignore it and continue on your way as calmly as possible. Odds are it will watch and forget about you when you are out of eyesight. Stay alert, and once away from the area where you saw the bear, pick up speed for a while and put some distance between you. If a bear follows, and if you can trust your horse to tolerate a little clamor from you, take advantage of how much bigger you appear to the bear and try to scare it off. Yell, clap your hands, flap a jacket toward it, anything to unnerve it and send it on its way. If you carry a firearm, and your horse is desensitized to shooting from his back, fire two or three rounds into the ground. Above all else, remain calm.

Bears are usually not dangerous, but they all have the potential to be. Check before riding in bear country to see if there have been recent reports of problem bears. If so, strongly consider another route to ride. There are documented cases of bears circling back and attacking humans.

COUGARS Cougars are less common than bears but can strike without warning. If riding in cougar country, keep your eyes UP. Cougars often rest on an overhead ledge or tree branch so they can drop onto unsuspecting prey. Don't let that prey be you.

If you make enough noise while you ride, odds are you will never see a large cat. But if you do, stop as soon as you notice it; face the cat; and, looking as large and dangerous as possible, yell (not scream in fright!), throw rocks, sticks, or lit fire-crackers, or fire your gun. Don't act afraid, don't run, and never try to approach a cougar in the wild.

SNAKES AND REPTILES

Find out, before you ride, if dangerous snakes and reptiles inhabit your area. If you ride in subtropical areas, such as parts of the Deep South, alligators can be a serious trail hazard. Though they can't catch you, much less your horse, on dry land, they can lurk at the water's edge and make a dive for your horse when he goes to drink. As with all predators, be cautious when riding in their environment. You're in their element, and they know all the angles.

Most horses have a natural fear of snakes, as you may know if you've ever tried to lead your horse over a garden hose. When riding in rattlesnake country, be aware of rattlers' likely hiding places: holes, the underside edges of rocks, and the shade of low brush or bushes, and never approach one sunning on a rock or out in the open. The warmer a snake is, the more energized and mobile it is, even if it appears to be dozing. Snakes are less aware, though not necessarily less dangerous, when their bodies are cold. They can strike out in confusion in any direction when startled.

Always wear heavy boots in snake country. You never know when you'll have to dismount and walk.

TRAIL TALE *Ditch the Berries!*

Keeping your head in potentially dangerous situations makes all the difference. When we were about 8 and 11, my brother and I were riding down a familiar logging road and came right up upon a black bear with two cubs. Our horses never batted an eye, but by that point they probably figured they'd seen it all anyway. We had been berry picking, and even though the bears hardly took notice of us, we loosened our berry baskets from our saddles and let them drop, while we kept riding as though we thought nothing of bears on the trail.

After we rode about 100 yards, we picked up the pace to put some distance between us and the bears, who were now feasting on the spilled berries, but that was about as exciting as it got. Had we panicked and run away, the bears may have pursued, but staying calm, and leaving something behind to distract them, pretty much guaranteed our uneventful escape.

STINGING INSECTS

The wild creature that is probably the feared most by trail riders is also the smallest. Though "bees" have a bad rap for stinging horses along the trail, the real culprit is most often a yellow jacket, with certain species of hornets coming in a close second. Yellow jackets and other wasps are at their worst in late summer and early fall. During this part of their life cycle, they are attracted to moisture and protein. A sweaty horse is a direct invitation, and you may often find a yellow jacket or two buzzing around you in circles. A heavy-duty insecticide helps to make your horse less aromatic, but often stopping and swatting the nuisance will be your only relief.

YELLOW JACKETS The problem with yellow jackets is that they nest in large groups in small, undetectable holes in the ground near trails. Very often one or two horses can pass by, or even directly over, a yellow jacket nest and be none the wiser. But pity that third or fourth rider. Because swarming wasps are none too polite about *where* they swarm, be sure to ride with your pants tucked into your boot tops to prevent them from buzzing right up your pant legs. Even if your horse starts to buck, the only thing to do is holler *"Bees!"* if there are other riders with you and get down the trail as fast as you can. Your horse can't outrun these flying fiends, but they won't fly far outside of their territory, and once you are well away from their nest, you can dismount and start swatting them off your horse.

Nothing is meaner than a late-summer yellow jacket. It will cling to your horse's legs and undersides, stinging him repeatedly until you can get it off. Unlike the mild-mannered honeybee, who loses her barbed stinger and dies on the first offense, yellow jackets have smooth stingers that don't detach so easily. They can and will sting your horse repeatedly. The venom itself contains a substance that alerts other yellow jackets to where a sting has occurred. They home in on this signal.

HORNETS Hornets also present a problem when you ride through nesting areas. Some types nest in trees, others in the open. Bald-faced hornets (which are really a form of wasp) are more than an inch long, fly like an F-18 (not coincidentally nicknamed "the Hornet"), and are very aggressive. All you need to do is ride near their nest, without even knowing you did, and they will come after you. Like yellow jackets, they are attracted to moisture and odors and may buzz your horse just out of curiosity.

COPING WITH STINGING INSECTS Try to resist swatting or smashing the nasty buggers near the nest site, as this releases pheromones that alert others from the nest to ATTACK! Once safely away from the nest, calm your horse as best you can and do a careful visual inspection of his entire body, from head to hoof. To prevent the stingers from working deeper into your horse's flesh and releasing more venom or possibly becoming infected later, carefully remove any from his skin. Pluck out the stinger, using tweezers or forceps, or scrape it off, using the blunt side of a knife or even your thumbnail. Avoid squeezing the bulb part of the stinger, as that will inject more venom into the flesh.

It's a good idea to carry a medicated "sting stick" or two in your gear. Dab a little on stings for both you and your horse.

Hornet

Wasp

Horsefly

Yellow jacket

Mosquito

ALLERGIC REACTIONS Some people experience allergic reactions to insect venom, especially when stung multiple times. Allergic reactions can range from mild localized swelling and itching at the sting site to a severe whole-body reaction known as **anaphylaxis,** or **anaphylactic shock.** *The latter must be treated as an emergency situation.* Such reactions can kill within 20 minutes of being stung and can occur up to 2 hours afterward.

If you have ever had a more severe reaction, you should always carry an EpiPen or a similar epinephrine-delivering device, and know how to use it. Available by prescription, the EpiPen injector is about the size of a permanent marker and easily packable. Immediate injection with epinephrine will open the airways and raise blood pressure, saving lives that might otherwise be lost.

Consult your doctor if you are concerned you might be allergic; you can be tested and then immunized over a course of injections. While fewer than 0.1 percent of people stung will develop anaphylaxis (according to the American Medical Equestrian Association), this accounts for around 100 deaths per year in the United States alone.

Even if you have no history of allergy, carry Benadryl and take it after a sting. This helps block the effects of a mild to moderate allergic reaction.

HORSES AND ALLERGIES Though rare, horses can have allergic or anaphylactic reactions, too. Symptoms can appear in as little as 2 minutes and up to half an hour after being stung. Itchiness or hives might characterize a mild allergic reaction, whereas excitement, trembling, fast pulse, and other signs of distress could signal a more severe reaction.

Antihistamines are not considered effective. Like humans, horses in anaphylactic shock are best treated with an intravenous or intramuscular injection of epinephrine (not subcutaneous, as the horse's body won't be able to absorb it while in shock), according to *California Veterinarian* magazine. The dose is from 4 to 9 milliliters (cc) of

Signs of an Anaphylactic Reaction

Be on the lookout for any of the following indications that someone is having a severe anaphylactic reaction to a sting.

- Blotchy skin
- Swelling of face or eyes
- Hives or itching
- Swelling and constriction of airways, making breathing difficult
- Coughing or wheezing
- Nasal congestion
- Disorientation and confusion, anxiety
- Fainting or dizziness
- Slurred speech
- Heart palpitations
- Rapid pulse
- Low blood pressure and weak pulse
- Abdominal pain or nausea
- Cyanosis: skin turns blue from lack of oxygen (most noticeable on lips and fingernails)
- Skin goes pale from shock

1:1000 solution for a 450 kg (roughly 992-pound) horse, following directions printed on the bottle.

If you are concerned that your horse may be allergic, ask your vet to perform a blood test to determine whether or not your fears are founded.

BITING INSECTS Flying biting insects, such as horseflies, gnats, and mosquitoes, may pale by comparison to the stinging insects that seem hellbent on your destruction. Nevertheless, they can still make for a miserable ride on a muggy day, and they can transmit deadly diseases such as West Nile virus and several varieties of equine encephalitis. Vaccinations are available for most transmittable equine diseases and highly recommended for trail riders, especially if you participate in group rides.

Deadly viral infections spread by biting flies are

far more common in the United States than one might think. **Equine infectious anemia** (EIA), also called **swamp fever** because of its prevalence in wet, warm areas where biting flies and mosquitoes flourish, is thought to be transmitted primarily by large blood feeders, such as horseflies and deerflies. It can also be passed from horse to horse by smaller biting insects and by houseflies attracted to sores or wounds. Symptoms of fever, weakness, and swelling limbs or belly may vary in intensity and there may be remissions, but there is no specific treatment, and affected horses must either be permanently segregated or slaughtered.

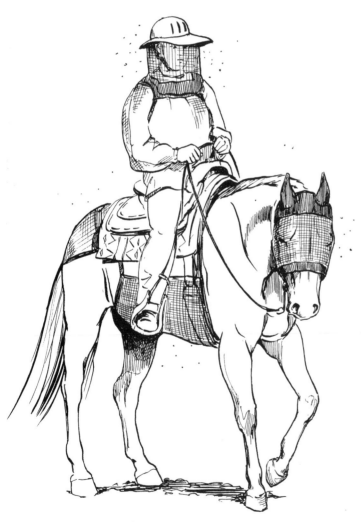

Although not pretty, an effective mosquito defense system will be one of the most welcome items in your saddlebags.

Although mosquitoes get the primary blame for the spread of **Eastern and Western equine encephalomyelitis** (EEE and WEE), a viral brain infection transmissible and generally fatal to both horses and human beings, the small, swarming species of biting flies may also play a role.

Those same tiny no-see-ums are believed to be among the vectors in the spread of **African horse sickness** (AHS), one of the equine world's most dreaded viral diseases. As the name indicates, the deadly cardiopulmonary infection is endemic to the African continent, but international movement of infected equidae can — and recently has — spread AHS to other parts of the world, where, undoubtedly, some species of *Culicoides* or other biting fly will be on hand to transmit the disease to local horses.

Flies offer an additional route for contagion for the many bacteria and viruses that can pass themselves along from horse to horse quite effectively without the help of flying intermediaries. The highly contagious microorganisms responsible for equine influenza, rhinopneumonitis, and strangles are transmitted when horses inhale them, usually from nasal and bowel discharges, but virus particles can also be carried by face flies and houseflies as they go from one set of nostrils to another. **Vesicular stomatitis,** a viral disease that causes painful sores in a horse's mouth, is another condition whose transmission is augmented by stable flies and houseflies drawn to sores or wounds.

All in all, a thriving fly population ups the opportunity for the spread of disease, no matter what role the insects play in the contagion process. Anthrax is among the most dreaded bacterial diseases transmitted by flies. Often confused with acute poisoning or snakebite, it is characterized by fever and sudden death, and it is frequently associated with dry, dusty conditions. Though biting flies can transmit the disease through blood contact, the infectious organisms, when exposed to air, form spores and may be dispersed by wind, water, scavengers, and nonbiting flies.

COPING WITH BITING INSECTS Although I hate chemicals, I still cover my horse generously with the best fly repellent I can find. Studies prove that N,-N diethyl-m-toluamide, marketed as DEET, is the most effective ingredient against mosquitoes and also protects against black flies, horseflies, deerflies, and ticks. It lasts much longer than all other products tested, from skin softeners, to citronella, to a range of commercially marketed concoctions. In a recent study commissioned by the state of Florida, a 7 percent DEET solution kept mosquitoes away for nearly 2 hours, while a 24 percent solution worked for more than 5 hours. In other studies, the only "natural-ingredient" repellents that worked for more than an hour were pyrethrin-based.

Consider also carrying a product that advertises "quick knock-down." These products work by instantly paralyzing an insect's nervous system (but not that of people or of horses) and are just the thing to have handy if you are the third or fourth rider over the yellow jacket nest. One quick spray and the loathsome things drop dead off your horse.

NONCHEMICAL WARFARE Fortunately, there are also nonchemical ways to battle flying insects. Some people have luck feeding their horse about ¼ cup of apple cider vinegar each day. And mesh guards, from fly masks to ear protectors to entire body shields, are available to physically bar the beasties from biting your horse. My horses may *look* silly with knee-high nylon stockings over their ears, but they feel great. Cashel Company (see appendix) has invented several bug guards to cover both you and your horse, from a face net that fits around the brim of your hat to a belly guard that protects your horse's vulnerable undersides.

CHAPTER 10

Trail Rider's Survival Guide

⊱─◈─⊰

EVEN THOUGH TRAIL RIDING IS A HEALTHY OUTDOOR pastime, it is still a sport fraught with possible pitfalls. Narrow the negatives by knowing what to watch for and how to respond. Your horse is trained and conditioned; you've done your homework, scoped out your trails, and are ready to ride. Before you take off, however, stop to consider what can go wrong. Murphy's Law applies to horsemen, but the reverse — whatever you are prepared for *won't* go wrong — seems to work too. In other words, if you cover your bases, you stand a better chance of making it home in one piece.

Worst-Case-Scenario Plan

No one likes to think about what might go wrong on a trail ride, but if you have a plan to cover the worst of possibilities, then anything less than an outright disaster is a good ride. Knowing that you can handle any situation that may arise lets you relax and enjoy the outing without worry.

Your plan doesn't have to be elaborate, just realistic. It must be tailored to you, your circumstances, and your horse. Page 161 lists things to carry along on trail rides; refer back to that general list and then think about any special circumstances your trails might present.

For instance, if you ride near quicksand, your plan might include carrying two long ropes, a cell phone, and the phone number of your nearest friend with a winch. Have a plan for how you will handle lameness, colic, a fall, altitude sickness, or whatever else you can think of that may apply to your situation.

Take the time one day (when it's too rainy, cold, or windy to ride) to make a complete list of emergency contact people and their phone numbers. Take one copy along in your pocket and post another where someone could find it in the event of an emergency (in case you can't make the call yourself). Taped inside a kitchen cupboard is a good spot. Make sure everyone who lives with you knows where it's kept.

Close Encounters

Depending on the trails you travel, there's no telling what other types of trail users might pop up around the bend. Hikers, bikers, dirt bikes, snowmobiles, dogs, llamas, donkeys, kites, guns, and other strange sights, sounds, and smells await you. Even though you hit the trails for that all-healing peace and tranquillity, you are not alone out there.

There are set "rules of the road" that apply on multiuse public trails (see box on page 230).

Emergency Information

Think through what kind of information people at home might need if you should run into trouble on the trail. Here's an example of a list of names and numbers to post in a conspicuous place. Make sure your key contact people know where it will be. You can photocopy your list and then customize it each time by adding specific information about where you are going and when you expect to be back.

❑ My cell phone: 884-4466
❑ Emergency contact: Sandra Thomas
    477-7982 home; 884-4588 cell
Backups:
❑ Mom (has 4WD pickup) 493-0925
❑ Joan Faber (has horse trailer) 477-1654

❑ Simon Corey (has winch) 884-4657 cell
❑ Jake Washington (neighbor; knows trails)
    477-2318
❑ EMT: Mountain Ambulance 477-6200
    (ask for Ed)
❑ Vet: Lee McTigue, 479-8643
❑ Fire: 911
❑ Extra truck key: in drawer by sink
❑ Cat food: bin in closet
❑ Joey Wright next door can feed animals if
    necessary, 477-8268
❑ Date and time I'm leaving: *Sat., 7/14, 10 a.m.*
❑ Trail I'm taking: *Cross's Lone Star*
❑ Trail head: *off Rte. 416 by Fisher's Creek*
❑ I expect to be back: *by 6 p.m. Sun.*

Realize, however, that even if *you* know the rules, the other guy may not, or may not care. Horses have the right-of-way over mountain bikers and hikers. If necessary, non-riders are to step off the trail to allow you to pass, even if this means they have to line up single file and wait for a few minutes. This allows you, the one with the greatest risk, to act according to the needs of the situation as you see them. Riders give way to pack strings, and downhill riders are to make way for uphill riders. Your main priorities are to stay in the saddle and keep yourself, your horse, and the other user safe — in that order.

Most other trail users are there for the same reason you are — to enjoy the trail. Nevertheless, often due to misunderstandings, conflicts sometimes happen. Here are some tips to make unexpected encounters as pleasant and safe as possible.

LISTEN AND LOOK

If you've ever driven with expired license plates, you know the vigilance you can muster in scanning the horizon for police cars. Put that same alertness to work in scanning for others on the trail. Listen for sounds of brush or dry leaves crunching, voices, bike brakes squeaking, motors, dogs barking, music, and anything else that signals other users nearby. In a lot of areas you will *hear* approaching traffic before you see it. Your horse certainly will.

Keep an eye on your horse's ears. Often he will hear or see other users before you do. If he's pricking his ears forward and looking intently in one direction, call out. Horses often warn us before they spook as they try to figure out what something is. If they hear a human voice answer, it can quickly defuse what a horse perceives as a scary situation. Daydream, enjoy the warm sun or the cool breeze on your face, but don't let yourself stray too far mentally. Never forget that you are the leader of a team, and that entails responsibilities. Focus on the trail ahead; glance around and over your shoulder from time to time.

SPEAK UP Keep it upbeat, but alert other users to your presence as soon as you notice them. A loud and friendly "Howdy!" gives fair warning to others that there be cowboys about. Half the time others on the trail are even more distracted than you are, talking, listening to headphones, or monitoring pulse rates. Following up with a friendly but serious "Just wanted to warn you that there were horses nearby" reminds fellow users that *they* aren't alone either, and that they need to be aware when approaching a horse.

It's always a good idea to ask about the trail ahead, especially to inquire if the person you have encountered is alone or part of a group. Offering information in turn on what you've passed is always appreciated (especially if it has anything to do with yellow jackets).

If your horse is shy of strangers, it helps to speak to people you meet on the trail. Let them know that he hasn't quite figured out what they are yet, and if they'd talk with you a bit, it would sure help to settle him down and reassure him that that big orange backpack isn't a horse-eating alien. Hearing a human voice gives the horse more information, and unfamiliar visuals become less threatening. Bouncy, loud, squeaky, and quick, kids can be a special challenge to meet on the trail and really require you to be on your toes, so that they don't wind up under your horse's. Talk with whoever is in charge and allow her to decide how close to your horse she wants her children to get.

Often folks will ask to pat a horse, and sometimes they'll just reach out to do so without asking. How to respond to this depends entirely on your horse and the situation. This can be a good opportunity to play equine ambassador and explain a few things about horses. Let curious hikers or bikers know that horses are prey animals and prone to some pretty goofy reactions by human standards. If your horse is a good sport, explain that horses like to be stroked more than patted, and that a gentle stroke along the neck is best. Ask that any wee ones be lifted up to where the horse can see or even sniff them (be ready for squeals and giggles!) and away from the horse's feet. If your horse isn't into it, be clear about that, and ask them to keep a safe distance.

SMILE Whenever possible, make eye contact with other trail users. That's the best way to know how your meeting has affected them. Don't forget that some people, for reasons only non-horsemen can understand, are genuinely afraid of large animals with the capacity to kill in a single hoof strike. Smile, be polite, and try to leave others on the trail with the feeling that they are glad they happened by that nice horseback rider.

MAKE YOURSELF SCARCE Despite the above advice, when I am riding alone, most other users never know I am there because I take evasive maneuvers. Every instance is unique, but the best policy is to put yourself and your horse in as little jeopardy as possible with the least amount of trouble. For me, that may mean moving off the trail or taking a side trail to avoid other users.

USE GOOD JUDGMENT Trail common sense is the same whether you're on a horse, on a bike, or on foot. I don't consider it my job to stop a pack of grinding mountain bikers and chastise them into creeping down trail in fear of coming across another horse. However, if I knew there were children down trail, or an elderly hiker, or a group of drunk hunters rambling about with guns, then I would be sure to stop any oncoming trail users and give them fair warning.

Never, however, try to block the path of another user. It comes across as aggressive and confrontational and can escalate into conflict. When circumstances warrant, do be firm in seizing his attention and alerting him to the trail conditions ahead.

Aside from sharing trail information, there are other ways you can earn that Helpful Trail Rider merit badge. You can provide directions, help the lost or exhausted, share a drink with a thirsty

biker, ride hard for help in emergencies, or pack out anything that can't get out under its own power. Remember, a horse is a powerful tool, so use it wisely.

WHEN STRANGERS AREN'T FRIENDLY

Strangers you meet on the trail are just that. Strangers. Statistically, women are more likely to be attacked on the trail than men, not only because they make up the majority of attack victims generally, but also because they make up the majority of trail riders.

Above all else, listen to your instincts. If someone makes you uncomfortable, don't allow him or her to approach. Anyone with dishonorable intentions will most likely grab for your reins; don't let him near enough to do that. Another ploy an attacker might try is to spook your horse in an attempt to grab or drop you from the saddle.

Trust your gut. Especially if you are riding alone, listen to that little voice, even if it's clucking like a big fat chicken. It's likely that your horse will pick up your feelings and fidget. Use his antsiness as an excuse to move on up the trail if you feel the need. Here's just one more reason why riding with a group is safer. You are much less likely to be singled out by an attacker on the trail.

Narrow Passings

At least once in your trail-riding career you are bound to come face-to-face with a mountain biker or llama packer overladen with weird-looking gear on a steep or narrow passage that leaves little space for getting around one another. Forced close quarters with a strange entity can put the calmest horse on edge, and if you are already on the edge (of a narrow trail), things can get dicey fast.

It's best to leave at least 3 feet between you as you pass. If necessary and possible, one of you should turn around and go back to a safer place to pass. Although the rule of thumb is for the downhill party to yield to the uphill party and for non-horse

Self-Defense for Trail Riders

If a stranger approaches your horse, how are you to know his or her intentions and what should you do?

Human predators (people who mean you harm) may try to lure you closer by gaining your trust or sympathy. ("Hey, I have a horse that looks just like this." "My puppy was just run over.") Don't be paranoid, but do be cautious.

When on horseback, never try to run over a would-be assailant as he blocks your path; most horses won't even come close to doing that. Never try to kick at or strike an attacker. It's far too easy for him to unseat you from your horse. Instead, get your horse's attention and be ready to take off.

A horse is a powerful weapon and has been used as such throughout history. When you turn his haunches toward a person who means you harm, you put a large, dangerous buffer zone between yourself and the troublemaker, and you prevent him from grabbing at your reins and taking control of your horse. Then you should make tracks outta there.

If you carry pepper spray for this type of situation, never spray into the wind or near your horse's face.

traffic to yield to horse traffic, the sensible thing to do is for the party with the least degree of danger to move back.

Let the other party know that it's safer for him to move to the downhill side of a trail while you pass him. A spooked horse is much more likely to head uphill than downhill.

Those chance meetings on the trail can be fabulous opportunities to share the rewards of horseback riding with non-horsey people or they can turn into impromptu auditions for Barnum and Bailey. Because other users have input as to where, when, and *if* horses are allowed on public trails, consider yourself an ambassador for us all when you meet them. I don't want to be barred from a trail because your horse stepped on a hiker any

more than you want to be ousted because I cussed out the Dirtbike Kid.

FELLOW TRAVELERS

Hikers are just people, but to your horse they can look like horse-hungry aliens. Creatures with large packs looming over their heads, runners pounding by, and bouncing, shrieking little people zipping back and forth all tend to unsettle horses that wouldn't think twice about the same people talking to them across their pasture fence. The best thing to do is say hello and keep moving. The more horses are with you, the more true this is. Horses stopped on the trail, especially packhorses with no rider to immediately control them, can get restless. (It's a good idea to practice stopping and standing on the trail for those occasions when it's necessary.)

Though the rules state that hikers should step out of the way, if it's easier for you to do that than for them, move on over. Your consideration will be appreciated.

VEHICLES Multiuse trails would be more fun if mountain bikers were required to wear bells. They and their bicycles can suddenly be upon you (usually in a place with nowhere to get off the trail quickly) before either of you realizes the other is there. All you're likely to hear is a whir and then maybe a thump, depending on how well you sit your horse and how well he reacts to sneak attacks.

Remember to keep an eye out ahead and behind for two-wheeled trail competition. Desensitizing to bikes at home before you hit the trail pays off, but practice with on-trail encounters is, unfortunately, the best medicine. If the biker doesn't stop or move off trail, then ride as far out of his way as the trail allows. Don't forget that distance is a comfort and that a nervous horse will lose some of his natural fear after seeing and hearing bikes whiz by at a safe distance.

Motorized vehicles, dirt bikes, snowmobiles, and all-terrain vehicles give you an advantage in that you can hear them coming down the trail and

In an encounter on a narrow mountain trail, the time-honored rule is that the downhill party should yield to the uphill party. However, it's often safer for one party to turn around and go back to a wider spot to pass.

retreat to a safe place to allow them to pass. Granted, you have the right-of-way, but if getting around each other and getting on with the trail ride is your objective, it's often easiest and safest to let them pass by with a wave and a smile.

In a perfect world, motorcycle riders and others on machinery would know to shut off their engines and allow a frightened horse to pass. The one time this happened to us, we were so floored at the courtesy of the two riders that we stopped and talked with them for quite some time. We found out they were also horsemen, but were enjoying their dirt bikes that particular day.

PACK ANIMALS

Pack animals often alarm horses on the trail. Even other horses can appear dubious when laden with pack gear, but mules, donkeys, llamas, and goats — especially if the species is unfamiliar to your

horse — can seem downright bizarre. Your horse may well be thinking, "I could accept how it looks, but did you *smell* that thing!?" Again, pre-ride preparation, by getting your horse as accustomed to as many different strange sights, sounds, and smells as possible, will help him trust that each new, strange thing is no more dangerous than the previous ones he's encountered under your protection.

Llamas seem to be a favorite terror of horses. We kept a few for years and our horses never batted an eyelash from day one. But our horses were introduced to them on their own turf, at their own pace. They watched as we unloaded the woolly things from a trailer, but they didn't have to approach them until they felt like it, which inevitably turned out to be right away. They often shared a pasture and basically ignored each other until it came time to shoo one away from a hay pile. Despite this experience, had I met a llama packer on the trail, I would never have assumed my horses would have reacted calmly.

DOGS

Dogs can be an even bigger challenge, especially since you are a lot more likely to meet them. My

Right-of-Way

Horses have the right-of-way over mountain bikers and hikers. If necessary, non-riders are to step off the trail to allow you to pass, even if they must line up single file and wait for a few minutes. Riders give way to pack strings, and downhill riders are to make way for uphill riders.

Rules of right-of-way are only as good as the people who follow them and the circumstances of the encounter. Many trail users act as though you are just another biker or hiker, not realizing that a horse reacts independently from your commands. Hikers can be tired and just not want to bother to get off the trail. Mountain bikers and ATV riders may not even see you until they are upon you. Even the most well-meaning snowmobiler can't stop his machine on a dime when he flies over a mound and spots a horse crossing the path.

Let your own horse sense dictate when you take the right-of-way. Personally, I never expect it, and accept it only when graciously offered. In those rare cases, I always thank the other trail user for her thoughtfulness and courtesy.

horses have put up with dogs all their lives. They are used to being barked at, run past, circled, snapped at, and generally harassed for no good reason. I once caught one tugging my husband's Quarter Horse gelding's tail. He looked at me as if to say, "Is this thing yours?" Oddly enough, even if their dog attacks your horse, a lot of people blame the horse if he kicks. Friendly dogs can be even worse if they think it's fun to jump up on people or horses.

On public trails, dogs are generally required to be on a leash, and if the dog seems to be under control, just give it as wide a berth as possible as you pass. Otherwise, or if you aren't sure of your horse's reaction, speak to the owner in a friendly tone and let him know your horse isn't used to dogs and it would be safer for all concerned for them to move off the trail a bit to let you pass.

Loose dogs can be a nightmare if they run toward your horse on the trail. It's just as much their instinct to chase as it is your horse's to run. But sometimes a horse will surprise you, as my gelding Rudy surprised me. He would turn, face the dog, and snort. If he so much as took one step forward, the dog would hightail it. This gave me the idea to turn and face loose dogs when on the road or trail.

Keep your horse's head toward the dog and watch him rethink the showdown. Most often the dog will retreat. If the dog moves around, keep turning to face it. Take a step or two toward it if it doesn't back off. I'm a dog lover and don't want to cause trouble for the dog or its owner (though some deserve a little trouble). The priority in such encounters is not to teach the dog anything, but to get past it safely.

If the owners are in sight, I will politely request that they restrain their dog. But if no one is around and a loose dog doesn't back off, I have had to chuck rocks and holler. Never show fear, and stay on your horse. The only thing worse than a spooked horse with a dog after it is a spooked horse running away while his rider is mauled.

Keep your horse facing the loose dog and then take a step toward it.

If you find yourself regularly riding past dogs that come after you, ride with a longe whip. Rub it all over your horse until he relaxes and realizes you don't intend to use it on him. Practice twirling and snapping the whip until he accepts the noise, transfer this to the saddle, and, when he calmly ignores your snapping whip, head out. The first time the lash makes contact with an offensive dog, both he and your horse will be impressed.

If you are likely to bring your own dog with you on a public or multiuse trail (see chapter 6), make certain that he is impeccably behaved, especially when meeting other riders.

Help! I'm Lost!

As you ride past a particular gnarly oak tree, marveling at how many of these ancient relics dot the hills, you notice that this tree has the exact same fork with a squirrel hollow in it as one you passed an hour ago. Then it dawns on you — you're lost.

As a kid, I got "lost" all the time riding the logging roads close to home. When I got tired of being lost, I kicked my horse forward and held on for the ride. Turns out I was the only one "lost."

But getting lost on a strange trail far from home is a much scarier proposition. Times like this make a barn-sour or herd-bound horse seem like a good companion. Some horses will carry you straight back to the trailhead, barn, or other horses no matter how lost *you* are. Test this by giving your horse his head and urging him forward. If he strikes out confidently, he may well know right where he's going. Or not.

If a *current* map of the trail you are riding is available, get one before you set out and study it. Assess turns, hills, creeks, and any marked landmarks in terms of minutes, not miles, and you'll have a good idea of what to expect on the trail. Here are some other basic rules of staying "found."

* Carry a compass and check it before you leave the trailhead; this way you'll know which direction to head on the way back.
* Mark your path by bending back any branches that protrude into the trail, or by flagging with surveyor's tape.
* When you come to a crossroad, look it over from the angle you will see it from on your return, even if this just means glancing back over your shoulder as you ride past.

✳ When you spot an obvious landmark, check your watch to note the time from the trailhead.

✳ If you are riding with a group, watch the trail for hoofprints.

If you do get lost, don't panic. If you've let someone know where you are riding, help can be on the way in minutes. If you carry a cell phone (and if it works where you happen to be), call 911. When lost, it's best to stay in one place. Riding or walking will help keep you warm, but it just may get you more lost, and if you keep going, you will eventually exhaust both yourself and your horse. If you must keep moving (because it's cold or because you are in an unsafe area), indicate the direction of travel for the benefit of searchers. Tie bits of surveyor's tape, bend back twigs, leave notes, anything to assist searchers.

EMERGENCY CAMP In colder seasons, your main concern is hypothermia; you need to stay warm and dry. You can last for days without water, possibly weeks without food, but only a few hours in cold temperatures.

Setting up a small camp with a fire not only is your best bet to stay warm, but also provides a smoke signal for searchers. Be aware that a fire itself is a tremendous responsibility and that without your full attention and know-how it can turn into an emergency situation all its own. In dry areas you run the risk of it getting out of control, but you also accelerate the rate at which you will be sighted if smoke is visible. It's a trade-off decision that you will hopefully never have to make.

Allow yourself an hour to get a fire going and up to 3 hours to build a shelter. This means stopping well before dark if you realize your situation in time. Try to find a shelter site with some natural protection and windbreak, access to firewood, shelter materials, and water. What passes for a shelter in one situation might not be possible in another. A low spot in the ground with your saddle over the top may have to suffice.

Find a place away from your shelter and fire to tie your horse. If you have a line to rig a highline, that's best, or at least tie him high on a sturdy tree branch. Lead your horse near your camp to graze if you can find any grass nearby. Your horse will be fine without food, but you'll feel better taking care of him.

See chapter 12 for more information on camping with horses.

Wrecks and Runaways

A confident rider on a good horse should never have to worry about falling off or having a wreck, but most do. If only to prove our susceptibility to gravity, horse wrecks happen. They range from the embarrassing to the life-threatening and can happen at any time, without warning. The best you can do is to be prepared and try to stay calm while you think your way through the situation.

FALLING

Falling is scary and can be dangerous. Falling *off* a horse is bad enough, but falling *with* a horse is more dangerous because he can land on you. If ever you have that split second to make the decision — as you feel your horse going down with you — bail off.

If you feel yourself losing your balance beyond your ability to correct it and stay on your horse, try to execute a controlled emergency dismount (see chapter 5). If at all possible, kick your stirrups free and bail away from the direction of the fall. But if you do hit the dirt, take a second to catch your breath. Often your horse will be on his feet before you can get to yours. Odds are your fall startled your horse as much as it did you, and if you lurch to grab his reins, you might scare him off.

If you are alone, call him to you and offer a treat. If you have a friend with you, have her slowly lead her own horse past you so that your horse must walk past you to follow. Then reach for him as calmly as possible.

Sometimes a serious fall means implementing your Worst-Case Scenario plan. Don't panic if your horse wanders off. Someone will notice him on the trail, at the trailhead, or back home, and be alerted that you are in trouble. Again, if ever you are alone out on the trail and can't get out under your own power, your primary concern is hypothermia.

A MORE SERIOUS FALL If your horse doesn't rise right away, approach him quietly and speak to him softly. He could be tangled in gear, afraid, wedged against something so that he can't free his front feet in order to rise, stunned, or hurt. Cautiously pull his saddle, clear any debris from near where he rests, and, if necessary, very carefully pull one front foot out in front of him. A horse has to stretch both front feet in front of him to get up. If he is on a hill, try to pull his head around to the downhill side and let gravity help him rock himself to his feet.

Once you get him up, give him a few moments to breathe while you check him over thoroughly. Ask him to move forward one step at a time. If he can walk, even tentatively, plan on leading him as far as necessary. If you can get to an access road, leave him there with a friend, or tied if necessary, and go fetch your trailer or call for help.

The worst thing that can happen in a fall is that your horse lands on you. Take a tip from Hollywood stuntmen and keep his head pulled around over his free shoulder and back around toward you, to prevent him from rising until you can be sure your feet are free of the stirrups. If possible, disconnect the cinch or girth, back cinch first, if you ride with one. (I seldom ride with a back cinch and always use a quick-release half hitch on the cinch in case my saddle and I need to part company with my horse. In nearly 40 years of riding, I've never needed to pull the release, but tomorrow is another day.) Slowly let up on the rein until he can straighten his head in front of him and try to rise.

If you are both down, focus on getting out from under him as calmly as possible.

If you should fall with your horse, try to rid yourself of your stirrups as you go down.

RUNAWAY!

After a wreck, a loose horse is the second scariest thing that can happen on the trail. A horse that comes when you call him will make you feel awfully lucky if he ever gets loose on the trail. If you carry treats, and he knows it, it will help to sweeten the deal. If you have another horse with you, lead or ride him off in the direction you just came from, and odds are the loose horse will follow. If the horse takes off, regardless of which direction he starts out in, plan on backtracking the way you have just come to find him. Unless you are headed home or back to camp and the horse knows this, he is most likely to turn back toward your original direction.

Recognizing Distress

Taking your horse's vital signs (see chapter 4) is an important objective way to measure his condition at any point, but something else is just as important — your personal knowledge of your individual animal. Often as not, a gut feeling first informs you something is wrong. Your horse may be "off" in subtle ways that, while you can't quite put a finger on it, tell you that he's not the same. This sounds vague, but that's precisely how it feels when you are faced with an undetermined problem. Think of this vague gut feeling as your early-warning radar system.

As soon as something seems off, stop, get off your horse, and check his vital signs. If they are normal, proceed at a walk back home or to the trailhead. If they are not, loosen the cinch and let him rest for 10 to 20 minutes, checking his heart rate every few minutes. You may be able to ride home, but you may have to walk or catch a ride with a fellow trail rider. Refer to your Worst-Case-Scenario game plan and be prepared to use it if your horse can't make it home.

FATIGUE

Fatigue is the first warning sign of distress and most people miss it.

How to recognize it. Often all you'll notice is a lagging attitude or perhaps increased stumbling. A tired horse is more likely to stumble because he doesn't lift his feet far enough off the ground. He may not seem to notice things he normally would. He'll seem grumpy.

What to know. The best method of judging your horse's state of fatigue is to check his heart rate before and after a 15-minute rest. If it doesn't drop below 72 bpm, he is very fatigued. (Ideally it should drop back to a resting rate of less than 42 bpm.) A longer rest, a cool drink, and if possible a soothing massage or sponge-down with cool water are in order.

What to do. Rest your horse frequently, and be sure to loosen the cinch so he can breathe easily.

What not to do. Never push an overtired horse. He is much more likely to strain a muscle, pull a ligament, or lose his balance and end up lame or very sore.

Use this quick-release half-hitch on your cinch so you can undo it from your saddle in an emergency. *Note:* This works only if your saddle has no back cinch.

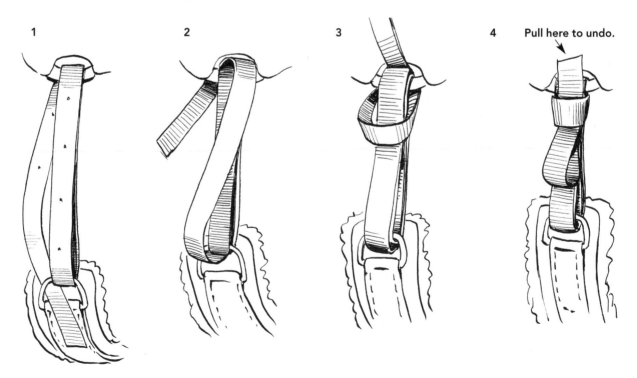

1   2   3   4   Pull here to undo.

LAMENESS

Lameness can result from an obvious trauma, such as stepping in a hole or slipping, or it can sneak up on your horse mysteriously. Either way, few miles are as long as those you walk leading a lame horse.

How to recognize it. Detecting lameness means paying attention. If he trips or slips, dismount and see if he can "walk it off." Otherwise, nothing beats your familiarity with your horse's gait, both when he is frisky and when he is nearing the end of his stamina, for warning you of possible lameness. You will likely feel a difference in the smoothness of the ride, or even hear a detectable change in the rhythm of his footfalls.

What to know. Some changes in gait are normal. An excited horse tends to take shorter steps with more lift. Once he gets down to work, he should loosen up and extend the length of his stride, but by the time he is tired, those steps will shorten again and have less lift. An off gait may also be due to something as simple as a rock stuck in his foot that you can easily dislodge, allowing you to remount and be on your way. Unfortunately, noticeable limping can also indicate more serious lameness.

What to do. If your horse goes lame during conditioning, take him back to the barn and treat accordingly. If he has pulled or strained a muscle, a massage with a good liniment and a few days' rest should help. On the other hand, if he has **graveled** a stone (forced a stone through the sole of his hoof, which travels through the hoof structure, often abscessing along the way, until it exits through the top of the hoof), you will have to wait it out before he can be ridden again. This can take weeks. Other problems may or may not necessitate a visit from your veterinarian.

Unfortunately, if you are out on the trail and your horse goes lame, you are either in for a long walk or must trigger your Worst-Case-Scenario plan. Your goal here is early detection and getting your horse home where you can treat him properly.

Checking for Lameness

If you suspect your horse may be going lame, dismount and check his legs carefully.

- When a horse feels pain in one leg, he will come down hard on the hoof on the opposite side, so first determine which leg is giving him trouble, even if you have to walk him around a few steps to figure it out.
- Then carefully look up and down both sides of the suspected lame leg and feel with your hands for any heat, swelling, or **filling** (an inflated feeling under the skin).
- If you find nothing obviously wrong, carefully lift his foot and examine his hoof for foreign material or any evidence of injury. Scrape away any dirt with a hoof pick and gently press with your thumb, first around the perimeter of the sole, then across the sole, and finally on the frog. Watch your horse closely for a reaction. He may only turn his head toward you, or noticeably flinch, or try to pull his hoof away if you hit a sore spot.

PREVENTIVE SHOEING Throwing a shoe on the trail is fairly avoidable, so if it happens, it's most likely the horse owner's fault. Be sure your horse's shoes are securely in place with plenty of wear left in them before you head out on a ride. Hooves grow faster in the spring and summer than in the winter, so check more often during these seasons. Lift each hoof and visually check and feel the shoes. Don't ride with a loose shoe, either: Get your farrier out to reset or replace it, or pull it yourself. A loose shoe shifting under your horse's weight could cause him to slip or stumble.

Keep tabs on your shoeing dates and plan ahead. Write your horse's shoeing schedule on a calendar (along with your trail-riding plans!). If you have a trail ride scheduled 6 weeks after your last farrier visit, have your horse reshod in 5 weeks (a week before your departure).

Because losing one shoe can ruin a whole

weekend for you and anyone who was counting on riding with you, you're better off shoeing a little sooner than planned rather than too late.

What to do. If a shoe is lost, there are a couple of options that will let you stay in the saddle, at least temporarily. One is to carry an Easy Boot, a removable horse bootie that you can slip on over the bare hoof. (Duct tape can also work, in a pinch.) The other is to continue on your way, riding only when the terrain allows for it. Lighten the horse's load if he is being used as a packhorse or carrying heavy gear. If rocky spots, gravel, or paved roads are part of the trail, get off and lead your horse. Nothing improves your memory of your shoeing schedule like a good long walk up a rocky hill.

DEHYDRATION

Dehydration is classified as mild, moderate, or severe. **Mild dehydration** (5 to 7 percent drop in body weight due to water loss) results in depression, dry mucous membranes (gums), and capillary refill time of more than 2 seconds. **Moderate dehydration** (8 to 10 percent water loss) can result in depression, weak pulse, capillary refill time of 4 seconds, decreased skin turgidity, and elevated heart rate. **Severe dehydration** (more than 10 percent water loss) leads to cold extremities, a depressed appearance, tenting of the skin, dry mouth, and sunken eyes and may result in multiple organ failure. Dark urine is another sign of dehydration.

What to know. Preventing dehydration means understanding how much water a horse needs and how he metabolizes it. On an average day, most horses will drink between 5 and 15 gallons of water. Exercise and temperature increase that, but a horse sweats out water faster than he can replace it by drinking. A horse can lose several gallons through normal sweating and urination. A horse that loses more than 4 gallons is considered dehydrated. A horse that loses 9 gallons is at risk of imminent death. A horse working in hot weather can lose nearly 4 gallons of water each hour.

How to prevent it. Of course, a horse should always have access to clean, fresh water when at liberty, and he should be allowed to drink at every safe opportunity on the trail. (Horses often don't drink enough water in the winter because it either freezes or gets too cold.) For reasons only hot, thirsty horses understand, they will often refuse to drink from cool running streams. Rather than risk your horse dehydrating on the trail, water him at home periodically from a collapsible pail and carry that with you on the trail. He is much more likely to drink from a familiar pail than from a suspect source.

When offering water to a hot or dehydrated horse, do so frequently but allow him to drink only small amounts at a time. Very cold water should not be offered to a hot horse, so if you are pumping water from a cold source, let it sit until the chill is off. A hot horse should never be turned out to drink on his own, or allowed to gulp down water. Colic or laminitis could result.

What to do. To keep your horse regularly hydrated, it helps to feed a high-fiber diet (grass hay as opposed to alfalfa or grain) because a horse drinks a gallon of water for every 2.2 pounds of dry

Equine Water Consumption

Whoever coined the phrase "He drinks like a fish" didn't know much about horses — or fish, for that matter. Horses require a lot of water to keep all their body systems operating smoothly.

At rest	5 to 10 gallons per day
Working (during conditioning)	10 + gallons per day
Hot weather	10 to 15 gallons per day
Working in hot weather	up to 20 gallons per day
Cold weather	5 to 10 gallons per day

hay eaten. This is held within the horse's large intestine, serving as a water reserve and helping to offset the loss of fluids (and electrolytes) from sweating. Grazing on fresh grass along the trail replenishes a little lost moisture. Keeping free-choice salt available also encourages water consumption. Hosing down your horse with water at the end of his workout also helps, as it provides the same cooling effect as sweating, without the water loss from sweating.

HEAT STRESS

Heat stress, which can escalate into life-threatening heatstroke, results when your horse can't dissipate enough excess body heat to regulate his temperature. Poorly conditioned horses are most at risk, but heat, humidity, a heavy load, and/or a steep trail can bring down even a well-conditioned horse. Heat stress or heatstroke can cause collapse, seizures, permanent brain or organ damage, or even death.

What to know. Often a horse in heat stress is already dehydrated and suffering from associated electrolyte imbalance (see box). These conditions alone can debilitate a horse, so be sure to carry water and electrolytes with you whenever you face a tough ride or hot weather. Heavy sweating depletes body cells, the gut, and even the bloodstream of moisture.

Heat and high humidity effectively cancel out your horse's ability to cool himself by sweating. When this happens, **respiratory heat dissipation** becomes critical, and the horse's respiration increases. Panting not only helps to draw in more cooling air and oxygen for the heart to distribute, but it also pushes out body heat. At the same time, blood flow is reduced from internal organs and the brain and increased toward dilated veins in the skin in the body's attempt to cool through radiant cooling (thermal energy moving from a small area of high heat to a large area of lower heat). The result can be a lack of oxygen and nutrients to the brain and internal organs and a buildup of toxins.

Electrolytes

Certain minerals, including sodium, potassium, chloride, calcium, magnesium, manganese, and copper, become electrically charged when dissolved in water — including the water in and between body tissues. These minerals, called **electrolytes,** are critical to the health of your horse because they help regulate fluid exchange, nerve and muscle function, and pH balance in your horse's system, just to name a few of their better-known tasks.

A horse's sweat actually contains a higher concentration of electrolytes than his blood plasma does. When a horse sweats excessively in an effort to cool his body, he loses vast quantities of these minerals, which can lead to imbalances. Imbalances can cause neuromuscular and systemic problems, including muscle cramping, tying up (see page 240), thumps (see page 241), and reduced sweating.

A diet balanced in electrolytes, including supplements when necessary, is the first step toward avoiding the problems associated with imbalances. Carrying prepackaged doses of electrolytes, easily administered in dissolved water on the trail, are an essential part of your trail readiness.

If you ride in hot weather, learn to keep an eye on the **heat index.** This number combines the air temperature with the percent of relative humidity. For example, if it's 70° out with 15 percent humidity, the heat index is 85, perfect for a comfortable ride. If it's 70° and the humidity is 75 percent, however, it's a different story. Whenever the heat index exceeds 125, heat stress becomes a serious concern. If the heat index exceeds 170, go swimming instead of riding.

How to prevent it. Try to avoid extreme exertion, such as bursts of speed or long, steep uphill pulls, during spells of high heat and humidity. Stop about every half hour (more often if necessary) to allow your horse's heart rate and respiration to return to resting levels, and offer water every 2 hours. A horse working in hot weather can drink up to 20 gallons of water in a day. Slowly cool your horse by walking and allowing him to drink small amounts frequently.

To avoid having to resort to desperate measures, always bring a horse sponge, bucket, and at least 5 gallons of water (individual milk jugs or plastic 5-gallon water-cooler jugs work great) with you when you haul your horse to the trails, and carry a half-gallon of water with you as you ride. (If you know you will be riding a specific trail on a hot day, see if you can scout it in advance and cache water if none is naturally available.) Save the best water to offer the horse, and if he will drink, add electrolytes.

How to recognize it. In hot weather, pay close attention to your horse's vital signs.

✳ Signals of **heat distress** progress from the barely noticeable to the extreme. The horse slows down, his reactions become slower, he has a pained or anxious expression, his nostrils flare and blush red inside, he may tremble, his breathing becomes shallow and quick, he stumbles or staggers.

✳ With **heat stress or -stroke,** the horse becomes reluctant to move forward, which could be confused with balking. Pushed beyond this point, the horse may collapse. A resting heart rate that doesn't fall below 60 bpm, respiration at more than 40 breaths per minute, and a temperature at or higher than 104°F are all signs of **emergency heat stress.** Dark red or purple-tinted gums are another sign.

What to do. If a horse exhibits these symptoms, get him out of the sun and remove his saddle and pad. Sponge him off with any available water, starting with the large prominent vein along the lower part of his neck (jugular vein). This helps cool the blood as it circulates through the veins throughout his body. RV tanks, bagged ice, coolers, canned or bottled drinks, creeks, mud puddles, toilet tanks, even radiators if there is no other water source available, all provide usable water reservoirs in an emergency. A shirt, socks, girth cover, or even a handful of moss can serve as an emergency sponge.

If a creek is close enough, try to get the horse to stand in it. Cool running water does wonders. Check his vital signs every few minutes, and continue sponging until his vitals return to normal. Afterward, lead or pony your horse out of the trail, waiting until the temperature cools off if possible. Stop every 15 to 20 minutes to monitor vital signs, and proceed only when they return to normal.

If your horse shows signs of heat stress, sponge him off with any available water, starting with the large prominent vein along the lower part of his neck (jugular vein).

COLIC

Colic is a catchall term for abdominal pain. The source can be intestinal gas, impaction of the intestinal contents at some point, or, most gruesome, a "twisted" gut in which the intestines themselves are physically twisted or moved out of place.

What to know. Because a horse's system is in delicate balance, it takes remarkably little to throw it off. Common causes are stress, diet change, and dehydration. The bustle and chaos of packing and hauling out for a trail ride might seem like an exciting adventure to you, but for a timid horse, or one that doesn't like to leave home, it can be stressful enough to send his body into trauma overload.

Remember that when a horse goes into "flight-or-fight" mode, his autonomic nervous system shuts down parts of the body not immediately on call to run or attack. Senses are heightened and blood flow to the muscles is increased, but his gut is all but shut down. Food passage stops. Even mere *preparations* for a trail ride are enough to colic some horses.

Because trail riding is a physical activity with inevitable changes in diet and hydration, there are physiological consequences that go along with it as well. If he is overworked on the trail (for his level of condition), a horse is at risk for colic. If a horse grazes for more than an hour when he is not used to it, he can stuff his gut with unfamiliar food, resulting in gas buildup and colic. A long ride with insufficient watering stops (especially if he sweats a lot) can rob the intestines of water needed to keep the contents moving, resulting in colic.

How to prevent it. There is no guarantee your horse won't colic even if you do everything right, but horsemen's wisdom has changed little over the ages in regard to prevention. Condition your horse before you work him hard. If you flat out can't get him in shape before a big group trail ride and you just *have* to be there, take it easy. Ride him only on short or easy jaunts. Allow your horse to become accustomed to new climates or altitudes before asking him to exert himself.

Pack in your horse's regular feed when horse camping or make any changes gradually during the week or two prior to the ride. If he will be grazing, find a spot near home to graze him for an hour at a time, gradually increasing his graze time until he can eat his fill. On the trail, offer water every 2 hours, and if he doesn't drink within 4 hours, rest him, then take him back home or to camp at a slow pace.

Preventing colic, or at the very least catching it early, is yet another reason to make checking vital signs a regular part of your trail-riding routine. How often you do so depends entirely on your circumstances: the demands of the environment and trail you ride, your horse's condition, even the weight he's carrying. Make a habit of checking him thoroughly before you ride out, again after a couple of hours on the trail, then again when you finish — or whenever he seems stressed. A resting heart rate (after 30 minutes) as low as 44 bpm, along with respiration of more than 20 breaths per minute, can signify distress.

How to recognize it. The classic image of a colicking horse is one that paws the ground, lies down and gets up, kicks at his belly, lies down and rolls, or just won't get up at all. By the time colic has progressed to this point, however, your horse's life can be in danger.

The first signs of colic can be easy to misinterpret or miss entirely. Your horse drops a manure pile that is drier than normal, or that has a thin mucous film over it (warning sign of dehydration), but you continue riding down the trail without looking back. He sweats a lot (he's working hard), but you don't realize that it's more than normal for him. He turns his head to look at his flank, but you assume he's looking at something behind him. He grinds his teeth or curls his lip, and you think it's because he's interested in the mare next to him. A horse at rest may stand stiff-legged with his head down, peering around at his belly or flank periodically. He'll refuse food, and sweat while just standing there.

Usually, it's an accumulation, and escalation, of signs that finally gets a rider's attention. But know that the earlier you catch most forms of colic, the better chance your horse has of getting through it.

What to do. At the first sign of colic, check the vitals.

✳ Check heart rate and respiration. If at any time during your ride you find a resting heart rate higher than 60 bpm and respiration of more than 30 bpm, realize that your horse is already in some form of distress, possibly from moderate to severe colic.

✳ Check his gums. A dark red/purplish color is a sign of progressing colic.

✳ Listen for gut sounds. Remember that if he has eaten recently or has a lot of water in his gut, sounds will naturally be more frequent and louder than his normal standing sounds; merely riding him can cause gut sounds to be quieter. Listen for gut sounds that are especially loud or still (see chapter 4).

✳ Call or send someone for your veterinarian. Keep checking vital signs every 10 minutes so you can give your veterinarian an accurate picture of what's going on.

✳ Give Banamine to help with the pain, but be sure to let your veterinarian know if you do, as it temporarily reduces symptoms (for about 30 minutes). NEVER give acepromazine to a horse in colic — it can cause a dangerous drop in blood pressure.

Keep the horse on his feet and walking slowly. Lead him home or to your trailer, keeping a close eye on him. Try to position him in soft footing if he looks like he's about to go down and you can't stop him. One of our mares that colicked did more damage to herself thrashing around on rocky ground than the colic ultimately caused. If you have to trailer a colicking horse, stop periodically to be sure he's still on his feet.

TYING UP

Also called azoturia, "Monday morning disease," paralytic myoglobinuria, and exertional rhabdomyolysis (ER), **tying up** is painful muscle cramping resulting from the breakdown of muscle tissue. (The name azoturia means nitrogen in the urine, a direct result of the breakdown of muscle tissue.) It is actually several symptoms combined, rather than a single condition. The pain can range from mild to excruciating and is sadly sometimes confused for balking, resulting in a suffering horse being punished. The end result is muscle degeneration and, often, kidney damage.

What to know. The name "Monday morning disease" comes from the days when workhorses became ill after a weekend of rest. Because their grain rations were not cut on their days off, their bodies continued to store energy in the form of glycogen in their muscle cells. Come Monday, the horses went back to work and began burning this stored energy, producing lactic acid as a by-product.

As horses burn that abundance of stored energy, lactic acid is produced faster than their bodies can flush it out. High levels of lactic acid disintegrate muscle tissue in a process that releases the muscle protein, myoglobin, which is then flushed out through the kidneys. Unfortunately, the kidneys don't process myoglobin well and the excess strain can lead to kidney failure. All this can happen in only 15 minutes, even with only moderate work.

Some horses tie up when fed lots of alfalfa or grain, especially when they aren't used to it. Another contributor is selenium deficiency, which inhibits normal muscle function. In some parts of the country (like mine) where selenium is naturally deficient in the soil, the grass or local hay is deficient, too.

How to prevent it. Good conditioning, regular exercise, and substituting rice bran for grain seem to help in preventing tying-up episodes. Resist the temptation to increase feed prior to a big ride. Horses don't need to "carb up" like human athletes do. If you live in a selenium-deficient area, provide a mineral block containing selenium for your horse. If he has tied up in the past or is from a bloodline that is known for it, your veterinarian may suggest you supplement his diet with vitamin E (500 to 1000 IU) and vitamin C (10 grams) to reduce muscle damage should an episode occur.

How to recognize it. Signs your horse may be tying up include suddenly stopping and refusing (or not being able) to move, sweating more than normal for the conditions, swishing his tail, tense or hard muscles in the hindquarters, pinning his ears, and trying to move away as you feel for or press down on painful areas. He may appear hunched up. Urine turns the color of coffee, a sign that muscle breakdown is in progress and that myoglobin is being expelled through the kidneys, most likely causing kidney damage in the process. If he does try to move, his gait will be stiff, due to extreme soreness. Again, a resting heart rate higher than 60 bpm and respiration of more than 30 breaths per minute confirm distress.

What to do. If a horse won't move and shows other signs of distress, dismount. Don't try to force him to continue or you will cause more damage to his muscles. Tying up isn't something a horse can walk off. Keep him still. Try to get the horse to drink; dehydration contributes to the body's inability to rid itself of toxins, which contribute to muscle breakdown.

If you know your horse is prone to tying up, consult with your vet before the riding season begins and ask him or her to dispense you an "emergency-response kit" along with clear instructions of what to use and when. Typical treatments include Xylazine or butorphanol to relieve muscle cramping and bute (phenylbutazone) to reduce inflammation and pain.

Only after all signs of tying up have subsided should you ask your horse to move. Walk him home slowly, stopping every 30 minutes or so for a 10-minute rest. For the next few days, watch his urine for dark discoloration, a sign of kidney damage, and stay in touch with your veterinarian.

A Mysterious Malady

The exact cause of tying up has long been poorly understood. Some horses have a tendency toward it. It seems that once a horse experiences an episode, he is at further risk for tying up in the future, but in many cases it is actually a genetic predisposition. Scientists with the Equine Genome Project are currently researching the method of genetic transmission of this as well as dozens of other genetically linked equine diseases. At this point, it appears that individual horses of some breeds inherit the tendency for different reasons than horses of other breeds do.

Because the genetic factors differ, so too do the apparent triggers. In Quarter Horse–type, draft, and Warmblood breeds, a cause is **polysaccharide storage myopathy** (or PSSM), an inherited tendency toward high blood sugar and insulin sensitivity. Susceptible horses should be fed a diet that maintains low blood sugar and low insulin and kept on a regular exercise routine. Feeding grain, confined rest, or sporadic exercise invariably results in a bout of tying up for susceptible horses of these types.

A different cause of tying up, found in some Arabians, Standardbreds, and Thoroughbreds, involves an irregularity in the movement of calcium within the cells during muscle contractions. For them, tying up tends to result from a combination of work and excitement, not from the amount of calcium in the diet. Extreme exertion, especially after the horse has been laid up, often starts the process.

THUMPS

So called because of the "thumping" noise the horse's diaphragm makes during an attack, thumps sound like rhythmic hiccups. More accurately known as **synchronous diaphragmatic flutter,** the sound is actually the result of the diaphragm contracting in conjunction with the heartbeat. It can range from being insignificant to deadly serious.

What to know. When a horse sweats, he loses not only water, but also electrolytes, which can quickly lead to an imbalance of calcium, potassium, chloride, sodium, and/or magnesium. These electrolytes are part of the normal conduction of nervous impulses. An imbalance compromises the nervous system, including the phrenic nerve, which lies directly over the heart. When the heart beats, the unstable phrenic nerve responds by firing, jolting the diaphragm with every heartbeat.

Thumps occurs in unfit horses and in fit horses that are worked hard in hot, humid weather before they get a chance to acclimate to it. Onset usually follows heavy sweating followed by drinking plain water, which further dilutes the remaining electrolytes present in the blood plasma. Other possible causes are blister beetle poisoning, a high-calcium (alfalfa) diet, and reaction to the diuretic drug Lasix (Furosemide).

How to prevent it. Prevention isn't a sure thing, but try to keep your horse's electrolytes in balance (see page 237). Be sure your horse's diet is balanced for calcium and phosphorus (1.2 to 2 parts calcium to 1 part phosphorus), as too much or not enough of either can cause metabolic imbalances. Carry an electrolyte (sodium, potassium, chloride, calcium, and magnesium) supplement with you and offer it in water to your horse before the ride and during the ride if conditions seem to warrant it.

How to recognize it. The most obvious sign of thumps is that the horse's flank twitches with every beat of his heart. Because the diaphragm is not working properly, the horse can't breathe in enough oxygen and may be prone to further problems. Even after a horse has been successfully treated for thumps, he should be carefully monitored, as recurrences are common, within hours to days after initial onset.

What to do. Treatment consists of administering electrolytes, either through drinking water or by intravenous injection with Ringers. Chloride and/or calcium therapy increases blood levels of calcium. (Chloride works by breaking the bonds that bind calcium to protein, making it unusable to the body.)

ALTITUDE SICKNESS

Altitude sickness is obviously only a problem in the high country. Few trails in the United States wind high enough to warrant concern, but those that do in Alaska and in the Rocky Mountains, as well as in the Canadian Rockies, are spectacular, drawing lowland riders from all over the world. For many of us, the experience just wouldn't be the same without our own trusty steed, so we go to the extra trouble and expense to bring our own horse. Be aware that altitude sickness can affect both of you, but you are more at risk than your horse is.

What to know. As of this writing, there are no available studies to cite for the effects of altitude sickness on equines, but a California Polytechnic State University study (involving six horses at elevations of 12,500 feet) is under way.

Two factors combine in horses affected by altitude sickness — effort and lack of oxygen. High-country trails are often extremely challenging, and before hitting the high country, horses should be in premium condition at home. At high elevations the "thin air" holds less usable oxygen, which makes physical exertion all the more demanding. Less oxygen for the lungs means less for working muscles as well.

It also causes the pressure within the blood vessels to increase and the blood acidity to decrease. In people, this can cause potentially lethal pulmonary edema (fluid accumulation and swelling in the lungs). Although blood pressure does rise in horses, pulmonary edema apparently is not a problem. People also suffer from headaches, nausea, weakness, dizziness, and disorientation, but it is not clear if horses develop the same symptoms. However, instances have been reported of horses shivering, stumbling, being less responsive to cues, and appearing more tired than the ride warrants.

How to prevent it. If you plan to take your horse into the high country, plan your excursion so that your horse gets from 1 to 3 days to acclimate to the high elevation before you ask him to work hard. Horses are incredible athletes, but extreme conditions mixed with extreme effort can tax him to his limits.

How to recognize it. As mentioned, keep alert for your horse shivering, stumbling, and generally seeming exhausted. Increased heart and respiratory rates means he is struggling. Keep an eye on vital signs and allow him to rest periodically until they return to normal resting values.

The good news for your horse is that, unless you are more acclimated to high elevations than he is, you are likely to suffer from the effects before he does. If *you* feel nauseous, dizzy, disoriented, weak, confused, disoriented, and/or sleepy, move to a lower elevation. Personally, I zonk out at 10,000 feet with little warning, but it's difficult to label specific altitudes to watch out for since everyone's tolerance is different. It's also hard to pinpoint your exact elevation on the trail unless you carry an altimeter (an instrument for measuring altitude). It's a good idea to add one to your "must-carry" gear if high-country riding is on your agenda.

What to do. The main priority when stricken with altitude sickness is to descend to a lower, more comfortable altitude as quickly and safely as possible. Once at an elevation that was previously comfortable to you (or your horse), find a spot to rest and recuperate until you are ready to proceed home. Drink plenty of water and (for humans) take ibuprofen for headache or body aches associated with altititude sickness.

If you must proceed through higher elevations, return gradually, advancing only as you are comfortable, with frequent stops to rest and rehydrate.

CHAPTER 11

Trail-Riding Competitions

——◦——

THERE ARE NUMEROUS WAYS TO COMPETE ON YOUR
trail horse. Ready for a challenge? Try Competitive Trail Riding. It tests your equine/human partnership over a variety of
courses, distances, and obstacles. Want to add some speed?
Try Endurance Racing. Other competitions include Ride and
Tie, where you partner up with another human, a horse, and
a good pair of running shoes, and Mounted Orienteering,
which adds the air of a treasure hunt to your trail-blazing
experience. If you love dogs, Mounted Field Trialing might be
your sport. Or brush up your skills, your duds, and your
horse's coat and hit the show ring in a Trail Class.

Competitive Trail Riding

Competitive trail riding is becoming more and more popular as people discover the deep satisfaction of conditioning, training, and riding their horse over a lengthy obstacle course on varying terrain while being judged on condition, manners, and performance. It is a crash course in horsemanship, without (we hope) the crash.

HOW IT STARTED

In one form or another, this type of competition has been around since people started riding, but in 1961 the North American Trail Ride Conference (NATRC) was formed to promote the sport formally on this continent. The NATRC set out to create awareness and interest in breeding and using sound, trailworthy horses of suitable type for the job, and to educate members as to the proper methods of training, conditioning, and caring for horses before, during, and after a long ride — in short, to promote good horses and good horsemanship.

THE RIGHT HORSE

Although Arabians have traditionally dominated the sport, Mustangs, Fox Trotters, Warmbloods, Quarter Horses, and even Pasos and an Icelandic have made impressive showings in recent years. Any breed or crossbred horse, pony, or mule can compete.

HOW IT WORKS

Competitive trail rides are timed, judged events that evaluate how well you and your horse are trained and conditioned. They combine the lure of the open trail with some of the challenge of endurance riding and the technical expertise of a trail class. They are not races. All horses must finish within a set time frame — not too fast or too slow. Judges monitor soundness before the ride, at checkpoints along the trail, and at the finish.

It's not enough to finish the course, ride well, and navigate all the obstacles perfectly to win a competitive trail ride. Your horse has to finish in better condition than the other horses do. Because all the horses negotiate the same trail and the same obstacles in a set period of time, judges can compare each animal's condition, soundness, and manners across the board. Excelling at this sport boils down to conditioning and training.

Each horse starts out with 100 points and is docked points over the course of the ride. The final score is based 40 percent on the condition of the horse, 45 percent on his soundness, and 15 percent on his trail ability and manners.

The horse with the fewest penalty points wins, and penalties can come up in many ways. If a horse doesn't recover a resting heart rate of fewer than 48 beats per minute (bpm) within 10 minutes, he will lose one point for each beat per minute over 48. Horses that don't recover within 10 minutes are "held" an additional 10 minutes, then checked again. Any horse that does not

Judges will monitor pulse and respiration ("P&R") at checkpoints along the trail and at the finish.

return to the target heart rate after three 10-minute checks is disqualified. A dehydrated or sore horse can also rack up penalty points, and a lame horse can be disqualified and eliminated from competition altogether. **P&R checks** along the way require the team to stop and check pulse and respiration. Horses are also checked for signs of dehydration, lameness, and injury.

TRAIL TALE: *Lost and Found*

Beverly Frick, from Conroe, Texas, may be what a lot of folks consider a late bloomer in the sport of Competitive Trail Riding (CTR). She had never even haltered a horse until age 52, and by the time she started competing on her little black Paso Fino gelding, Ocho, she had already celebrated her 60th birthday. But she was determined to do her best, and wound up winning many regional awards, as well as the Paso Fino Horse Association's Novice of the Year award, in part for her success in CTR.

Like anyone who loves this sport, Beverly has many stories to share. "On about my fourth ride as a Novice," she recalls, "after crossing some small streams that almost required Ocho to swim, I wandered off the trail somehow and ended up on the Open trail. We came to a tiny ditch with a trickle of water so narrow I could step across it. Ocho wasn't about to cross it. I tried a switch, I tried getting him over from the other side, broke a rein, etc. Remember, this is a timed event and for 45 minutes I fought and struggled to cross a teensy ditch. I came close to tears. Finally several Open riders came along and using three horses pushed and pulled him across.

"Because I'd lost so much time, I had to gallop him in to the finish. We had never cantered before, much less galloped. I just grabbed his mane with one hand and let him go. Ocho loved it. When we crossed the finish line, I had poor brakes and came in like a madwoman. I think we lost only four minutes, which cost us four points off Ocho's score, and he still finished the ride in third or fourth place."

Getting lost isn't easy, because trails are usually quite well marked for these events, but it's not impossible either, as Beverly found out more than once: "I was given the white cane award several times for getting lost. Once I got hopelessly lost in the forest. I couldn't figure out the map and for an hour I kept going back to a reference point and then trying to follow the map in. A lady on a four-wheeler came to find me, as all the other riders were in by then, and she pointed out the trail. Someone had pulled up the markers in the grass. I was a little past the two-mile marker and again had to come galloping in to try to make up for lost time. Everyone had to get out of the way because we still needed a brake job. We lost only a few points, and once again Ocho placed in spite of his rider.

"Everyone helped me. After all, when you get a blonde senior citizen riding a fire-eating horse that takes 5,000 steps a minute, that person *needs* lots of help. Ocho's feet went farther than the other horses' did. I was teased about him a lot: They called him a windmill, an eggbeater, and said they couldn't see how he could finish the course. But they also admired the heart and strength of the little horse with the heavyweight rider."

Horse and rider are judged as a team for the ride. If one is disqualified, the other is automatically out as well. Reasons for team disqualifications include when riders abuse or drug their horses, refuse drug testing, engage in conduct unbecoming a competitive rider, use abusive language, or violate the rules. Horses can be disqualified if they require veterinary treatment that interferes with evaluation, are unruly, or complete the ride more than 30 minutes before the minimum time. Carefully monitored requirements and standards keep competitive trail riding at the highest levels of sportsmanship and competition, making it a truly family-oriented activity.

HOW THE SPORT IS JUDGED

There are three types of rides and three divisions in NATRC competitive trail riding. Rides are designated as one-day (type B), two-day (type A), or three-day (type AA) events. The trail course varies from 15 to 40 miles per day on a carefully monitored schedule based on riding division. Open Division riders face the toughest and longest course. Competitive Pleasure and Novice riders ride the same course, with Competitive Pleasure riders completing more challenging obstacles along the way. Juniors (riders age 10 to 17) have no weight requirements unless they ride in the Adult Open Division, where they fall under the same rules as other Open riders. Junior riders (regardless of which division they compete in) must wear approved ASTM/SEI helmets while mounted and cannot compete on stallions.

According to the NATRC Rule Book, divisions are based on the age of the horse and further divided by weight class.

Open Division. The horse must be 5 years old (or older) as of actual foaling date on ride day. Weight divisions:

✴ Heavyweight — rider and tack combined equal at least 190 pounds
✴ Lightweight — rider and tack combined equal 100–189 pounds

NATRC

The North American Trail Riding Conference (NATRC) has the following goals:

1. To stimulate greater interest in the breeding and use of good horses possessed of stamina and hardiness and qualified to make good mounts for trail use.
2. To demonstrate the value of type and soundness in the proper selection of horses for competitive riding.
3. To learn and demonstrate the proper methods of training and conditioning horses for competitive riding.
4. To encourage good horsemanship as related to trail riding.
5. To demonstrate the best methods of caring for horses during and after long rides without the aid of artificial methods or stimulants.

Source: NATRC Rule Book

Competitive Pleasure. The horse must be at least four years old. There is no weight requirement.

Novice. The horse must be at least four years old. Weight divisions:

✴ Heavyweight — rider and tack combined equal at least 190 pounds
✴ Lightweight — rider and tack combined equal 100–189 pounds

Junior. There is no weight requirement (unless competing in Open Division; see above).

Riders are also independently judged on their horsemanship, and each event awards the highest-scoring rider. Scorecards to evaluate horse and rider performance are filled out by judges for each obstacle encountered along the trail. A rider can learn a lot about his horsemanship by reviewing these cards.

A team of at least two judges, one veterinarian and one horsemanship judge, are posted at intervals along the way to evaluate each horse and rider. Riders are judged on their overall horsemanship and on how they negotiate obstacles. Obstacles can be natural or man-made and may include steep hills (up or down), water crossings, bridges, gates, dense brush, backing/sidepassing or otherwise negotiating man-made obstacles, and crossing logs.

Endurance Riding

To finish is to win!

That is the internationally recognized motto of a sport that was extreme before "extreme sports" were cool. One famous example is the Tevis Cup race, in which riders wind through 100 miles of the Sierra Nevadas between Squaw Valley, Nevada, and Auburn, California, on one horse — in 1 day.

What the American Endurance Riding Conference (AERC) so modestly describes as "an athletic event with the same horse and rider covering a measured course within a specified maximum time" is actually one of the most grueling competitions known to equestrian sport. Endurance races pit painstakingly conditioned horses and riders against each other and each horse's threshold for exertion.

Horses are raced over predetermined distances that they must finish within a maximum time. Unlike competitive trail riding, there is no minimum time limit. For instance, 50-mile races must be completed in 12 hours, 75-milers in 18 hours, 100-milers in 24 hours, and races that exceed the 100-mile mark are run in 50-mile increments per day for a maximum of 150 miles. Longer rides, such as the 250-mile Shore-to-Shore race from Lake Huron to Lake Michigan, used to be completed in 5 days, but revised rules (2004) have cut back to the 150-mile maximum allowable distance. AERC rides also sponsor "limited distance rides" of 25 to 35 miles for beginners. Since all sponsored same-distance rides are held to the same time standard, what sets one race apart from another is the degree of difficulty of the terrain itself. Sand, rocks, and hills all add to the challenge.

Veterinarians carefully monitor horses at designated rest stops, where they are evaluated for soundness and metabolic stability. On a 100-mile ride, each horse is allotted only 3 hours total rest, and the rider, practically speaking, has hardly any rest time.

Herein lies the twist: The first horse across the finish line isn't always the winner. To win, a horse must qualify according to criteria set down by ride veterinarians. If a horse is deemed unsound or stressed beyond the designated limitations, he is disqualified. Horses stop every 10 to 15 miles throughout the ride and are checked over by veterinarians, who can eliminate a horse from the race at any point along the course.

These stops are serious business. It is not uncommon for horses to die from colic before, after, or during endurance races. Intense exertion, combined with other stress factors such as dehydration, excitement, food and water changes, and discomfort, creates a prime scenario for colic. This is no sport for the unprepared.

In endurance riding, the only judges are the clock and the attending veterinarians. An award for Best Condition goes to the one horse out of the fastest 10 finishers that is in the best condition after the ride. The veterinarians take into account the horse's speed and the total weight carried. But if none of the horses meets their criteria, the award is not presented.

In a sport already known for its difficulty, some rides such as the Tevis Cup and the Old Dominion Trail in Virginia are renowned for being especially punishing. Because it is so incredibly brutal, just completing a ride like that with your horse in good condition, regardless of where you place, is a genuine victory. Hence, the motto.

HOW IT STARTED

Endurance riding dates back centuries in horse cultures around the world. The sport had a reputation of pushing horses until they dropped, prizing the skill of the rider who could get the most mileage from his mount. By the late 1800s, it had fallen into disrepute due to mistreatment of horses.

One race was organized in 1893 to prove the mettle of the Western stock horse. A man named John Berry, on his horse Poison, won by covering the 1,000 miles between Chadron, Nebraska, and Chicago in 14 days. That's averaging more than 70 miles per day for 2 weeks straight. In 1908, a race crossed 500 miles of rugged mountains between Evanston, Wyoming, and Denver. About 2 years later another "endurance ride" took place, traveling from New York to San Francisco in 60 days (averaging 60 miles per day), but it wasn't techni-

Sponge cool water under your horse's neck and inside his legs.

cally a race. It involved two riders, riding together as a team for a prize of $10,000 if they made it in time. They didn't: They lost their horses in the Salt Lake desert and spent 3 or 4 days searching for them on foot. They arrived in San Francisco 2 days after the 60-day deadline. The riders were seven and nine years old!

These and other such races stressed horses to and beyond their limits. In the early 1900s, the Morgan Horse Club introduced rules to protect the horses during its rides in Vermont. Calvary-sponsored rides did likewise. With the founding of the AERC in 1972, the sport took on official regulations and standardized rules.

Today endurance riding is still standardized and sanctioned (in the United States) by the AERC. Riders rack up points as well as miles throughout the year toward year-end awards. Many riders accumulate thousands of miles on a single horse. Regional organizations offer their own recognition, as do several breed organizations, including the Arabian, Appaloosa, Morgan, and Paso Fino breed associations. The Arabian Horse Association sponsors championship rides around the country.

Endurance riding is not limited to the United States. It takes consistent high placing to qualify for international competition, such as the World Championships or the Pan American Championships. In Australia and the United Kingdom, the sport is nearly an obsession. Famous rides such as the Quilty in Australia and the Summer Solstice

Organized in 1955, the Tevis Cup ride covers 100 miles in 1 day.

and the Golden Horseshoe in Great Britain (along with the U.S. Tevis Cup) draw world-class contenders. Although the international Fédération Equestre Internationale (FEI) awards medals for endurance riding, it is not an Olympic sport — yet.

THE RIGHT HORSE

So what type of trail horse does it take to make an endurance horse? One with a crazy — or at least extraordinarily dedicated — owner.

Arabians rule the sport, but you can begin conditioning the horse you have right now and be able to finish 50-mile, or longer, races within a year or so. Any breed or unregistered horse is eligible to compete, and Quarter Horses, Morgans, Mustangs, Appaloosas, and Fox Trotters have all made respectable names for themselves in this discipline. When considering an endurance prospect, top contenders scrutinize a horse's hooves, pasterns, cannon bones, leg conformation, shoulders, heart girth, back, hindquarters, head, and neck (see chapter 2).They also look for a good, willing temperament and the ratio of the miles the horse can cover to how fast he covers them, and then, usually, they consider the breed.

Body type counts more than registration papers. Bulky, muscular horses build up too much heat in their muscles to sustain the effort. Generally, smaller, "drier" horses with ample flat bone and large joints hold up best to the rigors of the endurance trail. In the 1990 Race of Champions (150 miles), the top seven finishers had lower body condition scores (see chapter 4) and less fatty deposits in the hindquarters than horses that wound up disqualified during the race. This implies that lean horses are more suitable than those with fat reserves.

Large heart muscle is an indicator of oxygen-to-energy-conversion efficiency. When the incredible racehorse Secretariat died, his autopsy revealed that his very healthy heart was more than twice the normal size (22 pounds as opposed to 9 for an average Thoroughbred heart). Some buyers order ultrasound examinations of their endurance prospects to measure heart size.

To compete in endurance, a horse must be remarkably sound, willing, and in phenomenal condition. It takes several months to a year to get a prospect in shape. The first few months maximize aerobic power, but it takes months beyond that to build up anaerobic tolerance (to maximize the metabolism of lactic acid). It takes years of consistent training to maximize the horse's efficiency in gait, stride, and balance. Because of the time it takes for a horse to mature and to achieve adequate conditioning, horses must be at least five years old to enter 50-mile and longer races.

HOW IT WORKS

Like CTR, endurance riding has different divisions for competitors based on age and weight. Juniors are riders under the age of sixteen as of the first day of the current season. (Ride seasons run from December 1 through November 30 of the following calendar year.) Unless they are older than fourteen, have completed 500 miles, and have been accepted as "unsponsored" riders by the ride management, all juniors must ride with a sponsor, an

Sometimes proceeding on foot is the best and safest way.

adult twenty-one years or older. All juniors must wear an approved safety helmet and provide written parental permission to compete. Senior riders are further divided by weight class:

Heavyweight. 211 pounds (or more) of combined tack and rider weight.

Middleweight. 186–210 pounds of combined tack and rider weight.

Lightweight. 161–185 pounds of combined tack and rider weight.

Featherweight. 160 pounds or less of combined tack and rider weight.

Riders can be weighed at any ride and fellow competitors can challenge the weight of any rider and request an official weighing.

Rides are very competitive, and rules are strictly enforced. At any given checkpoint, horses must meet the preset criteria established by the ride vet-erinarians before they can continue. This includes standards of maximum allowable pulse and respiration, which can be set either high or low for the given course and conditions at their discretion. No medication or veterinary treatment is allowed during a competition. The AERC proudly states, "Endurance equines must compete entirely on their natural ability."

Other disqualifying activities include bouncing your entry check, equine abuse (including drugging and continuing to ride a horse without express permission after it has been pulled by a ride veterinarian), arguing with the ride veterinarians, breaking past them or blocking other riders on the trail, and moving trail markers or any other form of cheating, such as taking shortcuts on the course or leaving a timed rest stop early. A badly behaved horse will also get the boot.

A TYPICAL RIDE

A typical endurance ride begins with your arrival at the ride camp the night before the event. Upon entering you will be issued a vet card and a number. Keep the vet card in a safe place and wear the number whenever you are on the ride course.

The next step is your horse's examination. A veterinarian will write down your horse's pulse and heart rate along with comments about hydration, gait, and whatever else he or she may notice on your vet card.

That evening there will be a meeting about the ride, which will include important information about the route itself, the rules regarding vet stops, and any changes to the rules. This is when riders draw for starting times. The riders tackling the longest distances depart first, beginning at about 5:30 A.M. A group of about 10 riders will then leave every 5 minutes until all competitors are on the course. After the meeting, be sure your horse is fed, watered, and secured, and try to get some rest.

"Endurance equines must compete entirely on their natural ability."
— AERC Rules of Competition

In the morning, feed your horse at least 2 hours before you begin the ride. Eat a light breakfast, then make sure your supplies, including buckets of water, sponges, and a sweat scraper, are set out. It's nice to have a helper to handle these things for you, and going along as a helper is a great way to learn the ropes of the sport. Saddle your horse about a half hour ahead of departure time and warm up. Apply bug spray and sunscreen to yourself and your horse, and be sure to wear lip moisturizer. Some riders wear bandannas or even painter's masks to keep from inhaling dust. Put on your number and wait where you can hear the announcer call it.

Rides are usually plotted in legs that loop back to base camp. Some riders do only one leg; others ride back out from camp after the first loop to continue. You can even "elevate" from one length of ride to an additional leg if your horse qualifies.

THE VET CHECK When you complete your first leg, your time is noted on your vet card. You have 20 minutes before your horse is vetted to determine his condition or if he is "fit to continue," the goal of every endurance rider. This is why water and sponges are waiting.

Sponge cool water under your horse's neck and inside his legs, but do not use cold water on the large muscles of his neck, back, and quarters. The chill could cause painful cramping, which can eliminate your horse from the race. Allow your horse to drink a few sips of clean, tepid water every few minutes. The goal is to get your horse's pulse and respiration back down before the veterinarian checks him.

The vet will also compare your horse's gait to how he moved before the race (or the first leg of it) and evaluate how well he is hydrated. He or she might also listen to gut sounds and check capillary refill.

After 20 minutes (or up to an hour after your final leg of the race), you must present your horse and the vet card to the veterinarian. This is a do-or-die moment; any abnormalities and you are out. If your horse is in good shape and you finished within the allotted time, you will be allowed to continue on with the time you leave noted or you qualify for a certificate of completion. At the end of your final leg, the veterinarian keeps the vet card.

FORMALITIES

After the ride there is a certificate ceremony, which all riders are encouraged to attend. This delay also allows your horse some well-deserved rest before the trailer ride home. Balancing on four tired legs can't be fun.

Ride and Tie

Let's say you and a buddy are enthralled by the idea of endurance riding, but between the two of you have only one horse. What's a team to do? Go ride and tie. (And that just happens to be the slogan of the Ride and Tie Association.)

HOW IT STARTED

It probably began centuries earlier, but the first written record of using "ride and tie" as a method of equine transportation is from England in 1742. That year, Henry Fielding published *History of Joseph Andrews,* which included an account of how Andrews traveled to London with a friend. Fielding called it "a method of traveling much used by persons who have but one horse between them." He explained that "two travelers set out together, one on horseback, the other on foot: now, as it generally happens that he on horseback outgoes him on foot, the custom is that when he arrives at the distance agreed on, he is to dismount, tie the horse to some gate, tree, post or other thing, and then proceed on foot, when the other comes up to the horse, he unties him, mounts and gallops on, till having passed by his fellow traveler, he likewise arrives at the place of tying."

Similar accounts exist from America in the 1700s, a time when horses were not readily available to people of all walks of life. Other stories credit "ride and tie" as having been invented in the old West. But as a sport, it got its dubious beginning in 1971, thanks to a Levi Strauss & Co. public relations employee named Bud Johns. Johns had read the Fielding account and thought a contest that paired horse and human teams against each other and the elements was just the sort of image to fit Levi's.

Dubbed the Levi Ride and Tie, the first event was sponsored as a promotion for the jeans manufacturer. The course ran about 45 miles through the hills and rugged trails between Saint Helena and Sonoma, California. The competitors were excited, but most had no clue about the limitations of their horses. One participant lamented the experience in the following words.

The start of a Ride and Tie Race can look like a free-for-all, but serious strategy is involved.

"Our first Ride and Tie had no vet checks. Everyone was new at this new sport. . . . Many of the riders did not realize the horse should be well trained and physically near perfect . . . also not to be pushed too hard. Well — needless to say we were in great trouble before the end of the race. Two beautiful animals died on the trail that day! They did their best, but their masters asked too much of them."

This rider credits Bud Johns, among others, for making sure it never happened again. Future rides included veterinary checkpoints, watering stations at every stop, and mandatory pulse and respiration recoveries. A horse whose pulse does not return to 72 bpm (beats per minute) or less does not continue the race.

In 1988, the Ride and Tie Association was formed to promote and regulate the sport. Members benefit from a mentor program, training videos that stress endurance-horse management, a matchmaking service that pairs up partners for competition, and practice events. The association also sponsors regional and national ride-and-tie competitions. The sport is most popular in California, but several other states also host events. Ride-and tie-events also have been held in Canada, England, France, Germany and Sweden, and there is even a World Championship Ride and Tie.

HOW IT WORKS

Ride and tie combines two sports, running and endurance riding, with the strategy of a fast-paced chess game. Deciding who runs and who rides along which stretches of the course and where the horse will be tied to rest and await the runner are the strategy points that make or break a winning race. Stretches of one-half mile to a mile are fairly common. Some runners prefer longer distances, some shorter, and the terrain plays a part in deciding when and where to tie up. Uphill legs are bound to be shorter than downhill.

Ride-and-tie courses range from 25 to 40 miles and are generally held over running trails, logging roads, and other remote pathways. (Novice or fun races are often much shorter, 10 miles or so.) They may be held in national forests or state parks as well as on private land. Organizers look for trails with trees or other safe anchors (such as gates, fence posts, and telephone poles) to which horses can be tied and left unattended. Riders and runners must keep to the marked course, and only one team member at a time can use the horse. Each team must tie up the horse and take turns riding and running at least six times during the race, but there is no maximum as to how many times they can rest the horse and switch over.

HOW THE SPORT IS JUDGED

Unlike its unfortunate debut, the sport of ride and tie now has many safeguards in place to protect the health and well-being of its equine athletes. Horses must be at least five years old to race. Pregnant and nursing mares are not allowed to compete. No drugs or medications (including analgesic ointments) are allowed within 72 hours of race time or within an hour of finishing the race. All medications administered within the 2 weeks immediately prior to the race must be disclosed in writing at the pre-ride vet check, which every horse must pass to compete. For each event, ride veterinarians determine specific criteria for pulse and respiration levels that each horse must meet at vet checks stationed along the course. Horses must pass a final vet check within 1 hour of finishing for the team to remain eligible for completion awards.

Races have a maximum time limit, but these are often generous. Serious competitors average about 10 miles per hour, finishing a 25-mile race in about 2½ hours, but the ride may allow for as much as 6 hours to finish, or up to 8 hours for a 40-mile ride. Ride organizers and veterinarians determine finish times based on the trail terrain, weather, and other conditions. Since a team's finish time is not clocked until the last member finishes, most teams plan to cross the finish line together, as a matter of teamwork and unity. Usually this means one member has to wait for the other to catch up.

A TYPICAL RACE

The starting line of a ride-and-tie race is organized chaos. Runners and riders line up in a wide, open area, or at a broad intersection when dirt roads are used for the course. Horses start in front of the runners to avoid stepping on anyone. At the drop of a flag (or shout), they all take off at once. The first mile or so is a mad dash for position, but as the horses and runners spread out, teams settle into their race plans. Horses quickly outpace runners and a part of the racing strategy is to reach your tie-off spot before someone else takes it. With from 10 to 50 teams competing, prime tying locations can get snapped up quickly.

Some races allow a helper to be stationed at the first tie-off point to hold the horse. This safety measure was instituted due to the nature of some trails and the excitement of most horses at the start of the race.

THE RIGHT HORSE

The best mounts for ride-and-tie races are fast but reasonably calm. They must be able to tolerate standing tied, alone, while other horses (and runners) zip past them. Another feature that is appreciated by tiring runners is a horse that is not too tall. Mounting a small horse is easier than scaling a tall one.

One veteran competitor comments that the horse quickly figures out what the race is all about. By the third or fourth time she catches up to her horse, he is turned around watching for her and may even greet her with an excited whinny!

Any breed is eligible, but as for endurance racing, body type counts more than papers. Lean, dry-bodied types do best, and here, as in endurance riding and competitive trail riding, Arabians excel. Because speed is a vital component, Thoroughbreds also do well, and Standardbreds should too. There have been successful Morgan, Quarter

> ### Where to Tie?
>
> Part of the challenge of the race is to find, and reach, a suitable place to tie your horse before someone else does, and courses are deliberately plotted with this in mind. Sometimes a rider has to go for miles to find something usable. Horses must be tied to features of the existing landscape, like trees, tree roots, and fence posts. (Artificial ties, such as a stake brought from home, are not allowed.) The horse cannot block the trail or be tied in specified "No Tie" areas.
>
> Riders must find things to tie their horses to that will securely hold their horses. Experienced ride-and-tie horses are held fast by as little as a clump of grass, but others, or horses fresh and excited at the beginning of a race, require a more substantial anchor to stay put.

Horse, and Tennessee Walking Horse contenders. As with endurance horses, the main criteria are soundness, efficiency of movement, and condition.

The human two thirds of this team must also be extremely fit, as well as possessing good horsemanship skills and the riding ability to be competitive. But anyone who can walk and stay on a horse can participate just for the fun of it.

Mounted Orienteering

Billed as the "thinking horse sport," competitive mounted orienteering combines the skills of orienteering with trail riding. Competitors use a map and compass clues to find objective stations that have been hidden within a prescribed area, often in wild country, with few or no trails. You'll feel just like Lewis and Clark, except *you'll* have a map.

HOW IT STARTED

Orienteering has long been a part of military training as a way for foot soldiers to navigate unfamiliar territory. Beginning as a military exercise in 19th-century Scandinavia, it was first organized as a sport in that country in 1918 or 1919 (accounts vary) by Bjorn Kjellstrom, who also introduced it to the United States. He and his brother Alvar, with their friend Gunnar Tillander, are credited with inventing the modern orienteering compass. According to the *History of Orienteering*, by Bertil Nordenfelt, the term *orienteering* was coined by the Military Academy in Sweden in 1886 to mean "crossing unknown territory with the aid of a map and compass."

The sport graduated to horseback in the midwestern United States. The new version of the old sport was called competitive mounted orienteering (CMO). In 1981, the National Association of Competitive Mounted Orienteering (NACMO) was formed. Four years later the sport had spread across the country to Washington state. Today, 24 states have been involved with CMO at one time or another, and Arkansas, California, Idaho, Illinois, Indiana, Michigan, Minnesota, Montana, Nevada, New Jersey, New York, Oklahoma, Oregon, Pennsylvania, Texas, Washington, and Wisconsin have active chapters at the time of this writing.

HOW IT WORKS

Organized as a family activity or a competitive sport, CMO events often have the air of a group treasure hunt rather than a competition. Each event comprises a short course, which is typically a five-station ride, and a long course, which can have five or ten stations. The goal is to find as many stations as possible, as quickly as possible. The general whereabouts of each station is circled on the map and every competitor receives an identical map at the beginning of the ride. Each circle

In mounted orienteering, the stations are usually hidden so that you can ride right past them and not see them. Thus, it is crucial that you find them by their coordinates.

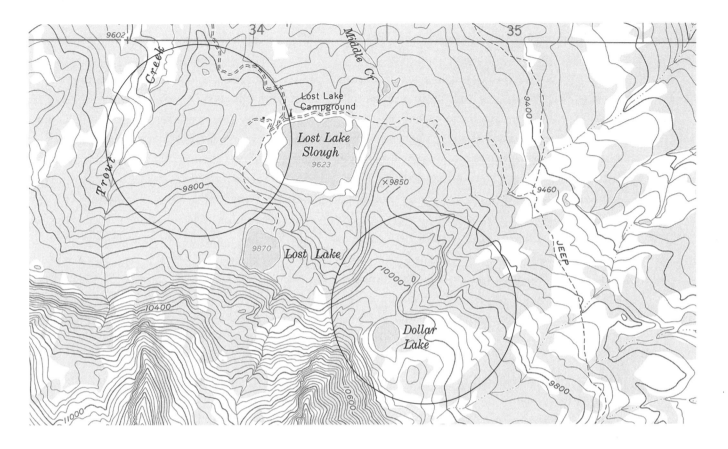

Each station is somewhere inside a ¾-mile circle on the map.

can cover no more than ¾ mile in diameter and must include the station somewhere within its area but not necessarily in the center. The station might be at the very outer edge of the circle, anywhere within its circumference, or right at dead center. After all, who'd think to look there!

Event organizers make it easy for newcomers. Each CMO ride begins with a seminar on map reading and compass use, and a practice objective station is hidden near the starting/finish line.

To find stations, competitors check the map and orient landmarks listed on the back of it with specific compass readings. Riders may work alone or in teams, depending on the rules for the event, but team members cannot split up to find different stations; they have to work together. Riders can look for objective stations in any order. Plotting the course to cover the entire area in the most efficient way is part of the strategy of the sport. Since winning depends on finding hidden markers,

competitors learn to be crafty, so as not to lead others to their discoveries.

Objective stations are 9-inch white paper plates with at least two letters and a number written on the back. Riders jot down the two-letter code and the number from the back of each objective station on their maps and proceed from that station to look for the next, using the clues on the map and their compasses.

The winner of a CMO event is the one (or the team) who finds the most hidden objective stations in the shortest amount of time. Time is counted from the second you receive your map until you (or the last member of your team) cross the finish line at the completion of the ride.

Courses vary in size and difficulty depending on the event and the natural terrain. A long course can range from 8 to 25 miles; a short course consists of much less territory. (Course routes can cover areas that range from 2 to 12 square miles.)

The distance and the terrain between stations challenge your horsemanship and your horse's condition. You can lose or gain a good deal of time in between stations, as well as by accidentally rushing past one and having to backtrack!

Events are timed and ideally last at least 2 hours but no more than 6. Upon crossing the finish line, each rider (or designated team leader) either hands in a written account of the code letters found on the back of the objective stations along the way or recites them verbally to ride management as proof of which stations have been discovered. Awards (and points) are given to the six highest-finishing teams, and points scored are forwarded to the NACMO, where they are tallied in a database for national point standings and year-end awards.

HOW THE SPORT IS JUDGED

The rules of mounted orienteering are less stringent than those of other trail-riding sports, but that doesn't mean the sport itself is less demanding. It all depends on the rider. Horses are not vetted, but pulse and respiration checks before and after are allowed. Anyone caught treating a horse inhumanely is disqualified.

An adult must still accompany riders under 18 years old, but those 14 to 17 may ride together if approved by ride management. Only registered members of the NACMO may compete, but you can join just for the day of a ride if you so choose. Helmets are not required and GPS systems are not allowed. Other rules are no tampering with the objective station markers, official landmarks, or clues on the course, and no interfering with other horses or riders.

THE RIGHT HORSE

Any breed is eligible for the sport, and horses as young as three years old are allowed to compete. Even though it isn't monitored during the event, your horse's condition should be good enough to cover the intended distance at speed. An orienteering horse should be a consummate trail horse, crossing all types of terrain (including hills, brush, water, wet squishy ground, bridges, and fallen logs) and standing quietly when tied.

Compared to some other competitive trail sports, orienteering places more emphasis on the brain of the human part of the team, but it also depends heavily on an able-bodied, quiet-minded horse. It is a family-"oriented" sport, and the different levels of ride provided at each event allow everyone to have a good time and compete as seriously as they see fit.

Reading a Compass

CMO enthusiasts recommend the Silva Type 7 compass (the same brand designed by the Scandinavian "father" of the sport, Bjorn Kjellstrom). Seasoned orienteerers recommend wearing your compass on a cord around your neck and tucking it into a shirt pocket to protect against jarring while in motion.

When reading your compass be sure:

- to avoid reading it near metal, including the metal frame of some saddle horns (which can throw the reading off by as much as 15 to 20 degrees), metal pipes, and bridges;
- it is not near any electronic device, including a cell phone or watch, which can alter a reading up to five degrees;
- to avoid overhead or underground power lines.

A Good Deal

Joining the NACMO has its perks. Not only can you participate in competitive mounted orienteering events, but membership also automatically covers all of your horses with a million-dollar liability insurance policy that is in effect 24 hours a day, every day.

Field Trialing

If negotiating and being judged on man-made obstacles, pushing your own or your horse's endurance to the limit, and getting lost are not your idea of fun trail-riding sports, then how about going to the dogs? Bird dogs, that is.

Hunting with dogs from horseback is a time-honored and distinguished sport. The sport is based on bird hunting, which by definition involves killing birds, so it is not a sport for everyone, although at many events the birds are not harmed and blanks are used instead of real shot. For competitors, field trialing combines the thrill of the hunt, the satisfaction of watching a well-bred, well-trained dog, and the pleasure of riding a well-trained horse.

HOW IT STARTED

Field trialing of bird dogs enjoys a rich and colorful history, particularly in the South and Midwest. The sport originated in the British Isles in the 1870s and quickly caught on in the United States. In 1884, the first recorded organized field trial in America was held near Memphis, Tennessee. A setter known as Knight, belonging to H. C. Pritchard, was immortalized as the first field trial winner.

Trials for setters and pointers grew rapidly under the aegis of the American Field, particularly in the southern states, until 1929. Throughout the Depression years and World War II, however, no more than ten field trials were held for pointing breeds in any given year. American Field is the oldest, the biggest, and in many competitors' opinion the best of the horseback-riding trials.

Conversely, for years the American Kennel Club (AKC), the major registry for purebred dogs, did not sanction mounted field trials or allow handling dogs from horseback in any of its existing trials. Professional trainers, many of whom had gained experience in American Field trials, felt that this restriction was highly detrimental to the improvement of the performance of their dogs. Many campaigned actively for the AKC to allow dogs to be handled from horseback, and in 1966 the AKC Standard Procedure for Pointing Breed Trials was amended to permit the optional handling of dogs from horseback. This victory helped to expand the popularity of AKC field trials for pointing breeds. The number of trials doubled to more than 450 per year, with more than 38,000 dogs competing annually. In recent years the sport has waned somewhat in the United States, due to strict state gun laws, game regulations, and limited access to large enough acreage for the trials.

In field trialing the horse is not judged, but he has to be extremely competent anyway.

THE RIGHT DOG

Generally only dogs that point game birds, such as German Shorthairs, Weimaraners, English Setters, Gordon Setters, Viszlas, Brittanys, German Wirehairs, Pointing Griffons, Spimonias, the occasional Beagle, and, of course, Pointers, are field-trialed from horseback, and to be blunt, the horses, while seemingly indispensable, are incidental in the eyes of the sport itself. Make no mistake, this is a sport about dogs and hunting; the horses are not judged or competing in any way.

Field-trial horses must not mind dogs running up behind them, around them, even under and into them.

Although only a small percentage of all bird dogs are worked from horseback, they represent the highest level of field trialing for pointing bird dogs. They cover more ground and compete under more stringent standards than do dogs that compete in "walking trials" with their handlers on foot. More people attend horseback trials than walking trials. Why walk when you can ride?

HOW THE SPORT IS JUDGED

Horseback field trials are divided into categories, or **stakes,** based on the handler's status (professional or amateur) and the dog's age. Stakes are run in **braces** of two dogs each. A judge on horseback follows each dog, and usually the two judges switch about halfway through the run to give each judge the chance to assess both dogs individually. Field-trial dogs are judged on how well they respond to their handlers and how well they cover their given area. A dog that scouts the edges, hedgerows, fence lines, and other areas that birds are likely to use as cover scores better than one that just runs around in circles.

Enthusiasm counts, as does accuracy on point. Does the dog find birds? How the dog points is measured. Style counts. Intensity gives the edge. Dogs are also judged on how bright their performance is, and on how much stamina they have left at the end of the brace. So what are the horses doing during all this?

THE RIGHT HORSE

Field-trial horses fill many roles. They are ridden by judges to keep up with the action, by handlers, by the **bird planter** (the person who carries live birds out to the field on his horse), and by field marshals and the **gallery** (people who are not directly participating in a particular brace but are just along to watch).

To be so versatile, these horses must possess many skills, and because this is not "their show," any horse that isn't serviceable is out. Field-trial horses must load and trailer flawlessly. They must stand tied or picketed, often for hours at a stretch, with no fuss. Obviously they must not be skittish around dogs and can take in stride dogs jumping on them and running up behind them, around them, and even under or into them. They must also be impervious to fluttering, squawking, and flushing birds. Field-trial horses cannot be spooky or gun-shy because guns are fired around them all day. They must also ground-tie reliably, as the handler must dismount to flush game for his dog multiple times throughout each brace. They must go where they are aimed and not be concerned about leaving other horses behind.

Field-trial horses are also used to **road** dogs, running them on a long leash and harness to get them into condition to compete, and to move them in a controlled manner off the course. If the dog gets tangled or bumps into the horse, the horse is expected to ignore it and keep moving unless told to stop by the rider. These horses must also tackle all types of terrain as part of a day's work, including mud, standing water, creeks, drainage ditches, brush, and hills.

Field-trial horses must be in excellent condition, as they are generally ridden hard for about 4 hours at a time. Most competitors use two horses — one for the morning braces and another for the afternoon braces. Field-trial horses are almost exclusively gaited, for two reasons. One is that field-trial rules stipulate that the horse must advance at a flat-footed walk. Gaited horses have that extra "gear," which *is* technically still a walk but just eats up the ground. The other reason is that gaited horses are so much smoother to ride, and anyone who spends an entire day — often days at a time throughout the season — in the saddle appreciates the difference in comfort.

Just about any gaited breed has made the grade as a field-trial horse, which speaks well of their mental abilities, as well as of their gait and stamina. Tennessee Walking Horses have long been the traditional mount for this sport, and Missouri Fox Trotters, Paso Fino, Mountain Horses, Peruvian Pasos, and Spotted Saddle Horses have all made reliable field-trial horses.

In fact, one entire breed was established and protected under the auspices of dedicated field trialers. In 1993, horsemen who also happened to be veteran field trialers set the wheels in motion to recognize the horses they had been breeding and using as field-trial horses for decades as a breed. The horses, named for the family that originally bred them, were descended from foundation stock for the Tennessee Walking Horse breed. The McCurdy Plantation Horse is now known all over the United States as a reliable trail horse with the extra advantage of a smooth saddle gait.

HOW IT WORKS

In a field trial the dogs and their handlers on horseback move out first, followed by the judges. Field marshals and the gallery (observers) ride up last. Some trials have as many as 70 members in the gallery, with up to 1,500 at American Field National Championships!

One key rider heads out before the competitors and the gallery hit the saddle. The bird planter rides out in advance to place birds in the area where the dogs will hunt. His horse must be unflappable — literally, because he carries the game birds, which are very likely to flap and squawk in protest.

Gallery Etiquette

To ride in the gallery is a privilege, and spectators must follow the longstanding rules of etiquette with regard to the dogs, handlers, and judges or they can be dismissed. Any behavior by a horse or rider in the gallery that distracts the dogs is a cardinal sin. All horses, including those of the gallery, which are in theory farthest from the action, must be dead broke to dogs. Any horse that is not trained for dogs or other field-trial conditions is not welcome. With prize hunting dogs worth $10,000 to $20,000 at stake, no one wants a horse around that might kick!

Showing in Trail Classes

You may ask what showing in a trail (or practical horsemanship) class has to do with trail horses. The simple truth is that any show horse will benefit from time spent on the trail, even if he does incur a bump or scratch. And any trail horse will indeed benefit from visiting the show scene. It is the mother of all proving grounds.

Shows are inherently exciting and distracting for horses. Just as a lot of people don't feel comfortable in crowds, horses that are used to the quiet of home or the open trail are often distressed, confused, and totally disoriented when they get to a show. Strange smells, the calls of unfamiliar horses, peculiar sights, smells, and people can put them into sensory overload. Your horse doesn't freak out intentionally to be bad; he just gets excited and winds up going into instinct overdrive. What better way to proof all that training you have put into your trail partner?

Don't kid yourself that your great trail horse can waltz right in off the trail and win a trail *class*. Things that don't count on the trail can count you out in the ring, but covering these bases isn't hard; it just takes some planning and work. You must know the rules, such as never putting two hands

A trail horse will benefit from experiencing a trail class, even if only once.

on the reins (unless riding in a bosal or snaffle class) and not changing hands on the reins (except at a mailbox obstacle or gate).

TAKE CARE OF THE VISUALS

To be competitive, you will need an attractive ensemble for you and your horse. This means more than clothes shopping; this means coordinating a look that will catch a judge's eye and make you look polished and professional, even if your horse doesn't execute a perfect sidepass. Though most people showing in trail classes traditionally show in Western tack and apparel, some exhibitors prefer to ride English. Just be sure all tack is clean, in good repair, and fastened correctly and that your outfit is smart.

Your horse also must be groomed to a tee. Proper grooming from your horse's perspective means a good roll in the dirt after a ride; from yours it may mean simply brushing him off or hosing him down to help cool him. From a show-ring perspective, however, it means putting every hair in place, even hairs you didn't notice before, such as those in his ears, on his muzzle, and under his chin. And as important as sound conformation is on the trail, an attractive, typey horse has a definite edge at a show.

Most of the things you encounter in a trail class are things that you would simply walk around or past on the actual trail. What trail rider in his or her right mind intentionally crosses a teeter-totter, walks through the centers of a line of tires, or steps into a box just to turn around and step out again?

| TRAIL TALE | *Reality Check* | |

It was 1969. I had just blown the gate and the tire obstacle at my first horse show, wearing a borrowed shirt and riding my cream-colored, blue-eyed trail horse. I knew I had lost the class and, rather than watch other riders go through (as I should have), I rode off the show grounds and down to a nearby river. The girl who had ridden before me, acing every obstacle, came along — as far as she could.

While I rode down the bank and into the water, she hung back. Truth was, her horse wouldn't go anywhere *near* the water. Later, when I (begrudgingly) congratulated her on winning the class, I kidded that it sure didn't seem fair that a horse that couldn't actually be trail ridden would beat out a true trail horse. She replied, somewhat smugly, that her horse wasn't just an old trail horse; he was a show horse.

But these and a multitude of other trail-class obstacles are meant to test your horse's training, focus, and obedience, not to simulate an actual trail ride.

HOW THE CLASS IS JUDGED

Trail classes are judged one obstacle at a time. Sometimes one judge follows a horse through the course; other times several judges work the ring at a time, each judging only one or two obstacles as multiple horses make their way through the course.

A map of the obstacles and the order and manner in which they are to be negotiated is posted before the class. It is the rider's responsibility to memorize the course and to complete the obstacles in the correct order and in the correct way. If you fail to trot over the poles instead of canter, or back through the L instead of sidepassing around it, it will cost you points. Completing obstacles in the wrong order can get you disqualified.

If you blow an obstacle (get a "no score"), keep going and do your best. You may be able to make up points, and continuing on will remind your horse that the fun doesn't stop just because he messed up (intentionally or otherwise).

ATTITUDE COUNTS A simple thing that makes a big impact on the judge, your horse, and even yourself is your own attitude. Think positively. Envision your horse flawlessly executing each obstacle. Sit as balanced and relaxed as possible and avoid tensing your body. To ensure that you're loose going in, alternately tense up one leg as tight as you can, then from the toes on up loosen the muscles all the way up. Repeat with the other leg, and then your arms. (Don't try to tense and release your entire body while sitting your horse or you could make him tense or confuse him.) Keep your eyes straight, since twisting in the saddle or looking down can inadvertently miscue your horse or throw him off balance. (For instance, don't lean over to see where he is stepping over

poles or along a back through or sidepass; you can cause him to step on the obstacle or trip.)

Don't forget that showmanship counts. If the other riders gingerly lift that bag of aluminum cans in the hopes that their horses won't startle at the sound and you can pick it up and give it a good shake while your horse looks on with mild interest, you will have made an impression. On the other hand, if he is slow and clumsy to sidepass, ask him to do only as much as is necessary to pass the obstacle, rather than goading him for more. And always remember to keep smiling! Showing your horse should be fun, so try to look as if you are enjoying yourself immensely.

How the horse handles himself is also critical. Judges look for a horse that works confidently and willingly, that neither drags through the obstacles nor rushes through them. Given a choice, however, between two flawless performances, one by a slow

A pattern like this one will be posted before the trail class.

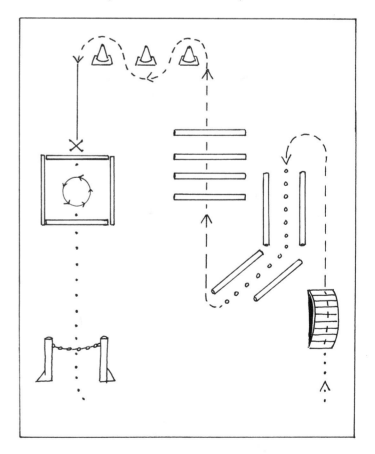

Trail-Class Obstacles

The first time you encounter a trail-class obstacle course you may wonder about the warped and demented mind that conceived it. However, these days trail-class obstacles are designed with more safety in mind than they used to be. In the 1970s there was a lot more emphasis on creativity and trying to spook horses than on training and safety. Here is a sampling of what you might find today.

- Slicker (ride up to a slicker on a post, take it off the post, and put it on)
- Walkovers (poles arranged on the ground to walk over)
- Jog-overs or lope-overs (same as walkovers, but at the speed required)

- Backing (between poles, in an L shape, in a pattern around traffic cones, for example)
- Sidepass (over a pole, around the outside of a square delineated by poles, across an L, or other pattern)
- Turn box (ride into a square that has been made by laying out four poles, turn around inside, then ride right back out)
- Trees, flowers, floating balloons, streamers (decorations in themselves can be obstacles!)
- Gate (rope or panel)
- Dismount/mount (sometimes you must also lift a hoof)
- Ground tie (dismount, leave your horse, wait, return, remount)

Mailbox (ride up open, take something out, ride on)

Water obstacle (sometimes just a tarp, sometimes a box about 6 inches deep is constructed and filled with water)

Bridge (usually wood, usually about 4 to 6 inches high)

horse and one with a little more speed, the horse that completes the course more efficiently will often place higher than his slower counterpart.

If your horse becomes flustered by an obstacle, move away from it and try it from a slightly different angle (as allowed by the course map). Ask him for first one step at a time, and then allow him to proceed if he is willing. Never push your horse through an obstacle at a show or allow yourself to get flustered. Better to accept a "no score" on any given obstacle than to get disqualified for "excessive schooling" or even abuse if you lose your cool.

In many shows, after the obstacles are completed, the entire class enters the arena for ring work. Horses are worked both directions, at a walk, trot (or equivalent gait), and canter (except for some gaited shows), and judged on the fluidity of their gaits, transitions, and responsiveness to their riders. Sometimes they are asked to line up and riders may be asked to back the horse or dismount.

SPECIALIZED SHOWS

Almost every breed has breed association–sanctioned shows that include a trail class. Be aware that each breed tends to have a look or image that it considers ideal. Quarter Horses are currently shown with their heads carried very low, but American Saddlebreds are expected to be more "upheaded." A purebred horse that doesn't project the preferred image of the breed does not normally lose points for that, but judges just seem unconsciously to score them lower than a horse that satisfies their eye.

In-hand trail classes, those in which a young horse is led through the obstacles, are gaining in popularity. Meant for weanlings through 2-year-olds, in-hand trail classes are a great way to introduce a young horse to the hectic atmosphere of a show and build a fabulous foundation for future education. Some shows even allow older horses to compete, and in-hand trail classes are a standard at Miniature Horse shows. Obstacles in in-hand classes might include trotting, backing, turning on the haunches or on the forehand, sidepassing, picking up each foot one at a time, putting a blanket on the foal, crossing a bridge, walking over ground poles, and even loading into a trailer.

Pack string classes are amazing to watch as the handler guides his saddle horse and two to five fully loaded pack animals (horses, mules, donkeys) through an obstacle course. He can physically control only his mount and the first horse in the pack string; the rest he must rely on to follow the leader in front of him or to respond to voice commands. If an animal misses an obstacle, refuses one, or knocks one down, points are deducted.

There are even "trail" classes in which you can drive your horse in a cart, though they are more aptly described as obstacle courses, in which many of the same types of obstacles are encountered. The Gambler's Choice classes are timed obstacles courses.

THE RIGHT HORSE

The most important thing to look for in a trail-class prospect is a horse with a well-balanced conformation, a willing, curious temperament, and an edge that will get him noticed in the ring. An attractive or unusual color, while not very important on the trail, will help your horse stand out in the judge's mind. An exceptionally smooth way of going, proud carriage, exemplary conformation, or, dare I say it, beautiful, kind eyes will also make your horse more memorable. Any breed or type of horse can excel in this class, and because competition can become addictive — especially when you win — you may find that showing in trail-horse classes is the perfect introduction for you to become involved in other classes or arena sports.

CHAPTER 12

Camping with Horses

JUST WANT TO RELAX AND GET AWAY? Here's how to ride off into the sunset and stay awhile.

For trail riders, camping with a horse beats staying in any fancy uptown motel, even without room service. This chapter will help you camp safely, comfortably, and responsibly. If possible, go on your first horse-camping adventure with seasoned campers.

Remember that others want to experience the wilderness just as you do. With more people using the backcountry, it can be hard to find that soul-satisfying solitude. The goal is to find it for yourself while still leaving some for others.

Respectful Camping

Although it is an incredibly freeing experience, camping with your horse also entails a great deal of responsibility. The most important thing to carry with you is an attitude of respect for your horse, the land, wildlife, and other wilderness users.

One important difference between camping with your horse and a day ride is the amount of damage your horse can do to the environment during an extended stay. In 2 days, two horses can eat every blade of grass in a 50- by- 50-foot paddock or corral; in less than a week they can trample the earth to dust (which will drift into everything downwind whenever they move around). Good planning is critical to an enjoyable and responsible camping experience. Be sure your plan includes how you will contain your horses and how you will keep your camp clean and free of damage. Leave it in as good and as natural condition as you found it.

For trail riders, the lure of the open trail is a siren song. The best of all possible worlds is a new trail.

Respectful camping means being aware of the impact your horse has on the environment and doing whatever you can to minimize it. Overgrazing, pawing up the ground, damaging trees, breaking down stream banks, and creating mud holes at water's edge or in marshy places are just a few of the ways horses and horsemen can damage the environment and their own chances of revisiting the area.

This is another reason why a good trail horse is so important. A well-trained, easygoing trail horse or packhorse will do less damage on the trail, in camp, and to your body than one that fidgets and fights, wanders on and off the trail, jigs, paws, pulls back or paces when tied, or fights with other horses. When considering the impact you and your mount(s) may leave on the trail or in camp, consider the horse(s) you have to work with. A calm trail horse is easier to care for and leaves less impact in his wake than a fractious one.

This chapter follows philosophies of respectful horse camping. Of course, it can't cover every possible scenario you'll encounter on the trail, but it will prepare you to make good decisions along the way.

THE LEAVE-NO-TRACE PHILOSOPHY

The terms Leave No Trace, Low Impact, and Minimum Impact Horse Camping refer to philosophies of environmentally responsible horse camping. The gist of all these labels is the same: You are both a guest and a steward of the land you ride. Take care of it accordingly. You should be able to ride through an area and leave no evidence that you have ever been there.

In early times, travelers often needed to hide their presence from possible attackers. Heavily loaded riders were easier to catch, and messy campers easier to find, than their more prudent counterparts. Imagine the Native, melting into the scenery, as trackers abandon his invisible trail. Imagine the stealthy soldier, slipping silently away from his frustrated foe. Traveling light and tidy has always had benefits.

Today's Leave No Trace (LNT) approach offers specific guidelines for riding and camping in the backcountry. Most of the ideas are common sense: Don't take more horses than you need; ride single file on existing trails to avoid damaging the trail's edges; camp and tie your horses well away (200 feet if possible) from natural water sources. Equally important is using common sense in your own unique circumstances. For example, LNT suggests that when riding in a wilderness area where there are no trails, a group should fan out to avoid creating one from the multiple impacts of many hooves along the same route. This may not apply when going through thick brush or over boggy ground. Leave No Trace, Inc. advises, "Consider your surroundings, local regulations, weather concerns, and your skill level when choosing the best way to Leave No Trace."

RESPECTING WILDLIFE

It's tempting to try to make friends by feeding animals or birds and to get close enough to get good photos. Resist those urges. Though you mean no harm, harassment of wildlife is a tremendous problem in the backcountry. In truly remote areas, some animals have not developed a fear of humans and you could wind up being harassed right back. Inviting animals into camp almost always winds up being more of a nuisance than it's worth.

My rule of thumb is never to get close enough to cause animals to change their behavior. If an animal notices us, we are on the line; if they run or approach us, we've crossed it.

The above goes double for your dog. Trail riding with a dog requires keeping a close check on his impact on wildlife. Don't allow him to chase, bark at, or tree birds or animals. In many areas it's legal to shoot a dog harassing game or other wild animals.

Respectful campers must also be aware of appearances. The impression left on other users can have a direct effect on future horseback access

to wilderness areas. A disheveled camp, manure allowed to accumulate until you get around to dispersing it, funky smells, an untended fire, and trash around camp are bad advertising for horse camping and have already had an impact on our rights. Be a good ambassador.

Horse Camping Guidelines

These guidelines were developed by Leave No Trace, Inc. (For more on LNT, see the appendix.)
- Plan ahead and prepare
- Travel and camp on durable surfaces
- Dispose of waste properly
- Leave what you find
- Minimize campfire impacts
- Respect wildlife
- Be considerate of other visitors

Avoid disrupting the behavior patterns of animals you encounter.

Plan, Plan, Plan

Advance planning is your best insurance for a great time camping with your horse. Read up on the area, know the rules and regulations of the area where you will stay (Are fires allowed? Can you pack in hay? Is water available?), buy maps, and try to plan ahead for everything you think you will need and do. Planning for horse camping is one time when obsessive behavior pays off.

Be realistic in your goals. Time is always a limiting factor, as is the amount of supplies you can carry. Some trail riders think nothing of a 100-mile trek over the course of a week; others are lucky to squeak out a weekend at a camping facility. Don't overestimate your time or your energy. Realize that rough terrain, steep hills, long trails, and lots of outdoor activity can wear you out faster than you might think. Allow yourself time to relax and just be.

WHAT TYPE OF CAMP?

If you intend to use a public camp, call ahead if possible. Reservations are often necessary during the peak seasons (which vary from region to region), and even with reservations it's a good idea to call and confirm before packing, loading, and hauling all the way to camp.

Two important decisions to make in advance are how long you will camp and whether you will break camp daily or ride out and return to the same base camp. The longer you stay, the more provisions you will need to take with you. Alternatively, you may arrange for someone to restock your

Camping in Bear Country

Traveling and camping in bear country means being vigilant, alert, and above all else tidy. Interactions with humans can be more dangerous to the bear than to people, because when "problem bears" learn to associate humans with food, they can become so aggressive that they must be shot to eliminate the "problem." Don't feed the bears, either on purpose or by accident. Black bears and grizzly bears can be dangerous.

- Situate cooking fires downwind of camp to avoid enticing bears into your sleeping area.
- Use a disposal hole for waste water that might attract bears through its scent.
- Don't cook enough to create leftovers; the scent will linger.
- Burn food residue in a tin can inside a hot fire to minimize the odor.
- Store food (including pet food or pellets and sweet feed for horses) in bear-proof containers. (Forest Service offices and the Interagency Grizzly Bear Committee (IGBC) often have containers available for rent.)
- Alternatively, hang food at least 10 feet off the ground 100 feet away from sleeping areas, trails, and areas of camp where you plan to spend much time.
- Burn feminine hygiene products completely in a very hot fire or triple-bag and pack them out. Never leave sanitary products near sleeping areas, but store as you do food, safely encased in a bear-proof box or hanging well away from camp.
- Throw fish entrails back into the water from which they came.
- Carry pepper spray.
- Don't play dead if attacked by a black bear. This might work with a startled grizzly bear, but not if he has his eye on you as lunch. FIGHT BACK! Yell, hit with sticks, and spray that pepper spray.

stores at a preset time and place during your stay.

Setting up a base camp and riding out on day excursions from there is the least work and requires the fewest provisions and therefore the fewest horses. This also means less impact on the camp as a result of your stay. If you'll be camping in one area in the backcountry, consider having someone come along to lead out excess horses for the duration of your stay to minimize impact on the site.

In some areas you can camp right with your rig. This allows you to take anything that will fit in a truck and trailer and to keep a close eye on your rig against theft or vandalism. Or you may decide to strike out into the wilderness, fully provisioned with a pack string, setting up camp wherever your heart desires and moving on whenever you please. That feeling of freedom compares to little else on earth. You can go as far, and for as long, as your horses and provisions hold out.

Pack It In, Pack It Out

Whatever comes into camp with you must leave with you, but nothing else. As the saying goes, "Take nothing but pictures, leave nothing but hoofprints."

How much you take with you on your day rides depends on whether you will be riding out from a base camp or packing it all with you from camp to camp. You can pack everything you need for a day ride in saddlebags or a cantle bag, along with a saddle horn pack for small, special items that you want to be able to reach quickly (camera, eyedrops, lip balm, water bottle). Packing into a remote camp (or camps) for more than an overnight trip may require a packhorse, or you can equip yourself with ultralight gear.

GOING ULTRALIGHT

While it's nice to take along some of the comforts of home, packing in can be greatly simplified by roughing it. Pack in what you truly can't survive without for the length of your stay and make good use of special lightweight supplies. Be sure to include at least a rudimentary first-aid kit, a compass, bedroll (a thick wool blanket or a high-tech lightweight compressible sleeping bag), water, a folding water bucket for your horse, food, gloves, a hat, a change of clothes, a pocketknife, a hoof knife, a working flashlight, a folding camp saw, matches, personal items (such as a toothbrush and comb), and, if usable in the area you ride, a cell phone.

WHAT YOU NEED VS. WHAT YOU WANT

You might think packing in with horses means you are limited to the bare necessities of life, but careful planning and packing allow you to take along almost anything you could want for a comfortable stay. Remember, however, that part of the experience is simplifying your life. Do you really need to check your e-mail on your wireless laptop while you are out on the trail?

The main things to consider are weight, size, fragility, and necessity. Take advantage of special lightweight camping supplies in order to pack more stuff with less weight. The less weight you have to carry, the less likely you are to need a packhorse, or the fewer packhorses you will need. Repackage food (and other items) into lightweight

Let Someone Know Your Plans

Once you have your route and itinerary planned, write it all down and leave it with park officials, family members, or friends. If you vary your routine, leave a note in camp, or let someone know if possible. It may sound a little counterproductive when you're trying to get away from it all, but you never know when you might want it all to find you again.

or burnable containers or paper. This not only cuts weight and packing space, but also leaves you with less to pack out when you break camp.

If you are packing gear on a saddle horse, here's a sample plan.

✳ Put the majority of your carry-on items in your side bags.

✳ Tie a lightweight sleeping bag behind the cantle.

✳ Use a cantle bag for toiletries. (Specially made "triple saddlebags" have a cantle bag built right into them.)

✳ Use saddlebags that fit over the saddle horn, or at the pommel, for a camera, lip balm, and sunglasses.

If using a separate packhorse, then the majority of the load will go in side panniers that must be balanced for weight. More can go on top of the load in **top packs** (bags that go on top of the load), but these should be kept low, as a tall pack will make the whole load more likely to shift.

Zippable plastic bags are a real boon to packing and keeping things separate and dry. Not only will they prevent a broken egg from oozing into your underwear, but they will even keep undies, socks, and CD players dry in a three-day rainstorm. They weigh nothing and take all the worry out of keeping dry things dry and wet things to themselves.

Zip-closure bags are essential on a trail ride. Take a few extra for unanticipated needs.

USING A PACKHORSE

Plenty of people rough it and do fine with what they can carry on their saddle horse, but a packhorse allows you lots of extras for just a little more work. Remember, though, that the less you pack in, the fewer horses you will need and therefore the less impact on the trail and campsites you will make. One pack animal should be sufficient to carry gear and food for two riders and all three horses.

Packing in with horses requires some special equipment and a new set of skills (see chapter 5). Packsaddles, panniers, Styrofoam inserts (to convert a pannier into a cooler), bear-resistant packs, and top packs can add up to a serious investment. The technology has improved tremendously over the past 20 years, and materials are lighter and easier to use.

A packhorse can carry 150 pounds easily (an average suitcase or backpack that YOU might carry on a trip weighs 25 to 30 pounds), which allows for a lot of amenities. In fact, you can up the initial load to 180 pounds as long as you aren't traveling too far too fast, because as you and your horses eat, the load will lighten every day.

PACKING THE HORSE To decide what to pack and how it will all fit in your panniers, create two piles of items, balancing them for bulk and weight. Start each pile with the essentials, then if space and weight allow, heap on the goodies. A packhorse can safely carry about 20 percent of his body weight, and that includes the packsaddle itself. Deadweight is harder for the horse to balance than is a rider, who can compensate for changes in the terrain by adjusting her balance.

Balance lightweight bulky items, such as a foam sleeping mat, sleeping bag, and puffy jacket, with small heavy or fragile items, such as that bottle of Merlot you plan to sip at sundown. While you are home and planning, it is easy to weigh each pile and rearrange until each load weighs the same as the other. If you mark each item with its individual

Things to Pack for Horse Camping

CAMP

- ❏ Tent
- ❏ Folding saw
- ❏ Shovel
- ❏ Ground cloth
- ❏ Sleeping bag(s)
- ❏ Solar shower
- ❏ Cooking supplies and utensils
- ❏ Dishes, bowls, and utensils
- ❏ Dish towel(s)
- ❏ Dish soap
- ❏ Can opener
- ❏ Coffee pot
- ❏ Food
- ❏ Cooking fuel and stove
- ❏ Lantern
- ❏ Folding camp table and chairs
- ❏ Camp toilet

PERSONAL ITEMS

- ❏ Toilet paper
- ❏ Soap (biodegradable), washcloth, and towel
- ❏ First-aid kit
- ❏ Clothes
- ❏ Gloves
- ❏ Hat
- ❏ Sunglasses
- ❏ Knife
- ❏ Matches
- ❏ Money
- ❏ Toothbrush
- ❏ Pillow
- ❏ Flashlight
- ❏ Medications
- ❏ Shoes, boots
- ❏ Emergency items: cell phone, contact information, etc.

HORSE

- ❏ Horse brush
- ❏ Hoof pick and knife
- ❏ Insect repellent
- ❏ Water bucket
- ❏ Sponge(s)
- ❏ Halter, lead, highline, hobbles and/or picket
- ❏ Feed
- ❏ Feedbag
- ❏ Saddle, bridle, and pad
- ❏ Breast collar and crupper
- ❏ Packsaddle, panniers, top packs, and pad
- ❏ Horse blanket for cool evenings
- ❏ Lariat and cover

EXTRAS

- ❏ Hammock
- ❏ Fishing supplies
- ❏ Radio or CD player
- ❏ Fishing gear and license
- ❏ Hunting gear and license
- ❏ Field guides
- ❏ Binoculars

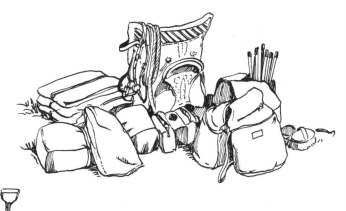

All the comforts of a well-stocked camp (left) can be packed (above) and carried by a single horse.

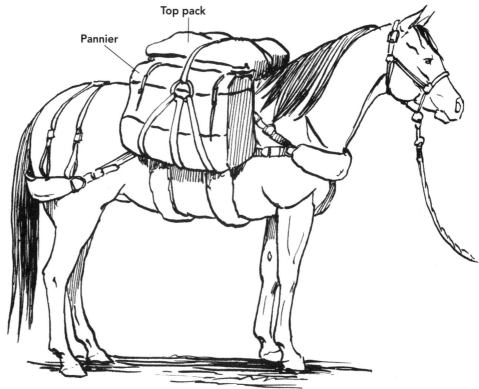

Top pack

Pannier

Packing in with horses requires special equipment.

Packhorse Safety Tips

A packhorse can carry 20 percent of his body weight, including the packsaddle.

- Balance the load on each side so that it doesn't shift.
- Arrange the pack contents so that nothing rattles, clinks, or clunks, to avoid spooking the packhorse.
- Don't lead the packhorse from your mount by holding the lead rope in your hand (as you would when ponying a horse for a short distance). Use a breakaway string (see *next page*) to attach him to your saddle.
- Don't allow a packhorse to become overtired. Rest often. Tired horses may stumble or slip, especially on steep, narrow trails.
- Accustom your packhorse to being ridden bareback. If he wanders off and you have to hike to find him, at least you won't have to walk back to camp.
- Don't run with a packhorse in tow if you can help it. Running can dislodge the load, spook your horses, and tear up the trail.

weight (or jot it down on a list), it will be easier to rebalance the load as you use up material and move from one camp to the next.

As you use up items and the packhorse's load gets lighter, you will have to readjust the weight accordingly. It's a balancing act you have to repeat often. An old trick to make this easier while on the trail is to add a rock or two to the "light" side so that you can continue on. At the next campsite, you can rearrange the entire load for balance.

LEADING A PACKHORSE Leading and controlling a packhorse requires a few skills and special techniques. Most critical is the rope you use for leading.

Rather than hold the lead rope in your hand, tie a 15-inch length of heavy-duty cord to the end of the rope and then to the D-ring near the saddle horn or pommel. One packer recommends parachute cord because it is strong, yet it gives at about 500 pounds of pressure, enough to release a packhorse that rears back or stumbles off the trail. This

breakaway string keeps your hands free to handle your own mount and prevents a packhorse from pulling you over in the event he spooks, slips, or falls. To connect packhorses together in a string, use breakaway strings tied to the arches of the packsaddle. Never attach them to the hip pad or to a horse's tail.

Leading a packhorse is much like ponying a horse (see page 143), and practice will make both your jobs easier. Leading while on foot requires the same basic horsemanship skills needed for leading any horse, except that you must be very aware of changes in the terrain. Train your horse in advance to lead a few steps directly behind you for those narrow places on the trail where you must walk single file. Keep the lead rope neatly coiled (so it doesn't accidentally drag and get stepped on) and hold it in a figure-8 with your fingers around it — never looped around your hand or arm. If a horse spooks or slips, you don't want to be tied to him.

WHAT WILL YOU EAT?

What to pack in for your own sustenance depends solely on your tastes and what you are willing to sacrifice in the name of gastronomic delights. One camp may revel in gourmet trail meals; another may choke down jerky while enjoying other amenities like a hammock and radio.

You can afford to go off your diet a little on a horse camping trip. The extra exercise you get while out horse camping will actually burn more calories. Besides, it's a short-term commitment and your normal diet awaits when you return to the "real world." So plan to enjoy your meals on the trail.

Pack in only foods you like, in the most convenient lightweight form possible. For instance, if you hate eggs, don't waste precious packing space by trying to take them along; on the other hand, if you can't live without them, consider breaking them and packing them in zippable plastic bags. You can carry a lot more dried apples (both for you and as a treat for your horse) than whole ones.

A Balancing Act

Learning how to balance a pack properly is especially important if you ride on steep, winding trails. An unbalanced pack will inevitably slip and slide at the worst possible spot on the way. This can cause more problems than just a lop-sided load. A lot of horses, even fairly experienced ones, will shy, buck, or bolt when their load tips.

Outfitters use scales to ensure that the loads are even. Each packed pannier is attached to the hook on the scale and gently lifted off the ground until the scale tab marks the weight. A few pounds of difference between the packs can throw your packhorse off balance and possibly tip the entire load. Adjust pannier weight by moving items between them.

If you don't have a pack scale, an old trick is to balance a pole over a big rock and sling each pack over the opposite ends of the pole, rearranging the contents between the two packs until the load balances.

Freeze-dried camp food appeals to some; others don't care for it.

For me, simple is best, but for some people the luxury of a steak simmering over a campfire is second to none. Packing in precooked foods simplifies food preparation.

BREAKFAST Mix precooked hot cereals with dried milk, a touch of sugar, or dried fruit (raisins, cranberries, cherries, or blueberries). Measure a meal's worth each into individual plastic bags, then just stir in hot water for a wholesome, warming breakfast. Many cereals and granolas make a good snack right out of the box liner, or mix with powdered milk in a plastic bag. When you are ready to eat, add cold water and shake. Warm a cup of instant coffee or tea and munch a few dried apple slices for a nutritious breakfast.

SNACKS Divvy up crackers, cheese, and pepperoni into individual snack plastic bags for a quick, high-energy break (keeping the crackers separately wrapped keeps them crisp).

High-energy bars are a good idea for in between snacks, and most states have laws in effect requiring that you pack in chocolate . . . or they should.

LUNCH AND DINNER Canned cooked chicken, tuna, and deli meats can be used as they are or fixed into more elaborate meals. Tuna or chicken salad, with celery, walnuts, and chopped apples, between bread slices or with crackers can serve as a meal any time of day.

Lunches and dinners based on prepared foods can be as simple or as elegant as you choose. Add sun-dried tomatoes, capers, pimentos, peppers, dried or canned meat, or other favorites to rice or

noodle dishes for an easy-to-cook, easy-to-enjoy camp meal. Dried soups can be very filling, especially if you add beans or other dried vegetables, noodles, or meat to fortify them.

WHAT WILL YOUR HORSE EAT?

It's always nice to plan a campsite around natural graze, as that means packing in less horse food. Certain areas, however, such as desert and alpine trails, just don't afford (or cannot tolerate) grazing, so be prepared to provide your horse's supper as well as your own.

Packing in horse food can be a quagmire all its own. In many areas, you are required to pack in certified weed-free feed. It's easier to pack in process pellets or cubes than hay.

If natural graze is not available, plan to take 10 to 15 pounds of cubes or pellets per horse per day. This will vary by several factors, including the size of your horse, how far you travel each day, and whether he is an "easy keeper." Even just 10 pounds per day will limit you to only two or three days on the trail for a single saddle horse (or as much as a week with a packhorse along to carry both his and your saddle horse's supper). Of course, your horse could survive on less (or nothing at all) for a few days, but putting your horse's welfare first is a good way to ensure your own safety and enjoyment.

If you plan to feed pellets or hay cubes, start offering them a few days before you leave for the trail. This will accustom your horse to his new diet in advance and lessen any chance of him refusing it or developing a stomach upset.

Take some grain along, whether or not your horse needs it to fulfill his nutritional requirements. Even a small ration, offered as your horse settles into a new campsite, will help him decide that this is where he wants to be. Nothing says home to a horse like a snootful of sweet feed.

Don't forget to include salt and electrolytes. A small, mineralized salt block will do for most rides, or take a loose electrolyte mix that you can sprinkle

---

Cowboy Coffee

For camp coffee, boiling makes the most potent brew for both flavor and caffeine content.

1. Put about ½ cup grounds per 3 cups water into a pot.
2. Boil for 10 or 15 minutes.
3. Pour in a cup of cold water.
4. Serve.

The cold water sinks the grounds to the bottom of the pot so that when you pour the coffee, the sediment will stay in the pot and out of your cup.

Another option is instant coffee, but it doesn't wake up the camp with that wonderful odor the way camp coffee does.

over feed. This encourages a horse to drink enough while in camp and on the trail.

High-fiber foods, such as compressed hay cubes, help hold water in the horse's intestines. This will help keep him internally hydrated on trails where water is not plentiful.

FEEDING TIPS

If you take salt for your horse, try to find a flat rock to set it on somewhere away from where you sleep. Salt attracts all sorts of wild things, and if you place it on the ground, any critters that find it will dig for more.

Feeding hay from the ground is iffy. It's okay in areas where horse use is light, but in public camps, you'll run much less risk of infesting your horse with parasites if you feed from a hanging bag. If horses are tied, be sure to hang hay bags high so that the animals can't get tangled up in them.

Feeding grain or pellets in a feedbag is a good way to prevent spillage (which will disappoint camp robbers such as jays and other crafty aerial thieves), but be sure to keep an eye on the horse. The bags are made so that horses can breathe in them, but they are not meant for extended wear. Never leave a feedbag on a loose horse, especially anywhere near water. It takes only a little bit of water in a feedbag to drown a horse.

PACKING IN WATER

Water is one of those limiting factors without which you cannot proceed very far. Most trails, even in wilderness areas, have natural water available. Finding it may be as easy as riding up to a trough or spigot or as difficult as digging around cactus roots (strongly discouraged except in cases of life or death).

Packing water in is hardly ever efficient. Each horse will drink from 10 to 20 gallons per day when working on the trail, depending on his condition, the weather, and the terrain. That translates into 80 to 160 pounds per horse per day! Each horse would barely be able to pack in his own allotment

Food-packing Tips

Try these suggestions so that your food is easy to find and still edible (or drinkable) when you need it.

- Split up food into plastic bags for breakfast, lunch, and dinner so you won't have to shuffle through everything to find what you want for each meal.
- Double-wrap frozen foods in newspaper and they will stay frozen 3 days or more in a cooler.
- Pack eggs in the carton, covered with a sealed plastic bag (just in case), inside a rolled-up mat or sleeping bag or nestled in with your horse's feed, pour into plastic bags as suggested above, or pack hard-cooked.
- Boxed wines are not that bad, and you can even remove the inner liner bag from the box to make them easier to pack.
- Other liquids can also be packed in plastic bags, but be sure to "double-wrap" them.
- Pack snacks on the outside of your panniers or in separate, easy-to-reach compartments on saddlebags for convenient access during rest stops.
- Make use of alternate packaging. Pour canned foods into plastic bags and remove the air by suctioning it out with a straw. The contents will be lighter in weight and more flexible to pack but more prone to getting smushed, so pack carefully.
- Take advantage of dehydrated foods. They cook up well over a campfire, and dehydrated fruits are healthy, lightweight, and easy to pack and carry.
- Pack sandwiches for day rides in containers with rigid sides to prevent them from getting mushed into doughballs.

of water for a day or two, and certainly little else.

Don't expect your horse to drink from a stream, however, if he is used to an automatic waterer. Horses have been known to dehydrate severely and still refuse to drink from creeks and other natural water sources. A lightweight, collapsible plastic water bucket can literally be a lifesafer.

Practice watering your horse from it occasionally at home and he will gladly accept a refreshing drink on the trail.

CLOTHING

Figuring out what to take in the way of clothes on a horse camping trip is like planning your wardrobe for a trip to the Oregon beach. It might be sunny. It might be cool and drizzly. It might be really windy. You never know until you get there.

Take an assortment of clothing and dress in layers. Remember to avoid cotton (even underwear) in cool or wet weather. I roll my clothes rather than fold them because it's faster and makes for neater packing. Rolled-up clothes wrinkle less, too, but on the trail, who cares?

PACKING OUT

What you pack out is just as important as what you pack in. Be sure you pack out all of your own trash and supplies. And since your load will be much lighter on your way home, make it a habit to pack out any litter you find left behind by others. Tiny bits of trash can be the most aggravating to pick up. Use a trash bag in camp for small items like twist-ties, gum or candy wrappers, Band-Aid backs, and cigarette butts.

What you pack in determines what you will have to pack out. Anything that can't be burned must be packed out. Choose containers with this in mind. For example, cans can be flattened and made more compact, but bottles can't.

Having a "carry-out" bag makes cleanup part of the process and saves you having to do it all at once when you are ready to ride out. It's smart to burn cans in the campfire before smashing them and placing them in your carry out-bag. The smell of leftover food attracts animals and flies; burning destroys the odor. Burn and smash cans, crumple up plastic bags and other containers, and keep them neatly stowed until it's time to break camp.

Fishermen and hunters have special considerations as to what they leave behind. Fish innards come with the territory and can be left for native wildlife to dispose of, thrown back into the water, or buried in a disposal hole to avoid other people finding them. If fishing on a day trip, take your fish home to clean them. Hunters should field-dress game as far from trails and water as possible and pack out immediately.

Some things should not be packed out. Don't remove native plants, interesting rocks, antlers, bones, or other natural or archeological artifacts. Leave the wilderness as you found it so that others can enjoy the same amazing discoveries that you did. In some areas, such as national parks, it is against the law to remove natural objects.

The same goes for removing any cultural artifacts, such as arrowheads, pottery, and tools, you find on public land (such as state and national parks and forestlands). The Archeological Resources Protection Act makes it a crime to remove such items.

Organic waste, such as human waste, wash water, and remains from fishing or hunting trips, must be disposed of properly. We'll discuss the specifics of what and how in the sections that follow.

Camp, Sweet Camp

The primary rule is to camp only in areas where horses are allowed. Finding such areas should be the number one priority of your obsessive planning stage. Horse camping facilities can be found all over the United States (see the appendix for resources). You can pull your trailer into a campground loaded with all the amenities, from restrooms and campfires to fine dining and golf courses, or you can leave your rig at the trailhead and ride out into the backcountry where the best camps are barely noticeable. The choice between facilities and the pristine wilderness is a no-brainer for some and a deal-breaker for others. Restrooms are definitely nice, but to some riders they just aren't worth it.

A well-stocked, comfortable camp, set up at an existing campsite, affords you a good time without unnecessary damage to the environment.

As part of your planning, find out about regulations for the area in which you want to set up camp and follow those rules.

WHERE TO MAKE CAMP

Choosing where you will set up camp is the first step in respectful, low-impact horse camping. If there is already an established campsite, such as at trailheads where facilities are provided, then the decision is much easier. Using existing camps is the best way to minimize camping impact. Established camps are easy to spot by the packed-down soil, lack of vegetation, and, in some cases, pens, fire rings, or other amenities. Making use of these campsites greatly reduces the impact on surrounding areas.

If you are camping in the backcountry there are more details to consider, including fragile native plants, thin soils, natural water sources, nearby wildlife, and the availability of firewood (more on

that later). Finding a site that will have a minimal impact on all of these calls for careful observation and consideration. The ideal spot is one that won't sustain damage. Look for a site well off the trail, with rocky or solid soil and little vegetation, at least 200 feet away from the nearest natural water source. In timber, camp away from the most delicate plants that inhabit the soft decomposing leaf and needle litter of the forest floor. In desert areas, look for a patch of dry sand or gravel.

Shielding your camp behind a natural buffer, such as a ridge of rocks or a screen of trees, will help ensure your privacy and peace if other trail users pass through. Pitching camp in an open area leaves you exposed to the elements and all passersby and can be detrimental to the land, as people and horses coming and going trample the grass.

Even in the backcountry, there are many established, well-used campsites. They can usually be found near water, good grazing, a prized fishing hole, or a knockout view, or just on a level spot in a protected hollow. Indications of a heavily used camp include denuded vegetation, packed-down soil, hitching rails, pens, and fire rings. If you come upon such a camp when you are ready to stop for the day, it's best to use it yourself, rather than creating yet another camp and spreading the damage farther.

Concentrate use in established camps; disperse it in natural areas.

However, if you find a backcountry campsite that shows signs of *minimal use,* such as grazed-down grass, trampled vegetation, compressed soil, and the beginnings of pathways, pass it by. Nature has amazing regenerative powers, and this site can restore itself. Once a certain level of use has been exceeded, vegetation can't grow back as fast as it is destroyed, soil erodes, and additional use can damage the site faster than it can recover. Some forests can sustain as little as 10 days of use per season before damage becomes significant.

How much use a site can sustain depends on the weather, soil type, natural vegetation, groundwater, and wildlife, as well as on human use. Avoiding campsites that are barely noticeable allows them to restore themselves to their natural splendor.

Don't camp in a marshy area. Dampness will soak into everything but your bones, and the ground will get torn up badly in no time. Mosquitoes may also be rampant, especially in spring. Be sure to set your camp back at least 200 feet from a lake or stream, even if a campsite is already established closer. We are doing better as conservationists nowadays and some of the older campers did not follow the same code of environmental ethics as today's horsemen.

SETTING UP How you set up camp is just as important as where. A neat, organized camp will help to make your stay as carefree as possible and leave a good impression on anyone who might wander upon it.

Pitch tents and set up your kitchen area on the toughest surfaces you can find, such as dry or hardpan soil, rock, and gravel, to keep damage to a minimum. A spot with a slight slope will provide natural drainage, so you won't have to dig an obtrusive drainage ditch around tents. Use tents that come with their own pegs to avoid cutting limbs for tent poles. Don't "clear out" the camp area by pulling up plants or cutting live trees or brush. It's okay to move rocks and deadwood out of the way, as long as you put them back to restore the natural look when you break camp. Because a camp kitchen (camp stove or fire, table, etc.) is the center of activity, set it up in an area that can take lots of footsteps without sustaining damage.

Clothing Checklist for Horse Camping

In warm weather, cotton layers are best. A sleeveless top or vest underneath a long-sleeved shirt gives you the option to strip layers as the sun heats up the day.

In cold weather, wear wool, down, or fleece, or any combination thereof, with a windproof outer layer. You'll also need:

- ❑ Comfortable, high boots to protect your legs in the saddle and while leading your horse on the trail
- ❑ T-shirts, sweatshirts, and long-sleeved shirts for layering
- ❑ Sweatpants or tights (these make comfy riding pants that won't chafe)
- ❑ Several changes of socks (cold, wet feet are not good)
- ❑ Chaps for brushy country
- ❑ A lightweight, waterproof windbreaker

FOR COLD WEATHER

- ❑ Long underwear
- ❑ A warm coat in addition to your windbreaker
- ❑ Stocking cap or other warm headgear
- ❑ Gloves
- ❑ Hand warmers

When you set up camp matters, too. Be sure to allow enough time to choose and set up an efficient, environmentally responsible, comfortable camp. Tired, aching muscles, bad weather, or impending darkness can lead to less than ideal camping decisions.

SANITARY FACILITIES

Many people consider toilet facilities a top priority; they can plan to stay at trailhead campgrounds with restrooms or portable toilets. Where restrooms aren't available, dig a toilet hole (1 to 2 feet deep) if you plan to stay a few days or a small hole (8 inches deep) to bury individual deposits. Set aside the sod and topsoil so that you can put it back in place when preparing to leave. Be sure to situate your personal facilities at least 200 feet (about 70 paces) from any water source, and equally far from your campsite. Look for areas that seem unlikely to be chosen as campsites by others.

Urine has much less natural impact, and dissipates much more quickly, than feces and need not be as carefully monitored. An accumulation, however, can give rise to an unpleasant odor, especially early in the morning when the air is moist, so it is still recommended to use toilet holes, or at the very least to venture well away from camp. Butterflies in search of natural salts occasionally congregate where humans (or others) have urinated.

Be stingy in your use of toilet paper and opt for natural-fiber "biodegradable" types, if possible, or plain white (with no dyes or perfumes). Dispose of it by burying deeply, burning in a hot fire, or packing out. Alternatives to toilet paper include such *au naturel* substitutes as leaves and moss.

Proper burial of such waste helps prevent pollution of water sources as well as of air quality in your immediate surroundings. It also decreases the spread of disease, as human waste decomposes quite slowly. Adding enzymes (such as those made for composting toilets) to these holes will help break down the waste and speed up the natural decomposition.

Be in Harmony

Respect the environment. Don't cut live trees, dig ditches around tents, drive nails into live trees, clear brush, or otherwise alter the character of the land.

FIRE-MAKING

Another priority is a fire. In cold, wet weather, a fire can make the difference between suffering and survival. Find out in advance from whoever manages the land you are riding if you can build a fire or if you should pack in butane or other fuel for cooking. Campfires are not allowed in many places, while some camps provide fire rings. Use them.

Always consider the dryness of your surroundings and wind conditions before starting a fire. Dry winds can quickly fan a quiet campfire out of control. Depending on conditions, alternatives are building up your fireplace to prevent the wind from scattering ashes, settling for a smaller fire than you might otherwise enjoy, and spending a chilly night in camp rather than risking a fire.

Be especially careful about fire during the summer and fall. If at all humanly possible, don't smoke on the trail. If you must, stop, dismount, finish your smoke, grind it out, pick it up, and pack it out.

COLLECTING WOOD Another concern is available firewood, which can be scarce in many areas. Always gather firewood by first picking up dead loose pieces, then cutting up dead downed wood, and finally cutting up dead standing wood. Don't even think about cutting standing live trees.

Look for wood well off the trail. Collect firewood from a broad area to avoid clearing out the immediate camp and giving it that "lived-in" look. Walk around the camp in no particular pattern, picking up wood as you find it, to avoid stripping any one area.

For minimum-impact camping, burn the smallest pieces of wood you can find, nothing bigger than 4 inches in diameter. These pieces will burn more completely than larger chunks and leave less telltale ash or cinders.

DOUSING THE FIRE Do this whenever you leave your camp unattended, not just when breaking camp to move on. Unattended campfires are a major cause of forest fires. Be sure all wood is burned down as much as possible and that the fire is cold before moving out of camp.

CAMPFIRE ALTERNATIVES In a remote area consider using a mound fire instead of a conventional campfire. It is easy to build and can be used almost anywhere, from flat solid rock to a grassy open area. Find a spot with sand, gravel, decomposed granite, or other mineral-based soil if possible. Mineral-based soils are usually found a few inches beneath the dark, crumbly soil of the forest floor or topsoil, so you may have to dig down a bit. Creek beds and rocky areas will also yield mineral-based soil.

With a small camp shovel or garden trowel, gather up this sandy or mineral-based soil onto a heavy-duty piece of tarp, about 4 feet square. Haul the soil on the tarp to your intended campfire site. Arrange the soil in a circular mound about 6 to 8 inches thick at the center of the tarp. The size of the mound should be wider than the fire you plan to make, and allow some extra space for the coals to spread out. Build the fire atop this mound. After the fire is out, roll up the tarp and disperse the soil and ashes.

Another alternative for backwoods fire building is a fire pan. Any metal pan with upright sides — the pan from a barbecue grill, a metal pan for draining crankcase oil, even a fortified garbage can lid — can serve. The sides should be at least 3 inches high, so a garbage can lid might need a strip of metal welded around the rim or to be build up around the edges with a ring of rocks (replaced later in their original locations). Set the pan on rocks or bank with mineral-based soil to avoid scorching the ground, then build your fire on the pan.

Finally, a camp stove makes a good alternative to the traditional campfire for cooking and heat. They help cut down on the number of campfires and the need to scavenge for firewood, although wood-burning models are also available.

USING WATER WISELY

Water is a critical part of any horse camp, and as part of your planning phase you will have found out where it is located. Be wary. Think of all water in the wild (even water provided in camp as "potable") as contaminated. Icky critters (better known as *Giardia lamblia*) thrive in many streams and waterways. They won't hurt your horse, but

---

Fire Rings

Unless you happen along an older camp that is in an inappropriate site (too close to water or some other objection), use established fire rings whenever possible. If you need to build a new one, dig up the sod or soil from the surface and set it aside so that you can replace it. Dig down several inches and set aside the dirt to refill the pit when you prepare to leave camp. Line the sides with rocks, if available. Go through the process in reverse when you break camp, putting rocks back where you found them, filling the hole, and replacing the sod, so that you leave no trace of your fire.

Dig down to the mineralized subsoil to create a fire pit so that your fire won't accidentally spread.

they can cause *you* serious illness that can linger for life. Either pack in safe drinking water, water purification tables (chlorine), a water-purifying pump filter system, or a pan in which to boil water. Outside of hauling in your own water (weighing in at 8 pounds to the gallon), boiling native water is safest.

Natural water sources can be fragile areas, with marshy ground, creek beds, and pond edges prone to erosion when trod upon. To minimize impact, water horses at established areas, at low graveled or rocky crossings, or with collapsible buckets well away from the water source.

WASHING AND SOAP Never confuse a creek with a bathtub, dishwasher, or laundry facility. Bathe (shower) and wash dishes well away from any water source. A solar shower offers a wonderful end to a dusty day in the saddle. Fill it with water, set it in the sun, and in a couple of hours you'll have a hot, albeit brief, cleansing shower.

Dump soapy water away from natural water sources and outside of your immediate camp. If you will be using the same camp for several days, dig a "gray water" pit to dispose of wash water. Most soaps are made with a form of tallow (or other natural fatty acids), which can lure small animals into your camp. Just the residue from washing dishes is enough to attract wildlife and bugs. Refill the water pit with soil when you break camp.

Soap breaks down slowly, especially in cool weather, so it's important not to allow it to filter into streams or ponds. You may find that you can live without dish soap, as most debris can be rinsed off if attended to immediately. Some soap can be tougher to rinse off than dried spaghetti sauce and leaves a chemical residue in its wake.

For personal soap, choose a biodegradable brand and lather up well away (200 feet) from any natural water source. Avoid washing clothes when in camp, and settle for a good thorough rinsing, instead.

STORING FOOD

Food storage is another key concern, especially in bear country — although even squirrels, deer, porcupines, and wild turkeys can do a number on unprotected stores overnight. In some areas you will need to store food in bear-safe, metal containers and hang it as high as possible in trees away from camp. Food attracts bears and you don't want to invite them into your sleeping area. Be sure to ask about any areas that might have potential bear problems.

Camp robbers (gray jays, who earned their nickname in the obvious way), squirrels, and other small critters can usually be thwarted if you keep your camp tidy and your food items put away. Storing food in the area between people and the campfire usually keeps even the most curious critters at bay. Otherwise, consider taking at least one metal-sided container to keep small animals from pecking, scratching, or nibbling their way to your stores.

Don't feed wildlife. Doing so can encourage some pretty rude and brash behavior (from the animals, too!). Dispose of "table scraps" well away from camp to avoid inviting in unwanted busboys. See box on page 270 for more tips for managing food in bear country.

MANAGING YOUR CAMP

When it comes to sharing the wilderness, keep in mind that horse campers can affect other users in many ways. We make visual impressions, in both our own appearance and our effect on the trail and campsites. Sounds and smells can also affect other users.

Sound travels long distances in open country and does some strange things in wooded areas. Hollering to one another, a donkey braying, a dog barking, or a radio blaring can disturb other users a mile away. Peace is part of the package: Revel in it, and camp quietly so that others can too.

Odd smells can be limited by running a tidy, sanitary camp. Non-horsey backcountry users may

Dos and Don'ts of Camp Management

The longer you stay at one campsite, the more diligent you must be to avoid damage and signs of use. You must pack in more feed, move pens or picket pins regularly to avoid overgrazing, and collect or spread manure to prevent flies and smells. Even in established camps at trailheads, try not to leave evidence that you have been there. Make it a point of honor that the next camper should find your campsite at least as pristine as you did.

- In established camps and campgrounds, DO stick to the paths and facilities already in place. By concentrating use in existing pathways, corrals, fire pits, and bathroom facilities, you will cause less impact.
- In more remote areas, where little or no evidence of previous camps can be found, DO use the opposite strategy and disperse usage as much as possible so as to leave no evidence of your visit.
- In the backcountry, DO camp on the toughest surfaces you can find with the least vegetation .
- DO avoid creating pathways by taking different routes to and from camp, kitchen, and latrine areas.
- DO move to a different campsite each night to avoid trampling or overgrazing a single area.
- DON'T damage the natural habitat.
- DON'T pound nails into trees, saw off live limbs, or allow tent twine or highlines to girdle the bark. Trees are not handy posts for nailing up your gear, mirrors, and so on, unless they come with conveniently positioned branches.
- DON'T let your horses chew on trees. In many places it is not legal to pick any natural vegetation, though in others, sampling native edible plants is part of the experience, for both you and your horse.
- DON'T pick more than 10 percent of what you find. Leave a few morsels of morels for the next camper.
- If camping with your dog, DO keep a wary eye on his adventures. DON'T allow him to dig holes and if he does, be sure to fill them back in.

not be comfortable around horses and, as mentioned before, will not appreciate the things horses leave behind or accumulate in camp. Aside from manure piles and the smell that accompanies them, horses can kick up a lot of dust, which other users will not appreciate any more than you do. Following the suggestions in this chapter will help minimize the effects of these and other perceived negatives of backcountry horse use.

Set aside a separate space to stow your gear. A tarp over a pole or length of rope between two trees will serve as a little tent to protect your gear from the weather and discourage nighttime nibblers from making a snack of your tack. Porcupines will chew on leather or anything with salt (or sweat) on it. Raccoons, possums, squirrels, coyotes, bears, and deer also can be attracted by the salty smell of sweaty gear.

At the end of each day's ride, place your saddle pads sweaty-side up in the sun. Not only does this dry the fabric, but the sun also kills germs and helps keep down the smell. (Never let the side that lies against your horse's back touch the ground, as debris will stick to it and gall your horse.) Be sure to put them under cover before dark. Some people tuck them under their sleeping bags for extra padding.

Many camps have strict requirements about horse manure. Some offer a pit or pile to dump it in; others require you to haul it back out with the horse that produced it. In the backcountry, spreading out manure piles helps them to decompose faster.

If you're lucky, nature's little helpers will carry away manure . A group of riders who traveled the Tevis Cup trail in a weeklong ride (rather than the competitive 100 miles in 1 day) were surprised to find out that coyotes made off with manure piles in the night. But if no such help is forthcoming, take along a collapsible rake or find a suitable branch to sweep the piles clear of camp. Even though horsemen don't notice a little poop, other users never miss it.

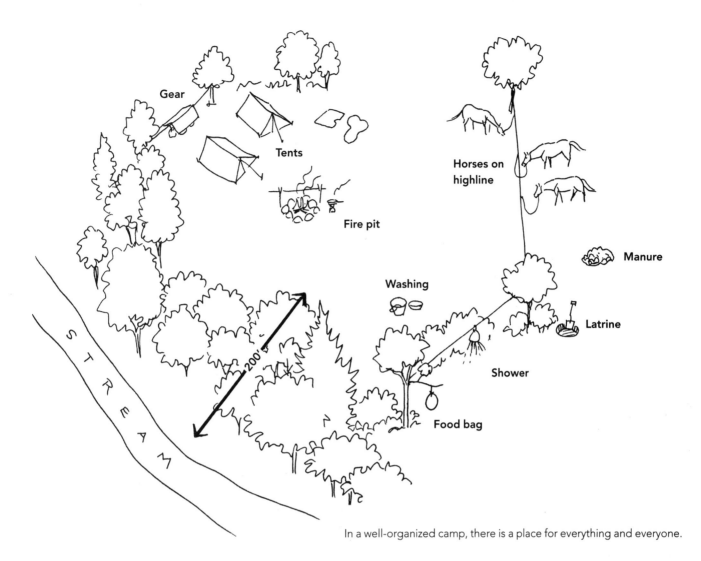

Gear

Tents

Fire pit

Horses on highline

Manure

Washing

Latrine

STREAM

200'

Shower

Food bag

In a well-organized camp, there is a place for everything and everyone.

Keep your camp clean and guard against environmental damage as much as possible. Consider yourself a steward of the land and never forget that complaints about damage by horses are the primary reason for the dwindling number of trails open to us. Obviously, the longer you camp in one place, the more prone it will be to damage from normal wear and tear.

Hold Your Horses

Providing for your horse in camp means keeping him safe and comfortable as well as preventing him from damaging the environment. How you manage all this depends somewhat on the camp itself. Some horse camps have small corrals available for campers, or they provide designated highline areas. Others leave you to your own devices, as when you're camping in the backcountry.

Station horses outside of the immediate camp, but close enough that you can keep an eye (and ear) on them. Your horses will sense visitors, welcome or otherwise, before you will. They will alert you to other riders, hikers, or wildlife. Proximity will help you monitor them so that they stay out of trouble and stay put.

Look for a spot where the breeze can pass through, downwind of camp if possible, to keep horses comfortable. Avoid leaving horses in direct sunlight or deep cover. Heat will dehydrate them, and heavy woods and brush are often home to swarms of annoying insects.

If you are camping in the mountains or early or late in the season when evenings can get very cool, take along a blanket for your horse. Without a winter coat, your horse can become chilled by frosts in these conditions and will be more comfortable with a little extra care on your part.

Portable pens can be a good way to contain horses near your campsite, but, except in very well-established campsites (those that are already far from a natural state), move them regularly to avoid damage to the environment.

CONFINING YOUR HORSE

There are several methods for keeping your horse where you want him. You can take along a portable pen, picket, highline, or hobbles or simply tie your horse up, but each of these has its perks and downsides. Often horsemen mix methods, allowing horses to graze hobbled or picketed in evening, then penning them up in a corral or tying them to a highline at night.

PORTABLE PENS Portable pens give you the most flexibility. Some are bulkier than others. These are best used at a onetime, well-established base camp, as they are cumbersome to set up, take down, pack, carry, and redo. The size and shape of these pens will depend on trees or other supports. A pen 30 to 40 feet in diameter will safely contain five or six horses overnight. The bigger the pen, the better, assuming all your horses can get along well enough to share the space.

Situate the pen away from water and marshy ground. Some riders roll up lengths of bright orange construction-barrier webbing and roll it out between trees or stakes for a quick, safe, fairly

sturdy instant corral. Others take a roll of electric horse fence webbing (webbing embedded with metal wires that conduct electricity) and a small solar charger to keep their horses close to home.

The biggest caution with a portable corral is to make sure ahead of time that your horse is used to it and will respect it as a barrier. Practice at home first. My dad's horses will stay in a pen made from two strands of baling twine, because he rotates grazing areas at home with this setup and the occasional hot wire so that they equate one with the other. The other caution is to move the pen periodically to prevent horses from tearing up the ground in a small space or overgrazing the area.

Electric pens are popular, as horses can be trained to respect them at home. They are lightweight and easy to set up, take down, and move around to minimize damage. They work well in areas that are too rocky or brushy for pickets or hobbles.

PICKETING Staking, known as **picketing,** is a method of tying horses out so that they have enough line to graze. Choose a spot free of horse-tangling debris, roots, limbs, jagged rocks, and the like. Some folks prefer to attach the picket line to a halter, others to a front foot by a half-hobble with a swivel snap. The trick with picketing is to find a place with good grazing to keep your horse content enough not to challenge the picket and clear enough of obstacles to prevent your horse from getting himself tangled.

Use ¾-inch cotton rope, about 25 feet long, for your picket line. Attach the end of the picket line to a swivel snap or with a knot tied in a nonslip loop so that it will swivel around the picket stake rather than wrap around it. One great way to make your own picket line is to run rope or cable through a garden hose. The hose protects the horse from rope burns and keeps the line from kinking.

The picket stake is a grand bit of bluff because most any horse can yank out of the ground all but a 5-footer sunk in solid granite. A 2-foot-long piece of rebar (used in cement work) with a ring welded to the top can be used, or prefab picket stakes are available. The trick is not to let the horse know it can be yanked. Elephants are trained to respect a foot chain when they are young and physically unable to uproot the stake. Though a full-grown elephant can easily yank free of its restraint, it doesn't know it can, so it doesn't. This is the same strategy to use with your horse. If you can't train him as a youngster, train him to respect a picket at home with a super-sturdy stake, or attach the line to a heavy log or other immovable object.

Some horses do better on pickets than others do. Some tend to fight the restraint of a foot chain; others accept it more readily. Use good equipment that won't tangle or burn and practice at home for short periods of time with good food within reach: These are the best ways to ensure that a horse won't resist and hurt himself. If picket time is always associated with good food, most horses will learn to look forward to it!

Most horses do best if picketed with a buddy. A horse left alone can get antsy and may paw, weave, dig, call out, or find some way to hurt himself. One

Hard-won Trail Wisdom

Always keep one horse tied in camp; that way, come what may, you have transportation. If you tie or picket the most dominant herd member, the others will stay close. Picketing is the next best choice, only because it limits horses to a smaller area, thereby concentrating the most potential damage in the shortest amount of time. Keeping a bell on loose horses may help you to find them should they wander.

Remember that a well-fed, well-watered horse, close to his buddies and comfy near camp, is least likely to wander off, paw, dig, or cause other damage.

good strategy is to picket a lead horse while leaving others hobbled in the area.

Whether on the trail or near camp, be sure to move the stake regularly — as often as every few hours — to prevent the ground from getting torn up and the area from being overgrazed. Because picketed horses can churn up soil and trample vegetation, picketing is not allowed in all areas. Check to be sure regulations allow it if you plan to restrain horses this way.

TYING There will inevitably be times when you have to tie up your horse near camp. Find something sturdy enough to hold a horse, with no fragile parts and no parts that could hurt your horse, away from the immediate camp area. The most common horse anchor is a tree, though odd-shaped rocks and exposed roots on overhanging outcroppings have come in handy, too.

The rules here are simple: Tie high and short, and only to something sturdy enough to hold your horse safely. If tying to a tree, find one with mature (thick) bark so that your horse can't damage it by chewing, then keep an eye on him to make *sure* he doesn't. If there are dead limbs sticking out from the tree (or on others nearby that could poke him), break or saw them off from just above your horse's eye level down the base of the tree. This won't hurt the tree and prevents a nasty gouge to your horse. Use a quick-release knot (see page 318) and be sure to tie the horse's head high enough that he can't reach his head any lower than knee level. Too many horses manage to get a front leg over a tied lead rope and suddenly realize they are tangled, only to panic, pull back, and at the very least give themselves some nasty rope burns, or worse, break a leg or neck.

Not all horses will stand quietly when tied, but odds are that after many miles of trail riding, your horse will be ready for a rest. But good tying manners are best first practiced at home, and part of our original list of things to look for, or train for, in a "broke" horse. You can reinforce good tying manners on the trail. If your horse tends to paw when

tied, hobble him to prevent him from tearing up the ground.

Apply bug spray if annoying insects are about. A lot of horses paw simply out of frustration and discomfort caused by bugs.

HIGHLINE A highline is a rope stretched high and taut between two trees. It is probably the easiest, most portable, safest, surest way to keep horses in place, but it too is best practiced at home (see chapter 5). It is considered an environmentally friendly method of restraining horses, giving them some freedom of movement but keeping them from damaging tree roots. Horses generally seem more relaxed tied along a highline than by other methods.

The best rope for the job is a multistrand ¾-inch polypropylene rope (boating rope). It stretches a little, but is strong and doesn't absorb water. Half-inch hemp works, too, and doesn't stretch out. Nylon stretches out of shape and sags,

A safely picketed horse can graze at his leisure. A swivel at the picket end of the rope and a garden hose covering the rope would be safer still.

Tying to a Highline: In Camp

If you have several horses, tie them at least 10 feet apart and so that the snap hangs about 2 feet above ground. This is long enough for a horse to lie down but short enough so that he can't step a leg over his lead rope and get hung up. It also prevents horses from grazing. Most folks tie up a little shorter at night than during the day.

1. Tie the rope about 7 feet above ground (see drawing). This height helps keep horses from tangling themselves or catching a saddle horn in the line if tied while saddled. This is also high enough so that horses tethered to it can't get their heads down to below their knees. NEVER tie a horse long enough that he can get his head down to graze, because he can become tangled and suddenly panic. A tied horse should never have enough rope to hang himself.

2. Don't tie the rope directly around the trees, since it might cut into the bark. Instead, wrap a 6-foot length of 2- or 3-inch webbing, a cut section of burlap, an old bicycle tire inner tube, or even your saddle cinch around the trunk and tie the rope to this buffer. Tree-savers, 2-inch-wide webbing devices, protect tree trunks from horses, hammocks, and anything else that might damage the bark or inner tissues from abrasion by dispersing the force of rope or twine over a broader surface area.

3. Attach individual lead ropes along the highline by tying loops in the rope and then tying one lead rope into each loop with a quick-release knot (see page 318).

4. If you are highlining a single horse, you can feed the rope through a ring or clip on a carabiner and tie the lead rope to it. The advantage of a sliding ring is that the horse can move around more freely, but most folks feel that a stationary horse on a highline is less trouble than one that moves around.

Tie the rope about 7 feet above the ground, and attach individual lead ropes to loops (step 3).

Horse-tracking Trick

As a safety measure, have your farrier add a dab of borium, from 1/8 to 1/4 inch thick, at the toe and heel of each horseshoe. This helps improve traction and also leaves an identifying mark in your horse's hoofprint should you ever have to track him down. If you don't ride trails regularly, have your farrier put on these "trail shoes" a week or so before a ride, and then pull them afterward to reuse later. They can last for months, even years, depending on how often you ride and in what type of terrain.

and can also inflict some nasty rope burns should it slide through your fingers. A light-colored highline or one with a glow-in-the-dark ribbon wrapped around it will show up best in the dark. Use only lead ropes with swivel snaps to prevent them from twisting or separating as the horse moves around. It's a good idea to use a leather halter. If a horse gets into trouble, leather is more likely to break than nylon or rope.

If your horse paws while highlined, consider hobbling him to break the habit. Just be aware: He won't be able to lie down to rest while hobbled.

HOBBLES Hobbles won't keep your horse from wandering away, but they will slow him down. If you use hobbles as a restraint in the backcountry, always keep the most dominant horse in the group tied or penned up while hobbled horses graze. Consider attaching a bell to the back of your horse's halter. In some terrain, a horse can be out of eyesight long before he is out of earshot.

Many outfitters prefer hobbles, as they allow horses to graze over an extended area, therefore causing less damage than when horses are limited to the smaller space of a pen or picket line. Keep an eye on hobbled horses; they can travel quite a distance. Usually, hungry horses will graze in an area for an hour or so before wandering off. Always offer your horse water before turning him loose in hobbles. Otherwise, he might wander off in search of water and could trip or even drown while trying to quench his thirst.

TO BELL OR NOT TO BELL Some outfitters recommend belling horses at night, although the tinkling can be a bit distracting. If ever a horse escapes into the dark, however, he will be much easier to locate if you have a musical clue in the background. Those with experience in the backcountry recommend belling mares and any horses with a tendency to wander or keep to themselves. You can find bells with different pitches and give each horse his own sound: The higher the pitch, the farther the sound will carry in the woods. Wind will mask the sound and damp weather will make it more noticeable.

Grazing

Allowing your horse to graze on native grasses is part of what makes the experience fun for him, too. Rotate the areas in which horses are allowed to graze to minimize impact. Also, be aware of any native plants that may be toxic to horses (see chapter 9 and appendix) and the signs of accidental poisoning. If plant life looks questionable, opt for a less verdant campsite.

Also check for debris from previous campers that might cause problems to you, your horse, or other traveling companions. Broken glass, ragged edges of tin cans left exposed, and other trash can be more than just a nuisance if your horse tries to eat it or you discover it with your bare feet in the middle of the night. At trailheads, leaky radiator fluid can be lethal to dogs (or cats) brought along for the ride.

Rather than ride on when trash is the problem, carefully pick up what you can and carry it out. Trail riders have seen it all out there, and it may be a good idea to carry a pair of lightweight plastic gloves just for trash pickup.

A horse can graze for 2 or 3 hours without so much as looking up. Be careful, however, if your horse isn't used to grazing, and limit him to an hour or two a day, as a sudden change in diet could upset his system and possibly even lead to colic.

Time grazing to take place just before a set evening feeding time. Even if your horse isn't particularly hungry after grazing, he will come for his regular ration of grain and be much easier to catch.

Avoid letting him overgraze any one area. Grazing areas should be left as lush as possible for the next camper; never let your horse consume more than half of the available graze before relocating him. Lush grass will stand up to grazing better than lean pickings will.

The more confined your horses are, the more likely they are to cause damage. Letting horses loose to graze, hobbled or free, is best. A good bit of advice is to hobble all, if any, loose grazing horses. A hobbled horse will hurt himself trying to keep up with horses that are not.

Breaking Camp

As you break camp, keep the next rider in mind. Strive to leave the camp as natural, clean, and damage-free as possible. Here are some reminders.

* Take down tent poles and stack them.
* Remove rope or twine from trees.
* Stack any unused firewood neatly (or disperse it the way you found it).
* Pick up all garbage.
* Cover toilet and gray water holes with the original sod.
* Fill in any holes dug up by dogs or pawed by horses and replace the sod when possible.
* Clean up or dismantle fire rings.
* Clean up after others if necessary.
* Scatter manure piles.
* Eliminate any signs that you were there.

In remote areas, be sure the site is as natural when you leave it as when you found it. This can mean replacing rocks, scattering collected firewood, and raking up trampled grass. The real test is that last look back, when you wish you could stay and realize that this is the perfect spot.

Leave camp as clean and natural as you found it, more so if possible.

APPENDIX: TRAIL MIX

TOXIC TRAILSIDE PLANTS

Many plants are not safe for horses to eat. Some cause immediate, severe reactions, others cause only mild discomfort, still others cause symptoms only when eaten in large amounts or over time. Even healthy forage can have dire consequences if your horse overindulges. Horses not accustomed to rich green grass or clover can colic or founder when let loose to graze on the trail. Fertilized fields can accumulate toxic levels of nitrates. Roadside plants may have been sprayed with pesticides or herbicides, which can be harmful in themselves or improve the taste of plants that horses would otherwise avoid, by converting starches to sugars.

The first thing to do if you suspect your horse has eaten a harmful plant is to prevent further ingestion and if possible pull any remnants from his mouth. Monitor his vital signs and inform your veterinarian as soon as possible if any symptoms appear.

A list follows of plants you are most likely to encounter on the trail or in public riding areas. In addition, keep your horse away from cultivated garden plants such as potato, tomato, castor oil plant, rhubarb (the leaves are poisonous), rhododendrons, and azaleas.

PERENNIALS

Boxwood *Buxus sempervirens*
Distribution: Throughout North America and Western Canada
Habitat: Cultivated. Commonly used as hedge
Toxicity: Highly toxic. Alkaloids; 1 pound of leaves can kill a horse
Symptoms: Gastrointestinal distress (colic), bloody manure, respiratory failure
Treatment: Supportive therapy as advised by your veterinarian; death can occur due to respiratory failure soon after symptoms appear

© ELAYNE SEARS

Bracken fern *Pteridium aquilinum*
Distribution: Worldwide
Habitat: Forests, overgrown fields, in a variety of soils, including poor, sandy, and clay
Toxicity: Moderately toxic. Thiaminase. Poisoning occurs after regular consumption for months; readily eaten, mildly/cumulatively toxic
Symptoms: Coordination is affected, depression, blindness, horse stands braced; thiamine deficiency
Treatment: Megadoses of thiamine, proper diet

REGINA HUGHES

Buttercup *Ranunculus* spp.
Distribution: Worldwide
Habitat: Marshy areas, fields, bogs, valley bottoms, creeksides
Toxicity: Toxic in large quantities. Ranunculin (turns to protoanemonin, an irritant, when chewed). Most toxic when in flower; horses dislike the taste, but if fed it before, sometimes seem to seek it out

REGINA HUGHES

Symptoms: Symptoms vary. Plant juices may cause sores on lips; depression, drooling, diarrhea, nervousness, abdominal pain, blindness, blood in urine
Treatment: No specific treatment; supportive therapy as recommended by veterinarian

Carolina jasmine *Gelsemium sempervirens*
Distribution: From Mexico, through the southern U.S. and along the eastern coast
Habitat: Wooded areas, from dry to damp
Toxicity: Highly toxic. Most toxic winter and spring, contains gelsemine and gelseminine, and other alkaloids related to strychnine; roots and flowers are most toxic
Symptoms: Weakness, convulsions, rigid legs and tail, respiratory failure, coma
Treatment: Intense supportive care; activated charcoal saline cathartics and IV fluids; successful recovery depends on amount ingested and level of treatment; can be fatal

BEVERLY DUNCAN

Clover, alsike *Trifolium hybridum*
Distribution: Cultivated and naturalized throughout the U.S.
Habitat: Roadsides, fields, open areas
Toxicity: Moderately toxic; phototoxin (not currently identified)
Symptoms: Trifoliosis; photosensitivity, red skin after exposure to sun, mostly around the mouth and hoofline; sores may become inflamed. Chronic poisoning leads to depression, colic, nervousness, diarrhea, liver damage, weight loss, jaundice
Treatment: Keep animals away from clover

Cocklebur *Xanthium* spp. (many species, all toxic)

Distribution: From Mexico, throughout the U.S. and Canada

Habitat: Disturbed soil, near water; prolific and persistent

Toxicity: Highly toxic. Seedlings (two-leaf) most toxic and most likely to be eaten. Fatal at less than 1½ percent of animal's body weight, or 15 pounds per a 1,000-pound horse

Symptoms: Gastrointestinal distress, depression, weakness, weak heartbeat, convulsions

Treatment: Mineral oil and activated charcoal followed by supportive therapy, IV fluids, monitoring. Treatment for liver damage may be necessary; chronic liver damage is a concern for survivors of acute poisoning; can be fatal

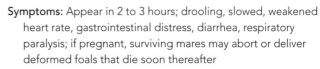

REGINA HUGHES

Death camas *Zigadenus* spp.

Distribution: Throughout the U.S. and Canada

Habitat: Damp, boggy areas, low hills, and wooded areas

Toxicity: Highly toxic, but rarely eaten; veratrum steroid alkaloids. Young shoots in spring most likely to be eaten

Symptoms: Symptoms vary; weakness, weak heartbeat, convulsions, staggering, drooling, nausea, coma

Treatment: Activated charcoal can help to prevent systemic absorption if administered soon after ingestion. Atropine sulfate and picrotoxin have been used by veterinarians with some success; can be fatal

© ELAYNE SEARS

Dogbane *Apocynum* spp.

Distribution: Throughout the U.S.

Habitat: Open areas and along streams

Toxicity: Alkaloids and cardiac glycosides; highly toxic: ½ ounce is enough to kill a horse; rarely ingested due to bitter taste

Symptoms: Fever, weak and elevated pulse, staggering, bloat, convulsions

Treatment: Veterinary action required, followed by EKG monitoring; recovery depends on amount ingested and speed of adequate veterinary intervention; can be fatal

BEVERLY DUNCAN

False hellebore *Veratrum viride*

Distribution: Throughout the U.S. and Canada

Habitat: Open areas, damp lowlands to high valleys; also cultivated

Toxicity: Highly toxic but rarely eaten. Steroidal alkaloids and glycoalkaloids. Unpalatable and unlikely to be eaten, except young shoots in early spring, when the plant is most toxic

BEVERLY DUNCAN

Symptoms: Appear in 2 to 3 hours; drooling, slowed, weakened heart rate, gastrointestinal distress, diarrhea, respiratory paralysis; if pregnant, surviving mares may abort or deliver deformed foals that die soon thereafter

Treatment: No specific treatment; supportive therapy as indicated

Fitweed *Corydalis* spp.

Distribution: From the Sierra Nevadas east throughout much of the U.S.

Habitat: A variety of habitats at high elevations (5,000–6,300 feet)

Toxicity: Highly toxic. Isoquinoline-structured alkaloids; all species are toxic at all stages

Symptoms: Rapid, shallow breathing, staggering, seizures, facial twitches, depression, and characteristic snapping at things with the mouth; death may occur within hours

Treatment: None noted; nonfatal cases tend to recover quickly

MALLORY LAKE

Foxglove *Digitalis purpurea*

Distribution: Throughout most of the U.S. and Canada, except areas with hot, dry summers; cultivated throughout, and wild in the western U.S. and Canada

Habitat: A variety of soils and conditions, sunny slopes, farms, fields, roadsides, open areas along wooded trails

Toxicity: Highly toxic. Saponins, alkaloids, and cardiac glycosides, including digitoxin, digitalin, and digoxin; only a few hundredths of 1 percent of a horse's body weight can be fatal, but horses rarely eat the plant

Symptoms: Colic, blood in manure, frequent urination, loss of appetite, pain, irregular heartbeat, convulsions

Treatment: Treat individual symptoms; no known antidote. Activated charcoal and saline laxatives recommended soon after ingestion; IV fluid therapy may be necessary, as may monitoring blood levels of potassium and other supportive therapy; can be fatal

MALLORY LAKE

Groundsel, common *Senecio vulgaris* and spp.

Distribution: The Southwest north into Utah, Colorado, and Wyoming

Habitat: High altitudes, 2500–7500 feet in arid mountain areas; prefers poor, dry soils

Toxicity: Highly toxic. Contains pyrrolizidine alkaloids similar to those in tansy ragwort; rarely eaten

Symptoms: Lethargy, loss of appetite, abdominal pain, weakness, red, watery eyes (especially when exposed to sun), crustiness

© ELAYNE SEARS

around eyes; animals may wander in a confused state or become agitated

Treatment: Once symptoms appear, too late to save the horse; can cause liver damage and failure to thrive without above symptoms

Horsetail *Equisetum* spp. (also known as scouring rush)

Distribution: Worldwide

Habitat: Drainage areas, low-lying wetlands, roadsides, sandy soils, marshes

Toxicity: Highly toxic (to horses). Thiaminase. More toxic to horses than other animals; depletes Vitamin B_1 which degenerates peripheral nerves

Symptoms: Weakness, erratic heart rate, abnormal gait, weight loss; once down, horses often cannot get up

Treatment: If given early, blood tests for thiamine deficiency and megadoses of thiamine if indicated

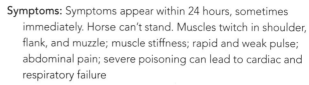

REGINA HUGHES

Jimsonweed *Datura* spp. (also known as apple of Peru)

Distribution: Throughout the U.S.

Habitat: River-bottom soils, fields, deserted farmsteads; also cultivated as an ornamental

Toxicity: Highly toxic. Solanaceous alkaloids (solanine, hyosyamine, hyoscine), which compromise digestion and the nervous system

REGINA HUGHES

Symptoms: Appear within minutes to hours. Excitement interrupted by sudden depression, colic, excessive thirst, diarrhea, low temperatures, convulsions, dilated pupils, coma, respiratory paralysis

Treatment: No specific treatment. Care for symptoms must be started early to be successful, including activated charcoal and laxatives to limit how much toxin is absorbed into the system. Physotigmine has been recommended. Death is common outcome; survivors may have compromised respiratory systems

Larkspur *Delphinium* spp.

Distribution: Throughout the U.S. and Canada

Habitat: Most problematic in the West; common in meadows, open areas in woods, roadsides, slopes

Toxicity: Highly toxic. Polycyclic diterpenoid alkaloids, most concentrated in young plants and later in seeds. Horses are usually poisoned in the spring or fall; tall plant spikes are least likely to be eaten

© ELAYNE SEARS

Symptoms: Symptoms appear within 24 hours, sometimes immediately. Horse can't stand. Muscles twitch in shoulder, flank, and muzzle; muscle stiffness; rapid and weak pulse; abdominal pain; severe poisoning can lead to cardiac and respiratory failure

Treatment: Stress to a poisoned horse can be fatal. Physostigmine is the preferred treatment, known to reverse the process of this type of alkaloid poisoning if given soon after poisoning. Activated charcoal and magnesium sulfate help to slow absorption of the poison into the horse's system; prognosis ranges from total recovery to death, depending on degree of poisoning and emergency response

Leafy spurge *Euphorbia esula*

Distribution: Throughout most of the U.S., Canada, and Mexico

Habitat: Varied and prolific

Toxicity: All parts toxic, moderately toxic but rarely eaten; diterpene esters

Symptoms: Blisters lips, tongue, and skin, may cause photosensitivity, irritates digestive tract; sap can irritate eyes if contacted while grazing among the plants

Treatment: Wash affected areas with mild soap if sap is present. No treatment other than removal from plants; recovery generally full and uneventful

© ELAYNE SEARS

Locoweed *Astragalus* spp.

Distribution: From northwestern Mexico through the western U.S. to southwestern Canada

Habitat: Dry, sandy soils, mountains and prairie lands in the West

Toxicity: Moderately toxic. Toxic in large amounts. Swainsonine (an alkaloid); some spp. also contain nitroamines (affect the nervous system) or concentrate selenium. Most toxic in late winter or early spring; symptoms appear after prolonged consumption

© ELAYNE SEARS

Symptoms: Dangerous because horses like it so much! Impairs cellular function or affects the nervous system. Weight loss, odd behavior (such as stumbling, falling, or suddenly charging) due to nervous system damage appear after weeks to months of consumption

Treatment: No treatment other than to keep the horse away from locoweed; once symptoms appear, prognosis is poor and the horse will always be prone to falling or other abnormal behavior

Lupine *Lupinus* spp.

Distribution: Throughout the U.S. and Canada

Habitat: Dry to damp soils, in cleared areas, meadows, open woods, mountains

Toxicity: From low to high. Quinolizidine, piperidine (alkaloids); nitrogen oxides. Not all species are poisonous; seeds are most toxic

Symptoms: Within an hour to a day, including depression, weak pulse, shallow respiration, nervousness, convulsions, coma

Treatment: Intensive supportive care as advised by your veterinarian; survivors often sustain permanent liver damage and never recover fully; can be fatal

Milkweed *Asclepias* spp.

Distribution: Northern Mexico, the U.S. (except the Pacific Northwest), and southern Canada

Habitat: Overgrazed areas, poor/dry soils

Toxicity: Highly toxic but rarely eaten. Galitoxin resinoid (an irritant) and cardiac glycocides. All parts of the plant are toxic. Species in Western states 100 times more toxic than those in the East; species with narrow leaves more toxic than those with broad leaves

Symptoms: Staggering, increased pulse, gastrointestinal distress, depression, weakness, seizure, bloat, difficult breathing; may all appear within hours of eating the plant

Treatment: Treat gastrointestinal distress and cardiac glycoside poisoning; sedatives, laxative, and IV fluids suggested. Intensive supportive therapy, including EKG monitoring, may be required. Prognosis grim to good depending on amount ingested, quickness of treatment, and completion of cardiac therapy; can be fatal

REGINA HUGHES

Mistletoe *Phoradendron villosum*

Distribution: Throughout the U.S., except the Great Lakes region and extreme Northeast

Habitat: Grows on trees in hardwood forests, especially oaks

Toxicity: Moderately toxic. Unidentified toxins. Some animals seek it out; horses grazing among or tied to oaks are at risk

Symptoms: Sometimes colic and diarrhea precede a sudden death

Treatment: No specific treatment, but activated charcoal, saline cathartics, and intensive supportive care may help relieve distress in nonfatal cases; can be fatal

LOUISE RIOTTE

Monkshood *Aconitum napellus*

Distribution: U.S. and Canada, except in areas with extreme high and low temperatures

Habitat: Wild and cultivated, in shaded, moist areas

Toxicity: Highly toxic. Aconitine and related alkaloids. All plant parts are toxic, leaves and roots are most toxic. Less than .075 percent of a horse's weight of root (about ¾ of a pound) has proved fatal to horses

Symptoms: Weakness, irregular heartbeat, nervousness, drooling, and lying down, unable to get up

Treatment: No specified treatment. Activated charcoal administered quickly after ingestion helps to slow absorption, and IV therapy has been used to counter cardiovascular effects; can be fatal

MALLORY LAKE

Nightshade *Solanum americanum*

Distribution: Throughout the U.S.

Habitat: Along fencerows, creek beds, clear-cuts, roadsides, and other areas where soils have been disturbed and neglected

Toxicity: Highly toxic. Rarely eaten. Glycoalkaloid solanine. Toxicity of plant parts varies, unripe berries considered the most toxic

Symptoms: Tiredness, muscle twitches, and other signs of neurological distress; bloating; congestion in the lungs

Treatment: No specific treatment for the toxin, and supportive care must start immediately to be successful. Activated charcoal and laxatives help slow absorption. Respiration support may be necessary; physostigmine has been recommended for severe poisoning

BEVERLY DUNCAN

Poison hemlock, Apiaceae family
Conium spp.

Distribution: Throughout the U.S., Canada, and Mexico

Habitat: Overgrown fields, roadsides, ditches

Toxicity: Highly toxic. Coniine and other alkaloids. Seeds are most toxic, followed by second-year leaves and stems

Symptoms: Dilated pupils, nervousness, shaking, bloat, weak heartbeat, reduced circulation, cold extremities, paralysis, coma

Treatment: No specific antidote. Mineral oil, activated charcoal, and saline cathartics, followed by intensive supportive care have been successful; often results in death

LOUISE RIOTTE

Sneezeweed *Helenium* spp.
(*Note:* related to sunflowers;
other species members of the
family Asteraceae also toxic)

Distribution: Throughout Mexico, the U.S.,
and Canada

Habitat: Meadows, damp slopes, swampy
areas, overgrazed pastureland

Toxicity: Highly toxic in quantity.
Sesquiterpene lactones (helanin) and other
toxins. Mature plant most toxic; all parts toxic,
including seeds

Symptoms: Convulsions, staggering, loss of
coordination, foaming at the mouth

Treatment: Activated charcoal and saline cathartics within
first hour or so of ingestion; supporting therapy

St.-John's-wort *Hypericum
perforatum*

Distribution: Throughout the U.S. and
Canada

Habitat: Common in disturbed soils,
poor, dry soils, roadsides, open areas

Toxicity: Moderately toxic. Hypericin. There
are 25 species and at least 6 are toxic.
All stages toxic, but new shoots most
likely to be eaten

Symptoms: Photosensitivity in pale or white
skin; horses may rub spots raw or roll trying
to relief the skin irritation; also fever,
elevated pulse, diarrhea, sensitivity to cold water

Treatment: Bring the horse indoors, out of direct sunlight.
Corticosteroids are often prescribed to reduce inflammation
and irritation. Antibiotics may be needed to combat secondary
infections due to extreme skin rubbing. Horses that continue
to graze St.-John's-wort and left in the sun continue to be
photosensitive and suffer; they may also go blind

Sweet pea *Lathyrus* spp.

Distribution: Wild and cultivated
throughout the U.S.

Habitat: Various

Toxicity: Mildly toxic. Beta
aminopropionitrile; seeds are most
toxic. It takes large quantities over
a few days produce symptoms.
Readily eaten; toxicity is
cumulative

Symptoms: Muscle stiffness, painful
motion; can be mistaken for laminitis or being "tied-up"

Treatment: Supportive care as advised by your veterinarian

Tansy ragwort *Senecio jacobaea*

Distribution: Coastal Pacific Northwest, also spots
in New England

Habitat: Moist soils (areas with substantial rainfall),
clay soils, open areas between wooded areas,
pastures, woodlands, logged-off areas

Toxicity: Highly toxic. Pyrrolizidine alkaloids, damage
to liver and central nervous system. "Animals eating
5 percent or more of their total daily diet of prebloom
tansy ragwort for periods exceeding 20 consecutive
days can be expected to die within a 6-month period"
(USDA Poisonous Plant Research Laboratory).
Flowering seed heads most toxic, but first-year plant
(leafy rosette) most likely to be accidentally eaten as
horses graze

Symptoms: Symptoms may not appear until 6 months after the
plant has been eaten. By then, it is too late to save the horse.
Loss of appetite, lethargy, weakness, trembling, dragging the
hind feet; horse may wobble around in confusion; crust around
the eyes and nose; eyes may be watery and red, especially
when exposed to bright sun; diarrhea or constipation, stomach
upset, cirrhosis of the liver, blindness

Treatment: None. Depending on the amount eaten, can be fatal
or lead to permanent liver damage

Vetch, hairy *Vicia villosa*

Distribution: Cultivated and wild throughout
the U.S.

Habitat: Fields, ditches, roadsides,
throughout the U.S. (and Europe)

Toxicity: Moderately toxic; toxic
components are not clearly
understood. Poisoning results after
consumption of large quantities or over an
extended period of time; readily eaten by horses

Symptoms: Horses with extensive areas of white skin may
experience photosensitivity. Drooling, runny nose, cough,
stiff limbs, swollen head and neck, rough and/or thinning coat,
weakness, convulsions, diarrhea; in pregnant mares, loss of foal

Treatment: None specified; liver and kidney damage may be
permanent

Water hemlock *Cicuta maculata*

Distribution: Throughout U.S. and
Canada

Habitat: Boggy, damp areas

Toxicity: Highly toxic. Cicutoxin.
Considered among the most toxic of
plants. One mouthful can kill a horse
within 15 minutes. Roots, new leaves, and
stems are most toxic plant parts; poisoning
most common in spring when tender new
shoots emerge

Symptoms: Violent convulsions, drooling, shaking, grinding teeth, pupil dilation, fever, abdominal pain, bloat

Treatment: Sedatives to ease pain. Flushing the intestines may help. Outlook grim; horses may die within minutes or after 8 hours of extreme pain.

Yew, Japanese (*Taxus cuspidate*), Western (*Taxus brevifolia*), English (*Taxus baccata*); also known as ground hemlock (*American yew*)

Distribution: Throughout the U.S., wild and cultivated. Japanese yew most common in northern areas, English yew most common in milder climates, Western yew in the Northwest

Habitat: Varied

Toxicity: Highly toxic. Taxine (alkaloid). Very dangerous because horses willingly eat it, but consuming only .1 percent of body weight causes symptoms

Symptoms: Horses have been known to collapse immediately beside the plant. Heart rate decreases, circulation fails, agitation, confusion, gastrointestinal distress, diarrhea

Treatment: Atropine suggested to restore heart function. Activated charcoal, saline carthartics, and IV fluids, as needed. Artificial respiration may be needed. Recovery is possible if symptoms are treatable prior to severe distress; can be fatal

GRASSES

Arrow grass *Triglochin maritima*

Distribution: Throughout the U.S. and Canada

Habitat: Salt marshes, boggy areas, low-lying, moist alkaline soils, shorelines

Toxicity: Toxic in moderate to large quantities. Prussic acid and cyanide, depending on growing conditions; .5 percent of body weight, or 5 pounds, has proved lethal

Symptoms: Consistent with cyanide poisoning, including weak pulse, rapid breathing, excitement, drooling, emptying the bladder and bowels, racing heartbeat, fainting, bright red gums and other mucous membranes, staggering, collapse

Treatment: Sodium nitrite, sodium thiosulfate (IV). Recovery depends on the amount ingested; Can be fatal

Fescue, Chewings *Festuca rubra* and Tall *Festuca arundinacea*

Distribution: Throughout the U.S.

Habitat: Chewings fescue grows wild in dry, rocky soils as well as cultivated in lawns; tall fescue grows in moist soils, bogs, swampy areas

Toxicity: Toxic only when infested. Chewings fescue may have nematode galls that develop in the seed and produce coryne toxins, which infect seed and grass; moderately toxic, problems are common. Tall fescue contains alalkaloids, perloline, and halostachine; also, an endophyte (fungus) that is toxic to horses infects the grass

Symptoms: Chewings fescue — trembling, incoordination, staggering, falling, abortion in pregnant mares. Endophyte-infected tall fescue — different symptoms depending on the time of year, and these may occur after a few days to months of grazing. Summer poisoning: fever, abortion or stillbirth, retained placenta, pregnancies that exceed due dates, infertility, reduced milk production in mares, poor growth rate in foals. Winter poisoning: lack of appetite, lameness, poor, rough coat, diarrhea, weight loss, and gangrene in the extremities

Treatment: No specific treatment. Kidney and liver damage may result in chronic cases of chewings poisoning; can be fatal

Foxtail grass, Squirreltail grass, various members of Poaceae (grass) family

Distribution: Throughout the U.S. and Canada

Habitat: A variety of conditions, often in overgrazed areas, fields, roadsides

Toxicity: Not toxic; harmful in that the seedheads are hooked and can work into the flesh of the horse's mouth, face, neck, and ears and cause abscesses

Symptoms: Loss of appetite, impaction colic, even blindness or systemic fever; one bite can develop painful consequences

Treatment: May require removal by veterinarian, colic treatment, or surgery

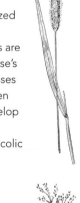

Johnson grass *Sorghum halapense* and other types of sorghum

Distribution: Texas, through the Southeast, and north to New York

Habitat: Open fields, disturbed and/or neglected soils

Toxicity: Highly toxic but rarely eaten. Prussic acid and sometimes high levels of nitrates. Cyanide concentrated when the plant is stressed (such as by drought or frost); highest when the plant is young and tender, lowest when tall and setting seedheads; leaves most toxic

Symptoms: Poisoning can be acute (sudden) or chronic (from prolonged exposure). Signs of acute poisoning: bright red mucous membranes, emptying bladder and bowels, weak pulse, rapid respiration, excitement, erratic heartbeat, staggering, collapse

Treatment: IV sodium nitrite and sodium thiosulfate for cyanide poisoning; IV 1 percent methylene blue for nitrate/nitrite poisoning; acute poisoning can be fatal

TREES & SHRUBS

Black locust *Robinia pseudoacacia*

Distribution: Northern Texas north into south-central and eastern U.S.

Habitat: Open areas in woods, roadsides; most prevalent in Appalachians and old Texas homesteads; prefers clay soils

Toxicity: Highly toxic. Glycoside robitin, and robin and phasin (phytotoxins). All parts, including bark, are poisonous; horses have been poisoned by chewing a small amount of bark when tied to the tree

Symptoms: Dilated pupils, weak, uneven pulse, paralysis in the hind end, weakness, cold extremities, stomach pain

Treatment: Treatment can be lengthy and needs to be regulated by your veterinarian. Activated charcoal and laxatives may help. Full recovery is common; rarely, death

Maple, red *Acer rubrum*

Distribution: Eastern U.S. and Canada

Habitat: River bottoms and any other areas with moist soil

Toxicity: Highly toxic but rarely eaten. Toxin unknown; leaves and bark can poison horses

Symptoms: Weakness, depression, pale gums (and other mucous membranes) and dark urine from severe anemia; pregnant mares may lose their foals

Treatment: Requires quick action by veterinarian, including IV fluids, oxygen, and blood transfusions; can be fatal

Mesquite *Prosopis glandulosa*

Distribution: Southwest through midwestern U.S. and northern Mexico

Habitat: Arid regions

Toxicity: Moderately toxic and physically damaging. Arabinose, most toxic summer and fall; thorns cause mechanical damage, pods cause impaction

Symptoms: Signs of colic, also drooling, constant chewing, nervousness, shaking, anemia; mouth, esophagus, and intestinal track may be damaged by thorns

Treatment: No known antidote. Supportive therapy for colic, including oil and fluids. Colic surgery may be needed; prognosis fair to good, depending on treatment

Mountain laurel *Kalmia latifolia*

Distribution: Eastern and northwestern U.S., cultivated. Common up to 4,000 feet; higher in the South

Habitat: Open woods, hillsides, rocky soils

Toxicity: Highly toxic. All parts contain resinoid adromedotoxin; leaves and smallest branches contain cardiac glycoside (arbutin). Grayanotoxins present in all parts. Ingesting .2 to .6 percent of body weight causes poisoning; most poisonings in winter or early spring, when other green food not available

Symptoms: Lack of coordination; watery eyes, runny nose, salivation; irregular breathing; bloat; weakness; trembling, increased heart rate, convulsions; coma; and death

Treatment: Activated charcoal via stomach tube, saline cathartics help prevent absorption. Atropine may be required to restore normal heart function. Can be lethal.

Oleander *Nerium oleander*

Distribution: Primarily cultivated in the Southeast, parts of California, and areas of the Southwest. Also Puerto Rico and the Virgin Islands.

Habitat: Cultivated in yards, parks, public gardens, road dividers, etc.

Toxicity: Highly toxic. Primary toxins are nerioside, oleandroside, saponins, and cardiac glycosides. All plant parts poisonous. A few mouthfuls can kill a horse.

Symptoms: [Similar to foxglove or dogbane]

Treatment: No specific treatment other than supportive therapy according to your veterinarian.

Privet *Ligustrum* spp.

Distribution: Throughout the U.S. and Canada

Habitat: Woods and bottomlands, abandoned home sites, along fence rows; widely cultivated as hedge

Toxicity: Moderate to high; leaves and fruit contain glycosides (specifically, ligustrin, syringin); gastrointestinal irritant

Symptoms: Colic, weak pulse, incoordination, partial paralysis, diarrhea, abdominal pain, convulsions

Treatment: Treat for dehydration and follow up with supportive therapy as advised by your veterinary; can be fatal

50 BEST TRAILS IN NORTH AMERICA

Important note: Be aware that if you are transporting horses out of your home state — in some states, from one region or county to another — you may be stopped by law enforcement and required to show: (1) a current negative Coggins test, (2) a health certificate from your veterinarian, and/or (3) brand inspection papers (western states). Contact the state veterinarian or brand inspection department of the state in which you intend to ride for details.

Though the information provided here is the best available at this time, trail conditions, regulations, and access can change without notice. Please contact trail authorities before you head out.

1

Location: Arkansas, Ozark National Forest
Name of trail: Moccasin Gap Horse Trail
Trails: Four major loops totaling 28 miles. Degree of difficulty varies from beginner to experienced horses and riders depending on which loop ridden. Trails are marked with color-coded blazes on the trees.
Facilities: The horse camp has 15 gravel parking sites with a tether post and fire ring. Facilities include municipal water, trash cans, and toilets.
Usage: Multiuse; horses, hikers, mountain bikes, and motorized vehicles.
Further info: Bayou Ranger District, 12000 SR 27, Hector, AR 72843; (479) 284-3150
Notes: Located 2 miles down Highway 7 is the private campground Mack's Pines; food, cabins, and hot showers are available here.

2

Location: Jasper, Arkansas
Name of trail: Buffalo River (Steele Creek Access)
Trails: 13 miles west of Jasper on Highway 74, proceed 2 miles down a steep, winding gravel road.
Facilities: Open year-round. April through October, drinking water is available. 26 tent sites with no hookups; flush toilets, fire grates, picnic tables, river access, equestrian campsites, and horse trails.
Usage: User's fee charged. Horses and hikers.
Further info: Park Superintendent, 402 North Walnut, Suite 136, Harrison, AR 72601-1173, (870) 741-5443; www.nps.gov/buff/ or e-mail buff_information@nps.gov
Notes: Not recommended for large trailers, buses, and RVs due to steep, winding road. Beautiful scenic bluffs.

3

Location: Arizona, north of Tucson
Name of trail: Catalina State Park, Coronado National Forest
Trails: 5,493 acres at elevations near 3,000 feet offer miles of outstanding, interconnecting trails. The desert in bloom is spectacular and the area is filled with strange and wonderful saguaro cactus.
Facilities: Horse campground, with water and 12x24 stalls. No electricity at horse camp. Shower and restrooms at non-equestrian campground. Hay and feed available outside the park. Picnic areas, grills, fire rings (bring your own wood), good parking, even a gift shop.
Usage: Multiuse.
Further info: www.pr.state.az.us/Parks/parkhtml/catalina.html; P.O. Box 36986, Tucson, AZ 85740; (520) 628-5798
Notes: 14-day user limit.

4

Location: Northern Arizona, Grand Canyon
Name of trail: 6 trails open to privately owned equine use
Trails: Rugged steep descents and ascents. Amazing transformation from the rim to the bottom.
Facilities: Campgrounds, showers, laundry, various accommodations.
Usage: Horses and hikers.
Further info:
www.nps.gov/grca/backcountry/private_stock_use.htm; Backcountry Office (928) 638-7875, North Rim (928) 638-7870, South Rim — Ronnie Gibson (928) 638-7809. www.kaibab.org/bc/gc_trail.htm#horsey
Notes: No llamas allowed. Group-size restrictions due to the fragile environment. "Animals must be kept on the trails and off the fragile areas along trail borders. Riders accept responsibility for their personal safety and for the removal of their dead or injured animals from the park. Notify park rangers immediately of any animal injury or fatality." These are not easy trails, with rapid changes in elevation over short distances and often extreme heat. Mules are recommended over horses.

5

Location: California, Humboldt Redwoods State Park, approximately 40 miles south of Eureka
Name of trail: Cueno Creek Horse Camp
Trails: 50+ miles of trails ranging from 2- to 20- mile rides on mostly easy trails
Facilities: 38 corrals/group and individual. Restrooms and coin-operated showers.
Usage: Horses.
Further info: www.humboldtredwoods.org/cuneo.htm

6

Location: California, 10 miles northwest of Corona
Name of Trail: Chino Hills State Park
Trails: There are miles of well-maintained and flat trails here.
Facilities: Picnic area, equestrian staging area, pipe corrals, a historic barn, water spigots, restrooms.
Usage: Most trails are multiuse.
Further info: www.parks.ca.gov/?page_id=648; 951-780-6222
Notes: No smoking due to fire danger. Fires limited to fire rings, prohibited during fire season. Park is shut down for 48 hours after ¼ inch of rain, as the clay soil becomes "greasy" and dangerous.

7

Location: San Diego, California
Name of trail: San Diego Sea-to-Sea Trail
Trails: 140 miles
Facilities: Lodging.
Usage: Multi-use; horses, hikers, mountain bikes.
Further info: www.seatoseatrail.org/; Sea-to-Sea Trail Foundation, PO Box 19413, San Diego, CA 92159-0413; (619) 303 6975; contact@seatoseatrail.org
Notes: Ongoing project to connect a trail system among all of the 48 lower states.

8

Location: California, 22 miles north of San Francisco
Name of trail: Point Reyes National Seashore
Trails: 120 miles of trails from mountain forests to meadows to white-sand beaches
Facilities: Various at different trailheads.
Usage: Multiuse.
Further info: www.pointreyes.net/activities/
Notes: "A trail that gives you the feeling of being where man has not touched, a bit of heaven on earth, surreal in some ways."
— Sharmaine Ege

9

Location: Clayton, California
Name of trail: Mount Diablo State Park
Trails: Short and well marked
Facilities: Campsites, exhibits, interpretive center, art center, restrooms, showers
Usage: Multiuse.
Further info: www.parks.ca.gov/; 96 Mitchell Canyon Road, Clayton, CA 94517; (925) 837-2525
Notes: Famous views from the Golden Gate, to Mount Lassen, to the Sacramento River Valley.

More trails and horse rentals in California:
http://totalescape.com/active/animals/rides.html

10

Location: San Juan National Forest (Pagosa District), Colorado
Name of trail: Turkey Creek Trail (580)
Trails: 20 miles to the Continental Divide at Piedra Pass, trail is fairly difficult, with streams to cross and some steep grades. Views are spectacular. Several trails shoot off from this one. The highest point on the trail is 12,000 feet, with a total ascent of 5,000 feet. The route that includes the Turkey Creek Trail, the Continental Divide Trail, and the West Fork Trail (561) is sometimes called the Rainbow Trail.
Facilities: Parking at trailhead.
Usage: Horses and hikers only, no bikes or motor vehicles.
Further info: San Juan National Forest, Pagosa Ranger District, P.O. Box 310, Pagosa and Second Streets, Pagosa Springs, CO 81147; (970) 264-2268

11

Location: Okeechobee, Florida
Name of trail: Kissimmee Prairie Preserve State Park
Trails: 46,000 acres, 110 miles of two-trail roads
Facilities: Open from 8 A.M. until sundown, all year round. Campground is 5 miles inside park gates.
Usage: Multiuse.
Further info: www.floridaparks.com/stprks/south_east/kissimmeeprairiepreservestatepark.htm; Kissimmee Prairie Preserve State Park, 33104 NW 192nd Avenue, Okeechobee, FL 34972; (863) 462-5360
Notes: No alcohol allowed in Florida state parks.

12

Location: Ocala, Florida
Name of trail: The Greenway
Trails: 110 miles of trails from the Gulf of Mexico through the heart of Florida
Facilities: Various facilities along the length of the trail.
Usage: From multiuse, to bikes only, to horse and hiker only, depending on the stretch of trail.
Further info: www.dep.state.fl.us/gwt/guide/cfgtrails.htm or call Office of Greenways and Trails, (850) 245-2052

13

Location: Micanopy, Florida
Name of trail: Chacala Trail, Savannah State Preserve (Paynes Prairie State Preserve)
Trails: 20 miles of unpaved trails, 2.6 miles paved road. Chacala Trail is most suited to equestrians, hikers, and bikers.
Facilities: Parking, picnic areas, restrooms, campsites.
Usage: Multiuse.
Further info: www.dep.state.fl.us/gwt/guide/regions/north/trails/paynes_prairie.htm; Paynes Prairie Preserve State Park, 100 Savannah Blvd., Micanopy, FL 32667, (352) 466-3397

Notes: Birds include a pair of eagles that nest in the preserve. "It is a rugged park for riding. But we like it as it is natural: wetlands, small lakes, tall grasses, pine, wax myrtle and small oaks, sand trails, and sometimes muck." — Darlene Wohlart

For more Florida trails, visit: www.floridahorse.com, www.florida stateparks.com, www.sfwmd.gov, www.dep.state.fl.us/gwt/guide/

14
Location: Fort Oglethorpe, Georgia
Name of trail: Chickamagua Battleground
Trails: 7 miles of easy trails, monuments and historical markers
Facilities: Restrooms, parking lot.
Usage: Multiuse.
Further info: www.nps.gov/chch/index.htm

15
Location: Haiku, Maui, Hawaii
Name of trail: Adventures on Horseback, private business
Trails: Safe for first-time riders
Facilities: Ride begins at private ranch with full facilities and breakfast served. Lunch is served during the course of the ride.
Usage: Horses only.
Further info: www.mauihorses.com/maui_horseback/index.html; e-mail: info@mauihorses.com; reservations: (808) 242-7445, ranch: (808) 572-6211, fax: (808) 572-4996; P.O. Box 1419, Makawao, Maui, HI 96768
Notes: Horses provided, maximum six riders plus guide. Riding on beaches is not legal. Weight limit 215 pounds, height minimum of 5 feet. Ride lasts approximately 6 hours. No smoking.

16
Location: Harrisburg, Illinois
Name of trail: Shawnee National Forest
Trails: 261,357 acres of trails, from moderately difficult to very challenging
Facilities: Several camps, including Camp Cadiz (618) 287-2201, Johnson Creek (for groups) 5.6 miles connecting to Kinkaid Lake Trail (618) 687-1737 and One Horse Gap (618) 287-2201, with varied accommodations. Visit Web site below for links regarding details.
Usage: Multiuse, though oriented to horseback riders because of the primitive surroundings.
Further info: www.fs.fed.us/r9/forests/shawnee/; Shawnee National Forest, 50 Highway 145 South, Harrisburg, IL 62946, (618) 253-7114 or 1-800-MY-WOODS (699-6637)
Notes: "Trails are just awesome, totally breathtaking, but very challenging." — Brian Helson

17
Location: Kanopolis State Park, southwest of Salina, Kansas
Name of trail: Several different trail names that intersect with each other
Trails: 25–30 miles of trail, varied terrain, some rather difficult areas that are rated rough
Facilities: Horse camp available with pipe corrals, picket line/tie-out area for each campsite, wash areas, heated bathroom with showers, full electric and water hookups for RV/campers, as well as primitive camping areas.
Usage: Multiuse; horses, hikers, mountain bikes.
Further info: KanopolisSp@wp.state.ks.us; (785) 546-2565
Notes: State park fee as well as nightly camping fees and vehicle permit.

18
Location: Pineville, Kentucky
Name of trail: Pine Mountain State Resort
Trails: 1,519 acress, including 8.5 miles of trails
Facilities: Lodge, cottages, primitive campsites, golf, picnicking, playgrounds.
Usage: Multiuse.
Further info: www.state.ky.us/agencies/parks/pinemtn2.htm; Pine Mountain State Resort Park, 1050 State Park Road, Pineville, KY 40977-0610; (606) 337-3066 or (800) 325-1712.

19
Location: Eastern Kentucky
Name of trail: Wranglers Camp at Land between the Lakes, and Willow Creek
Trails: Over 70 miles of horse and wagon trails, and currently undergoing expansion. Billed as the Southeast's premier horse camp; rolling hills and lakefront trails
Facilities: Campground includes stalls, hitching posts, hot showers, and more. Stable available.
Usage: Multiuse (horses restricted from hiking trails, as well as cemeteries, agricultural fields, and camping/day-use trails).
Further info: For Land between the Lakes (Forest Service, National Recreation area), visit www.lbl.org/HORSTrails.html. For stable, call (931) 249-0452
Notes: Willow Creek, just around the corner, is a little more secluded. Good campground, restaurant, not as many trails. Both are easy to access.

20
Location: Michigan, Lake Huron National Forest
Name of trail: Michigan Shore to Shore Trail
Trails: 220 miles, winding between lakes, woodlands, and waterways
Facilities: Campgrounds with privies and wells approximately every 20 miles. Most of the camps overlook lakes or rivers.
Usage: Horses and hikers.
Further info: www.kerchevalave.com/mtra/sh2sh.html

Notes: Maintained by the Michigan Trail Riders Association, sponsors of the Michigan Shore to Shore Long Distance Endurance Ride.

For more information on riding trails in Michigan, contact: The Michigan Horse Council, PO Box 22008, Lansing, MI 48909-2008.

21

Location: Minnesota, southeast of St. Paul
Name of trail: Afton State Park
Trails: 5 miles, accessible in the summer only
Facilities: Picnic area, water, winter "warming house" with woodstove and restrooms.
Usage: Horses, hikers, snowshoes, skiing, camping.
Further info: www.dnr.state.mn.us/state_parks/afton/rec.html; 6959 Peller Avenue, South Hastings, MN 55033; (651) 436-5391
Notes: "Sits on a bluff above the Mississippi River with an elevation high enough to be used as a popular ski resort. Winds along the edge of a birch forest. A canter path brings you out of the woods and on to a grassy plateau." — Joan Lucas

22

Location: Houston, Minnesota
Name of trail: Outback Ranch
Trails: 50 miles of groomed trails in the beautiful bluff country of Minnesota
Facilities: Primitive campsites and electrical hookup sites. Cabins (for a rental fee).
Usage: Camping and horses.
Further info: www.outbackranch.net; (507) 896- 5550

23

Location: Birch Tree, Missouri
Name of trail: Jack Fork River Trails (part of Ozark Mountain Scenic Riverways system)
Trails: Over 80,000 acres of public land, trails are rugged and scenic
Facilities: Various campground facilities along the river.
Usage: Horses, hikers, and canoes along the waterway.
Further info: http://gorp.away.com/gorp/resource/us_river/ mo_ozark.htm; Ozark National Scenic Riverways, Superintendent, Ozark National Scenic Riverways, P.O. Box 490, Van Buren, MO 63965; (573) 323-4236
Notes: Described by *Life* magazine as "one of the world's most scenic float, fishing streams." Very wild and scenic.

24

Location: Eminence, Missouri
Name of trail: Two Rivers
Trails: 5.4-mile loop
Facilities: Parking area.
Usage: Horses and hikers.

Further info: Call (573) 323-4236 ext. 0 for directions
Notes: Eminence is the home of the largest group trail rides in the country, with many trails, facilities, and events.

25

Location: Dale County, Missouri
Name of trail: Hulston Mill, owned by the Missouri Conservation Department and the Corps of Engineers. Maintained by the Dade County Historical Society
Trails: 14 miles with cut-across trails
Facilities: 55 electric hookups, and water. Portable toilets, a large cinder-block building with his and hers restrooms (flush toilets, sinks, showers with hot water, and electricity).
Usage: Horses and hikers.
Further info: www.ridehulston.com; Dade County Historical Society President Jim Dodson, (417) 637-2522
Notes: "About half of the trail is along Stockton Lake, very scenic." — Richard E. Maxwell

26

Location: Kalispell, Montana
Name of trail: Bob Marshall Wilderness Complex (encompasses Flathead, Helena, Lewis & Clark, and Lolo National Forests)
Trails: Hundreds and hundreds of miles of trails in these 1.5 million acres, with many routes doable in a day and others that can take a week to 10 days or more
Facilities: Various at various location, though most are primitive. Most have water, feeding bunks.
Usage: Horses, hikers.
Further info: http://wildlife.visitmt.com/categories/moreinfo; Flathead National Forest, 1935 Third Avenue East, Kalispell, MT 59901; (406) 758-5200
Notes: Recognized as one of the most "completely preserved mountain ecosystems in the world, the kind of wilderness most people can only imagine: rugged peaks, alpine lakes, cascading waterfalls, grassy meadows embellished with shimmering streams, a towering coniferous forest, and big river valleys." Caution: This is grizzly bear country.

27

Location: Libby, Montana
Name of trail: The Kootenai National Forest encompasses millions of acres and more than 1,400 miles of trails
Trails: Includes five major trail systems
Facilities: Remote and primitive.
Usage: Horses and hikers.
Further info: www.libbymt.com/outdoors/trails.htm
Notes: Backcountry or wilderness permits are not required here. The backcountry is remote and expansive. In the event of emergency, help could be hours or days away. Jaw-dropping wilderness beauty, rugged and breathtaking.

28

Location: Cheshire County, New Hampshire
Name of trail: Pisgah State Park
Trails: 13,500 acres of rugged forest, high ridges, and wetlands; 6 trailheads
Facilities: Parking.
Usage: Horses and hikers.
Further info: www.nhstateparks.org/ParksPages/Pisgah/Pisgah.html; Routes 119 and 10, Route 63, Chesterfield, Hinsdale, and Winchester, NH 0347; (603) 239- 8153, or State of New Hampshire, Department of Resources and Economic Development, Division of Parks and Recreation, (603) 271-3556
Notes: Open year-round, free to the public.

29

Location: New Jersey
Name of trail: Island Beach State Park
Trails: 3,002 acres
Facilities: Interpretive center, programs, ocean swimming, bathhouses, wheelchair access to ocean, canoeing, fishing, waterfowl hunting.
Usage: Multiuse.
Further info: Island Beach State Park, Route 35, Seaside Park, NJ 08752. Phone: (732) 793-0506

30

Location: Northern New Jersey (Sussex County)
Name of trail: Wawayanda State Park
Trails: 60 miles of well-marked trails over sand and dirt roads, rocky/hilly terrain
Facilities: Designated trailer parking. Park may relocate trailers on busy weekends. There is adequate parking and maneuvering. Restrooms at swim and boat areas. No overnight camping allowed.
Usage: Multiuse.
Further info: Wawayanda State Park, 885 Warwick Turnpike, Hewitt, NJ 07421. Phone: (973) 853-4462, www.state.nj.us/dep/parksandforests/parks/wawayanda
Notes: Day fee Memorial Day to Labor Day. Maps available at park office. Horseshoes recommended. Water on some trails for horses, bring rider water. Bear country. Many trails, but horses are not permitted on the Appalachian, Cedar Swamp, and Pump House Trails.

31

Location: Madison County, New York
Name of trail: Brookfield Trail System
Trails: 130 miles of moderate to difficult trails, some steep, but generously wide
Facilities: Free camping, covered tie stalls, water, nearby store for meals as well as supplies.
Usage: Horses, hikers (snowmobilers and skiers in winter months), camping.

Further info: www.dec.state.ny.us/website/dlf/publands/stateforests/reg7/brookfield.html; New York State Department of Environmental Conservation, 625 Broadway, Albany, NY 12233; DEC Region 7 (includes Madison County) Regional Director: Kenneth Lynch, 615 Erie Blvd. West, Syracuse, NY 13204-2400; (315) 426-7403; maps available from NYS Department of Environmental Conservation, Region 7, P.O. Box 594, Sherburne, NY 13460-0594, (607) 674-4036

32

Location: New York, Adirondack State Park
Name of trail: Otter Creek State Forest
Trails: 65 miles of interconnecting trails, mostly easy, flat, sandy
Facilities: Free horse camps, no picketing, tie stalls provided.
Usage: Horses, hikers, (snowmobiles and skiers in winter).
Further info: www.dec.state.ny.us/website/dlf/publands/stateforests/reg6/ottercreek.html; New York State Department of Environmental Conservation Lowville office, (315) 376-3521

33

Location: Blowing Rock, North Carolina
Name of trail: Many within a close radius
Trails: Many, varied
Facilities: B&Bs, resorts, campsites
Usage: Multiuse.
Further info: www.ncguide.com/outdoors/horseback.htm

For more trails in North Carolina, visit:
www.nchorsecouncil.com/HorseTrails.htm or
www.cs.unca.edu/nfsnc/recreation/horsetrails.pdf

34

Location: Medora, North Dakota Badlands
Name of trail: Maah Daah Hey Trail
Trails: 96 miles of scenic, rugged, marked trails
Facilities: Places to camp and keep your horse.
Usage: Horses, hikers, mountain bikes.
Further info: www.nps.gov/thro/tr_mdhtrail.pdf; U.S. Forest Service, Medora District: (701) 225-5151; 161 21st Street W., Dickinson, ND, 58601
Notes: Weed-seed-free feed required.

35

Location: Oregon, western slope of the Cascade Mountains
Name of trail: Willamette National Forest
Trails: 1.6 million acres of National Forest, including 1,700 miles of trail; many trails are in wilderness areas
Facilities: Multiple camps and facilities, to primitive backcountry.
Usage: Multiuse.
Further info: USDA Forest Service, 211 East 7th Avenue, P.O. Box 10607, Eugene, OR 97440; (541) 225-6300; e-mail: Mailroom_R6_Willamette@fs.fed.us
Notes: Seven major volcanic peaks, fir forests, rivers. Gorgeous territory. Easy access.

36

Location: Southeastern Pennsylvania, linking Valley Forge to the Appalachian Trail

Name of trail: Horse Shoe Trail

Trails: 140 miles marked by yellow blazes

Facilities: Various along the route, near many towns along the way. Side trails to hostels and attractions marked with white blazes.

Usage: Horses and hikers.

Further info: Horse Shoe Trail Club, www.pagreenways.org/db-orgdetails.asp?ORG_ID=450; 863 Tallvho Drive, Hershey, PA 17033; (717) 533-2612, and www.pagreenways.org/db-Greenway details.asp?GW_ID=8

37

Location: Northwestern Pennsylvania

Name of trail: Allegheny Snowmobile Trails, Allegheny National Forest

Trails: 159 miles of marked equestrian trails and more than 300 miles of snowmobile trails used by horses in the "off season"

Facilities: Various along the route.

Usage: Multiuse.

Further info: www.fs.fed.us/r9/forests/allegheny/; Allegheny National Forest, P.O. Box 847, Warren, PA 16365; (814) 723-5150.

For more trails in Pennsylvania, visit:
www.pa-conservation.org/horse.html

38

Location: Tennessee, Cedars of Lebanon State Park

Name of trail: Cedar Trail

Trails: 12 marked miles, 100+ miles of forestry trails, varied degrees of difficulty

Facilities: Corrals, water, parking, bathhouse available at rental barn. Trail use; parking is free. Stall fee, plus rental horses available.

Usage: Horses and hikers.

Further info: ww.state.tn.us/environment/parks/parks/Cedars/index.php?activity=Hiking+Trails; Cedars of Lebanon State Park; 328 Cedar Forest Road, Lebanon, TN 37090; office: 615-443-2769, toll-free, cabin reservations: 800-713-5180, horse rentals (615) 444-5465

Notes: Open fires prohibited, no motor vehicles allowed on trails.

39

Location: Natchez Trace State Park, Wildersville, Tennessee

Name of trail: Natchez Trace

Trails: 200 miles of historic trails, 444 miles of parkway, and 63 miles of developed trails

Facilities: Cabins, camping, bathhouses, garbage drop-off, electrical and water hookups, rental horses available May–October

Usage: Multiuse.

Further info: www.nps.gov/natt/; Natchez Trace State Park, 24845 Natchez Trace Road, Wildersville, TN 38388; (901) 968-3742

40

Location: Wartburg, Tennessee

Name of trail: Lone Mountain and Frozen Head Park

Trails: 14 to 15 miles each of moderate to very advanced trails, stream crossing, beautiful views, streams

Facilities: Primitive at Lone Mountain; no overnight horse camping. Campsites, bathhouse, picnic area. Playgrounds, horseshoes, sports fields, even a stage that can be reserved at Frozen Head.

Usage: Multiuse.

Further info: www.state.tn.us/agriculture/forestry/stateforests/12.html; 302 Clayton Howard Road, Wartburg, TN 37887; (423) 346-6655 and www.state.tn.us/environment/parks/parks/Frozen-Head/; Frozen Head State Park, 964 Flat Fork Road., Wartburg, TN 37887; (423) 346-3318

41

Location: Vermont

Name of trail: Merck Forest and Farmland Center

Trails: Miles and miles of trails in excellent condition, fit for novice to experienced riders

Facilities: Parking is limited. Cabins with wood-burning stoves and bunks, shelters, tent sites, outhouses, water.

Usage: Horses and hikers only, no wheeled vehicles.

Further info: www.merckforest.com; P.O. Box 86, Route 315 Rupert Mountain Road, Rupert VT 05768; (802) 394-7836; e-mail: merck@vermontel.net

Notes: No fee, but donations are welcome. This is a unique environmental education center, with lots of interesting things to do after the ride, and for non-riding members of your party.

42

Location: Mount Rogers, Virginia

Name of trail: Many

Trails: 120,000 acres of National Forest land within the George Washington and Jefferson National Forests, including Mount Rogers, Virginia's highest point (5,729 feet), 400 miles of maintained trails, including 60 miles of the Appalachian Trail, 18 miles of the Virginia Creeper Trail, and 67 miles of the Virginia Highlands Horse Trail.

Facilities: Nine developed campgrounds; three are set up for horseback riders.

Usage: Multiuse.

Further info: www.damascus.org/mra.html; Route 1, Box 303, Marion, VA 24354; (276) 783-5196 or 800-628-7202; USFS@NETVA.com

43

Location: Western Washington

Name of trail: Capitol Forest

Trails: 170 miles of trails, with 80 miles reserved for nonmotorized users. Mostly easy trails, some views, beautiful scenery within the woods, some stream/bridge crossings

Facilities: Several campgrounds, with 90 campsites, some with water, corrals, restroom, garbage pickup, manure bunker. Campsites free to use, first-come, first-served, limit of 7 days per year per user.

Usage: Horses, hikers, and mountain bikers (motorized-use trails are separate from nonmotorized trails at north end of forest).

Further info: www.dnr.wa.gov/htdocs/adm/comm/nr04_027.htm; DNRs Pacific Cascade Region (360) 577-2025

44

Location: Washington coast
Name of trail: Long Beach
Trails: 21 miles of sandy beach
Facilities: No camping allowed, but restrooms, restaurants, and various facilities within ½ mile of the beach all along its length. Lodging and horse boarding available nearby. Horse rentals.
Usage: Public access, October through April, open as a state highway.
Further info: www.funbeach.com; (360) 642-3676 for horse rental
Notes: Stay off the clam beds during low tide (near the surf).

45

Location: Ontario, Wisconsin
Name of trail: End of the Trail campground between Wildcat Mountain and the Kickapoo Reserve
Trails: 15 miles of color-coded trails that connect in loops, 20+ miles of trails on Wildcat Mountain, 40 miles of trails in Kickapoo Valley Reserve
Facilities: Horse campgrounds; 24 sites, 20 of which can be reserved through the Wisconsin Department of Natural Resources (WDNR). Campground has picnic tables, fire rings, drinking water, vault toilets, a corral, hitching posts, parking pads, loading ramps, and a large parking lot. Electricity at each site, wonderful split firewood, hot showers; guided tour, if you want, of the reserve.
Usage: Horses and hikers.
Further info: http://dnr.wi.gov/org/land/parks/specific/wildcat/trails/; (608) 337-4775; also www.endofthetrailcampground.com; (608) 337-4738
Notes: "For those who can't ride for 8 hours, they also will help shuttle trailers. You can ride to the Rockton Bar, where you can tether your horse, and go in and enjoy either a wonderful chicken dinner on Sundays or a great burger. Then you can trailer back to camp. This trip takes around four hours." — Melanie Ganta

46

Location: Wyoming, Big Horn Mountains
Name of trail: Wyoming High Country Camp
Trails: 350 square miles
Facilities: Cabins, no electric, horse pens provided, rental horses available.
Usage: Horses and hikers.
Further info: www.gordonsguide.com/cattle-drives/wyoming highcountry/index.cfm; Wyoming High Country, P.O. Box 306, Lovell, WY 82431; toll-free: 877-548-2301

MULTISTATE/PROVINCE TRAILS

47

Location: Western Canada to Mexico
Name of trail: Pacific Crest Trail
Trails: Nearly 2,500 miles through three states (California, Oregon and Washington), 3 national monuments, 7 national parks, 24 national forests, and 33 federally mandated wildernesses
Facilities: Various along the route.
Usage: Mulituse, including camels.
Further info: www.pcta.org/; Pacific Crest Trail Association, 5325 Elkhorn Blvd., PMB # 256, Sacramento, CA 95842-2526; (916) 349-2109
Notes: "From desert to glacier-flanked mountain, meadow to forest, the Pacific Crest Trail (PCT) symbolizes everything there is to love — and protect — in the western United States." — from pcta.org

48

Location: Big South Fork, Tennessee and Kentucky
Name of trail: Big South Fork Park
Trails: Hundreds of miles of marked trails, varying in difficulty over 125,000 acres
Facilities: Lodging, campgrounds, stables.
Usage: Multiuse.
Further info: www.bigsouthforkinfo.com/

49

Location: Cross country from Delaware to California
Name of trail: American Discovery Trail
Trails: 6,800 miles of trails across 15 states
Facilities: Varies in different locations.
Usage: Horses, hikers, and mountain bikers.
Further info: www.discoverytrail.org/
Notes: Not all trails affiliated with this system allow horses.

50

Location: Montana to Mexico
Name of trail: Continental Divide Trail
Trails: The Continental Divide Trail follows the rigorous peaks of the Rocky Mountains from Canada to Mexico. It passes through meadows and deserts, and some to the most primitive backcountry in the United States, including the high point of 14,230 feet in Colorado. It's 3,100 miles of wild trail cross through 5 states.
Facilities: Various along the route.
Usage: Horses and hikers.
Further info: www.cdtrail.org/map.html; P.O. Box 628, Pine, CO 80470 (303) 838-3760 or (888) 909-CDTA
Notes: Established in 1978, most of the route is not marked on the ground. It is still a work in progress. Only hikers and horses allowed in wilderness areas.

Note: Some parks and National Forests require users to purchase use permits or trail passes in advance.

50+ TOP OUTFITTERS AND ORGANIZED TRAIL RIDES

ALABAMA

1

Seven Springs Lodge

Where: Northwest Alabama

When: Throughout the season

Contact: Seven Springs Lodge, 1292 Mt. Mills Road, Tuscumbia, AL 35674

Phone: (877) 370-7218 or (256) 370-7218

Web site: http://homepages.about.com/sevenspring

E-mail: springlodg@aol.com

2

Cherokee Trailride

Where: Natchez Trace Parkway, NW Alabama

When: Call for details

Contact: 13010 Mt. Hester Road, Cherokee, Al 35616; (256) 359-4423 or (256) 810-2087

3

McCurdy Plantation Horse Fall Trail Ride

Where: Near Selma, Alabama

When: First Saturday in October

Contact: McCurdy Plantation Horse Association, (903) 677-4858

Web site: www.mccurdyhorses.com

Notes: Overnight accommodations available; open to all horse breeds

ARKANSAS

4

Ozark Mountain Trail Ride

Where: Timbo, Arkansas

When: 5-day rides throughout the season

Contact: Ozark Mountain Trail Ride, Box 336, Mtn. View, AR 72560; (870) 746-4300

5

Circle K Ozark Scenic Trail Ride

Where: Clinton, Arkansas

When: 5-day rides monthly, April through October

Contact: Circle K Ozark Scenic Trail Ride, (501) 745-7513

ARIZONA

6

Arizona Horseback Experience

Where: Tucson, Arizona

When: Throughout the season

Contact: 7759 W. Amber Sky Lane, Tucson, AZ 85735; (520) 883-6807

Web site: http://horsebackexperience.com

Notes: Supplies horses

CALIFORNIA

7

Rock Creek Pack Station

Where: Bishop, California

When: Throughout the season

Contact: P.O. Box 248, Bishop, CA 93515; (760) 872-8331

Web site: www.rockcreekpackstation.com/

Notes: Horses provided. "We furnish stock, packers, cooks, tasty meals, tents, and camping equipment. Length varies from 4 to 12 days."

8

Ricochet Ridge Ranch

Where: Fort Bragg, California; beach and redwood forest

When: Throughout the season

Contact: Ricochet Ridge Ranch, 24201 N. Highway 1 Fort Bragg, California 95437; phone: 707-964-7669; fax: 707-964-9669

Web site: www.horse-vacation.com; e-mail: larishea@horse-vacation

Note: *Outside* magazine included this company in their list of top "25 Trips of a Lifetime."

CANADA

9

Saddle Peak Trail Rides and Pack Trips

Where: Alberta, Canada, near Banff National Park in the Canadian Rockies

When: Throughout the season

Contact: P.O. Box 1463, Cochrane AB T4C 1B4; (403) 932-3299

10

Horsin Around Trail Rides

Where: Fish Creek Provincial Park, Calgary, Alberta, Canada

When: From May through October 31

Contact: 13946 Woodpath Road, Fish Creek Provincial Park, Calgary AB; (403) 238-6665

Notes: Hay- and sleigh rides in winter

11

Trail Riders of the Canadian Rockies

Where: Banff National Park or the eastern slope of the Canadian Rockies, Calgary, Alberta

When: Eight 6-day rides, plus a fall ride throughout the season

Contact: Box 6742, Station D, Calgary AB T2P 2E6; (403) 684-4086

FLORIDA

12

Ho's Ponderosa Rides
Where: Bushnell, Florida
When: Call for details
Contact: Ho's Ponderosa, 7804 SW 90th Avenue, Bushnell, FL 33513
(800) 794-2768; (352) 793-9044
Web site: www.hponderosa.com/Default.htm
Notes: Full-moon rides; entertainment

13

Doering Ranch Rides
Where: Alachua, near Gainesville, Florida
When: By reservation
Contact: Doering Ranch (Tennessee Walkers and Spotted Saddle Horses), (386) 454-7865; 10520 NW 234th Street, Alachua, FL 32615-7850
E-mail: doeringranch@hotmail.com
Notes: Board your horse while you see the sights, then ride nearby trails

GEORGIA

14

Blanche Manor Rides
Where: Ellijay, Georgia
When: Throughout the season
Contact: Blanche Manor, (706) 455-7433 or (423) 496-1060
Web site: www.blanchemanor.com
Notes: Hayrides, dinner, bonfires; bring your own horse or use theirs

INDIANA

15

Midwest Trail Ride
Where: Hoosier National Forest, Indiana
When: Spring, summer, and fall
Contact: RR 2 Box 80A, Norman, IN 47264; (812) 834-6686
Web site: www.midwesttrailride.com/
Notes: Show facilities, stalls, restrooms, campsites, nightly entertainment, meals

KANSAS

16

Ride Kansas
Where: Augusta, Kansas
When: Throughout the season
Contact: Kelly Mosley, (316) 733-5769 or kmosley@feist.com
Notes: Western entertainment and country trail–style cooking always available

17

Country Boys Carriage and Prairie Adventures
Where: Flint Hills, Kansas
When: Weekend adventures and day rides throughout the season
Contact: Country Boys Carriage and Prairie Adventures, 1504 South Rock Road, Newton KS 67114; (316) 283-2636
Web site: www.KsCoveredwagon.com
E-mail: cbcpa@kscoveredwagon.com
Notes: Wide-open vistas all around, all-you-can-eat lunch

18

Gyp Hills Trail Ride
Where: Gant-Larson Ranch, Medicine Lodge, Kansas
When: Two rides held in May each year and private rides throughout the year
Contact: Gant-Larson Ranch, Bob or Charlene Larson (620) 886-5390
Notes: Primitive camping (horse water available and portable toilets); an extreme ride through beautiful gypsum hills on private land

MAINE

19

Ellis River Riders
Where: Western Maine
When: All seasons
Contact: P.O. Box 332, Andover, ME 04216; (207) 674-3593
Web site: www.ellisriverriders.com
E-mail: mbean@exploremaine.com
Notes: Also hunter paces; barn, food, water, and lovely trails

MICHIGAN

20

Brighton Trail Ride
Where: Brighton, Michigan
When: Monthly, April through October
Contact: Brighton Trail Riders Association
Web site: www.geocities.com/brightontrailriders

MISSOURI

21

Cross Country Trail Ride
Where: Eminence, Missouri
When: Throughout the season
Contact: James D. Smith, P.O. Box 15, Eminence, MO 65466; (573) 226-3492
Web site: www.crosscountrytrailride.com/
Notes: Swimming, showers, indoor arena, horse events, rodeo, restaurant, tack store, nightly events. "Visit us, and you will enjoy three meals a day, horse shows, dancing, swimming, horse sales, tack sales, Nashville entertainers, and much, much more!"

22
Golden Hills Trail Ride & Resort
Where: Raymondville, Missouri
When: April, May, June, July, August, September, October, and Labor Day Weekend
Contact: Golden Hills Trail Ride & Resort, 19546 Golden Drive, P.O. Box 98, Raymondville, MO 65555; (417) 457-6222
Web site: www.goldenhills.com/
Notes: Ozark Mountain riding

23
Ozark Trailrides Inc.
Where: Hartville, Missouri
When: Scheduled rides throughout the season
Contact: Ozark Trailrides Inc., P.O. Box 55, Plato, MO 65552; (888) 474-0450
Web site: http://ozarktrailrides.net/
Notes: Also truck & tractor pulls, bull rides, & bluegrass festivals

24
Fourche Creek Trail Rides
Where: Doniphan, Mark Twain National Forest, Missouri
When: Monthly trail rides
Contact: Fourche Creek Trail Rides, P.O. Box 97, Neelyville, MO 63954; (800) 457-3025
Web site: www.fourchecreek.com/
Notes: Also RV hookups, stalls, showers, fishing

25
Panther Creek Trail Rides
Where: Tuscumbia, Missouri
When: Throughout the season
Contact: Panther Creek Trail Rides, 152 Opal Drive, Ulman, MO 65083; (573) 369-2655, (573) 369-2441, (573) 793-2372 (during rides)
Web site: www.panthercreektrailrides.com/
Note: 100 miles of trail over 4000 acres of trail-riding land, 30 miles of trails for wagons, 80 campsites with meals, shower house, covered stalls, and entertainment

26
Meramec Trail Riding Vacations LLC
Where: Bourbon, Missouri
When: Throughout the season, including a 7-day "inn-to-inn" trip
Contact: Meramec Trail Riding Vacations LLC; Carol Springer, 208 Thickety Ford Road, Bourbon, MO 65441; (573) 732-4765
Web site: www.meramecfarm.com/
Notes: Bring your own or ride one of the tour's Missouri Fox Trotters or other gaited horse

NEVADA

27
Rough Riders Trail Ride
Where: Las Vegas, Nevada
When: Second Sunday of each month
Contact: Rough Riders Trail Ride, mule@anv.net

NORTH CAROLINA

28
Lake Mattamuskeet Trail Ride
Where: Hyde County, North Carolina
When: Second week in April
Contact: Mark (Hyde), (252) 926-9961; Rick (Rocky Mount), (252) 883-7114; Steve (Duplin), (910) 298-5125

29
J.O.Y. Riders Saddle Club Trail Ride
Where: Dudley, North Carolina
When: Second week in April
Contact: Larry King, (919) 273-7474; Mr. Williams, (919) 734-7264

30
Little River Trails Spring Ride and Dinner
Where: Little River Trails, North Carolina
When: Late April
Contact: Lori Lanier, (910) 893-4351

31
Trail Ride
Where: Greensboro, North Carolina
When: First week in May
Contact: Ed Hawkins, (336) 449-4471

32
Triangle Trail Riders Trail Ride
Where: Raleigh, North Carolina
When: Early June
Contact: Cornell, (919) 231-3897

NORTH DAKOTA

33
North Dakota Badlands Trail Riders Annual Trail
Where: Little Missouri State Park, 22 miles north of Killdeer, North Dakota
When: Labor Day weekend
Contact: North Dakota Badlands Trail Riders Annual Trail, Linda Morrow Schauer, 4425 Pleasant Valley Road, Mandan, ND 58554
Web site: www.angelfire.com/nd2/badlandsriders/index.html

OHIO

34

Smoke Rise Horseman's Resort and Cattle Drives
Where: Ohio
When: 5-day rides in April through August, September and October
Contact: P.O. Box 253, Murray City, OH 43144-10253; (800) 292-1732 or (740) 76-RANCH
Web site: www.hockinghills.com/smokerise/
Notes: Ride hosts also offer camping, cabins, RV hookups, roping, team penning, sorting, dances and meals.

OKLAHOMA

35

Indian Mounds Trail Ride
Where: Clayton, Oklahoma
When: Seven organized rides per year
Contact: Jess Johnson, Indian Mounds Horse Camp, HC60 Box 62, Clayton, OK 74536-9700
Web site: www.indianmoundshorsecamp.com/
Notes: "Best pie in Oklahoma available at the local café in Clayton"

OREGON

36

Steve Evans Back Country Trips
Where: Near Medford, Oregon, covering over 3 million acres of Forest Service land
When: Throughout the season
Contact: Steve Evans, 4261 Avenue H, White City, OR 97503; (541) 826-7165

PENNSYLVANIA

37

Cook Forest Scenic Ride
Where: Summerville, Pennsylvania
When: Weeklong rides and 3-day rides May through October
Contact: Dude Ranch & Campground, Summerville: R.R. #2 Box 113, Summerville, PA 15864; (814) 856-2081 or (814) 226-5985
Notes: Rental horses available. Square dancing, live bands, tack auction, horse games, swimming pool, Jacuzzi, playground

38

Annual Horseshoe Trail Ride
Where: Cold Springs to Valley Forge, Pennsylvania
When: Mid- to late June; 6-day ride covering 160 miles
Contact: Circle T Trail Riders, Elaine Batdorf, (717) 949-2213; ebatdorf@localnet.com
Notes: Meals provided or bring your own; horses/mules recommended to be in good shape and shod with borium and possibly pads

SOUTH CAROLINA

39

New Ellenton Riding Club Trail Ride
Where: New Ellenton, South Carolina
When: Spring and fall
Contact: (803) 642-8410
Notes: DJ on Friday night and band on Saturday

SOUTH DAKOTA

40

Plenty Star Ranch Rides
Where: Pringle, South Dakota
When: Throughout the season
Contact: Plenty Star Ranch, John and Isa Kirk, P.O. Box 106, Pringle, SD 57773; phone/fax: (605) 673-3012
Web site: www.plentystarranch.com/
Notes: Rental horses available

TENNESSEE

41

Bucksnort Trail Ride
Where: 2887 Poplar Grove Road, McEwen, Tennessee
When: 5-day rides, April, June, October, and weekend rides April through October
Contact: Linda and Tony Baker, 9080 Old Charlotte Road, Pegram, TN 37143; (615) 662-7512; for reservations: Bruce Frederick, 1015 Garners Creek Road, Dickson, TN 37055; (615) 740-9199
Note: Electric hookups, bathhouse, covered stalls, nightly entertainment

42

Loretta Lynn's Trail Ride
Where: Hurricane Mills, Tennessee
When: 5-day rides, June and September
Contact: Loretta Lynn, 44 Hurricane Mills Road, Hurricane Mills, TN 37078; (931) 296-7700
Web site: www.lorettalynn.com/ranch/trail_ride.html
Notes: Yup, *the* Loretta Lynn

43
Buffalo River Trail Ride
Where: Waynesboro, Tennessee
When: 5-day ride and camp March, June, August, and October
Contact: (931) 722-9170

TEXAS

44
Indian Hills Outfitters
Where: Burkeville, Texas
When: Guided rides throughout the season
Contact: Indian Hills Outfitters, (409) 379-8479
Notes: Current Coggins required

45
Dead Man's Corner Trail Rides
Where: Aspermont, Texas
When: All-day ride on or around March 19 and November 20
Contact: Patricia Penrod, (806) 254-2326
Web site: www.geocities.com/deadmanscorner

UTAH

46
Hondoo Rivers and Trails
Where: Colorado River Plateau of Utah
When: Throughout the season, custom rides or regular schedule
Contact: P.O. Box 98, Torrey, Utah 84775; phone: (800) 332-2696
E-mail: hondoo@color-country.net
Notes: Provides horses. Sponsors family and all-women rides in addition to traditional

VIRGINIA

47
Carolinas and Virginia Wagon Train Association
Where: North Carolina, Virginia
When: Weekends, spring through late fall
Contact: 3031 George York Road, Randleman, NC 27317; (336) 498-3411
Notes: Entertainment and food

48
Graves Mountain Fall Trail Ride
Where: Blue Ridge Mountains, Virginia
When: Fall, late October
Contact: Trail Ride, c/o Overnight Wilderness Outfitters, General Delivery, Syria, VA 22743; (540) 786-7403
Notes: All meals provided

WASHINGTON

49
Methow Valley Backcountry Horsemen's Annual Spring Trail Ride
Where: Okanogan Territory of Washington state
When: Last weekend in April
Contact: Methow Valley Backcountry Horsemen of Washington: (509) 4802 or nancyp@methow.com or Ann Port (509) 997-5491

WEST VIRGINIA

50
G.R.E.A.T. Rides
Where: Greenbrier River Trail (Rails-to-Trails), West Virginia
When: 2-day to 6-day rides throughout the season
Contact: G.R.E.A.T. Rides, P.O. Box 60, Harper, WV 25851; (800) 934-7674
Web site: www.greattrailrides.com/

WISCONSIN

51
Wilderness Pursuit
Where: Clark County Forest, Wisconsin
When: 6-day rides throughout the season
Contact: Wilderness Pursuit!, N. 5773 Resewood Avenue, Neillsville, WI 54456; (715) 743-4484
Web site: www.wildernesspursuit.com
E-mail: wpwpw@tds.net

WYOMING

52
Outlaw Trail Ride
Where: Thermopolis, Wyoming
When: Mid-August
Contact: Outlaw Trail Ride, P.O. Box 1046, Thermopolis, WY 82443; Vince Hayes, trail boss, (888) 362-RIDE toll-free in the U.S., or (307) 864-2287
Web site: www.rideoutlawtrail.com/
E-mail: outlaw@trib.com
Notes: First night's camp is the famous Hole in the Wall camp of Butch Cassidy and the Sundance Kid

RESOURCES

The following write-ups are taken directly from the Web sites or promotional material of the associations or services themselves.

HORSEMEN'S ASSOCIATION: GENERAL

American Horse Council (AHC)
The national trade association representing the horse industry in Washington, D.C.

The AHC works to represent your equine interests and investments. Organized in 1969, the AHC promotes the industry by communicating with Congress, federal agencies, the media, and the industry itself on behalf of all horse-related interests.

The AHC mission is to promote and protect the equine industry by representing its interests in Congress and in federal regulatory agencies on national issues of importance; to unify the equine industry by informing industry members of regulations and pending legislation, and by serving as a forum for all member organizations and individuals; and to advise and inform government and the industry itself of the equine industry's important role in the U.S. economy.

American Horse Council
1616 H Street NW, 7th Floor, Washington, DC 20006
Phone: 202-296-4031
E-mail: ahc@horsecouncil.org
www.horsecouncil.org/

HORSEMEN'S ASSOCIATIONS: RIDING

American Trail Horse Association (ATHA)
An association dedicated to promoting and improving the once overlooked/unrecognized equine breed of the great American Trail Horse.

Through education, and registration, we prove that one of the greatest disciplines in the equine world today is Trail Riding. By giving identification to equines of known and unknown parentage, we are striving to protect them from theft as well as helping reunite owners with their escaped, lost, or stolen equines. By joining forces with today's trail rider programs around the country, we provide presence of the Trail breed/discipline, and help protect our trails. Our slogan: "We know no boundaries."

ATHA, Inc.
P.O. Box 293, Cortland, IL 60112
Phone: 877-266-1678
E-mail: info@trailhorse.com
www.americantrailhorse.com/start.htm

Back Country Horsemen of America (BCH)
BCH has a threefold purpose: to volunteer service in the backcountry, to educate horsemen on minimum- impact horse handling, and to get involved in land- use planning.

This organization of recreational stock users is committed to the perpetuation of the commonsense use and enjoyment of horses in America's backcountry and wilderness. Back Country Horsemen has more than 8,500 members divided among 75 chapters in 11 Western states. Educational programs include: Tread Lightly, Gentle Use, Back Country Etiquette, and Minimum Impact Horse Camping. Service is a key component of Back Country Horsemen philosophy with nearly 1 million of documented volunteer work on public lands in 1993. The organization is dedicated to preserving the historical use of recreational stock in the backcountry commensurate with our heritage.

Contact the BCH to find the chapter in your state.
Back Country Horseman of America
P.O. Box 1367, Graham WA 98338-1367
Phone: 888-893-5161
www.backcountryhorse.com/

Long Riders' Guild
The world's first international association of Equestrian Explorers and the largest repository of equestrian travel knowledge in human history.

The Long Riders' Guild Web site — combination museum, bookstore, tack room, and Guild Hall — contains the world's largest collection of equestrian travel information. A visit inside will introduce you to the amazing men and women who have ridden horses in search of mounted adventure in every conceivable country and climate, ranging from Africa to Antarctica. For the first time ever, a host of these Long Riders have shared their "Stories from the Road" to inspire and amuse you. You may ride alongside Equestrian Expeditions currently out on the road or watch those preparing to set off into the unknown. If you are planning an expedition, then study our Equipment pages for independent firsthand information gathered from Long Riders in 30 countries. Or visit the publishing arm of The Guild, HorseTravelBooks.com, where you can enjoy the largest selection of equestrian travel titles in the world.

Our goal is to demonstrate that you and your horse can undertake a life-changing equestrian journey of your own. That is why this massive Web site is a commercial-free, open source of information designed for global distribution. It is a gift to the world from the equestrian Argonauts who are members of The Long Riders' Guild.

E-mail: longriders@thelongridersguild.com
www.thelongridersguild.com/LRG.htm

North American Riding for the Handicapped Association, Inc. (NARHA)

Promoting equine-facilitated therapy and activity programs in the United States and Canada.

Currently, more than 650 NARHA program centers serve some 30,000 individuals with disabilities. Each year, dozens of new centers initiate new programs and thousands of individuals profit from these beneficial activities.

Since 1969, NARHA has ensured that therapeutic riding is both safe for, and accessible to, those in need. In that time the field of therapeutic riding has expanded along with the numbers of individuals profiting from involvement with horses. Today NARHA represents a growing number of equine-assisted therapies and activities, including recreational riding for individuals with disabilities, hippotherapy, equine-assisted psychotherapy, driving, vaulting, competition, and other therapeutic and educational interactions with horses.

North American Riding for the Handicapped Association, Inc.
P.O. Box 33150 Denver, CO 80233
Phone: 800-369-RIDE (7433); fax (303) 252-4610
E-mail: NARHA@NARHA.ORG
www.narha.org

HORSEMEN'S ASSOCIATIONS: SPORT

COMPETITIVE MOUNTED ORIENTEERING

National Association of Competitive Mounted Orienteering (NACMO)

The association devoted to the "Thinking Horse Sport."

Competitive Mounted Orienteering (CMO) is one of the most challenging and exciting equestrian sports — for the competitive as well as family horse rider! The NACMO sponsors rides, tallies points for awards, connects riders with each other, and provides a resource for riders for information.

NACMO
Executive Director, Walt Olsen
503 171st Avenue SE, Tenino, WA 98589-9711
Phone: 800-354-7264; fax: 360-264-4890
E-mail: arabnacmo@thurston.com
www.nacmo.org/index.tpl

COMPETITIVE TRAIL RIDING

North American Trail Ride Conference (NATRC)

The association that sanctions competitive trail-riding events. The Web site will keep you abreast of rules, rides, other news, and other related associations and links.

NATRC
P.O. Box 224, Sedalia, CO 80135
Phone: 303-688-1677; fax: 303-688-3022
www.natrc.org/

ENDURANCE RIDING

American Endurance Ride Conference (AERC)

The national governing body for long-distance riding.

The American Endurance Ride Conference (AERC) was founded in 1972 and over the years has developed a set of rules and guidelines designed to provide a standardized format and strict veterinary controls. At the same time, it has sought to avoid the rigidity and complexity so characteristic of many other equine disciplines.

From its beginnings in the American West, the AERC has spread roots both nationally and internationally. The AERC sanctions more than 700 rides each year throughout North America. In 1978 the Fédération Equestre Internationale (FEI) recognized endurance riding as an international sport, and since that date the U.S. and Canada have regularly swept the team and individual medals. In 1993 Endurance became the fifth discipline under the U.S. Equestrian Team (U.S.E.T.).

In addition to promoting the sport of endurance riding, the AERC encourages the use, protection, and development of equestrian trails, especially those with historic significance. Many special events of 4 to 6 consecutive days take place over historic trails, such as the Pony Express Trail, the Outlaw Trail, the Chief Joseph Trail, and the Lewis and Clark Trail. The founding ride of endurance riding, the Western States Trail Ride, or Tevis, covers 100 miles of the famous Western States and Immigrant Trails over the Sierra Nevadas. These rides promote awareness of the importance of trail preservation for future generations and foster an appreciation of our American heritage.

American Endurance Ride Conference
701 High Street, Auburn, CA 95603
Phone: (916) 823-2260
www.aerc.org/

See also these related Websites:

Endurance Long Distance Riding International Conference

Web page giving general information on endurance riding as well as results and standings of endurance rides at the international level.

www.eldric.org/

Endurance Riding

www.endurance.net/

Riding for Sport Endurance

Information on endurance riding, tack and grooming, the endurance horse, main competitions, and a list of related links.

www.riding-for-sport-endurance.com/

Research literature related to Endurance Riding.
www.wsu.edu/~chisman/endbibf.htm

FIELD TRIALING

American Kennel Club
The registry for purebred dogs, including most, if not all, bird dogs used in field trials.
AKC
5580 Centerview Drive, Raleigh, NC 27606-3390
www.akc.org/dic/events/fieldtrials/gundog04.cfm

American Field Publishing Company
Publisher of American Field: The Sportsman's Journal
AMERICAN FIELD *has followed the field trial sport in America since 1874, including horseback stakes.*
542 S. Dearborn Street / Suite 1350, Chicago, IL 60605
Phone: (312) 663-9797; fax: (312) 663-5557
E-mail: amfieldpub@att.net
www.americanfield.com

American Field Trial Dog Stud Book
542 S. Dearborn Street, Suite 1350,
Chicago, IL 60605
www.americanfield.com

Amateur Field Trialing Club of America (AFTCA)
Bylaws, field trial judging, club applications, list of clubs, schedules, results, championships, sponsors, and more.
E-mail: aftca@aol.com
www.aftca.org/

Field Trial News
Providing up-to-date information on field trials, hunt tests, and shows, sponsored by pointing dog clubs.
www.fieldtrialnews.com/

English Springer Spaniel Field Trial Association
Includes a map of field trialing clubs throughout the United States.
www.essfta.org/ESS_Field_Trial_Clubs.htm

RIDE AND TIE

Ride and Tie Association
Disseminates information about the sport of ride and tie to new and potential participants.
The Ride and Tie Association was created in 1988 to provide stewardship for the sport. It sponsors research, analysis, and education to ensure improvements in the level of competition, horsemanship, and athletic performance, and establishes rules and standards for ride-and-tie competitions for the protection of the human and equine contestants.
The Ride and Tie Association
987 Crows Nest Lane, El Cajon, CA 92019
Phone: 619-445-4485; 650-949-2321
www.rideandtie.org/

TRAIL GUIDES AND INFORMATION

Access to Federal Land
Specific trail information in your region, complete with a weather report and maps.
Western settlers explored much of America on horseback. Today, many of our parks, forests, and wilderness areas can still be explored on the back of a horse for a unique natural adventure. This Web site shows federal recreation areas that offer trail riding as well as off-trail riding.
www.recreation.gov/horses.cfm?myActivity=horsebackriding

American Trails
Working to enhance and protect America's network of interconnected trails.
We support local, regional, and long-distance trails and greenways, whether in backcountry or in rural or urban areas. Our goal is to support America's trails by finding common ground and promoting cooperation among all trail interests.
American Trails
P.O. Box 491797, Redding, CA 96049-1797
Telephone: (530) 547-2060; fax: (530) 547-2035
E-mail: trailhead@americantrails.org
www.americantrails.org/

Equestrian Land Conservation Resource
Dedicated to promoting access to and conservation of land for equestrian use.
Loss of open land has been identified as the greatest threat to the future of all equestrian sport, recreation, and industry. By educating horse people and encouraging partnerships with conservationists at the local level, the Equestrian Land Conservation Resource is mobilizing thousands of equestrians to work for land access and protection in their communities. We recognize that without such concerted efforts, the equestrian world as we know it is at great risk.
ELCR
126B North Main Street, P.O. Box 423, Elizabeth, IL 61028
Phone: (815) 858-3501; fax: (815) 858-358
www.elcr.org

Horse and Mule Trails

A collection of trails and places to camp and ride submitted by trail riders and organized by state.

This page lists trails, trailheads, horse campgrounds, overnight hosts, places to stay, 5-day rides, and BYOH (bring-your-own-horse) trail rides that are open to the public.
Charles Olsen
2655 Bay Place, Nashua, IA 50658
www.horseandmuletrails.com

Horse Trails and Campgrounds Directory

A camping and trail-riding resource for equestrian trail riders (horse, mule, donkey).

Provides information about bridle paths, trailheads, horse campgrounds, overnight stay facilities, and B& Bs, including ratings of horse trails and campgrounds and trail-specific weather. We hope you will find some great trail riding and horse camping places that have been described by others, and we invite you to share your experiences by rating trails and adding trails and campgrounds to this trail riders' database.
www.horsetraildirectory.com/

National Reservation Reservation System (NRRS)

A one-stop reservation service for public outdoor recreation facilities and activities operated by the USDA, Forest Service, Army Corps of Engineers, National Park Service, Bureau of Land Management, and Bureau of Reclamation.

With more than 45,000 reservable facilities at more than 1,700 locations, the NRRS is the largest outdoor recreation reservation service in the country. Whether you are heading north to Alaska's Tongass National Forest, south to Florida's Lake Okeechobee, east to North Carolina's Blue Ridge Parkway, or west to California's Los Padres National Forest, you can reserve your place under the stars with the NRRS.

The Web site offers convenient, round-the-clock access to the Online Reservation System. You will be able to search by state or facility name and also check availability among the many functions available.
Phone: 877-444-6777; TDD: 877-833-6777; international: 518-885-3639
www.reserveusa.com

National Geographic Maps

Offering topographic maps of areas ranging from around the corner to around the world.
National Geographic Maps
P.O. Box 4357
Evergreen, CO 80437-4357
http://maps.nationalgeographic.com/trails/

National Park Service (NPS)

Information on U.S. national parks.

Through the NPS Web site you can find out about trails and campsites in our national parks, as well as see how the NPS preserves America's history in parks and communities.
National Park Service
1849 C Street NW, Washington, DC 20240
Phone: 202-208-6843
www.nps.gov

Online Guide to Public Lands

Includes a clickable map to all trails in the United States, a gift center, gear store, bookstore, maps, and a newsletter.
Interactive Outdoors, Inc.
312 AABC Suite D, Aspen, CO 81611
Phone: 800-741-1717; 970-920-7097; fax: 970-920-9680
www.wildernet.com

Two Horse Enterprises

Providing trail and trail-riding information, books, maps, and other items.

Order our trails reference guide containing over 1,000 addresses of where to write for horse trails and horse camping information across the nation. Write for a free catalog.
Two Horse Enterprises
P.O. Box 15517, Fremont, CA 94539
Phone: 510-657-5239; fax: 510-683-9162
E-mail: twohorse@horsecamping.com
www.twohorseenterprises.com

Recreation.gov

A great online resource to find public lands and match them with the type of activity you are interested in.

Match a variety of activities to public lands where the desired activities are available. Click on any state on the map for a listing of recreation areas, and get real-time weather advisories and updates for your selected area.
www.recreation.gov

Riding on Public Roads

Collects statutes and administrative regulations that deal with riding or driving horses on public roads.

Most states have statutes or regulations dealing with this subject. Public roads include the full public right-of-way from fence to fence, including ditches and shoulders, not just the paved or graveled portion on which motor vehicles travel.
http://tarlton.law.utexas.edu/dawson/roads/roads.htm

United States Forest Service

The Forest Service manages public lands in national forests and grasslands.

Established in 1905, the Forest Service is an agency of the U.S. Department of Agriculture. Gifford Pinchot, the first chief of the agency, summed up its mission as follows: "to provide the greatest amount of good for the greatest amount of people in the long run." National forests and grasslands encompass 191 million acres (77.3 million hectares) of land, an area equivalent to the size of Texas.

USDA Forest Service
1400 Independence Avenue, SW Washington, D.C. 20250-0003
Phone: 202-205-8333
www.fs.fed.us

United States Geological Survey

Detailed contour maps of every area of the United States.

Phone: 888-275-8747
www.usgs.gov

TRAVELING WITH HORSES

Horse Motel

A complete listing, by country, province, and state, of horse motels anywhere in the world.

If you're traveling and need lodging for your horse(s), check our Web site for a facility along your way. We accept only high-quality facilities to ensure our customers a safe, comfortable overnight stay. If you are a traveler and have comments about your accommodations, feel free to e-mail us; we welcome your feedback. Facilities are listed alphabetically by city within each country, province, or state. To keep your horse(s) at a listed horse motel, current health papers and a negative Coggins test are required.

Dick Beck
P.O. Box 230373 Las Vegas, NV 89123
Phone: 888-468-1302
E-mail: dickbeck@horsemotel.com
http://horsemotel.com/

The Equestry Inn

A listing of facilities that will provide accommodations on a daily basis for those traveling long distances with horses.
www.worldaccessnet.com/~kozy/eqinn.html

Horse Trip.com

A state-by-state directory of stables, horse motels, equine-friendly camping, and bed and breakfasts that will stable your horse after a long day on the road.
www.horsetrip.com/

MAGAZINES

Trailblazer

4241 North Covina Circle, Prescott Valley, AZ 86314
Phone: 866-818-4146

The Trail Rider

730 Front Street, Louisville, CO 80027
Phone: 303-661-9282
www.trailridermagazine.com

TRAIL-RIDING GEAR

Cashel Company

Unique and innovative products.

Durable, high-quality products, the majority of which we make by hand (often from ideas you have suggested), designed with your and your horse's comfort and safety in mind. A staff of knowledgeable horse people will answer your questions.

Cashel Company
446 Gore Road, Onalaska, WA 98570
Phone: 800-333-2202; 360-978-4330
www.cashelcompany.com/

Long Riders Gear

Top-quality horse products and supplies for the endurance, competitive trail, and distance rider.

Offers an online catalog, a mail-order catalog, and appointments. Gear for both horse and rider.

Long Riders Gear
P.O. Box 2525, Pismo Beach, CA 93448
Toll-free: 888-420-GEAR; 805-474-1400; fax: 805-474-1402
E-mail: info@longridersgear.com or longridersgear@charter.net
www.longridersgear.com

Outfitters Supply

Horse tack, Western saddles, horse supplies, and horse riding equipment.

Quality is the most important characteristic of an Outfitters Supply product. We use only the best materials, including the best leather available, to make sure there are no surprises while you enjoy the great outdoors. Our mule tack and horse pack equipment make horse packing, mule packing, and horse camping a pleasure.

Outfitters Supply
7373 U.S. Highway 2 E, Columbia Falls, MT 59912
Phone: 888-467-2256
www.outfitterssupply.com

Outdoor Provisions
Camping equipment at competitive prices.
Find tents, backpacks, sleeping bags, lanterns, and much more. Free shipping.
www.outdoorprovisions.com

Wyoming Outdoor
Innovative low-impact packing supplies, trail saddles, camping supplies, wilderness supplies, equine gifts, hunting, calling supplies, and more.
Wyoming Outdoor Industries, Inc.
1231 13th Street, Cody, WY 82414
Phone: 800-725-6852
www.wyomingoutdoor.com

OTHER IMPORTANT RESOURCES

Self-Defense for Trail Riders (video)
Scot D. Hansen, former mounted police officer
Phone: 206-227-5007
E-mail: ScotHansen@Horsethink.com
www.HorseThink.com

To write your state representative in Congress
U.S. House of Representatives
Washington, DC 20515
Phone: 202-224-3121
www.house.gov/writerep/

For further information about toxic plants:
The Horse Owner's Field Guide to Toxic Plants Publishing, Breakthrough, 1996
www.vet.purdue.edu/depts/addl/toxic/byanim.htm
www.nwcb.wa.gov/ (Washington State Noxious Weed Control Board)
www.pprl.usu.edu/Poisonous_Plants.htm (USDA Poisonous Plant Research Laboratory)
http://plants.usda.gov/cgi_bin/topics.cgi?earl=plant_profile.cgi&symbol=NEOL
www.ansci.cornell.edu/plants/alphalist.html (Cornell Poisonous Plants Informational Database)
www.vth.colostate.edu/poisonous_plants/report/

For more information on finding trails:
Find more trails by contacting your local Forest Service or Parks Department, or by searching the Internet, beginning with these Web sites: www.horseandmuletrails.com/Va.htm
www.recreation.gov/horses.cfm?myActivity=horsebackriding
www.trailhorsedirectory.com

National Trails Day
The first Saturday in June has been designated National Trails Day, a celebration by trail users of all kinds. Ride on that date and then send a report card to trail authorities to let them know trails are in use and keep them informed as to conditions. A pack of Trail Rider Comment Cards can be ordered from:
Two Horse Enterprises
P.O. Box 15517, Fremont, CA 94539
Phone: 510-657-5239; fax: 510-683-9162
E-mail: twohorse@horsecamping.com
www.twohorseenterprises.com

QUICK-RELEASE KNOT

Here's a knot that is quick to tie and even quicker to release, but will hold your horse safely in the meantime.

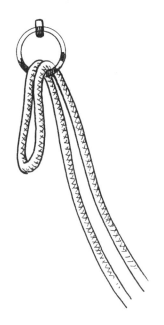  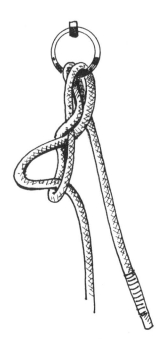 

1. Make a loop about 8 inches long, leaving 6 inches of the end of the rope free. Pass the loop through the tie ring.

2. Twist the rope a couple of times, leaving an opening at the end.

3. Make a short loop in the rope that goes back to your horse and pass it through the opening at the end of the twist.

4. Make a fold in the free end of the rope and pass it through the second (horse end) loop. Pull on the horse-end of the rope and draw the knot snug.

To undo the knot, just pull on the free end of the rope; it will release in an instant.

EMERGENCY INFORMATION

Photocopy this form, take a copy with you, and leave another copy at home in a prominent place in case someone else needs to find it.

Date and time I'm leaving: _____

Trail I'm taking: _____

Trail head: _____

I expect to be back: _____

My cell phone number: _____

Emergency contact:

Name: _____

Phone number: _____

Back-ups:

1. _____

2. _____

3. _____

Four-wheel-drive pickup: _____

Horse trailer: _____

EMT: _____

Vet: _____

Fire: _____

Other information:

_____

_____

_____

INDEX

References in *italic* denote tables or boxes.
References in **bold** denote illustrations.

barn-sour or herd-bound horse, 199–201, *200*, *200*, *201*

bolting, whirling, bucking, rearing, 186–192, *188*, *189*, *189*, *190*, *191*, *193*, *193*

calling out, 199

dominance, challenging, 180

habits, avoiding bad, 180–181

head tossing, 193–195, **195**

jigging, 197–198

nature of, 180–181, *181*

shying, 182–186, *182*, *183*, *184*, *185*, *187*

snacking, 198–199

stumbling, 195–197, 234

Vision of horse

eyes, assessing, 36–37, *37*

and head tossing, 195

and shying, 182–183

Vital signs of horse, checking. *See* Condition of horse, assessing

W

Water. *See also* Dehydration

when camping, 277–278, 282–283

crossing, 202–205, **202**, **204**, **205**

Weanlings, working with. *See* Training

Weather

darkness, 215–216

gear, 78

heat, 211

rain, 212–213

snow and ice, 213

thunder and lightning storms, 213, 215, *215*

wind, 211–212

Weight of horse, estimating, *3*

Western and Eastern equine encephalomyelitis (WEE and EEE), 222

Western saddles, **54**, 54–58, **55**

Whirling. *See* Vices of trail horse

Whistles, 79, **79**

Wildlife, encountering, 217–223, **217**, **219**, **220**, **221**, **222**

"Wind, broken," 39

Wind, riding in, 211–212

Windpuffs, 37–38

Withers, back, and ribcage, assessing, 34–36, **35**

Woods, riding in, 209

OTHER STOREY TITLES YOU WILL ENJOY

101 Arena Exercises: A Ringside Guide for Horse & Rider, by Cherry Hill. A ringside exercise book for riders who want to improve their own and their horse's skills. Classic exercises and original patterns and drills presented in a unique "read-and-ride" format. 224 pages. Paperback. ISBN 0-88266-316-X.

Easy-Gaited Horses, by Lee Ziegler. An in-depth guide to working with gaited horses by one of the world's leading experts on the subject. Includes line drawings and diagrams. 256 pages. Paperback ISBN 1-58017-562-7. Hardcover ISBN 1-58017-563-5.

Horse Care for Kids, by Cherry Hill. An introduction to safe, responsible horsekeeping for young riders, including selecting a horse, feeding, grooming, and stable management. 128 pages, full color. Paperback ISBN 1-58017-407-8. Hardcover ISBN 1-58017-476-0.

The Horse Conformation Handbook, by Heather Smith Thomas. How to judge a horse for soundness, athletic potential, trainability, longevity, and heart. Analyzes all aspects of conformation in regard to a horse's performance and suitability for particular functions. 400 pages. Paperback ISBN 1-58017-558-9. Hardcover ISBN 1-58017-559-7.

The Horse Doctor Is In, by Brent Kelley. Combining solid veterinary advice with enlightening stories from his Kentucky equine practice, Dr. Kelley informs readers on all aspects of horse health care, from fertility to fractures to foot care. 416 pages. Paperback ISBN 1-58017-460-4.

Horsekeeping on a Small Acreage: Facilities Design and Management, 2nd edition, by Cherry Hill. Horse trainer Cherry Hill describes the essentials for designing safe and functional facilities. 320 pages, full color. Paperback ISBN 1-58017-535-x. Hardcover ISBN 1-58017-603-8.

The Rider's Fitness Program, by Dianna R. Dennis, John J. McCully, and Paul M. Juris. A six-week program (85 exercises) focusing on the muscles riders use, improving overall balance, flexibility, and coordination. 224 pages. Paperback ISBN 1-58017-542-2.

Starting & Running Your Own Horse Business, by Mary Ashby McDonald. This essential guide shows readers how to run a successful business — and how to make the most of their investments in horses, facilities, equipment, and time over short- and long-term periods. From general business tips to saving cash on stable management, this book quickly pays for itself. 160 pages. Paperback ISBN 0-88266-960-5.

Storey's Horse-Lover's Encyclopedia, edited by Deborah Burns. This hefty, fully-illustrated, comprehensive A-to-Z compendium is an indispensable answer book addressing every question a reader may have about horses and horse care. 480 pages. Paperback ISBN 1-58017-317-9.

These books and other Storey books are available wherever books are sold, or directly from Storey Publishing, 210 MASS MoCA Way, North Adams, MA 01247, or by calling 1-800-441-5700. www.storey.com